Janet Flanner's World

BOOKS BY JANET FLANNER

The Cubical City

An American in Paris

Pétain: The Old Man of France

Men and Monuments

Paris Journal: 1944–1965

Paris Journal: 1965–1971

Paris Was Yesterday

London Was Yesterday

*Janet Flanner's World:
Uncollected Writings,
1932–1975*

Uncollected
Writings
1932-1975

EDITED BY IRVING DRUTMAN

JANET FLANNER'S WORLD

Introduction by *William Shawn*

Harcourt Brace Jovanovich

NEW YORK AND LONDON

Design: Dorothy Schmiderer

Printed in the United States of America

LIBRARY OF CONGRESS CATALOGING IN PUBLICATION DATA

Flanner, Janet, 1892–1978
Janet Flanner's world.

I. Drutman, Irving.   II. Title.
PS3511.L285A16   1979   814'.5'2   79-1820
ISBN 0-15-146154-6

First edition

B C D E

Contents

IV

Acknowledgment

When I suggested to Janet Flanner a new volume of her numerous *New Yorker* pieces written from cities and places other than Paris or London and not yet collected in book form, we immediately thought of Irving Drutman, who had edited two earlier volumes of Janet's, to make the selections. I was reluctant to ask him, however, because he was seriously ill. But his admiration for Janet was such that I felt he would be interested in the project and it might prove helpful to him as well. Indeed. Irving worked with dedication, even from his hospital bed, and delivered an edited manuscript only a few days before his death.

To his memory goes my deepest gratitude. If Janet were still with us, she would join me in saying thank you.

NATALIA DANESI MURRAY

Introduction

This collection of Janet Flanner's journalistic writings, edited by the late Irving Drutman with great sensitiveness and devotion, contains Letters and other articles written for *The New Yorker* between 1931 and 1976. Although Janet Flanner is best known for her Paris Letters, published by *The New Yorker* over a period of a half century, she also wrote many pieces from England, Germany, Austria, Italy, Holland, and elsewhere. Her domain was spacious, and without national boundaries. She was most, and equally, at home in France and America, but she managed to put down roots wherever she happened to be: she arrived in Rome or Salzburg, went to her hotel room, looked out the window, took further bearings, and, as soon as she had opened her typewriter, was on her way to a journalistic dispatch that would someday be seen as literature. Most of the pieces in this volume were written in Italy and Germany, and include her prophetic 1936 Profile of Adolf Hitler, her report on the Nazis' 1936 Olympic Games, and her notable series on the Nuremberg Trials in 1945 and 1946. There are also portraits of Thomas Mann, Ingrid Bergman, and Bette Davis. The unmistakable Flanner touch is everywhere. The book begins with a report from a bankrupt Berlin in 1931 and ends with Janet Flanner's last Paris Letter, written at the age of eighty-three: a lyrical tribute to a small garden of roses.

The colors, the shapes, the sounds, and the textures of this earth, whether they were arranged by nature or by artists, enthralled Janet Flanner, just as words and the play of ideas enthralled her, and political and cultural events, and scenes on city streets, and, finally, and fundamentally, people, whoever they were. A stranger to fatigue, boredom, and cynicism, she met the world with rapture and wrote about it with pleasure. As a writer of prose, she was a virtuoso, yet she never let herself be carried away by her own brilliance; some essential humility—a humility that often goes hand in hand with genius—led her to place all her powers at the service of the information she wished to convey and of what she believed that that information meant. Though she was one of the least literal-minded of writers, she loved particularities. Beneath the elegance of her style was the plain speech that went back to her Quaker upbringing in Indiana. Embedded in her enormously sophisticated manner was a Hoosier common sense.

New information resides nowhere until it has been identified, objectified, assembled, and communicated by one or another kind of reporter; and every reporter sets out on every quest more or less in the dark. At first, there is little to go on except instinct; but at last, as fragment after fragment falls into place, the information materializes and some light, with luck, is cast. What distinguished Janet Flanner from her colleagues was the sureness of her instinct, the individual mind in which her reports took shape. Her mind was an exquisite mechanism, awhirr with wit, warmed by reserves of passion. Her reporting methods were eccentric—seemingly haphazard. Facts came to her out of the air, and turned out to be the facts that she needed and that counted. As if by inadvertence, she wrote political, social, and cultural history of the first order. She looked beyond what the ordinary eye could see, and she heard vibrations too delicate for the ordinary ear. She picked up signals, intimations, atmospheres, dim forms, ambiguous voices, and out of all this she constructed as accurate a representation as we have had of what was going on in Europe between 1925 and 1975. Her insistence upon never writing in a predictable, or even a convenient, way, her compulsion to reach for unusual phrases and rhythms, reflected not simply a fondness for surprise and ornament—although that she had—but a refusal to allow her thought to fall into molds or patterns. She had a dread, it appears, of the commonplace. Nominally, she was a reporter, a journalist, but in the intensity of her response to what she observed, in her peculiar, nearly explosive mixture of intuition and intelligence, in her imagery, in her verbal fun and audacity, in her inspired distillations, in her bizarre and marvellously controlled elisions, in her dependable gravitation toward the heart of the matter, she was, above all and abidingly, a poet.

WILLIAM SHAWN

Janet Flanner's World

I

੩੨

Über Alles

BERLIN, DECEMBER 28, 1931   It is perhaps unfortunate that Germany's bankruptcy, as seen in its capital city, still lacks the professional pictorial touch. Even with Ufa directing, it is unlikely that the debacle would screen well. For if one may judge by what one sees, national failure is being conducted—and how grateful the traveller is—with business in *gemütlichen Weinhäusern*, theatres, and night clubs going on as usual. Nowhere in Europe is there a capital where overeating, fine restaurants, mocha, tobacco, music, flowers, and courtesy so warm the tourist's heart. Up till frost fell, Berlin's miles of broad residence streets were colored by the womanly touch of purple petunias cascading from balcony and window-box. In the business centers, *Konditorei* terraces were perfumed by the manly scent of Havana cigars. As the hard winter has drawn in, night and day life, both expensive, continue to be conducted with a heavy air of habit. Concerts, operas, and their beer-and-sausage entr'acte bars are hungrily attended. After all, the performances are government-subsidized to the tune of twenty-two and a half millions of marks annually and ought to be patronized if only as a form of patriotism. And if banks close down for weeks, cabarets rarely do before dawn.

Somewhere in the town are workers without work and capitalists without capital, but on the sidewalks are neither apples nor unemployed. Only a few war heroes with matches to sell, a few war heroines with nothing to sell, and the steady tramp of well-fed, worried, blond citizenry—the new Berliners, strong where they used to be stout, affable where they once were formal, affectionate to adult foreigners as they used to be only to their own children. And all sure that their country is going to the dogs.

However, they personally are going to the theatre first, and, considering the excellence of what they have to see, it is a good idea. The three biggest operetta hits of the world and the two most talked-of new operas all hail from bankrupt Berlin. For not since "The Merry Widow" or "Rose Marie" has an operetta had the success accorded to the now-classical Charell-Reinhardt "Das Weisse Rössl," which has been playing to capacity in London as "The White Horse Inn," and anticipates a similar triumph after the holidays in Paris, where it will be called "Au Cheval Blanc." Certainly no song-show ever made such a hit on such unimportant music. It has encouraged *Schuhplattler* to *schuhplatt* even at the Casino de Paris and has launched a new manner in revue-directing: a combination of Viennese sentimentality, Prussian military precision, American dancing, and German mechanics.

Also "Die Schöne Helena," once out of Meilhac-Halévy-Offenbach, now more out of Reinhardt-Korngold, who between them have done something to the libretto and score, is still to be seen at the Theater am Kurfürstendamm, touted on its recent construction as the Continent's most artistic playhouse, and a charming jerry-built muddle of Wienerwerkstätte and Schönbrunn rococo it is. Cochran has taken an English version of what is left of Offenbach to London, and New Yorkers are supposed to have it soon after, in German, with its masked chorus, plus, if they have luck, its enchanting discovery, Fräulein Friedel Schuster as Prince Orestes.

The third of the Berlin operetta trio worthy, musically and financially, to be sent to other lands is "Viktoria und Ihr Hussar," also scheduled for New York. Its composer, Paul Abrahams, is Viennese and definitely possesses the light, melodic touch which leads some critics, pretentiously perhaps, to compare him to Lehár.

The rest of the theatrical news, though more recent, is even more Reinhardt. This winter he controls, in addition to six theatres in Berlin, a pair in Vienna, the Festspiel in Salzburg, and a private stage on his nearby estate at Leopoldskron, all of which can be used as summer tryout stations for what the German capital later sees. His present season opened at the Deutsches with Ernest Hemingway's "Kat," which is German for "A Farewell to Arms," a play which Mr. Hemingway liked less than the critics, perhaps because he had read the novel, and despite the presence in its cast of Helene Thimig and Käthe Dosch, the two Lynn Fontannes of the German stage. The rest of his winter productions entail the new Molnár comedy called "Jemand," a new Hauptmann piece called nothing so far, a translation of Giraudoux's "Judith," which could easily be better in German than it was in French, and "Der Grosse Gefangene," a Napoleonic episode of Helena days which has just had its tryout at Hamburg. This last was written for and by the undersized star, Moissi, and is probably a mistake for both little men.

* * *

The biggest item in new serious music, outside of the continued popularity of "Schwanda" and "Wozzeck," was the world première of Stravinsky's new violin concerto, written for Dushkin, a piece more classical than the "Sacre," richer than the piano capriccio, and melodically dating somewhere near last year's "Symphonie de Psaumes."

As for the repertory war horses given at the State operas, they are led with such finesse in conducting, move with such dash and ensemble, that they seem new. The only stage in Europe where "Le Mariage de Figaro" is properly presented as an improper French story is the Berliner Oper, where Teutons in buffons whisper the plot in flawless recitative, like silk-clad musical gossips animated from a canvas of Watteau.

The cinemas, however, seem to fail to fare well. Ranking on the Continent, because of Ufa, along with Moscow in celluloid intelligence and technique, Berlin, outside of Charell's super-production of "Der Kongress Tanzt," has taken a back seat. Anyhow, it has never had enough cinema seats to go round. There are fewer movie houses in all Berlin than in three *arrondissements* of Paris. Paris may make some of the worst films in the world, but it goes to see them; and the French may be thrifty, but they have time to go to the movies all day and half the night, as America has taught them. In Berlin the giant *Kinos* have only two shows daily, one at seven and one at nine, with a Sunday vesper meeting at five. Nor are the Berliners missing much. Lang, who made "Metropolis," aroused expectations which his "M" (the initial standing for child-murder) failed to satisfy. Pabst's "Dreigroschenoper," his reel version of the "Beggars' Opera," with modern music by Kurt Weill, has in both French and German versions disappointed many, among whom would be counted Mr. Gay were he to hear of it. Richard Tauber, in "Die Grosse Attraktion," proved to be little when he first opened near the Zoo. With his increasing gramophone fame, this piece was rigged up to be the musical travelling salesman of the year, but outside of the records for the charming "Du warst mir ein Roman," probably won't go too far, in Europe anyhow. As a spectacle it is a typical star vehicle hitched up to a singer with a strong tendency to embonpoint and lately (in his London season, particularly) a weak larynx.

Nor has art been much of a business. Modern French canvases, always gobbled when good enough by Berlin, are a drug on the merchants' shelves. The only German painter (and he is Swiss) who finds any takers is Paul Klee. The sole other salable art is any work of Renée Sintenis, the exotic and over-popular young sculptress deft in the matter of colts, boys, and other adolescent animals.

But the best in the way of art is not for sale. It is also, in its new

3

arrangement, the best in the world. No other museum has ever done for the Greek and Trojan war what postwar Berlin has done in its new Pergamon Museum, where a hall seventy feet high and one hundred and fifty feet long, culminating in a vast flight of steps topped by a fake temple, has been built to house a major portion of the famous fighting frieze (discovered in Asia Minor by Humann and probably dating from 180 B.C.). The bas-relief came into Germany's possession under the Kaiser, but even that grandiose man boggled at the idea of the expense involved in appropriately placing it. Owing to local as well as foreign criticism of such an outlay at such a time, the cost of its recent habitation is not available. However, the value to aesthetics is also incalculable.

The beauties of night life, however, flourish. In the Jockey, in the Lutherstrasse, Berlin now has a night club where one is liable to meet everyone one knows, a delicate danger that has not been encountered in Paris since the old days of the first Bœuf-sur-le-Toit. The Jockey's décors are a few *démodé* theatrical posters, its entertainment one gentleman at a piano, who on big nights becomes two gentlemen at two pianos, placed, with the aid of a ladder and a platform, one above the other. At the moment, it is probably the most pleasant club in Europe, certainly the only one where good manners and good conversation, gentle drinking and gentle jazz, seem sufficient attraction for staying up half the night.

The only other midnight rendezvous of equal quality is the Eden Hotel Bar. Here is an atmosphere of die-hard ease and Semitic chic, monocled men, waltzes heard over popping corks, and an odor of bankers' boutonnières mingling with Prussian cocottes' French perfume. The wine is yellow and old, the ladies blonde and young, the goose-livers Gargantuan, the scene civilized. Something imperial still collects about this gathering of overlords of a bankrupt country, something racial, powerful, first-class, like German liners, toys, industry, and patriotic obedience in the days when Germany set a standard for them all.

The rest of the night life centres around Kurfürstendamm and Kleiststrasse out to Nollendorf Platz, honeycombed with dreary little imitations of Montmartre and Manhattan, as dull and well patronized as if they were really in Manhattan or Montmartre.

But at any rate the integrity of Friedrichstrasse, that street of sin, has not altered. Indeed, what with the panics and Puritanism that have finally swept over Europe, the nightly parade of prostitutes on this blazing thoroughfare comes with the shock of an anachronism. As a survival it is unique. Serious as psychiatrists, devoid of the gaiety or gallantry of the girls who once livened the Roaring Forties and the French *promenoir*, the Teutonic *fräuleins* tread their heavy nocturnal path, their special occupation solemnly ticketed by their costumes. From eight till midnight, without any but foreigners stopping to stare, the gathering files and counter-files, as unreal, unromantic, and literary as a sample page of Rowlandson's illustrations for some book that is bound to be dull.

However, the real feature of night life in Berlin is eating. It is also the real feature of day life. As if in surprise, Berliners admit that their restaurants are both dear and packed. Sometimes in the half-hour wait needed to get into any expensive eating house, they try to puzzle the thing out for the foreigner. Probably the hardest thing to explain is the nightly presence of what the management estimates as three thousand diners in the Haus Vaterland, recognized as the biggest restaurant on earth. It's a mixture of Turkish coffee salons, Japanese tearooms, Swiss-châlet *bistros*, Spanish *bodegas*, Neapolitan *trattorie*, and Wild West American bars with waiters dressed as cowboys, hat-check girls as geishas, and *Weinkellner* rigged up as Castilian bloods; there are bands and cabarets at every turning, and in the Bavarian dining-room an orchestra in Oberammergau shorts that alternately blasts on the brass and obliges with yodels during a storm scene with real water and calcium lightning playing, with cloud effects, over a panorama of the Alps. *Ach, wie herrlich!*

There must be, it is true, terrible want in certain quarters in Berlin. True, there is similar want in all capital cities of the world. And true, in Berlin as everywhere, workers want work and new gramophone records if they can manage it, capitalists want a fair return on capital, and, though they'd be glad to get it again, they don't mean a safe five per cent. Germany's estimated unemployment figures for this winter would be terrifying to New Yorkers if they had not themselves seen apples and unemployment. The jobless will rise to at least seven million, which, Germans being as sentimental as they are, means babies and other dependents to the tune of twenty million. In thrifty France, if there were seven million men out of work, having been specially thrifty as regards their own generation, the dependents wouldn't amount to ten million. However, if there were seven million Frenchmen out of work, they'd all be busy making a revolution.

In the meantime, though perhaps otherwise unemployed, the Berliners are busy making a new race. It may be that the fat-necked prewar German was killed in the war and the fat wife who matched him died of grief. In any case, they have disappeared from the capital city. They are seen only in cartoons there; and sometimes in Bavaria and occasionally in Brooklyn. Or occasionally they can be located among the provincial types who, in fair weather, take the Untergrundbahn out to the *Flughaven* that overlooks the flying field at Tempelhofer Feld. Here the Kaiser used to hold his annual military reviews, here Count von Zeppelin (his grandson won't get into one of the things and refused Dr. Eckener's invitation to fly free to America on the ship's maiden transatlantic voyage) came zooming through the clouds to be greeted by army and emperor, and a hysterical populace. The roof of the air station is a popular outing place still. Refreshments—as if anyone would refuse to buy them—are obligatory, one can leave one's beer and take a trial flight, listen to orchestras on the loudspeaker, or the field steward's announcements as to which commercial or private planes are taking off or coming down. Out in the grass a smudge fire continuously burns, to show which way the wind is blowing. The grandstand faces south. To its east lies a locust-like horde of Gothas, Moths, planes big and little, at the moment commercial and all on the ground, but military and up in the air if the hour arrives. Somewhere to the south lies France. England to the west. And somewhere in between the two lies Belgium, so little that once it wasn't worth flying over and an army simply walked through.

There is almost a literary touch in the fact that of all the nations', Germany's unknown warrior was the last to be entombed. Owing to factional disputes among politicians and art critics he has only recently found his final resting place. But the choice of the fought-over site is in the end his military victory. He now lies in Unter den Linden in the little old guardhouse, become a true Pantheon by opening the circular roof to the sky. The whole edifice could be placed between the columns surrounding the *Soldat Inconnu* in the Arc de Triomphe, could be fenced in by a wing of the pillars from the hemicycle at Arlington, would be lost among the mounting tiers of the war monument in the Piazza Vittorio Emanuele in Rome. Here, bare to all weather, flanked by flambeaux, topped by a wreath hammered from the multicolored metals of guns, and merely inscribed "1914–1918," rests a great, black, stone tomb. Within lies an anonymous German military man with only a date for his epitaph.

Führer

FEBRUARY 29, 1936 Dictator of a nation devoted to splendid sausages, cigars, beer, and babies, Adolf Hitler is a vegetarian, teetotaller, nonsmoker, and celibate. He was a small-boned baby and was tubercular in his teens. He says that as a youth he was already considered an eccentric. In the war, he was wounded twice and almost blinded by mustard gas. Like many partial invalids, he has compensated for his debilities by developing a violent will and exercising strong opinions. Limited by physical temperament, trained in poverty, organically costive, he has become the dietetic survivor of his poor health. He swallows gruel for breakfast, is fond of oatmeal, digests milk and onion soup, declines meat, which even as an undernourished youth he avoided, never touches fish, has given up macaroni as fattening, eats one piece of bread at a meal, favors vegetables, greens, and salads, drinks lemonade, likes tea and cake, and loves a raw apple. Alcohol and nicotine are beyond him, since they heighten the exciting intoxication his faulty assimilation already assures.

As *Reichsführer, Reichskanzler, und Höchstkommandierender der Armee* of Germany, Herr Hitler, by reason of his high offices, occupies the building in the Wilhelmstrasse in Berlin which was called the *Reichskanzlerpalais* until recently the Nazi government, to avoid any monarchical implications, renamed it the *Haus des Reichskanzlers*. Devoid of appetite for luxury, he inhabits the palace in agitated simplicity. His physical wants are few; he dislikes servants, and maintains only a skeleton domestic staff of five. Four of them are friendly, political comrades of earlier days who now serve him as chauffeur, chef, major-domo, and aide-de-camp. Brigadier Schreck drives the Führer's handsome black Mercedes touring cars for him. Hitler often borrows his friends' motors. He likes automobiles generically, enjoys riding in anything so long as it's fast and open, and has the German impatience with slow, stuffy limousines. He prefers to sit in front with the driver, except when he stands up in back, receiving the cheers of his public. His cooking and housekeeping are done for him by a couple named Kannenberg, who are old acquaintances. Kannenberg is a well-known, jovial character who used to run a smart, small, Behrenstrasse restaurant. Owing to Hitler's diet, about all Kannenberg can do for him now is to act the court clown, play the accordion, and sing funny Bavarian songs, for which the Führer still has a taste. If Hitler goes on a cross-country tour, one of the cars is fitted with a kitchenette, and Kannenberg goes along as musical cook. Being a Bavarian, he knows the recipe for Hitler's favorite South German gruel, or *Brennsuppe*—a kind of porridge soup made of browned flour, butter, and caraway seeds, seasoned with salt and a little vinegar. Hitler's aide-de-camp is Oberleutnant Wilhelm Brückner, a former Wimbledon tennis star of military family; genealogically, he sets the tone for the establishment. Hitler has no valet. Adjutant Schaub, a large fellow who wears the black uniform of the S.S., or *Schutzstaffel*, acts as major-domo. Though he lays out Hitler's clothes, neither he nor anyone around the palace has ever seen the Führer in slippers and dressing gown; Hitler's modesty verges on the morbid. In the morning it takes him fifteen minutes, from the time he gets up, to get dressed and be ready for breakfast. He usually appears in his favorite costume—black trousers and a khaki coat cut in the pattern of what German officers call a *Litevka*—the traditional military lounge jacket without insignia. He never wears jewelry. He has always been frantically neat, clean, and of tidy habits; his clothes wear forever. Most of his wardrobe consists of uniforms, but there are a few civilian garments. He scrupulously chooses a second-rate tailor. Schaub orders most of his things. They are sent to the palace, where Hitler tries on and selects; he can't go into a shop without its being mobbed by his Nazi admirers and hasn't bought anything in the normal way for three years.

The Führer sensibly gets up in the morning according to the hour that he went to sleep the night before, which is irregular, depending on what he's had to do or what's on his mind. Being a sufferer from insomnia, he does a lot of his thinking in bed. He has no mania for fixed hours or early rising and is more flexible in his routine than is supposed. Though his day is limited by certain scheduled events, when he wakes he manages to select some shape for it, is liable to change his plans, usually secret in any case. For self-protection he always arrives deviously at a rendezvous, even with his public. When in Berlin, he lunches promptly at 2 P.M., as is the city's custom, and at this palace meal entertains frequently in a modest way. Guests are usually Party colleagues, *Gauleiter* up from the provinces. They get a sturdy soup, a hearty meat, potatoes, second vegetable, and salad, served all at the same time, in German fashion; and for dessert, oftener than not, some South German sweet such as *Schmarren* with stewed fruit, the only course their host can join them in. On Sundays they get only a pot stew, since Hitler observes *Topfsonntag*, or the fat-and-food-economy Sundays which he recently inaugurated. Because of his diet, Hitler hates banquets, doesn't approve of them anyhow, as "emphasizing the immense disparity between riches and poverty" in a Spartan state; rarely accepts invitations to meals in private houses, because, like most *Süddeutscher*, he prefers to eat in public in some favorite spot.

When in Munich, he still goes to the quiet little Osteria-Bavaria Restaurant, which he has used for years, and occasionally he drops in for *Jause* at the Carlton tearoom, which is the nicest in town. When he eats a meal at the elegant Vier Jahreszeiten Hotel, it's in the modest back room, not in its Walterspiel restaurant. The Walterspiel brothers, two of the greatest *gourmets* of Europe, are old friends of his, and concocted Hitler's onion-soup recipe especially for him. When in Nürnberg, Hitler still stops at the second-rate Deutscher Hof, which was grandeur for him in the old days and which he thinks today is grand enough. He likes places he's familiar with, where people know his habits and let him alone. With his shadows, the elegant Brückner and the lowly Schaub, he often goes in Berlin to the

Kaiserhof in the afternoon for a glass of milk and his favorite *Linzertorte*, a walnut cake. He has a sweet tooth.

The few Chancellery palace formal dinners Hitler gives are stiff affairs with roses, candles, and the menu written out. While General Göring, when he gives a Berlin dinner, calls in Horcher's restaurant, rival of Paris's Larue as the finest *traiteurs* left in Europe, Hitler's catering is done in the house. Guests are drawn from the Party men and their lucky wives, and from the *Kulturkammern*, or the Nazi so-called intellectual world; i.e., the committees on censorship, press, propaganda, and the graphic arts, in addition to folk-art organizers, opera-house functionaries, and occasional state actresses or soprani in unshakably respectable standing. Hitler still has a provincial's naïve admiration for the Thespian and prima-donna types. As entertainment after dinner, he usually shows movies with a projection machine he's had installed in the palace. He's crazy about films, especially when historical, sees all the news weeklies of himself, and occasional earnest foreign films, and is apt to sit on the floor in the dark when they are being shown. When he takes a fancy to a picture, he has it repeated and invites those he thinks it should interest; he is sincere about trying to get the right films and guests together. When he discovered the Schubert "Unfinished Symphony" movie, he gave a party to bring it and Wilhelm Furtwängler together. But in spite of these occasions, Hitler, like all people who have no talent for it, has never had time for a good time.

He also has no gift for intimacy. Neither his enemies nor his best friends (who perhaps tried even harder) have been able to bring forward any mistress out of his past. Upper-class women were among his first sympathizers at a time when housemaids thought him a freak. To these same housemaids he is now a hero and *der schöne Adolf*, and his photo hangs over their washbowls. Like many small, dominant men, when he chooses he has a talkative charm with women; even in the parlor, he has the orator's instinct for adapting his conversation to his listener. He loves to laugh in company, enjoys obvious jokes, and occasionally makes solemnly funny remarks. For a self-conscious man, easily flustered by memory of his early, burning deficiencies and enviously impressed by diplomas and social distinctions, he has learned in three years of power to forget himself somewhat and has gained a relative ease of manner. When in company, he long ago added to his provincial politeness the more worldly gesture of kissing the ladies' hands as greeting, though among the non-aristocrats the custom is now usually derided as anti-Nazi. Conversation excites him. In anything approaching serious talk, his sapphire-blue eyes, which are his only good feature, brighten, glow heavily as if words fanned them. His principal gesture is a shrug of the shoulders. If he's really interested, he is likely to walk up and down the room, and in arguments he becomes violent.

Years ago, when young and unsuccessful, his rather heavy political conversation was delivered with such complete concentration on his topic that it attracted older or intellectual women who had learned patience. He made his worldly début as a thin, neat unknown, in the famous Munich salon of Frau Katherine Heine Hanfstaengl, whose mother was a Sedgwick of New York. For the past fifteen years Hitler's greatest woman friend has been Frau Victoria von Dirksen, formerly a fashionable hostess in her Margaretenstrasse mansion in Berlin, and now stepmother of the German ambassador at Moscow and widow of the magnate who helped to build the Berlin *Untergrund*. It was in her salon that the secret, Frau Hermine Hohenzollern–Hitler meeting took place when the question arose of which should be presented to which—the second wife of the ex-Kaiser of the former German Empire to the Nazi Führer of Germany's Third Reich, or vice versa. (Hitler tactfully kissed the lady's hand before anyone could introduce either, and then tactlessly refused her plea that her exiled husband be allowed easier terms from the land he'd once ruled.) Frau von Dirksen gave most of her late husband's fortune to promoting Hitler's career. Their friendship has not been interrupted by his success or by her recent quarrels with his Party. When in Berlin, he still loyally takes tea with her every fortnight.

Hitler's less wealthy feminine friends include a small, distinguished gallery which anyone could know about and most of upper-class Germany does. He has been photographed at official functions with Frau Winifred Wagner, widow of Richard Wagner's son, Siegfried. Having succumbed to Wagnerism and "Lohengrin" at the age of twelve, when poor and Austrian, Hitler could not, as later leader of Germany, resist the meeting with Frau Wagner. There was talk of their marrying, but it was a canard instituted by the foreign press. Friends now feel that celibacy is part of Hitler's natural career. Frau Wagner was an early Nazi devotee. She was not rich, but on the strength of her name she persuaded others to give fortunes to the Party. Leni Riefenstahl, former cinema star, is another well-known German woman whom Hitler knows. He confided to her the editing, and worked with her over the cutting, of his 1934 Nazi propaganda film, "Der Triumph des Willens," which he refused to show publicly outside of Germany, since, as he himself said, "national fervor cannot be exported." He still thinks her competent to handle enthusiasm for home consumption, and she will officially photograph the forthcoming Berlin Olympic Games, as she did last summer's Nazi Nürnberg Congress. (The latter film was recently shown in Berlin under the title "Tag der Freiheit.") At the tremendous, opening Shovel Parade of the *Arbeitsdienst*, she was not only the sole motion-picture director, she was also the only woman on the great parade field—one white linen skirt moving freely before fifty-four thousand green-woolen, mechanical men, one professional woman on her job, and so rare a sight in masculinized Germany today that among the quarter-million spectators assembled, there wasn't a person who didn't know who she was. She is unique, and the white-skirted figure couldn't have been anybody else.

Other exceptional figures commented on in Hitler's entourage are two English women, Lord Redesdale's daughters, the Honourable Mrs. Bryan Guinness, who in London had already been converted to Sir Oswald Mosley's Black Shirt Fascism, and her younger sister, the Honourable Unity Mitford. Both sisters are blonde, handsome, speak excellent German, and use the Nazi salute. The younger is Hitler's favorite, because more devoted to the German cause. She and he frequently lunch together at the Osteria restaurant whenever he's in Munich, as English, rather than German papers, point out. Another admiration of Hitler's is Frau Viorica Ursuleac, dramatic soprano of the Unter den Linden Opera, who moved from Dresden to Berlin when the Viennese director Clemens Krauss became the more complacent successor to Furtwängler, after the latter's insistence that Jews were also musicians.

Though chief of a political party which doctrinally enforces the domestic submission of women to "men's natural rule as illustrated by the Wagnerian heroes like Wotan and Siegfried," Hitler prefers the Walküre type of lady who gets around on the public heights. He also likes women who are well dressed. Though it would be officially denied, Hitler opposed Frau Göbbels' recent patriotic boycott of French dress models, a blacklisting which, since Germany has no dress designers, nearly ruined the foundation of Germany's ready-made garment trade. This is the largest in Europe, and is three times the volume of Germany's coal industry. Owing to Hitler's pressure, the ban was lifted, and today one-third of the five leading Paris couturiers' model business is with Berlin. Having been recently argued into white tie and tails for his rare Opera appearances, Hitler nearly ordered the women auditors to dress also, but renounced the idea as Napoleonic. He has a holy horror of Bonapartism.

Hitler has only one close friend among men—Rudolf Hess, formerly appropriately the Führer's secretary, now his personal deputy. It is to be noted that Corporal Hitler's early political companions, now highest in power, must have chosen him rather than have been chosen, since they were his superiors in military rank, society, or education. Hess, now called "the preferred companion," who knows Hitler best and idealizes him most, was born in Alexandria, Egypt, son of a well-to-do exporter, but was educated in Europe under the geologist Haushofer. Hermann Göring, formerly a flight-captain, is now a general and Minister of Air. He came of rich, Prussian county-family stock. As war ace, he received the highest German decoration for bravery under fire, and on von Richthofen's death took over the command of his famous Flying Circus. Anti-Nazi writers have said that after the war he became a temporary morphine addict. Today, Göring is the German masses' hearty ideal, and is the only big Nazi they hail by his first name. He is supposedly already selected by Hitler to succeed him in the event of the Führer's death. Göring says he is "Hitler's skin and hair," whatever that means.

The last of the Nazis now important in the Party to join Hitler was the little, clubfooted Dr. Joseph Göbbels. He came from the Rhineland, in his youth was an unruly scholarship student at seven universities, and later became a journalist and wrote some indifferent poetry and plays. He is now Minister for National Enlightenment and Propaganda—more of the latter than of the former, German jokesters whisper.

Dr. Ernst Sedgwick Hanfstaengl, known on both shores of the Atlantic as "Putzi," is now Chief of the Foreign Press. He is American on his mother's side, and on his father's side came of a cultivated family of art publishers. He is a graduate of Harvard, a scholarly author of medieval German history, an apt musician, a considerable comedian, and godson of Duke Ernst II of Saxe-Coburg-Gotha, brother-in-law to Queen Victoria. Hanfstaengl was an early Hitler devotee, and in 1923 lent the Party $1,000, a vast sum when the mark had fallen to thousands for a dime, which made possible Nazi control of the powerful *Völkischer Beobachter*, still the official Hitlerian newspaper. Hanfstaengl and his hospitable family were Hitler's first social mentors. "Putzi's" clowning and piano-playing were relaxations appreciated by the Corporal. As a participator in the Munich Beer Putsch in 1923, Hanfstaengl, with prison hanging over him, was for two years a voluntary exile in Austria, where he lived as Herr Schmidt. His recent propaganda film on the life of Horst Wessel (for which Hanfstaengl also wrote the theme music) was not allowed to feature Wessel's name and was little shown in Germany, owing to Göbbels' jealousy of Hanfstaengl. (Göbbels, as Minister of Propaganda, felt that Hanfstaengl was intruding on his field.) Hanfstaengl edited the famous book of Hitler cartoons, the only humorous Nazi publicity to date. Because of his linguistic gifts and worldly education, it was supposed when the Nazis came to power that Hanfstaengl would be named Foreign Agent. He was not, however, and Hanfstaengl's relations with the Führer have apparently of late become strained, because, it is said, he courageously criticized Nazi's curtailment of intellectual liberties. He has recently won a libel suit against the London *Daily Express*, which reprinted from the American weekly, *Time*, the following statement attributed to Hanfstaengl: "Damn those Oxford professors! I'll send some of our swine to burn down their Oxford." Hanfstaengl satisfied the English court that he had never said any such thing.

In spite of the worldwide rumors to the contrary, there seems no reason to believe that Herr Hitler is homosexual, outside of the fact that, until he finally had most of them shot, there were pederasts among his Party friends and file. But in Europe, where, as one of the frantic postwar phenomena common to capital cities of both the Allies and the Central Powers, homosexuality paraded in all walks of life, this is not sufficient reason to substantiate the charge. There is a rumor that Hitler was wounded genitally in the war. Whatever the cause, his real abnormality apparently consists of the insignificance of his sexual impulse, probably further deadened by willful asceticism. Emotionally, Hitler belongs to the dangerous, small class of sublimators from which fanatics are frequently drawn.

Being a man with no talent for friendship, Hitler's gift for disloyalty has been developed by the dramas of his career. Von Hindenburg at first considered that the Bohemian Corporal, as he called Hitler, could never keep his word and that as an unreliable rising young policitian might be safely elevated to the position of Postmaster General—but no higher. Had Hitler become Postmaster, dozens of his early comrades might still be alive. Of the many violent deeds which were part of the Nazi Revolution, the one for which Hitler was most bitterly reproached was the assassination of his old friend Captain Ernst Röhm, who in 1928 had written a pro-Nazi autobiography ironically entitled "The Story of a Traitor." In 1934, he was shot as one. Röhm was Hitler's first important convert to Nazi in the early days, was next to Hitler in strength as organizer, enthusiast—and troublemaker. In one of his many quarrels with Hitler for domination of the S. A. militia, Röhm resigned from the Party, and became a lieutenant colonel in the Bolivian Army. The death of Hitler's oldest friend was officially laid to Röhm's having secretly talked to "a foreign statesman," probably French—a crime which Hitler oddly said was punishable by death "even if they were only discussing the weather and old coins."

In over sixteen years' struggle for power and its maintenance, the Führer has been loyal only to one man—Adolf Hitler.

MARCH 7, 1936 So complicated is the German Führer's Austrian genealogy that it was finally charted in a Nazi exhibition, aptly entitled "The Wonder of Life." Apparently, Hitler's ancestors were long-lived, intermarrying, pious, Roman Catholic peasants who, wherever they dwelt and however they varied their surname (it took the three forms of Hiedler, Hüttler, and Hitler), mostly died in Spital, a town once near the Bohemian, now the Czechoslovakian, border of the mountainous Austrian Waldviertel district. Adolf Hitler was born of a lusty father past his prime —was, indeed, almost born Adolf Schicklgruber, since the father, a love child, was not legitimatized into a Hitler until his fortieth year. Adolf's mother's great-grandfather was his father's grandfather. The father's and mother's common ancestor was a farmer, Martin Hüttler (born 1762). Old Martin's grandson, and Hitler's father, was a cobbler, known by his mother's name, Schicklgruber. When he was forty years old and the husband of an elderly, well-to-do peasant woman, his wife bought him a job as customs officer and purchased the papers that gave him the civil right to his father's name, which he transmuted into Hitler. This Alois Hitler, in his fifty-second year and his third marriage, fathered Adolf Hitler of Germany today. Adolf's mother, Klara Pölzl, whom he looks like and loved, was a gentle, determined, youngish creature with sad eyes, who as a girl had worked as servant in Alois's house during his first marriage. They were related, because she was also a direct descendant, though one generation further removed, of Martin Hüttler. Thus Klara's Alois was not only her husband but also slightly her cousin and uncle, and certainly old enough to be her father as well. Adolf Hitler's inbreeding is as specific as that of any Austrian Hapsburg.

Adolf was born in the Austrian border village of Braunau-am-Inn, April 20th, 1889, in a house, now a cheap hotel prosperously pink-plastered, which must originally have been impressive with its fine rows of eighteenth-century, rounded windows, topped with stucco fans. Next to the building is a regimental barracks marked, ironically, with a plaque stating that there the martyred Austrian Chancellor Dollfuss had done his military service. At the town's edge rushes the river Inn, and over it passes the old bridge that has for so long marked the bitter boundary between Austria and Germany. On the Austrian side, the gigantic, wrought-iron, imperial Hapsburg eagle that was there in Hitler's childhood is still preserved, but today, at the German end of the bridge, the Führer's Nazi soldiers are the only decoration. His father's office, as Austrian customs inspector, is also as it was—a cubicle the size of a coat closet, hanging out over the cold river and still warmed by Alois's pretty, white porcelain stove.

The old man, who was ambitious and truculent, moved on to successive posts at Passau and at the city of Linz, where occurred two contacts which marked his son's life: the boy fell on a German history book detailing the glories of the Franco-Prussian War, and a history teacher who was a rabid

Pan-Germanist. The result was that, at the age of twelve, little Adolf officially announced that he had become a Pan-Germanist, and that he had "learned to understand and penetrate into the true sense of history."

As a schoolboy, Hitler thought his "talent for drawing indisputable," was good at geography and history, poor at all else, unpopular with other children, liked to roam the fields, wanted to be an artist, and had the courage to quarrel with his heavy-fisted father, who wanted him to be a civil servant. When Hitler was thirteen, his father died, and two years later his mother. Then Adolf, who had just recovered from lung trouble, set off for Vienna and art. Turned down by the Imperial Academy as indisputably without talent, he remained in Vienna and became a hod-carrier who preferred political reading and Wagnerian music to manual labor, and for seven friendless years nearly starved. Hunger, he later said, was his companion. He read gluttonously at this period, though exactly what only he knows. From later remarks, he apparently read enough Goethe to dislike him for criticizing the Germans; adored Schiller, that patriot's poet; and devoured all he could find about Bismarck, still the Führer's sentimental hero. What is more important, Hitler clearly read up on the Hapsburg Empire's lamentable history, thus founding his angry, racial Nazi *Weltanschauung* of today; he certainly also read the French Count de Gobineau, from whom he got his notions of Nordic race superiority. (The author's grandson, Serpeille de Gobineau, was an honored guest at the recent Nürnberg Nazi Congress.) He obviously read the philologist Max Müller, and not carefully, since Hitler's use of the adjective "Aryan" to describe race instead of language is as muddled, Müller had already pointed out, as to refer to "a brachycephalic dictionary." Most influential of all, Nietzsche must have been read by Hitler at this critical time. A recent Weimar photograph shows the Führer staring, maybe with gratitude, at the philosopher's statue. For Nietzsche's "Remember thy whip," Hitler later substituted his own "Heads will roll," but he took over intact Nietzsche's doctrines of the strong over the weak, and the right of the sacred individual to rule the vulgar mass. Hitler also says that in Vienna for the first time he came across anti-Jewish literature; Jews may be interested to learn that, according to Hitler himself, he struggled for two years "against being converted to anti-Semitism." Communists may be informed by his statement that he got through "Das Kapital" in two weeks. He also learned to dislike the proletariat, whom he found friendly to "free beer checks and inaccessible to abstract ideas"; to disapprove of the bourgeois mind as "being like cod-liver oil," or difficult to swallow; to liken parliamentarians (or government by representation) to "cackling male geese."

In these important, formative, Viennese years, young Hitler borrowed enough from the *Zeitgeist* around him, and from second-hand books he brooded over, to assemble—with the addition of a page or two he later took from Mussolini—the mental equipment he still uses today. Hitler early wrote that "in a man's youth appears the essential of his creative ideas." He has spent the past twenty-five years proving it.

In 1912, urged by his Germanophilia, Hitler left Vienna for Munich. Of his two years there before the war nothing is known, except that by day he painted houses, by night painted aquarelles and tinted postcards to sell, and studied at architectural drawing. For him the war was opened by his kneeling to thank heaven he was alive to fight for Germany, closed by his weeping in a hospital to hear Germany had lost. Because of a letter he wrote to King Ludwig III of Bavaria, Hitler, though Austrian, had been allowed to volunteer in August, 1914, in the 16th Bavarian Infantry Reserve, whose uniform he wore for the next six years. Hitler fought and was wounded in Flanders, got his second wound on the Somme, was gassed at Ypres, temporarily blinded, and, as lance corporal, was awarded the Iron Cross, First Class, rarely given to men of that rank. Apparently, he was mostly detailed to the lonely, dangerous service of carrying front-line dispatches; there's a story that he used to embellish them with flourishing, patriotic phrases when he considered their style defeatist or dry. He was disliked in the trenches; the soldiers thought him courageous but queer.

What he and his career are today sprang from post-bellum German demoralization. With the war and Kaiser lost, the results were a Weimar Republic, a Munich Soviet, Berlin governments of all colors popping up and down, money going only down, food scarce, national faith scarcer, and all over the land, little groups of men, each with a new brand of patriotism which, if they could only build it to power, was to be the country's single salvation. It was thus, in 1919, as an army lecturer to bolster morale, with the side duties of spying on these sometimes subversive political groups, that Corporal Hitler met up with the obscure national *Deutsche Arbeiter Partei* via its Munich unit, composed of six poor members. The club's funds consisted of seven marks fifty pfennigs when Hitler joined as seventh member, attracted by the party's belief that the World War was not yet over, since Germany hadn't won, and by a rather Socialistic pamphlet on productive vs. nonproductive (or bankers') capital, which the party had issued. This pamphlet Hitler read at 5 A.M. in the company of some mice whom he used to feed, and who shared his quarters. It was the turning point of his life. Under Hitler's immediate dominance, this modest workingman's club expanded into the *Nationalsozialistische*

Deutsche Arbeiter Partei and, eventually, became the rich, powerful, Nazi German government of which he is the Führer today.

The high points of his career are, briefly, as follows: In 1920, he resigned from the German Reichswehr to orate for himself and Nazi, then comprising thirty members; the following year, by a struggle, he had himself elected Party president and founded his *Sturmabteilung*, or S. A. Brown Shirt militia, then hardly more than a handful of men, now grown to 800,000. In 1923 took place the fatal Munich Beer Putsch. In retaliation for Nazis' having kidnapped the city's ruling Commissioner and forced him to proclaim a new government, the Commissioner, when released, collected troops and in a street battle routed the brown shirts. Sixteen Nazis were killed, or afterward died; Hitler and his friends fled, he being later captured at Uffing in the country cottage of Fräulein Erna Hanfstaengl, a sister of Ernst Hanfstaengl. Nazi members were by this time 15,000, its funds 170,000 gold marks. Hitler was tried for treason, pleasantly imprisoned for nine months with a typewriter, easy chairs, and friends, and finally had time, so he said, to write "Mein Kampf."

By 1927 the movement had changed, was more middle- than lower-class, and began shortly to be even smart. In fear of Bolshevism, one of the Kaiser's sons finally joined; the Kaiser gave funds, as did Thyssen of the Mulheim Steel; von Schröder and Wolff of Cologne, banker and iron magnate respectively; Bohde, of munitions; Kirdorf, of Rhineland mines; and many mistaken, rich Jews. Henry Ford, because of his anti-Semitism, was also asked to contribute. There is no reason to believe that he complied. The S. S., or the new, black-uniformed Schutzstaffel, a conservative and aristocratic Hitler militia (as against his khaki, radical, more plebeian S. A.), was ostentatiously organized. In 1930, Nazi sent one hundred and seven deputies to the Reichstag, had six and a half million votes, and was so powerful that frightened foreign bankers flatteringly called in their German loans. 1932 was the bad year for the party. Internal dissensions and over-hasty organization, treacheries and over-optimism, almost led Nazi to a collapse. President von Hindenburg, at the head of a coalition government, received Hitler for the first time, but didn't even ask his visitor to sit down, let alone offer him a government seat. The S. A. and S. S. were suppressed as *coup-d'état* plotters upon the discovery of a code telegram for the zero hour, which read "Grandmother dead." But after two years of adroit political maneuvering, Hitler's position had so strengthened that he was named Chancellor by Von Hindenburg and asked to form a cartel government. In 1934, on the old General's death, Hitler announced that he was combining the offices of President and Chancellor and that he himself was the incumbent of the new office. (With a similar sweeping gesture, Napoleon Bonaparte with his own hands once crowned himself Emperor of France.) At the same time Hitler made official his title of Führer, or Leader, first informally bestowed on him by a Nazi comrade. It is difficult for foreigners to understand what Nazi ideology consists of. In Hitler's own words, its "principles are based on a racial conception of the world," and it is a militant, hierarchal form of responsible, patriotic society with "the good of the State before the good of the individual," "with obedience going upward, authority going downward." Its original twenty-five-point platform demanded the abolishment of unearned incomes, the "breaking the bondage of interest," and the communalization of the big department stores. More recently Hitler has revised his economic theory somewhat, stating that "Capital is useful to trade, and trade is useful to capital."

Point 4 of the twenty-five contains Hitler's famous anti-Semitic decree: "Only those who are of German blood can be considered as our countrymen, regardless of creed. Hence no Jew can be regarded as a fellow-countryman." In the German business world, the results of Point 4 have been two: (1) In big shops, such as Berlin's greatest department stores, the Jewish owners have been retained as managers. Firing them from their own premises might result in incompetent management of the business, perhaps even bankruptcy and closing, and thus more Christian unemployment. Nazis do not state how much the Jewish ex-owners are paid for this new work. The large Jewish banks have been similarly reorganized. (2) In small Jewish shops, the owner is not retained as manager, since the small shops are ordered closed, and therefore need no managing. Christian shops have also been reorganized, as to their advertising, anyhow; in the provinces, especially, one sees window displays featuring "Aryan wool," "Aryan pork sausages," Aryan anything and everything. After a cattle fair near Düsseldorf, a scandal was caused by a cow's being led to her new Nazi barn by a poor Jewish peddler, her former owner; the cow was declared to be non-Aryan, capable of producing only non-Aryan milk, cheese, and calves. The Woolworth five-and-ten-cent stores in Germany were boycotted because Woolworth was declared to be a typically Jewish-American name. It is in the provinces, particularly in Bavaria, that villages display the signs *"Juden Sind Hier Nicht Erwünscht"*—"Jews Are Not Wanted Here." In an unprosperous hamlet near Rothenburg the sign reads, "Jews are like moths in the coat closet, like mice in the cupboard. They are not wanted here." Jews who in 1934 voluntarily fled from Germany to become refugees, principally in Switzerland and France, are now possessed of expired German passports, which the Nazi government will not renew;

this means the refugees are not only people without a country but, what is worse in bureaucratic Europe, people without identity papers. Thus they cannot obtain visas, and have to travel on *laissez-passers*, as in war times. The Jewish problem Hitler has raised is a vast one in emotional importance, both in and outside of Germany; numerically, from the German point of view, it is a small one. In 1934, there were less than six hundred thousand Jews in all Germany for the twelve million Nazi Party members to accuse of dominating the sixty-five million German Gentiles; today there are not quite a half-million Jews still in the Reich. It is difficult for inhabitants to leave a land from which they are permitted to take only ten silver marks to embark on a journey as momentous as crossing the Red Sea must once have seemed.

In the past year, Herr Hitler's official statements likely to affect public opinion in other countries have definitely mellowed. It is a matter of astonishment, even to anti-Nazi Germans, to learn of America's bitterness —greater than all Europe's combined—toward Nazi Germany. The American antagonism comes from the fact, Hitler says, that United States banks, business, press, and cinemas all are Jewish-owned. It is difficult to estimate how much Hitler really knows of other countries' reactions. In large German cities, most of the leading American, English, and French daily newspapers are for sale, though there have been times when such papers as the Manchester *Guardian*, the Parisian *Le Jour*, and the New York *Times* were banned. For his own information, Hitler employs private foreign agents, the most noted of whom is Herr von Ribbentrop, Hitler's roving personal Ambassador-at-Large.

While Göring tips his chauffeur for every funny new Göring story the driver can collect, Hitler dislikes jokes at his own expense, whether native or foreign. Political wisecracks are forbidden in music halls. Monologists with Hitler patter have been repeatedly imprisoned, except the fat Bavarian beer-hall actor, Weiss Ferdl, who nightly convulses Munich audiences with his sly Führer gibes. No one knows why he isn't in a concentration camp with Claire Waldorff, first famous for having discovered Marlene Dietrich and more recently noted, until her imprisonment, for her spirited cabaret songs about the Nazi chief. There are a few dinner-table jokes about Hitler, most of which begin with "It seems that Hitler was dead and went to heaven and—" The best of these jokes goes on to add that, at the pearly gates, Hitler said to God, *"Heil Hitler, lieber Gott!,"* to which God answered, *"Grüss' Gott, lieber Hitler!"*

At the moment, Herr Hitler's relations with heaven, as exemplified by his treatment of both Roman Catholic and Protestant churches, would certainly seem to be slight. The medieval Nordic mythology which Hitler, in spite of his own Catholic inheritance, has allowed to be officially called more satisfactory as a religion for modern Germans than the Judaically-based Christian faith is a notion which he undoubtedly got from Ludendorff, whose wife, by converting the old General to paganism and opening a bookshop for pagan literature, started the present Dark Ages cult. Physically, it is satisfying to many of the Hitler Jugend groups; politically, it is useful to the more mature Hitlerian leaders as a means of breaking up the obstinate unity of the two Christian faiths. Hitler has also suppressed the open practice of Freemasonry in Germany. Intolerance, he has always stated, is the measure of any movement's strength. "What would you think," he has asked, "of an advertisement for soap which stated that other soaps were also good?"

MARCH 14, 1936   As ruler of a great European power, Herr Hitler is the oddest figure on the Continent today, but even as a humble individual, he would still be a curious character. With a limited mind, slight formal education, a remarkable memory for print, uncanny powers as an orator, and a face inappropriate to fame, in fifteen years he planned, maneuvered, and achieved an incredible career, which was personal to him and has now become intimate in the lives of sixty-five million German people. His brain is instinctive, not logical, and has a feminine quota which, as a man of action, he has mobilized. Lacking the cerebral faculty of creating new public ideologies, as a fanatic he has developed his unusual capacity for adapting those of others. Being self-taught, his mental processes are mysterious; he is missionary-minded; his thinking is emotional, his conclusions material. He has been studious with strange results: he says he regards liberalism as a form of tyranny, hatred and attack as part of man's civic virtues, and equality of men as immoral and against nature. Since he is a concentrated, introspective dogmatist, he is uninformed by exterior criticism. On the other hand, he is a natural and masterly advertiser, a phenomenal propagandist within his limits, the greatest mob orator in German annals, and one of the most inventive organizers in European history. He believes in intolerance as a pragmatic principle. He accepts violence as a detail of state, he says mercy is not his affair with men, yet he is kind to dumb animals. He becomes sick if he sees blood, yet he is unafraid of being killed or killing. He has mystical tendencies, no common sense, and a Wagnerian taste for heroics and death. He was born loaded with vanities and has developed megalomania as his final decoration. He is an unstereotyped statesman, a specialist in the unexpected; as a politician, he nullifies opposition by letting friends oppose each other and by suppressing enemies. As a bureaucrat, he dawdles for months over minor decisions, and overnight forces large issues; he dislikes paper reports and loves oral information. He is garrulous; in interviews, the interviewer often fails to get in a word edgewise. Momentarily influenced by colder, harder minds, he is ultimately convinced only by himself. His moods change often, his opinions never. Since the age of twenty, they have been mainly anti-Semitic, anti-Communist, anti-suffrage, and Pan-German. He has a fine library of six thousand volumes, yet he never reads; books would do him no good—his mind is made up. Alternately polarized by indolence and furious energy, he can outwork his colleagues in a crisis. He has the mediumistic time sense of the imminent which is special to dictators. His disordered nervous system gives him a psychic superiority over the healthy and plodding. By his intimates, his fits of weeping are undenied and unexplained, and give none of them an advantage over him. At such moments, the neurasthenia of the Führer, with tears on his cheeks, but life and death in his hands, is too serious to be trifled with.

Today, music is the only medicine for Hitler's frayed nerves; it gives them their sole relaxation and gives him his greatest aesthetic pleasure. He has a passion for the piano, used to be inclined to beat time with his head at concerts, loves Schubert in song, Beethoven in symphonies, Wagner in opera. He also likes manly marches. For safety's sake, he is now accompanied everywhere he goes by his officers or secret-service men. Since he prefers to go alone to concerts, he therefore goes out increasingly rarely to good music. At the Munich Opera, the program, at his request, begs the audience to pay no attention to him if he is present. He has also had to give up his long, solitary walks, which were his only sport. (A dictator on foot is easily assassinated. It is now a penal offence to toss flowers in the Führer's path, for fear the bouquets may explode.) Like most Germans, Hitler loves the theatre. Since he came into power, his favorite plays have been the Lessing Theatre's long-run peasant comedy "Krach um Jolanthe" (Jolanthe being a sow), which he saw twice. His other favorite was "Tovaritch," which the censor had first forbidden, because it was by a Frenchman. When it finally was produced, Hitler went to see it, but asked the management to warn him five minutes before the final curtain so that he and his row of secret police could sneak out privately in the dark. However, he became so enthusiastic over the plot, which concerned the superiority of White over Red Russians, that he finally stayed on to the end to applaud heartily.

Probably because he failed to become either painter or architect professionally, Hitler has since compensated by regarding himself as Germany's governmental art arbiter, with some, though not enough, reason. Certainly he has talked nonsense about art history. "There is no such thing as

21

Chinese or Egyptian art," he said in one speech. "I've told you already that there exists no art except Nordic-Grecian." Yet despite the Vienna Art Academy's contempt, Hitler's early pencil drawings of cottages and trees are definitely gifted in the English album manner. As an amateur architectural draftsman, he supervised the plans for the Munich *Braune Haus*, or national Nazi headquarters. He also had an important finger in designing the new museums and government buildings now making Munich's charming old Pinakotheker Platz unrecognizable. Hitler's knowledge of German eighteenth-century romantic art is considerable. He appreciates good canvases. He recently gave Göbbels a canvas by Spitzweg, a period painter now becoming the vogue. For a wedding present for General Göring and Frau Emmy Sonnemann, Hitler ordered a copy painted of the Berlin Correggio called "Leda with the Swan." (He had first, for propriety's sake, ordered the marriage.) While he is constantly giving presents to his friends, he himself has no acquisitive hobbies or collections. His only two volitional possessions are a couple of police dogs, whom he adores. He always remembers the birthdays of his early Party comrades with gifts of fine books or minor objects of art. He himself constantly receives amazing and difficult donations from his people: a flock of black ducks which he passed on to the Munich Zoo; a streamlined locomotive (he hates trains); forty-one airplanes for his forty-sixth birthday; part of the Guelph Treasure, valued at two and a half million dollars. He has just been presented with a fabulous thirteenth-century monastic manuscript, illustrating early Germanic scroll writing. Such things as this he gives to his pet Munich museums.

In redecorating the Berlin chancellery palace for his use, Hitler's artistic ameliorations consisted mostly of a few fairly modernistic rooms, plus some Nordic mythological tapestries for the Great Hall which depict Wotan Creating the World. Last spring, with more enthusiasm, he redid his small Munich flat in his favorite baroque blue, white, and gold, according to plans he made and was proud of. This bourgeois flat in the unfashionable end of Prinzregentenstrasse is part of Hitler's odd passion for privacy and is probably also a symbol of his municipal loyalty to Munich, the city where he made his start, and which he considers the gem, for art and architecture, of all Germany. Being ethnologically a South German, and hence anti-Prussian, he has never thought highly of Berlin. The Munich flat, which he uses as a *pied-à-terre* in his frequent Bavarian trips, of late years harbored his half-sister, Frau Angela Raubal, a plump, simple widow who, until her recent marriage to Professor Doctor Martin Hammizsch, ran Hitler's Haus Wachenfeld mountain cottage for him. This once bucolic peasant châlet, now suburbanized by garage, sun parlor, rock garden, lawn parasols, is a few miles' climb above Berchtesgaden, situated next to the highest peak in the frontier mountains. From his German windows, down a long, low vista of green mountain meadows, hemmed in by gray, towering crags, Hitler can look over to the distant roofs of Salzburg and into that Austria he left and never loved.

What was once the peaceful hamlet behind his cottage is now a busy Nazi pilgrimage centre, with hawkers selling souvenir medals, beer mugs, and colored photos of *der Führer*. Beer is vended from what were once peasants' front porches, and milk is sold like holy water from the dairy that the Führer patronized when he was a poor political recluse. To control the motor traffic on the narrow hill road to his village, private cars are forbidden, and only local taxis and buses are allowed to pass, in thirty-minute one-way shifts, all going up on the hour or coming down on the half-hour. Since Hitler refuses to accept any salary from the government, his nonofficial homes, the Wachenfeld chalet and Munich flat, plus the brotherly subsidy he accords Frau Angela, and another he is reported to give to a reported full sister, Frau Paula Wolff, now in Vienna and formerly a stenographer, come out of his author's royalties from his printed speeches and "Mein Kampf." Hitler is supposed also to have a half-brother, Alois, whom he apparently doesn't keep, since Alois is alternately reported dead in Hamburg or else running an inn in Berlin. Frau Angela is the only relative whom Nazi publicity features.

It is impossible to estimate what Hitler's German "Mein Kampf" royalties might be; in Germany, the book's first two-volume edition was reported as two million copies, a publishing record. By 1933, only seven hundred and fifty thousand copies had been sold. Thousands have been given away as propaganda to young bridal couples; two thousand copies alone are now on the German cruiser Karlsruhe to be presented to natives of the Canary Isles, China, and the U.S.A. during a round-the-world run. The English translation of "Mein Kampf," also reprinted in America, was made by Captain E. T. S. Dugdale, who is a great-nephew of Macaulay, the historian, and a cousin of Lord Balfour. This translation, with the German publisher's permission, condensed Hitler's rambling work so the book might be sold at a moderate price. On the American edition, Hitler gets the customary author's fifteen per cent; about seven thousand copies have been sold here, which is a respectable sale but no landslide. The English and American editions contain the major anti-Semitic and anti-French remarks. In the official French translation, the troubling comments anent "destroying the French hydra," and "We want to wipe out France," have been deleted. They are, however, contained in an unauthorized verbatim translation, instigated by the late Maréchal Lyautey, who says it was "a book all Frenchmen ought to read." Not many Germans have read through "Mein Kampf" either; it runs to nearly a half-million words in its full form, and is a curious, earnest jumble of Danubian politics, dadaist art, racial theories, Germanic patriotism, Nazi ideals, random thoughts on the beauties of motherhood and autocracy, the shames of social diseases, suffrage, silly movies, Semitism, Bolshevism, selfish capitalism, and equally selfish proletarianism, all superimposed on some remarkably interesting politico-philosophical formulae. (Since Hitler became a god in 1934, and since hurried, official Party books about him agree in praise rather than in dates or detail, his "Mein Kampf" is still the soundest pro-Hitler work to be found in Germany. The soundest anti-Hitler works, not to be found in Germany, are Konrad Heiden's remarkable "Geschichte des Nationalsozialismus" and "Geburt des dritten Reiches.")

Though Hitler takes the worst photographs in the world, there are seventy thousand of them, all different poses, in the Berlin files of *Reichsbildberichterstatter* Heinrich Hoffmann, who is the official Nazi photographer. He and Hitler first met sixteen years ago, when Hoffmann was still anti-Nazi and—what was worse for a photographer—when Hitler still wisely refused to be photographed. It was Hoffmann's persuading Hitler of the propaganda value of the camera which led to Nazi Germany's using the lens more concentratedly and professionally than any other region on earth except Hollywood. Weekly news photos over the years show that Hitler's face has changed, and from month to month is still changing. The first official portrait (1921) shows a lean, serious, intent visage with nothing funny, fat, or fatuous about it. It shows a portentous, determined mouth; a mustache, brief but without humor; hair without a forelock and neatly roached back in a straight browline. In the last year alone, Hitler has gained fifteen pounds, less publicly visible in the waist (since his uniforms now include a compassing jacket instead of the former revealing Nazi Brown Shirt) than in the face, where weight shows in ounces of pouches beneath eyes and mouth, caricaturing the facial construction. His receding hair he has, like many mistaken middle-aging men, brought forward in a wiglike wad which nearly conceals the left eye. In photographs, his gold tooth fortunately does not show. Because of the nervous lines now drawing down his upper lip, his mustache has lately taken on a Kaiserlike tilt. In real life, what is physically most noticeable about Hitler, especially at a distance, is his hurried dogtrot and, close to, his quick, forced smile; both have that disjointed, rather comic quality seen in a film which is being run too fast. In repose, Hitler locks his hands low over his abdomen. His best likenesses are the unofficial snapshots taken by his Berchtesgaden mountaineer neighbors of him and their offspring. When he is alone and at ease with children, Hitler's face has the avuncular tenderness of the man who has not had babies of his own. After five minutes, little girls especially show a disposition, which petrifies their parents, to romp with the Führer.

Because of his passion for his châlet and for South German touring by automobile, a superb motor speedway, connecting Berchtesgaden with Munich, was constructed through the Alps to shorten by several hours the last lap of the Führer's run from Berlin. Time is precious to Hitler; he travels by air and road, far and fast, and with fantastic endurance. For example, after a midnight torchlight parade in his honor, he once left a Westphalian *Arbeitsdienst* camp by motor at 2 A.M. en route for a flying field near Bonn, where he took a plane for Munich, arriving at 4; by dawn he was setting out again by motor for Wiessee, close to the Austrian frontier, which he reached by breakfast. After an hour he motored back to Munich for lunch (which he couldn't eat), made a private speech, dictated a national broadcast statement, and flew to Berlin, arriving at 10 P.M. This, it is true, was not a usual but a special twenty-hour routine, being that of June 30th, 1934, or the day Captain Ernst Röhm, and seventy-odd other official traitors, were shot at Wiessee, Munich, or Berlin. Hitler's interest in flying has greatly encouraged German aëronautics. His favorite machines are a tri-motor Junker and a silver-and-black steel Immelmann, both monoplanes. He is as conversational about motors in general as an American boy, will explain how freewheeling is wrong for small, and sensible for big, cars. Franconia is his favorite motoring province; he likes to stop at noon by the roadside, spread a robe on the meadow grass beneath trees, and have a picnic lunch.

Almost two years after having come to supreme power, the Führer is still the most protected man in Europe. His latest special Life Guard, or black-uniformed *Leibstandarte*, even wear his name embroidered in full in silver script on their cuffs. These guards, patterned on Frederick William's gigantic *lange Kerle*, are supposed to be six feet tall, and, as members of the aristocratic S. S. militia, must observe special oaths and conduct. Chosen socially and physically among the élite, they are to found Germany's new racial, eugenic Nazi nobility; they cannot marry without permission or until both they and their fiancées, back to the fourth generation, are proved, on examination, to be both Nordic and fit for matrimony. All S. S. men are supposed "never to meddle," to "preserve an aristocratic silence" in public argument, to hold monthly meetings (in full uniform), when they may not smoke or leave the hall during speeches, and at closing they must sing their corps song, "Though All Should Prove Unfaithful," standing at attention during the last verse. They are also supposed to carry in their pocket, for propaganda distribution, three copies of the day's *Völkischer Beobachter* Party newspaper. They are to act as "the most model Nazi Party members that can be imagined." It isn't known how many of these models form Hitler's Life Guard, its strength never having been given out.

Since Hitler's coming to power, the phrase *"Heil Hitler!,"* with the Roman arm salute (originally a password among his militia), is now the social greeting *de rigueur* among Germany's civilians. It is officially called "the German greeting," in distinction to the old *Bürgerliche Gruss*, or bourgeois *Guten Tag*. In Bavaria, where the greeting used to be *"Grüss' Gott,"* Hitler's name has been substituted for that of God. As most German aristocrats still click their heels, kiss the ladies' hands, and, if in uniform, add the old-fashioned military salute, these, plus the Nazi arm-flinging, make modern German salutations fairly acrobatic affairs. The latest civilian rulings are as follows: "Between people of the same station, it is correct to bend the right arm at the elbow to an upward angle so that the palm shows. Then say *'Heil Hitler!'* (or at least *'Heil!'*). To people distant in the street, lifting the hand is enough, though for personal greetings in a room, *'Heil Hitler!'* should definitely be added. Should you meet someone who through social or other circumstances is not of your rank, then don't bend the right arm but stretch it out straight on a level with your eyes, at the same time saying *'Heil Hitler!'* Always *heil* with the left arm if you are leading a lady with your right."

By Hitler's decree last summer, his swastika flag was declared to be Germany's sole official emblem (von Hindenburg had previously authorized its general use, except on barracks and boats). In "Mein Kampf," Hitler states that he chose the swastika as sign of Nazi's "struggle for the triumph of Aryanism." (Hitler doubtless copied his emblems from the *Hakenkreuz*, or swastika, on the coat-of-arms of Abbot von Hagen, which decorated the Lambach monastery, where, as a once good Catholic, young Hitler was a choir boy.) As for the design of his flag, Hitler states that "a dentist from Starnberg" suggested its white circle, to which Hitler, "after repeated experiments," added the background of red, "the color which most infuriates one's opponents." The proportions of Germany's flag today are based on Hitler's measured designs of 1920. It was also as long ago as 1920 that he conceived the publicity value of those colorful decorations which have put Nazi Germany's mass meetings and parades into the front rank of European theatrical performances. Hitler's use of flags, banners, scarlet, gold, of music, of singing, and of marching, massed men, made last summer's Nürnberg Nazi Congress a week of unusual sights—especially to the two hundred foreigners he allowed, by special written invitation, to attend.

Because of his incessant speech-making, last spring two nodules were cut from Hitler's vocal cords, an operation common to hard-worked opera singers. There is now talk that another operation is imminent. Ten years ago, when he was making eleven speeches nightly, when his goal was to talk in every German city, when he was orating daily for hours and without pause before hundreds of thousands, in wind, rain, or smoky beer halls, he was warned that his voice could not last. It lasted long enough to talk his Party into power. Hitler is a born spellbinder of the emotional type, who produces in crowds the excitement he produces in himself. His oratorial powers were the bases of his career. From the first, Hitler was the kind of public speaker who, when heckled, could find an explanation quick as lightning and make it sound like thunder. He has always talked in prophecies and rhetorical numbers: "After fifteen years of filth and mire . . ." or "One thousand years from now, when the superior Nordic race . . ." He loves words like "destiny," "honor," "place in the sun," "pollution," "purity," "my comrades," "our enemies." Though he makes few gestures, his oratory used to wilt his collar, unglue his forelock, glaze his eyes; he was like a man hypnotized, repeating himself into a frenzy. Today, his goal gained, he is calmer on the speaker's tribune; his voice, restored by the operation from his former sinister screaming and croaking, is now a pleasant, barking baritone. His accent and vocabulary are still inelegant Austrian. Though his sentences are sometimes too involved to make grammatical sense, his meaning is always clear.

Public speaking is Hitler's real passion. As a little boy he made speeches to other little boys. The first time he addressed a crowd of two thousand, he says, he thought his heart would burst with joy. "I knew how to talk!" he later triumphantly wrote from prison, where, sure enough, his undeniable gifts for political oratory, plus other violences, had led him. Hitler has moved up to his present supreme power on words. Where most newcomer autocrats in history have rushed into rule by a *coup d'état*, Hitler rose slowly to Reichsführer by fifteen years of lecturing. "What I do and say are matters of history," he has stated. Actually, he and his Nazi Party mounted less on their actions, or even on the troubles of the country, than on his propaganda lungs. Success hasn't silenced him; he still addresses his millions. Anyone on the Continent with a radio can, if he chooses, often hear the bang of the Führer's favorite "Battle of Badenweiler March," which exclusively heralds his approach, hear the roaring *"Heil Hitler!,"* and hear the master's voice. Adolf Hitler still talks more than any other man in Europe.

The Olympic Games

BERLIN, AUGUST 16, 1936 Anyone who attended the XI Olympic Games conscientiously for two weeks spent eight hours daily in the open air, rain or shine; sprinted miles from swimming pool to polo field, from hockey stands to jumping pits; and became as lean and strong as an athlete. The Games did us non-competitors a lot of good.

While the Stadium's track and field sports dominated the first week, the swimming pool was the sell-out of the second. Under the floodlight of the sun, the pool took on the intimate, sensual quality of a backstage scene in a musical-comedy theatre, with the pool's orchestra blaring waltzes and the nearly naked international stars, male and female, parading their forms and talents with professional half-unconsciousness. Most Olympic women track and field athletes lacked gender; all lady swimmers were the contrary. The Japanese were the most exotic aquatic troupe. America's blond high diver, Wayne, was the pool's Apollo. Our Mrs. Hill diving through the air, our Medica swimming through the water, and any Japanese in a relay race caused the most turbulent tension. The German starter invariably first screamed at the swimmers and then fired his gun, after they had been frightened into the water. At the high divers' daily practice, the pool's borders filled with athletes of all nations, come to watch in their gay team clothes. Only the Americans, in their blue serge suits and blue-banded straw sailors, looked like small-town travelling salesmen. Other nationals looked like country swells. The Hungarians had red jackets with gold-embroidered coats of arms, and green hats with strange sprays of feathers; the Canadians had scarlet blazers with a white maple leaf; the Swedes appeared in lemon yellow and sky blue, and the Germans in chocolate; the Mexicans wore their national sombreros and sandals; the Hindus had rose turbans; the Japanese were in mouse gray with comic caps, and the French in blue tricots and berets.

There were many surprises in the events themselves. Germany's brilliant rowing on the Langer See; her supremacy among the twos and fours, with and without coxes; her trial-heat defeat of the English double scullers, her licking Switzerland, which had beaten the British at Henley, and her nearly licking Washington, astounded everybody. Washington won, in dirty shirts and filthy rain, with a sprint up to the line that nearly killed all Americans present, including the crew. They were heiled by the Olympics' greatest assemblage of what Berlin calls its royal family—Herren Hitler, Goering, Göbbels, von Blomberg, Frick, Darré, and von Papen. Equally astonishing was Poland's fine fencing in the thirty-three day and night fencing séances Foreign fencers shout when thrusting, and argue and gesticulate with all five officials, who argue and gesticulate back. Another surprise was the Hindu hockey team, and its handsome, sari-clad womenfolk. The surprise in polo was the poor attendance. The only real crowd was that drawn by the team from Hamburg, one of the few provincial cities rich enough to support the proper ponies and turf. The yacht racing at Kiel also lacked éclat, though the German fleet attended and fired guns. Reported rough weather kept ticket-holders from boarding the steamer which followed the sails around. The awards themselves were troublesome. Great Britain got the gold medal in the six-metre class only after Norway had entered a protest against the Swiss boat; Italy won in the eight-metre class only after a stormy session among the judges. The other outstanding Olympic unpleasantness was at the opposite end of the social scale—in boxing, which took place nightly in the beautiful half-glass Deutschlandhalle. The boxing was bad, the judging worse; nationalism was rampant.

Even the higher ranks had to be reminded what they had come to the Games for. In his official box at the Stadium, Herr Hitler was seen to flap his hands affably to silence the over-talkative King Boris, and to point to the four-hundred-metre relay race as being more sport than political small talk.

After a day of the world's hardest military equestrian jumps and some postprandial Beethoven, the 1936 Games were over, and a half-million provincial Germans and foreigners, in Berlin for the weekend, were facing Monday morning and home.

The Germans have been criticized by everyone, including certain Germans, for too lustily cheering their victories and sometimes their rivals' failures. Considering the megalomaniacal nationalism which Germans have recently been taught, it should in honesty be reported that they never groaned, as did some folk, at the monotony of the American victories, but each time rose to the Stadium orchestra's "Star-Spangled Banner" and heiled the hoisted Stars and Stripes with protocol politeness. The best German sportsmen were the proletarian bicycling fans, who hailed the

French hundred-kilometre winner with the sporting upper-class cheers that Olympiads are supposed to promote every four years, and usually don't. Certainly the press was prejudiced; it headlined minor German victories at the expense of major Olympic news.

There will probably be significant changes here after the Games. One, surely, will be in the Döberitz Olympic Village, where the male athletes dwelt, which will become an important demonstration centre of Germany's new "organized career" theory, which will require every man aiming for a top position to learn his job from the bottom up. In the Döberitz *Offizier Schule*, young officers, instead of being granted a commission at once because of blood or brains, will first serve one year as buck privates, pass their technical exams, be made *Fähnriche*, or cadets, and then, as lieutenants, go into the Reichswehr. There has already been a small military experimental school at Dresden; the ex-Olympic Village camp will be the first great formal test of the theory of totalitarian education for the new Army's new leading men.

The other changes, which everyone prophesies, will probably be similar symptomatic socializations. They will be toward what early Nazi theorists termed the Left, will aim at continuing capitalism and checking the accumulation of riches, and will expand popular paternalisms, such as the *Kraft durch Freude's* vacation-fund bus voyages, now being visibly enjoyed by working-class Germans on every picturesque German highway. Secondarily, the changes may include a redistribution of real estate, now valuable for the first time since the inflation, and, in Berlin especially, still dominantly owned by non-Aryans. The real-estate adjustment will probably be unlike that which was made in the case of the banks and department stores, formerly just as dominantly non-Aryan-owned, since the land, one hears, will be sold outright through a board oddly similar to that of our wartime Alien Property Custodian. The third rumored change will be the lowering of restrictions on admission to the select small Nazi Party— the first time fair-weather members will have been admitted since the Party came into power. Ironically, German businessmen, who since 1933 have become sold on the Nazi government, because business is better, are the ones who aren't going to want to join, because they are too busy and being a Party member can take a lot of time.

Certainly business, which means money, is now almost more important here than ideology. Germany's recent 700,000,000-mark loan, subscribed within ten days instead of the month the banks expected, was, after all, not a fresh floating of capital but a refloating of part of billions of marks of old short-term notes in the shape of a new long-term loan. The Olympic Games helped some. The government permitted Berlin hotels a substantial price boost, so that foreigners with the half-priced registered mark practically paid for their lodgings at the usual rate. Furthermore, foreigners were forced by the German government to purchase their Olympic Games tickets in foreign currencies, which brought in dollars, pounds, francs, etc., as unguents for Germany's dried-up credit system. Indeed, the Games were managed as a brilliant banking coup which, with the excitement about how far and fast athletes could run and jump and swim over and under things, no one seemed to notice.

Owing to Germany's recent record of slow but sure material success within and sudden diplomatic victories outside her borders, the average German's reaction to his government has audibly changed. He now has a mild tendency to criticize, almost comfortably; to regard Herr Hitler with diminishing hysteria and increasing admiration; to give the Leader the praise, to give the machinations of certain of his intolerant friends and the machinery of his Party the blame. For Germany, in more than one sense, 1936 has been an Olympian season. Though still stumbling over the downtrodden bodies of the churches (fuller than ever of churchgoers), synagogues, science, and fallen currency, the III Reich has in its third year got into what seems its adult stride. Only a determined deaf-and-blind visitor to any corner of this land could fail to see and hear the sight, the sound, of Germany's forward march.

The Schauspielhaus gala of "Hamlet," starring, and produced by, Gustav Gründgens, afforded visitors [to the Olympic Games] three-quarters of a remarkable theatrical evening. Here was a new and strictly Nordic version of the melancholy Dane, with his castle built of rough logs, his rampart guards wrapped in fur raglans, with wool mufflers tied over their ears, and not one ghost but many, doomed to walk the earth amidst shadow and macabre light effects. Never has Shakespeare's most thoughtful play seemed so violent. Gründgens' Hamlet is a prince who wears revenge and madness rather than poesy and speculation as his sombre dress; he shouts, he whispers; his mother and stepfather scream with weary woe; Ophelia in her floral madness climbs tables and chairs distributing her rue. To further heighten excitement, a revolving stage is used, and about its pivot one sees the protagonists circle and wander to their final sad tableaux. Gründgens' finest readings seemed marred by his narcissism; the spotlight on his handsome hands, further brightened by reflections from the odd tin table used in the family-supper scene, was a vulgar if beautiful distraction. From the gravediggers' comedy on, the whole well-calculated production slipped into disorder, and Gründgens' death scene, endlessly prolonged by marching soldiers, trumpets, and presenting of

31

arms, seemed almost local burlesque. One visitor, at least, left the Schau-spielhaus with the impression that Hamlet was going to be given a fine Party funeral.

Salzburg Music Festival

AUGUST 27, 1936   At the Salzburg Music Festival, now drawing to its close, Arturo Toscanini and Lotte Lehmann are still in the lead, with Verdi and Wagner running second, and Mozart coming in a poor third. The Maestro's presence in the Festspielhaus has made musical history that will last for many moons. New York, Paris, and London have recently had him as a concert director, but only in Salzburg does he direct operas now. His direction, in his sixties, of the opera "Falstaff," written by Verdi in his seventies, has been a triumph for the older generation and an incalculable treat for those of all ages to whom this gorgeous gay music, too rarely produced, is nearly unknown. In his domination of this opus, Toscanini established himself by his tempi as the Greenwich of musical time, by which other directors must set their batons. He so synchronized the Vienna Philharmonic Orchestra in the pit and the Italian-language singers on the stage that an opera made from English Shakespeare's "Merry Wives of Windsor" became a unique Austrian unity. The female cast was special both for face and for voice, with a handsome unidentified American, billed as Franca Somigli, enacting Mistress Ford. Angelica Cravcenco, as Mistress Quickly, looked like a Palma Vecchio portrait. Mariano Stabile, of the Scala, probably found Falstaff the ideal rôle of his career, in spite of his too ugly makeup.

Toscanini's second triumph was in "Die Meistersinger," thanks to his new second-act terminal tempo, to his reducing of choruses to the small whisper of a woodwind, and, above all, to his bringing Lehmann's voice to full glory in the quintet. Though the rôle of Eva suited her in Salzburg no better than it has anywhere else on earth, nowhere has her isolated artistry ever assumed more character of its own. Variable in mood and rhythm, criticized here last year and hailed here this season, Lotte Lehmann has been the outstanding female and vocal personality of the Festival season. In "Fidelio" (more Lehmann's and Toscanini's than Beethoven's in its dramatic speed), in those spoken lines which most singers fall down on, she lifted herself to histrionic heights. Toscanini's morning concert of

Brahms' Deutsches Requiem; Lehmann's *Lieder* recital with Bruno Walter at the piano, in an intimacy which musicians loathe and the public loves; the Shostakovich Symphony, directed by Rodzinski of the Cleveland Orchestra, and certain of the Dom concerts finish the list of Salzburg's performances.

The Salzburg seasons were once intended to feature Mozart in the town where he was born. He could have been born in China so far as the importance of this year's "Don Giovanni" was concerned. Probably the most interesting spiritual Mozart work, closer to that studious ideal for which the Mozarteum was founded, and which has since been forgotten, was "The Goose of Cairo," a rediscovered comic-operetta manuscript, tenderly sung and enacted at the shabby Stadttheater by a student group called Internationale Opernstudio, and directed by Alberto Erede, who has worked with the Christie private Mozart theatre at Glyndebourne.

Salzburg's one operatic novelty this year, Hugo Wolf's "Der Corregidor," built on the same libretto as the "Ballet of the Three-Cornered Hat," and conducted by the too affable Bruno Walter, seemed no more momentous in the Festspielhaus than when it was given in Vienna and London. But English patronage is important to Salzburg's cashbox. Wolf is *chic* in England. He seemed less so in the Salzkammergut.

The sinister snobbery which suddenly marked the Salzburg Festivals three years ago, and which since 1933 has helped the management pull itself out of the red, still obtained this summer, though the hangers-on have been less choice. As if they have come to stare at wild animals, the local townsfolk still line the curb across from the Festspielhaus and in broad daylight watch the *haut monde*, in tail coat and décolletage, descend, usually in rain and mud, from limousine, taxi, or plain one-horse Salzburg surrey. With some operas starting at five, by four the smart Oesterreichischer Hof lobby is filled with ladies with bare backs, and the river bridge is lined with young bucks in dinner jackets and Tyrolean hats. For going native is part of going to Salzburg. The famous Café Bazaar is filled from breakfast to midnight with women from all over the world in dark bodices, Gretchen blouses, gay aprons, calico skirts, and flowered kerchiefs. Their menfolk are rigged up in embroidered leather shorts, mountaineers' jackets, and cerise handkerchiefs. If the sight doesn't cut your appetite, the Bazaar offers the best complicated cakes and coffee with whipped cream in town. Owing to the frenzied fashionableness of Salzburg, hotel prices are fantastic. Eight dollars a day for a room without bath seems fantasy in a countryside where charming inns furnish a single bed, also without bath, but with breakfast, for a dollar. For night life, there is gambling till three in the morning, and Count Alfred Salm has opened a restaurant, but the operas begin so early and last so long that by eleven-thirty every sensible soul is in bed—and *in extremis* after all the gossip, crowds, and social and artistic hysteria. It would seem that, as a serious world musical centre, Salzburg is weakened socially by the presence of the rich, without whom it couldn't have kept going, and who by inflating prices have kept the poor from coming. Artistically, the Festival seems in danger of being sapped at its source by the combination of envy, interference, and dawdling which is as indigenous to Salzburg as its beautiful, bewildering baroque.

Bullfighting at Nîmes

JULY 28, 1937 Because men are tragically fighting men in Spain, the best of Spanish bullfighting this summer is being done in southern France. The Fascists hold Andalusia and Salamanca, where blooded fighting bulls grow, the Loyalists have held out in Madrid, to whose ring great bullfighters go. In order to get together, both *matadors* and animals have passed over the border for special French *toros* at Bordeaux, Bayonne, Dax, Béziers. Especially for one who prefers good architecture to good bullfighting, the handsomest of the recent *corridas* was that at Nîmes, in the magnificently preserved antique Roman arena where Christians used to be killed for sport. The Nîmes program was special, offering eight rather than the usual six bulls, with, as matadors, Vicente Barrera and Domingo Ortega, two of Spain's most noted today, plus, as extra attractions, two *novilleros*—Juanito Belmonte, natural son of the great Belmonte who revolutionized modern bullfighting technique, and Luis Ortega, Domingo's adolescent brother. As sprigs of famous fighting families, both youths genealogically disappointed. Belmonte, aged twenty-one, wearing green embroidered with gold, had his father's lack of physical grace, without his grace of mind; had the paternal underhung jaw and shambling gait, but was himself nothing but vulgar show. Luis Ortega, aged seventeen, tall, slim, with a face like a blond angel, dressed in rose and white, was an unformed caricature of his brother. He finally achieved his second kill, amidst boos, with five whacks of the *descabello*, the *coup de grâce* sword.

In Barrera and the senior Ortega there was more chance to see what *aficionados* adore and others abhor—that stylized, highly technical, dangerous drama between silk-clad men and a well-horned beast, with the long-drawn-out and disciplined *repartie* of pose, pace, defense, death.

Ortega's work with the *muleta*—his specialty, rather than the cape—was called fine, his first kill done with enough style for him to be given the ears, tail, and a delirious Nîmoise ovation. According to experts, his repertory is limited but he gives much emotion; he fights bad bulls best; his great ability to dominate the animal is a matter of instinct, not knowledge. Other critics think him a perfect mechanic rather than the complete artist. Barrera's opening *veronicas* were admired for their calm, and he was superior in ring organization. He's credited with unusual knowledge of bulls—what they'll do next, etc. *Aficionados* never agree on anything; in general, however, they agreed that both *matadors* gave about a thirty-per-cent performance, with their *faena* marred by the high wind that is always blowing out of the empty cerulean sky in the Midi.

Le Toril, best French bull-ring paper, said that the eight bulls (from the famous *ganadería* of Count de la Corte) were "two middle-sized, two small, and four indecent animals." In the last twenty-five years, bulls have been bred smaller and less dangerous than before Belmonte, who, around 1908, because of his weak legs, invented his famous modern technique of bringing close to him the bull he could not actively pursue. To make up in drama for this loss of wide action, fighters since Belmonte have developed what's called the repertory—passes with the cape like the *mariposa* invented by Lalanda, or Manolo Bienvenida's *veronica* done on one knee. This has given fighting a fancy gypsy turn. Killing with the *descabello* instead of with dignity, danger, and the true swordsman's *estoque*, has also added to the present degeneracy. Since the beginning of the Spanish war, even the money end has weakened. Few Spanish matadors now fighting in France receive more than 25,000 francs for a performance. The Loyalist government at Valencia has just announced it will suppress bullfighting in its provinces entirely.

Because the peasants couldn't leave their work in the vineyards, the midsummer *corrida* was less patronized than the October fête, when the grapes are safely in the vats. English *aficionados* came to the fight from London but Americans were scarce. Though most people don't know it, France has had bullfights since 1853, when the first combats to death were organized at Bayonne for Napoleon III. It's still against the law to kill bulls in the ring and promoters just cheerfully pay the death fine. The horses all wear *caparazones*, or mattress protectors. We always close our eyes during the horse business in a bullfight, but heard that all the horses left the Nîmes ring alive.

Sidney Franklin, America's unique and fine bullfighter, says that till the war in Spain a matador got 25,000 pesetas, or $5,000, for killing two bulls, but that his clothes and outfit—three *banderilleros*, three *picadores*, a valet, their traveling expenses, plus bribes to journalists, which was a high item—had him down $2,000 before he marched into the ring. A swell fighting suit (*traje de luces*, "suit of light," so-called from its gold or silver embroidery) costs from $300 to $500. A popular *matador*, with ladies after him and a big public to please, has at least six suits. The embroidery is done by nuns who otherwise specialize in making priests' copes. A fighter has to be valeted, the clothes being too heavy and tight to get into alone. It takes a full hour to dress him carefully in the following unvarying routine: First, three pairs of stockings—elastic, thick white cotton, then rose silk ones ($12 the pair). Then longish drawers with knee tapes to hold up the stockings. Then a linen shirt, formerly of embroidery but now pleated plain, and with strings to prevent its riding up (a hanging shirt-tail can catch a bull's horns and bring death). Then the trousers, thick tricot and so tight that the valet hauls up while the *matador* jounces down. The trousers have further stocking-holding knee bands, also an inner abdominal girdle to hold in the fighter's stomach; his shape is important in the ring. Next the eyeleted pumps, artfully made to turn up at the toes when empty but flattened by the fighter's foot so they don't slip off. Then the false *coleta*, or pigtail, fastened to the back hair by a chenille-covered metal button. Then the sequined vest and finally the coat, weighing twenty-five pounds, of three thicknesses of buckram beneath massively embroidered stiff satin. The sleeves are not sewed in, but are left free under the arms for action and sweat, and are attached to the coat's shoulder by cords running through eyelets. The cape for the march into the ring is pale satin, often embroidered with pansies, morning-glories, rosebuds.

The day of the Nîmes fight, the leading butcher shop advertised that during the week it would sell to its exclusive clientèle the meat of the superb bulls killed in the local arena that hot Sunday afternoon.

Preparing for War

MUNICH, SEPTEMBER 1, 1937 There are three developments in Germany which even the tourist can note. Firstly, Germany is storing enough of what it already has to last out a two years' siege (just in case Russia marches through Czechoslovakia); and what Germany hasn't got, it is brilliantly inventing. Thus articles marked *Reine Wolle* (pure wool) now contain twenty-five per-cent pure wool and seventy-five per-cent pure something else. Automobile tires are an *Ersatz* composition of old rubber and a coal-oil compound, are very good indeed, cost ten per cent more than the real article, and, like it, are at the moment unprocurable. Copper, which Germany lacks, is being substituted for by aluminum, whose components Germany hasn't either. German businessmen are making money, but they can't make raw materials, which are nationally more important. Though edible grains may no longer be fed to livestock, even this summer's exceptionally fine wheat, rye, barley, and oats crop will not suffice for man, and winter bread will contain corn. However, no potato shortage will be permitted to provoke the populace, as one did last winter in Berlin and Hamburg. Germany's gold reserve, for import purposes, is mounting. Principally owing to America's purchases, Germany's balance of trade last month was for the first time in five years markedly favorable; also, Germany has annexed (and paid for in marks) about one-third of German investors' foreign holdings which pay in dollars, pounds, etc.

Secondly, the painful struggle between Church and State has been temporarily stalemated by pro-Vatican Mussolini's recent private protests. That the Pope is considered by chancelleries to have lost holy ground by blessing the Ethiopian campaign means nothing to pious Bavarians, to whom faith means all. Bavarians owe their last rich architectural and artistic inheritance to the eighteenth-century Catholic princes, priests, and bishops who supplied them with rococo in palace and church—a rich aesthetic legacy that lets Bavaria deplore Prussia as parvenu, Protestant, and poor in mind, and makes northern Nazi paganism seem antipathetic to southern soul and sight. Munich churches now display a yellow placard which begins *"Bewahre den Glauben"* and ends *"Ich bin und bleib' Katholisch"*: "Guard the faith ... I am and remain Catholic."

Thirdly, there's a growing bewilderment in the public mind. Despite the "no war" promises of their Führer, on whom, rather than on his advisers or their regime, the people's devotion and belief still loyally concentrate, Germans see their efforts, hopes, abnegations, and productions all going into the molding of a war machine and mentality. The young Germans already lost in the Spanish war have added grief to the confusion. The average simple German feels, not because he thinks Nazism a failure but precisely because he believes it a success, that it ought now to relax on its laurels and give the citizens a rest. Since 1914, Germans have been making sacrifices, and always only for themselves. Thus their nationalism has become tiring to others and tribal to themselves.

Here, close to the frontier which divides the two German-speaking nations, southern Germany talks hopefully of the *Anschluss* which certainly northern Austria wants. As the Austrian folk admit, they love liberty, but you can't eat it. They are eager to trade what freedom they have left for food and the *Ersatz* work with which Germany, rather than give idle relief, supports its unemployed.

Across the other frontier, bordering France, there pass daily nice German cars filled with fortunate German families en route to the Paris Exposition. At the French end of the Kehl boundary bridge over the Rhine, the French have just finished constructing a sort of turret, which, if it contains anything, contains something that, if popped out, would aim straight toward the German sentries at the bridge's other end. Maybe not only England's but everybody's boundary is on the Rhine.

Wagner at Bayreuth

AUGUST 21, 1938 This being the one-hundred-and-twenty-fifth anniversary of Richard Wagner's birth, his late and early works are being featured in expansive festivals all over Germany this summer. In his home town of Leipzig, his *juvenilia*, "Die Feen" and "Das Liebesverbot," operas rarely brought down from the attic, have been given gala revivals. Munich has presented "Die Fliegende Holländer"; Dresden and Zoppot have specialized in Wagnerian spectacles. To honor the maestro's birth, Bayreuth, world centre of Wagnerianism, has conscientiously presented "Parsifal"—as usual, with the Ring and "Tristan" thrown in. Mme. Germaine Lubin of the Paris Opéra has been the Kundry of the season; foreign artists are not unheard of here. Bayreuth started giving "Parsifal" as a novelty in 1882, when Wagner was still alive. It's too late to change now. Bayreuth's Wagnerianism has nothing to do with the calendar. It's a cult.

Bayreuth's Wagnerianism also has nothing to do with chic. Bayreuth today is not Salzburg as Salzburg was yesterday, filled with international snobs in evening clothes. In the late-afternoon sunshine, just before the traditional trumpeters blow the first act's leit-motiv as a curtain warning, the Germans gather to parade, in the unstylish best they've got, around the ugliest great opera-house exterior in Europe. They have gathered not for modes but for good music, and they get it.

In the three performances we heard (two of them six and a half hours long), signally the best stretch was the second act of "Tristan." Indeed, it really was wonderful Wagner, with the mature Frida Leider singing superbly as Isolde, Margarete Klose in glorious voice as Brangäne, and the super-Aryan Lorenz at any rate acting handsomely as Tristan. Though Bayreuth was the maker of the Wagner tradition, the stage business was strangely unorthodox. Isolde was first discovered on the right rather than on the left of the ship, and Tristan and Isolde sang the guilty-love duet walking, and not while embracing on the garden bench. However, "Tristan's" new décor followed the geography of the original maquettes, which are preserved in the Wagner Museum here. Thus the set supposedly depicting Cornwall was a meticulous portrayal of the lovely forest landscape of the Muggendorf-Bayreuth highroad.

We also noted that in "Parsifal" the Christian crosses are now left off the Crusaders' backs, and that the Holy Grail is no longer illumined from above, as from heaven, but operates, like a flashlight, on its own earthly power. And motion-picture effects replaced "Die Walküre's" former realistic fire and steam jets, though the antique steam machinery, still housed in a humble shed behind the Festspielhaus's stage door, was smoking like mad all day.

Most of the performances begin at four and end at ten-thirty. There are two entr'actes of an hour each for the supposedly underfed Germans to snatch a bite at the Opera's park restaurant, where three German portions of cold cut and salad sufficed after "Tristan" for the two American ladies and three Frenchmen at the table next to ours. "Das Rheingold," being the shortest of the shows, began at five and was over at half after seven. The best-dressed Germans we saw in Bayreuth that night were the Wotan family. In fact, the costumes for all the productions were in tailoring and coloring altogether admirable.

By tradition no applause is permitted in the Festspielhaus, where a respectful silence is supposed to obtain. The handclapping is done later in the restaurant across the road when the singers make their famished appearance for supper. By tradition also a table in the restaurant is still marked *"Reserviert für Fr. Wagner,"* in recollection of the days when old Frau Cosima Wagner built up Bayreuth's financial backing there, principally by wisely inviting the rich to sup and the poor only to have an entr'acte glass of beer. The family honors this season have been shared by three of the composer's four grandchildren—a portly miss who inherited her full share of her grandfather's nose, and two grandsons, strange, unworldly blond youths in provincial black suits. One of them, Wieland Wagner, designed last year's sets for "Parsifal."

Each of the half-dozen great opera houses of the earth puts its special signature on its productions of grand operas which are otherwise common to all. The Metropolitan has costly star voices; Salzburg had glamour. The mark of Bayreuth is its laboriousness. Here, through the sonority of the orchestra, through the traditional score-reading, through the earnest, scholarly singing of mature stars, the listener senses the tremendous labor that Wagner's genius entails to this day. Here stars, like professors, can be middle-aged and fat and be forgiven; they have devoted half a lifetime to the study of their notebooks. Bayreuth's Wagner is in the great, windy, meticulous racial tradition of the composer. Wagner elsewhere may be more entertaining, more brilliantly vocal, gayer. Here it is the real solemn thing.

Salzburg

AUGUST 29, 1938 It's a pity to strict Mozart music-lovers who for seasons have been decrying the Salzburg Festspiele's international snobbery as all wrong didn't turn up for this year's performances. Certainly Salzburg's festival is now national and unsnobbery. Indeed, maybe the *Anschluss* has turned Salzburg into the bigoted Mozart-lover's dream —a beautiful, dreary, unfashionable rain-soaked baroque town, offering excellent summer opera to simply dressed, easily impressed visitors of Mozart's race and faith. The famous Café Bazaar is no longer packed with Salzkammergut peasant costumes, since the American and English gentry who used to go peasant there have taken themselves someplace else this year. You can now get a seat and *Schlagobers* on Tomaselli's terrace even in a downpour. There are no foreign motorcars paralyzing the streets, which are *Sturmabteilung*-policed and one-way; there's no quaint horse-and-carriage traffic jam on the bridge at the opera hour, for the German visitors walk to their Mozart and take their umbrellas. The Bristol Hotel has become the Nazi *Generalkommando* headquarters; the other smart hostelries have philosophically sliced their prices; and we were able to buy a ticket for "Don Giovanni" one hour, instead of one month, before the curtain went up. There is nothing left of the Salzburg Music Festival except the music.

For "Don Giovanni," the house was nearly full and partly papered. The singers were as good as formerly—Pinza was the fine-voiced seducer, Lazzari was Leporello, Elisabeth Rethberg a shrill Donna Anna, Luise Helletsgruber a deliciously complaining Elvira—but all of them were slowed down by the worthy routine conducting of the Nazi newcomer, Karl Böhm. Singers, not conductors, used to be Salzburg's star drawing cards. It is unlikely that visitors will come from the ends of the earth to see Munich's young Hans Knappertsbusch substitute for those great absentees, Toscanini and Bruno Walter. Their absence this year has left Furtwängler as an isolated magnet. The Nazi management has literally turned the Festspielhaus hind side before. The enlarged stage is now where the balcony used to be, and the seats are new, more numerous, and don't squeak—all great improvements. The Vienna Symphony is functioning here intact for the last time. Its racial purge will occur after its seasonal utility is over, when its best fiddler and 'cellist, along with a dozen other non-Aryans, apparently all in the strings, will be dismissed. The brass-and-wind section —as usual, Christians—will remain untouched.

No foreigner except a fool could expect to get at the inner politics of a city which has just been through what it still calls a revolution. And no democrat except a dolt would deny that the Germans have a talent for organization, the lack of which apparently gave the Austrians their chief charm. And surely no Marxian to whom Communism has become a theology should fail to comprehend that to millions of Austro-Germans, Nazism is a violent economic religion in which Hitler, like Lenin, is revered as the new order's savior and the exterminator of the opposing cult. The Salzkammergut was a known northern Nazi stronghold. A combination of desperate hope for work and a long-starved Teutonic instinct for hero worship made Herr Hitler's surprise Salzburg visit after the *Anschluss* the greatest postwar emotional event in the lives of most of the population, all of whom, whatever their convictions, were at the end of their political and economic resistance. Salzburg could count on its Festspiele tourist season to provide only three months' work in the year. Jobs for the town's eight thousand unemployed have principally been supplied (at lower wages than under the pre-Dollfuss Socialist regime) by the twenty-four-hours-a-day work on the local *Reischsautobahn*, or motor highway, which already runs from Munich to Reichenhall and will, Hitler promised the Salzburgers, reach Vienna in 1941—three years after he got there. Such magnificent four-lane roads now ribbon all of Germany. They have been Herr Hitler's chief WPA project and are not reserved for pleasure cars but serve also as camion routes, since the bulk movement of materials and men is of strategic importance in Germany's place-in-the-sun policy.

Contrary to outlanders' suppositions, the Austrian peasants are Hitler's most passionate supporters, although they are also in certain Catholic districts his bitterest resisters. The local *rentier* upper middle class, which is linked to the aristocracy, has slowly disappeared with the postwar collapse of investments. The lower middle class, the Salzburg shopkeepers, is pro-Nazi because it is pro-cashbox. The *Anschluss* has stimulated business by opening the nearby frontier to free trade. Even as tourists, the Germans, though not spendthrift, are not to be sneezed at. They pack the small inns, where they eat and drink more than the Austrians have been able to afford in years. The Austrian resorts like Badgastein, however, have been hard hit by the *Anschluss*, the American and English boycott, and the enforced lack of Jewish visitors.

In the Salzburg countryside, the peasants have been frightened for two weeks by talk of impending European war. It cannot happen, they say with fanatical ardor. Their Leader has said he wants no war. His new followers believe him.

Vienna

SEPTEMBER 5, 1938   It takes a long time to change what has been a popular, indolent, proud Central European capital city. The Viennese have never been in a hurry. They are in no haste to become German today. Vienna's surface seems little changed by the *Anschluss*. Because to say "Heil Hitler" is still a novelty, the Viennese say it more often than Berliners bother to at this late date, but as for getting down to hard work—which was what the *Anschluss* was created for—work is still something the Viennese haven't got the hang of, though they're talking about it as they sit in their pleasant coffeehouses. The original Party members, previously in prison, are now openly and heavily Nazi. The bewildered bulk of non-political middle-class people, who are pinning their faith on Hitler rather than on his Party's methods, ardently long for the *Anschluss* to succeed. As they say, it's their country's last hope. After all, the *Anschluss* isn't a new idea. It's so old that the Treaty of Versailles specifically forbade it nineteen years ago.

The most noticeable Nazi manifestation in Vienna is a display called "The Eternal Jew," the largest anti-Semitic demonstration, aside from pogroms, ever held in Christendom. It is the Nazis' first propaganda exposition here and is currently on view in the vast Nordwestbahnhalle. There prints, photographs, models, electric signs, graphs, fine typography, and sales talks are used not to make consumers buy a product but to make the public boycott a race. There is a movie, with loudspeaker comment, of a kosher calf-killing. There are ethnological wax masks, and photographs of living international and local Jews, the latter grouped according to those spheres of activity the Viennese Jews governed, apparently without the slightest difficulty—the theatre, law, medicine, the dress trade, violin-playing, banking, etc. As the founder of *Bolschewismus*, Karl Marx Mordechai, so-called, gets a whole wall; as, apparently, the equally reprehensible founders of *Kapitalismus*, the Rothschilds get two walls, one of which displays their increasingly distinguished family tree. Among the pictures of the international intelligentsia to be shunned are portraits of Charles Chaplin, Heine, Mendelssohn, and, more oddly, Layton and Johnson, an American Negro jazz team. Posters of the exhibition are displayed on the Viennese billboard pillars along with ads of American movies, for it is considered one of the summer attractions. "The Eternal Jew" is visited daily by thousands of Austrian Christians. On their faces is a strange expression which pagan faces doubtless wore when watching exhibitions at which Christians were thrown to lions.

On their doors, Vienna's Christian shops show a swastika and a sign, "*Arisches Geschäft*"—"Aryan Business." Absence of the sign establishes the unhappy identity of Jewish shops. Jewish doctors and lawyers are being deprived of their right to practice, but Jewish shops, rich and poor, are still open to trade. We bought non-Aryan stockings in the humble Mariahilf Jewish wholesale district and a non-Aryan washrag in the smart retail Kärntnerstrasse. There is no Austrian money any more; the *schilling* has been replaced by German money sent from Berlin by the trainload a week after the *Anschluss*. Though wages are lower than in Germany, business taxes, and hence prices, are about three times as high. What Viennese Christian business hopes to gain from the *Anschluss* is Germany's tax, price, and profit levels, which could perhaps make Vienna's desperately needed financial comeback possible. Because of its economic peculiarities, Vienna has always been in the position of a kept lady. Indeed, one of the reasons for the great Austro-Hungarian Empire was that it enrolled nearly everybody in Central Europe to help keep Vienna in the style to which she was accustomed—and without which she literally and tragically can't make her economic ends meet. Some critics fear (and others hope) that Hitler, in attempting to absorb the population that gave Vienna her famously shiftless charm, has bitten off more that is insolubly Austrian than even he can chew.

Intelligent Viennese are disappointed that German, rather than Austrian, Nazis have been given the new government jobs and grieve that Austria, once an empire, is now called Ostmark and is a province. But they accept their position as part of the new German Empire's *Drang nach Osten*. As a defeated German people, they are rather proud of it, and think that if there is a war, this time they will be on the winning side, since they believe that

43

no matter what it is that Herr Hitler plans to do (and they don't know what it might be any more than if they didn't belong to him), nothing can stop him now. The psychology of the defeated nations has as much as economics to do with their trends today.

Whipped cream and pastries still flourish in Viennese coffeehouses; Schöner's Restaurant remains costly and well patronized; Sacher's is less well run than when old Frau Sacher made it hum. The famous *Kipfel* crescent rolls are still white but will probably soon be an adulterated gray. As a means of conserving meat, Germany is going to send North Sea fish to the Viennese, who don't like any fish except the fresh-water varieties and certainly won't trust any foreign fish that has been on a train. Except for their blue trout and *fogosch*, the Viennese prefer noodles, which they won't get, as a substitute for meat. Deep-sea products are unfamiliar to them. As the Viennese say, few of them have ever tasted the corner of an oyster.

Over three hundred thousand modest Viennese, principally of the working class, have already applied for a K.D.F., the midget German motorcar that bears as its name the initials of the *Kraft Durch Freude* movement it is to exemplify. When it comes out, it will cost only 950 marks, which may be paid in installments of 5 marks weekly. It will go 14 kilometres on a litre of gas and use an eighth of a litre of oil per 100 kilometres. People who earn 500 marks or more monthly will be forbidden to buy the car, which is intended for the small earner. In Vienna, an annual vacation of two weeks with pay has been instituted by the Nazis, and waiters now work nine instead of fourteen hours a day. Hitler's increasing concern for the proletariat generally and his growing harshness toward their bosses have placated the masses as much as they have frightened the owner class. The recent severe slump on the Berlin Bourse, almost the only uncontrollable indication of what really goes on in Germany, probably partly came, as the German propaganda stated, from the enforced liquidation of Jewish businesses. As the propaganda didn't state, the slump also more than probably was caused by the panic of manufacturers of war supplies, who can no longer hope to make fortunes in case of hostilities, as their factories certainly will be nationalized. Their fears are perhaps a sort of message from Mars.

It now appears that though the Germans' swift occupation of Vienna was a complete surprise to the Viennese—and to some of the smartest foreign journalists in Europe—a forty-eight-hour secret warning had been given Austrian Nazi chiefs. There's a rumor that before the *Anschluss* Schuschnigg told visiting ex-President Hoover, who must have sympathized, that he expected eighty per cent of the population would vote against him. Some foreign observers think that Schuschnigg and Hitler would each have received a twenty-five-per-cent *Ja* vote if the balloting had been honest, but it is conceded that each would have had the ballot boxes stuffed and that Hitler would have won. Nobody except argumentative fanatics, of which there are already thousands, thinks the ninety-nine-per-cent pro-Hitler vote was natural. Most foreign observers think that Hitler had sixty per cent of the people in his favor. It must be recalled that voting means little to the Viennese. They weren't allowed to vote under either Schuschnigg or Dollfuss; their parliament has long been suppressed; they are used to accepting dictators without consulting the voting booth.

Near the baroque pilgrimage church of Maria-Taferl, a pleasant hundred kilometres from Vienna, lies the Schloss Artstetten, once the residence of the Archduke Francis Ferdinand of Austria. He is buried in its adjoining private chapel. The Schloss has four fine towers and a handsome roof. Had the Archduke remained beneath it, he would not have been assassinated by a Serbian at Sarajevo on June 28, 1914, and there would have been no last great war. No one seems to know what will provoke the next great war. This ignorance today is Central Europe's only bliss.

Budapest

SEPTEMBER 17, 1938 Up to a week ago Budapest had largely busied itself with religion. For two months the city buzzed with a Eucharistic Congress and festivals celebrating the nine-hundredth anniversary of St. Stephen's death. Now Budapest, like all its neighbors, is occupied with wondering about war. War wouldn't seem especially ungodly in these parts. Hungary belongs not so much to the Western World as it does to the East. Moreover, for a thousand years the same war has been intermittently going on between the same tribes. Whereas the English and French would be fighting for a Czechoslovakia they'd never laid eyes on, Hungarians would be fighting against a Czechoslovakia which they've known well since the Treaty of Versailles and which is conveniently next door. As a result of the last World War, there are seven hundred thousand Hungarians living in Czechoslovakia—a minority, forbidden to speak its own language in its schools. For these seven hundred thousand, a million or more Hungarians are prepared to die.

Because Hungary stands at the borders of the East, where Britain has always been so influential, faith in England's power as a mediator was until recently limitless. Hungarian hopes rested on Lord Runciman purely because he was British. Then, in a pinch, he stated that he had prayed to God that there might be no war. To Hungarian ears, this sounded more like something left over from the Eucharistic Congress than like help from Downing Street.

The best way for the Budapest visitor to understand why he will never understand the present Central European situation is for him to cross the border into what used to be part of Hungary and is now Czechoslovakia. Here he will discover that in any big country house the owner is an aristocratic Hungarian, usually broke; that the house servants are Slovaks; that the tradesmen they buy from are Czechs; that the estate farmers are Jews; that the stablemen are Magyars; and that the gamekeepers are Germans, originally imported by Queen Maria Theresa, mother of Marie Antoinette. Each of these peoples has at some time, physically or financially, conquered or been conquered by one of the others. None of them has ever forgiven or forgotten. This is the old setup that makes the Central European problem of today. The problem's only novelty consists in the fact that of all these groups, who as underdogs desire the complete autonomy which as top dogs they always refused to give, only one, the Sudetens, have a Herr Hitler behind them. One suffices. Because of this one, the frontier roads into Czechoslovakia were this summer blocked at the border by *chicanes*—great concrete blocks forming a maze through which a peaceful car had to meander and which no military tank could crush. In the meadows at either side of the road the barbed-wire entanglements already lay waiting.

History looks queer when you're standing close to it, watching where it is coming from and how it's being made. The Hungarians think that President Wilson had a mother-in-law who was a Czech and that that is why he converted Czechoslovakia into a ruling state. Certainly Clemenceau favored presenting the Czechs with the Sudetens because he believed that in one generation the Sudetens would become loyal, loving Czechs and thus form a dandy bulwark against Germany in the next war. In Central Europe, history not only looks queer; sometimes it looks funny.

The Hungarian nobles have their economic problem and their own limited way of solving it. At a really smart Hungarian dinner party, the gentlemen are all deaf after a day shooting on their game preserves. Shooting, exporting the bags, and renting their shoots to foreigners have become a regular business now with most Hungarian nobles, great landowners, and bishops. About 150,000 pheasants and 100,000 partridges are taken out of Hungary by French, American, and English sportsmen yearly; the supply of Hungarian game is the largest left in Europe. The birds, being bred wild, on an average fly higher and faster than in England. Hungarian stag-stalking makes Scotch stalking seem tame. The Hungarian animals are huge in size and the stalking is done from mountain huts. The biggest stags are available in September, the rutting season. At a rented shoot, the first stag costs $750, subsequent animals $500. The biggest supply of water birds is usually found on the Hortobágy, a vast Hungarian marsh also populated by horses, long-horned gray cattle, cowboys, and shepherds. It has one inn for sportsmen and can offer literally millions of wild geese at this time of year. From the high road, in an hour our borrowed Ford flushed several thousand ducks, flocks of snipe, clouds of wild geese, and dozens of indignant storks, dallying on their way to Egypt.

Of all the Entente nations, Hungary alone never went through a postwar food shortage. In August, Hungary's countryside is one great grain, melon, and corn patch. About sixty per cent of the peasants are well off, in that primitive, rural, eighteenth-century manner which one finds east of Western Europe. In the town of Mezökövesd, famous for the elaborate costumes of its peasants, we saw women paying tidy sums for superb cerise silk skirts. The pretty skirts are losing popularity, however. In general, the most modern thing about the Hungarian peasants today is their ugly, up-to-date, ready-made clothes. It's the living conditions that remain in the costume period.

The Hungarians don't know what will happen to them if Herr Hitler makes war. They don't know what will happen to them if he doesn't make war. They'd rather be dead on the field of battle than absorbed. The farther east one goes in Europe, the farther east one finds the people fatalistically suppose Hitler will go. In Hungary, for instance, the peasants don't think he'll stop with Czechoslovakia. They think the Führer will push on to Istanbul.

War

BORDEAUX, SEPTEMBER 24, 1939 The news of Russia's entry into Poland seemed as staggering an announcement as the news of Europe's entry into war. Reacting to Russia's move, the French newspapers were full of questions, not answers. Few experts knew what to think; most of them, in the first moment of grim shock, tried not to think at all. Probably this is a moment in Europe not to think but only to feel, since events have passed beyond rationalization. Only two things seem clear: Russia's German-inspired seizure of Poland has augmented the confusion, mental and military, which all Europe, including Russia, Germany, and Poland, now must be prey to; and circumstances have created a crazy chaos in which those people who believed neither in Nazism nor in Communism are the most shocked, ideologically, at the opportunist union of Europe's two ideological enemies.

There is no sense in discussing the war physically, especially considering its momentarily stagnant condition. Its psychological possibilities, which time alone will develop, are the only sources of possible illumination. These psychologies can merely be guessed at, not known. Foremost will be the German people's mental reaction to the new pragmatic association with the Russian "Red Devil," which Germans have for six years been trained to fear and loathe. Second will be the Germans' economic reaction to the stringencies of a war which few wanted. The possibility of a German civil revolution is the most important factor, capable of being delayed by any victories and specifically by the victory in Poland. The other psychological elements are mixed but coherent. Though conquered in whole or in part, what are the Poles, Czechs, Slovaks, Moravians, and even the Austrians going to do now, and how many German regiments will be required to watch them? What will be the psychology of the Baltic (and even some Balkan) states which have been brought into the line of menace? Only an idiot could deny that in the last three years Germany has been the one European state, new or old, to attract adherents through the pull of success and fear, as well as through brilliant, active plans. But only Herr Hitler himself could now fail to see that, alarmed as certain European countries are at the thought of Russia's power thrown in Germany's favor, there is also a new feeling of desperate relief brought about by the possibility that Hitler had made his first, typically Teutonic psychological error and made it earlier in this war than the Kaiser made his mistake in the last. On millions of European neutrals, Russia's entry into Poland had the same emotional repercussion as the sinking of the Lusitania. Like all men of destiny, Hitler has been surrounded by an aura of infallibility. Now, no matter what battles he may win, he has begun to suffer a certain loss of those who trusted him and an even greater loss of those who only feared him. When the war on the Western Front finally enters into its full bloody horrors, it may well slow down, or perhaps speed up, all or any of these psychological ingredients, which are an important part of the war's ammunition.

In Bucharest there is now being distributed a German map dated 1938.

It announces for the spring of 1938 Germany's conquest of Austria, and for that autumn the taking of Czecho-Slovakia; for the autumn of 1939 the taking of Poland; for the spring of 1940 the conquest of Yugoslavia, and for that autumn the taking of Bulgaria; for the spring of 1941 the triple taking of France, Denmark, and Switzerland, and for the autumn of 1941 the possession of the Ukraine. This last may be a typographical error which Russia can now correct. France is full of mobilized Frenchmen who will never believe in the completion of this preposterous, Napoleonesque plan of Germany's.

Many of the thousands of North and South Americans concentrated in Bordeaux, from which port their homebound ships now exclusively sail, are short of funds, having waited in Cherbourg or Havre for English, French, or German ships which never appeared. For a fortnight there has been total confusion at the office of the United States Lines. Americans, prevented by police from entering the building, have had to stand on the sidewalk to wait for their baggage tags. Some of them have stood there for a week, with time off only for meals and sleep, in order to have their return sailings, peacefully purchased four months ago in Chicago or St. Louis, properly verified. Meanwhile, the American Consulate has functioned admirably, patiently, and paternally.

To help evacuate the Americans *en bloc*, French formalities have been suspended in Bordeaux. Old visas need not be renewed. Our nationals are spared the hours of waiting required by the prefectures elsewhere to have identity cards stamped for arrival and departure, nor have they, as formerly, had to furnish photographs for a special slip retained to molder in France as evidence that one more foreigner has departed hastily in the tragic sequence of world events. Bordeaux cafés are overrun with the visitors from the Americas, and with the animated local population. Though the town is blacked out at night, gas masks have never been distributed; by day all shops are open and busy. Americans, French officers, and rich Brazilians patronize the Hôtel Splendide's terrace bar; the more modest drinkers populate the cafés along the handsome Allées de Tourny. Among the more celebrated *évacués* are Toscanini and Hubert Fauntleroy Julian, the Black Eagle, who plans to fly something for somebody in the war if he can get things fixed up in Harlem first.

The Bordeaux-Paris trains are now running on their regular ten-hour schedule. Last week they took twice that time bringing most of the refugees down here. Those who travel by motor carry, if wise, gigantic tins of gasoline in their luggage because fuel may be lacking in certain localities.

In the centre of France, we saw big green auto-buses from Paris waddling along country roads, piled with furniture for barracks, or with soldiers' kitbags, or with fodder for horses. We saw big guns being drawn by sextets of superb Percheron stallions. We saw lines of whippet tanks, painted in camouflage, rattling along forest highways. In chalk, on the necks of the tanks, the drivers had scrawled their best girls' names—Lulu, Marie-Louise, Simone, Beb. In name, anyhow, the girls, too, were all going off to war.

Paris, Germany

DECEMBER 7, 1940 Paris is now the capital of limbo. It is a beautiful French city on the banks of the Seine which only Berlin, the capital of Germany, knows all about.

This was to have been remembered as the century of perfected human communications—of swift air-mail letters flying over oceans and lands, of radio stations comfortably crackling sparks of news into the night, of wireless-telephoned headlines presumably announcing that mankind was all well, and of streamlined trains hustling across continents with unimportant postcards. From Poland, from Denmark and Norway, from Holland and Luxembourg and Belgium, there have been few communications in recent months. Johannesburg, South Africa, however, recently reported capturing storks which had just migrated from Holland. Around the birds' legs had been wrapped messages that read, "The German occupation of Holland is hell" and "The Dutch people are dying under injustice." As there are not many storks at any season in France, as French carrier pigeons have been forbidden to fly by the Nazis, and as French postmen may not, under penalty, cross the boundary from the Occupied Zone into the Unoccupied, written communications, even smuggled, have been rarer from Paris and the rest of Occupied France than from any other German-conquered territory. In the autumn of 1940, the French of Nazi France communicate even with each other principally by word of mouth. With the rest of the world, they don't communicate at all.

Information about Paris brought back to America by French refugees, American expatriates, members of volunteer ambulance units, and the like, is also only oral. With their tongues they tell you what they saw and heard with their own eyes and ears, but they have no papers to prove it. The only documentation on Paris today is in Berlin. Still, on three or four particulars, all these informants agree.

First: Anybody who loved Paris and grieves at its plight is fortunate not to see it now, because Paris would seem hateful.

Second: Parisians permit themselves exactly two words to describe their conquerors; Parisians say that the Germans are *corrects* and that they are *emmerdeurs*. This superficial adjective and this scatological substantive, taken together, are probably important historically. By *corrects*, the French mean that physically, militarily, one might almost say socially, the Germans have up to now conducted themselves with disciplined decorum. By the second word (now used as practically political terminology by polite Parisians who never before used such a word for anything), Parisians mean that they find the German mentality, its shape, its principles, its whole Teutonic mentation, boring to a malodorous degree. These two curious words so far represent merely the intellectual periphery of a vocabulary not yet filled in with words for the despair and anguish which some of the conquered French are beginning to feel not with their brains but with their stomachs and hearts.

Third: Owing to the Germans' mania for systematic looting—for collecting and carting away French bed linen, machinery, Gobelin tapestries, surgical instruments, milk, mutton, sweet champagne—the French will have to become a race of liars and cheats in order to survive physically. For example, milk is now sold only for babies, pregnant women, and people over seventy. Parisian housewives stand outside dairy shops for hours with rented babies in their arms, or with pillows stuffed under their apron fronts, or with borrowed grandparents hanging on their shoulders. In the old days, soldiers, Christian or pagan, looted with disorderly enthusiasm—raping, robbing, staggering down roads with booty and with blood on their hands. In the new Aryan looting manner, Nazis ring the French front-door bell while an Army truck waits in the street, and soldiers do the job of fanatical moving men.

Fourth: The German passion for bureaucracy—for written and signed forms, for files, statistics, and lists, and for printed permissions to do this or that, to go here or there, to move about, to work, to exist—is like a steel pen pinning each French individual to a sheet of paper, the way an entomologist pins each specimen insect, past struggling, to his laboratory board. For years, Parisian liberals had suspected that their Republic's increasing tendency toward petty bureaucracy was weakening France. As totalitarians, the Germans seem sure that their bureaucracy, organized on the grand scale, is their strength. Even the suburban fisherman now must

51

have written permission to fish in the Seine, though they haven't caught anything in generations worth writing a line about. As one old fisherman cried, "Soon even French minnows will have to learn to read and write German!"

At least three conscious psychological attitudes characterize the German treatment of Paris. The first attitude is that of moderation, almost of consideration, toward Parisians, provided such moderation gets a good name for the Germans. Their treatment of the French has the quality of a cruel but polite *opéra bouffe*. With political shrewdness, and out of racial egomania, they want the French to refer to them as *des braves types, tout de même* ("nice fellows, after all"). This cynical moderation is part of a carefully calculated publicity program. By chance, it often slightly benefits the French, but if it doesn't help German publicity more, it's cut short. Or, to quote the French, "The Nazis offer us, let's say, twelve grains of rice and then take away from us eleven potatoes. But if they're not praised by the populace for donating twelve of something small and taking only eleven of something large, they take both the rice and potatoes, which makes the score twenty-three to nothing." The rice and potatoes are purely figurative. Rice is so scarce that it is not given out except on a doctor's certificate, pure starch having already reached pharmacopoeial ranking. As for potatoes, by August the Germans had their soldiers guarding the fields while the potatoes were still in the French ground. The French rarely see potato bugs, which they elegantly call *doryphores*. This summer there was a pest of them, and of German soldiers, whom the French grimly nicknamed after the bugs. "*Ja*," admitted one German soldier, "we're the *doryphores*. We will eat the potatoes and you will eat nothing."

The second psychological attitude of the Nazis is that Parisians must be equalized. There is an effort to reduce the individualistic French to a common level. For example, a French doctor who has been an expensive heart specialist is forced to become a general practitioner at small fees; a lawyer who has been used to pleading only before the highest courts is forced to handle petty litigation. This equalization policy is also applied materialistically. Because German *Hausfrauen* lack bedsheets, since German looms have been working only for the Army, many Paris housewives have been forced to give the Nazis all their sleeping equipment except two pairs of sheets, one blanket, and one mattress for every occupied bed in their homes. If the sheet owner lives in a château and possesses, as one old chatelaine did, sixty pairs of fine yellow linen sheets left from her trousseau, the Germans do not even leave one pair but take them all as punishment for her plutocracy. By this policy of equalization, the Germans hope to unsettle the modest French into hating the clever or rich and into admiring the Nazis for what Nazis call their special sense of social justice.

The third psychological attitude of the conquerors applies only to themselves, but it enormously affects the French. Oddly enough, each local German *Kommandant*, or *chef*, is free to interpret Nazi policy according to his own judgment or temperament. Thus the German *Kommandant* in one Paris *arrondissement* took bedsheets from every house on only one side of the street, whereas another took them from every other house on both sides of the street. Such uncertainties add to the demoralization of the unhappy French. A *Kommandant* in Neuilly expressed his individuality by charging his French mistress's new wardrobe and his florist bill to the *mairie*, which, after a scandalized protest, was forced to pay. On the other hand, the *Kommandant* of a town near Saint-Malo has become noted for his strict honesty and justice toward the French. The *Kommandant* at Fontainebleau, however, has another notion of justice. He punished the mayor for having fled his post of duty when the Germans arrived, forcing him, on his return, to quit his mayoral mansion and live in a furnished room. Because an insouciant little Fontainebleau boy made a *croque à jambe*—stuck his foot out—and tripped a German soldier, all citizens of Fontainebleau are compelled to step into the gutter when a Nazi approaches them on the sidewalk.

In the application of only one of their better-known Nazi psychological devices have the Germans been remiss in Paris. Though addicted, when at home, to book-burning and the destruction of criticism in print, not until the last of July, five weeks after they marched into the capital of highly literate France, did the Germans get around to suppressing anti-Nazi books. In all, only one hundred and sixty-two books, including, as a belated addendum, "France and Its Army," by Charles de Gaulle, now of the Free France movement, have been put on the index, though for the five years before the collapse France was fuller of anti-Nazi literature than it was of any other means of self-defence. As for German *Lieder* and other German music, only Germans are permitted to perform them in Paris, since foreigners, the Nazis say, would demean both the racial melodies and the noble language. A stranded American baritone who offered to sing Schumann's "Dichterliebe" at a private concert was informed that he might sing only degenerate music, such as Debussy or Ravel.

Before the German Occupation, Paris was the world's greatest news-publishing and news-reading centre, having eighteen major daily newspapers, one of them, the *Paris-Soir*, with the Continent's largest daily circulation—two and a half million. Only a handful of the papers remain, and all of them function entirely under the German eye and reflect its news squint, though the actual writing of the Paris newspapers is done by French journalists, since a job is still a job. The *Paris-Soir* had the distinction of being the only paper to have its printing plant (which was a new one and considered the best in Europe) actually handed over, with the door keys, to the Germans immediately after they made their entry into Paris. The rich gift was tendered by *Paris-Soir*'s Fifth-Column Alsatian elevator man. Prepared for any emergency, however, the Germans had brought to Paris with them several fonts of French type—easily distinguishable from French-manufactured type—which they now use to print their official Paris daily, *Les Dernières Nouvelles*. Under the Germans' solemn efficiency there are, comically enough, two editions of *Le Matin*—a morning *Morning* and an evening *Morning*. The Nazis have also started a labor paper, sternly entitled *La France au Travail,* which is a substitute for the old sitdown-strike backer, the Communist *L'Humanité*. Except when a sort of crazed hunger for news, even false, seizes the Parisians (a new neurasthenic phenomenon which can visit a civilized population straitjacketed for months, cut off from world communication), most of them refuse to buy the Nazi French papers, because they don't believe the news.

The most blatant of the new Nazi papers is the anti-Semitic, anti-Free Mason weekly *Au Pilori*, which already has acquired a reputation for the obscene cartoons it publishes. It is sold on the street by the young Gardes Françaises, the new French Hitler Jugend, to which all French girls and boys from twelve to fifteen must now belong. The July 26th *Au Pilori* contained an editorial entitled "Egalité," which opened, "The democracies only govern by lies. They've made us swallow that fantastic yarn that one man is as good as another." The policy is against "anonymous and international capitalism," favors the so-called "capital-labor" of National Socialism, demands that the French admit France erred and deserved her fate, and features a "Noblesse de Ghetto" society-chat column which accuses a Prince de Ligne and a Duc de Gramont of having married Rothschilds. In an article headed "No; No Trials!" it argues against letting lawyers fuss to defend the former French leaders at Riom and begs instead for "the good, rapid, direct, ineluctable justice of the street . . . the death of Blum, Daladier, Mandel, Renaud and Paul-Boncour" by "*lynchage.*"

Utterly different, infinitely more delicate as propaganda, is *Signal*, the "*édition spéciale de la Berliner Illustrirte Zeitung.*" This is a pictorial weekly containing some excellent color photographs and astonishingly dignified text which refers to the French as "the enemy," and which furnishes remarkable documentation on the Battle of Flanders, the March into Paris, the French refugees, and other similar subjects. Photographs show the inefficiency with which "the enemy" blew up its bridges and the skill with which France's enemy reconstructed them within an hour. Photographs also show London jobless in their lying-down-in-the-streets strike of 1938 and London hovels in the East End over the caption, lifted from Lord Halifax, "If Hitler wins, it will be the end of all that makes life worth living." Various editions of *Signal*, printed in Paris in English, French, German, Portuguese, and Spanish, have been put on sale in Lisbon, so that people, many of them leaving Europe forever, can take it with them as a souvenir of what happened in France, according to the Germans, in the summer of 1940.

In general, a strained air of venality hovers over Paris. The Germans who are there have money in their pockets for the first time in twenty-two years and can buy French luxuries the like of which some of the younger Germans have never laid eyes on since they were born. For centuries, *les élégances de Paris* have been regarded all over Europe as a sort of civilized, fabricated soul of France. This particular soul of France is perforce for sale for German cash. Like termites that have been walled in for years and on a diet, the Germans, since the middle of June, have steadily advanced through the Paris shops, absorbing, munching, consuming lingerie, perfume, bonbons, leather goods, sweet silly novelties—all the chic, charm, and *gourmandise* of Parisian merchandise. In order to save for themselves what little they themselves have allowed to remain in the city's stores and warehouses, the Germans have just decreed that all the big Paris shops and department stores must close from noon till two o'clock, hours in which French employees normally go out for lunch and shopping, but also hours in which the Germans are housed in their garrisons or *Speiselokale*, eating their slowest, largest meal. Under the new ruling, the empty-handed French go back in to work just as the Germans, digesting, come out to buy again.

With their curious capacity for convenient metaphysics, certain of the more educated Germans see in their ability to purchase unlimited French silk stockings the operation of an almost occult law. When recently a Frenchwoman in the Trois Quartiers protested against her being forbidden, in the interest of conservation, to buy more than one pair of stockings when she wanted three, while at the same moment a German officer was buying a dozen pairs to send home to his wife, he explained to her in his puffy French that because French legs had worn silk while Germans had worn only cotton, it was now, as a matter of philosophical justice and moral evolution, the Germans' turn.

In a more vulgar manner, Paris has been frankly presented as the Promised Land to the common soldier lucky enough to be detailed there. Bliss takes queer, violent forms in young people who, through force or fanaticism, have for years been practicing self-denial. Eyewitnesses say that some of the earliest German soldiers in their first free hour in Paris stuffed their mouths with oranges and bananas without taking the skins off and spread butter on their chocolate bars. All one Austrian soldier wanted of Paris was to eat tinned pineapple and to moon over Napoleon's tomb. In the Paris cafés, the German soldiers still order what was their first favorite series of drinks—a beer, then a coffee, then what they generically call "*liqueur*." When the French *garçon* asks, "*Mais quelle liqueur?*," they simply repeat, uncritically, "*Liqueur*." During an evening they will mix whatever the waiter brings—Chartreuse, Bénédictine, Cointreau—with gluttonous indifference.

The German officers go in wholeheartedly for champagne. It's like a liquid symbol of their conquest of Gay Paree. Having a naïve belief in the Nazi theory that French degeneracy was brought on by high living, they demand and expect champagne wherever they go. As one peasant said, "*Ces cochons*, they come into my cottage and ask me for champagne—I, who have never given myself anything better then a bottle of *mousseux*, even for my son's first Communion."

Whatever the German soldiers buy in Paris, it's really the French who pay for it by footing the staggering occupation bill, which includes the unusually high pay given to Nazi soldiers in Paris. The mark which the Germans print in Paris, expressly for use in France, on presses they brought with them, is used concurrently with the franc in Paris business transactions. In a restaurant, a French diner may hand the waiter a hundred-franc note to pay his bill and have to take two German marks and some French centimes in change. The French marks are cleared through the Banque de France. There are probably about twenty thousand Nazi men in uniform in Paris. No official figure is known. All the French do know is that there are too many. The Nazi soldiers are constantly shifted to prevent fraternization with the French. The ratio of officers to men is unusually high; Germany discovered that even the model Nazi soldiers failed to remain model, in France, if left without strict supervision.

On June 10th, just before the Occupation, a *sous-directeur* of the Hôtel Ritz phoned Minister of the Interior Mandel, saying that he was nervous for Mme. Ritz's sake and hadn't they better close her hotel. Mandel replied that the Germans would not be in Paris before the fourteenth and that if the Ritz closed, the German officers would requisition it as being unused, whereas if it remained open, it would probably get the German *Kommandantur* as paying guests (paying guests at the expense of the French government, as it has since turned out). The staff was warned that those who left would not be taken back and that those who remained would sink or swim together. A number of them left. In a dignified, traditional manner, to fill the vacancies, the elevator men became concierges and the pageboys became elevator men. Olivier, most famous maître d'hôtel of Europe, is believed to be still at his post, because the restaurant service remains impeccable. One old French waiter said that between overwork and anguish he lost ten pounds the first week the Germans were there, but that it was no moment in the history of France to let the Ritz service down, too.

At first the Rue Cambon side of the hotel was closed. Now the long passage between the Cambon and the Place Vendôme wings is shut, but the Cambon side has been opened again, for the use of non-Germans only. The Germans have the exclusive use of the Place Vendôme wing. Before its porte-cochère stand two Nazi soldiers on guard, with a third to signal "Psst!" as a warning to present arms when an officer approaches. The small writing room, to the left on entering, is now a checkroom for rifles and pistols. The old mixed bar is reserved for men only. In the big, formal dining room no one but the *Kommandantur* and guests now dine; the regular officers' mess is in the famous back room, which is shared by the few remaining French patrons, who maintain a wide, empty space, which they consider *de rigueur*, between themselves and the Germans. It is thought bad form for loyal French to recognize the Germans socially when in the Ritz, though the same Frenchmen may have been struggling for better terms with them in their *bureaux* all day. For the first time, the Ritz serves a sixty-franc table-d'hôte dinner; it begins and ends with whipped cream. Caviar, which had been missing since the beginning of the war, came back to the Ritz with the Germans; brioches appear on the breakfast menu on Thursday, Friday, Saturday, and Sunday, but the delicious little *croissants* are no longer there. The French and foreigners who, by habit, continued to live at the Ritz were criticized by their friends for dwelling amid the enemy—until the friends realized the Ritz guests were bringing them a certain amount of unprinted political news. By tradition, the Ritz room keys always hang, when not in use, in the elevators. The sudden absence from their hooks of ten or twenty keys on a single floor meant that a mysterious delegation of somebodies had arrived from somewhere to see the Germans about something—delegations of Spaniards, say, who were there to sign on the dotted line, to try to wiggle off it, to palaver, to protest, to promise, to try and take part, with or without hope, in changing the trembling boundaries of the new map of Europe.

57

War and conquests are, in some small ways, humanizing disasters. The Ritz staff, formerly trained to show not even indifference, under conquest (and with the door closed) now sometimes show their beating hearts. That is to say, recently one old French room waiter, first asking permission of Madame, rolled up his trouser legs to show his battle wounds from Verdun and wondered aloud if his son had received the same or worse, or had indeed been killed, when the cathedral at Beauvais was bombed. One old chambermaid showed snapshots of her peasant sisters, who had fled from the Ardennes family farm as refugees and of whom there had been no news since; she also asked Madame's permission to consume the second brioche and the part of the café-au-lait which Madame always left.

For a soldiers' mess, the Germans have taken over the Champs-Elysées Taverne Alsacienne, which had doubtless been a Fifth Column station, since, significantly, it was opened only a few years ago, with German beer, waitresses in Alsatian costume, and not enough French patronage to warrant staying in business. The upstairs room of Bofinger, formerly the Bastille businessmen's *fin-bec* eating place, has also been taken over by the Germans. The French may still lunch downstairs, provided the Germans don't overflow. The de-luxe Rex and Marigny movie houses have been made exclusively German, both as to patrons and pictures; American films are forbidden and there aren't any new French films. This segregation of the Germans from the French is sought by the German command in as many ways as possible. One way has been to tell the German soldiers that all French women are diseased.

The German soldiers, because of the high pay they receive in Paris, come into closer public contact with their officers than they ever did before in the German Army. Whereas the Nazi soldier at home receives per diem one German mark (about forty cents), in Paris he gets two French marks, which is fifty times what the French soldier was paid for active service in the current war. This pay is probably the highest ever received by Continental troops in Europe's military history. In the World War, our A.E.F. got a dollar a day and ranked as millionaires. As a result, the Nazi ranks turn up often enough in the same cinemas, cafés, and restaurants as their superiors. In theory, the Nazi soldier eats in his cheap *Speiselokal*, where he absorbs the heavy German victuals that are deemed to be Nordic and virile, as distinguished from the degenerate, tasty French diet. Nevertheless, they stray. Eyewitnesses tell about two bewildered German soldiers who found their way into the Crémaillère, formerly international society's hangout and now patronized by the *Kommandantur*. On leaving, the soldiers pulled down their tunics, stiffened, and got ready to goose-step and *heil* two German officers seated by the door. The officers made embarrassed signs, to signify *"Um Gottes Willen, nein."* The acrobatics of the German salutes, the presenting-of-arms outside the officers' hotels (with little French boys capering in imitation), the integral, muscular, Teutonic solemnity which meant so much morally to the Nazis at home have been found to mean nothing, beyond the snicker they arouse, to the French. This baffles the Germans.

When the Radio-Paris, which the Nazis have taken over to blare out their official news, is broadcasting, French children sing, to the tune of "La Cucaracha," *"Radio-Paris ment, Radio-Paris ment, Radio Paris est al lemand"* ("Radio-Paris lies, Radio-Paris lies, Radio-Paris is German"). To Parisians, the most trusted radio news is what they get from the American short-wave broadcasts; strangely, the French are still permitted to listen to all short-wave programs, though only in private. Some of the bitterer Parisians have begun to head their letters to each other "Paris, Germany." *"Veni, vidi, Vichy"* is the only bon mot Pétain has produced. Apparently, the best thing about Parisian morale is that Parisians remain, under the Germans, just what they were under the French. Parisians grumble, argue in cafés about the new politics as they did about the old, are logical, critical, disgusted, sardonic, witty, realistic, civilized as they always were, but they have an earnest, a desperate and humble, hope that is new. The blackout is severer under the Nazis, though Paris has not been bombed by the English, than it was under the French when they were still at war with Berlin. For carelessness during blackouts, the Germans warn a householder twice. The third time they fire a pistol shot through the offending lighted window. *Ils sont très corrects.*

Outside of Paris, the roads to Senlis, Laon, Beauvais, Les Andelys, and Vernon are deserted except for occasional bicycles. These towns are deserted in proportion to the destruction they suffered. Along the roads still lie the debris of the catastrophic refugee trek. Through the summer there also lay the remains of French soldiers, unnamed, unmarked, half earthed-over where they dropped. With that appalling efficiency which still leaves the French speechless, the German dead were neatly buried wherever they fell, whether in some villager's chrysanthemum bed or in some peasant's wheat field, always beneath wooden crosses which the Germans, who apparently thought of everything, brought to France with them. The graves are marked with name plates and German helmets are placed on them, like headstones. If several German dead lie together, there is often a German spread eagle decoratively patterned in pebbles on the well-tended, well-heaped earth.

The new French morale, the reaction that will permanently count, will surely consist not only of what the French see of the Germans at close range but also of what the French, when their bitterness dies down, re-

59

member about themselves. In the meantime, the rich French industrialists, whom the French Communists accused of being pro-Nazi, are, naturally, getting from the Nazis the treatment which the Nazis at one time would have dealt out only to the French Communists. That is, the rich French industrialists are being systematically ruined. Ninety million francs' worth of machinery in the Hispano-Suiza factories has been earmarked for shipment into Germany, and the French Ford plant (belonging to the Matford company, in which the American Ford company has a controlling interest) has already lost about fifty million in machinery. In Lyon, the fine-textile centre of Europe since the fourteenth century, looms have been ripped out and shipped to Germany. What silk printing is still being done is restricted to two colors; formerly up to fifty colors were used. Designers trained through generations for delicate artistic invention are ordered to experiment with fabrics made only for durability and often of *ersatz* yarns. The great French dressmakers, around whom literally hundreds of thousands of French workers revolved in ramified industry, have been invited to work in Berlin. The 1940 autumn dress collections in Paris were made up in fabrics left from the autumn of 1939. This autumn, when the Paris stores and shops should have been displaying wool and furs in their windows, the display of beach frocks and sandals dragged on. Paris *couture* had been bought up, cleaned out, cut down before it was ready to sell, even to the Germans.

Biarritz is the secondary Promised Land for the Germans. As a reward for being German, troops by the hundred are sent down in trucks for a look at Biarritz. During the summer, German generals strolled the beach and other German officers on holiday leave renewed their domesticity with their dowdy wives, dazed at having a good time. The majority of Germans have never seen the ocean. Nazi youth has been taught to swim in the tideless German rivers. At first, in the chilly, treacherous Biarritz surf, many German soldiers were drowned. Then a system was worked out. In September, an American on the beach watched a platoon of German soldiers march out on the sand, led by an officer, who ordered them to stand in three rows, facing the sea. At a command, they all stripped to their shorts, folded their clothes in a neat pile in front of their boots, and, crossing their arms and ankles, sat down behind their boots. The officer, advancing from his own piled-up wardrobe, walked knee-deep into the ocean and tested the water's swish and temperature with his hand. He then commanded the first row of soldiers to march into the water to swim, while he kept paternal watch. After their plunge they filed out and sat down behind the two dry rows of soldiers, who, one row at a time, then took their turn. Finally, all the soldiers, on command, dressed, pulled on their boots, and marched away. These are the boots, this is the system, marching around half of France.

Mona Lisa

SEPTEMBER 31, 1942   Probably the most famous Parisian personality in southern France today is Mona Lisa. She is in the town of Montauban, in the little municipal museum, crowded. in among several thousand other choice masterpieces from the Louvre. The "Venus de Milo," on the other hand, is guarded by German soldiers about a hundred miles southwest of Paris in the Occupied Zone, in the Château de Chambord, which is now principally populated by the Louvre's sculptural treasures. The refugee trek of Louvre art was less publicized than that of French citizens, and better rehearsed. In the last four years the Louvre has moved its most valuable things four times. The first time, which was Munich, the contents were merely whisked downstairs into the basement. The curators had planned so well that it took twenty minutes flat to pop the museum's absolutely first-class movable treasures into the *sous-sol*, which was built as wine cellars for Francis I, Henri II, and Catherine de' Medici, and has bomb-proof, sixteenth-century, nine-foot-thick walls. Among these treasures were "Mona Lisa," Fouquet's "Charles VII," Manet's "Olympia" and "Le Déjeuner sur l'Herbe," Ingres' "Odalisque Couchée" and "Le Bain Turc," Uccello's "La Bataille," Dürer's "Portrait de l'Artiste," Giorgione's "Concert Champêtre," and Delacroix's "La Mort de Sardanapale." "Venus" was too heavy for the twenty-minute job. Second-class treasures included Ingres' "Odalisque Assise Vue de Dos" and two dozen Corots. Among the third-class treasures were six dozen Corots. It took ten days to wrap up all three classes in the basement, but the moment Chamberlain sounded his peace-with-honor all-clear, the French government ordered the Louvre to get things unwrapped again within seven days. A closed Louvre was bad for public morale; a rapidly reopened Louvre looked like government efficiency, peace, and even a diplomatic triumph for Daladier. Being economical, and maybe cynical, the Louvre saved all its Munich wrappings for the next *alerte*. The wrappings were expertly devised, complicated, and fire- and water-proof. Cloth was first wound around the paintings, to prevent scratching; next excelsior, as a cushion against shock; then asbestos, against fire; then tar paper, against water. Each precious package was finally berthed in wooden cases on wooden pegs, the purpose of the pegs being to prevent vibration, worse than a bullet hole for a painting.

By the time the second and real *alerte* came, in September, 1939, the Louvre had already been moving its masterpieces fast and far away for two weeks. Lesser works were left in the museum, where they remain today. The goals toward which the treasures were headed were carefully selected, dry, privately owned châteaux around Tours and Le Mans. Having learned, from the evacuation during the war of 1870, that big paintings chip when rolled up, and, from the war of 1914, that the Germans move fast, the Louvre called on the Samaritaine department store for forty-three of its swiftest packers, including two who were expert scaffolders. French scaffolds are still made medievally, of ropes and poles, without nails, are calculated by the eye rather than figured out on paper, and work fine. For one whole morning the scaffolders, in their blue denims and sabots, sat in the Salon Carré eying Veronese's "Les Noces de Cana"—thirty-two feet long, twenty-two feet high, and weighing two and a half tons (with original frame)—and silently cogitated and smoked. The curators had proclaimed that the men must not smoke and they had proclaimed that if they didn't smoke they couldn't cogitate. Thirty workmen got the Veronese off the wall, without rolling, by making the most of a scaffold, a rope trick, some pulleys, and the picture's own weight (including two hundred pounds of dust accumulated since Renaissance times). It took forty-two Samaritaine packers, plus one who walked backward and semaphored signals for the shoulder-balancing act of the *copains*, to carry Géricault's gigantic "Le Radeau de la Méduse" upright through the Louvre's customary painting-evacuation door, the Napoleon III portal, which is the highest. The Napoleon I portal, the broadest, is used for sculpture. Though airplanes, because they don't joggle, are the ideal vehicles for transporting pictures, the Louvre was glad to settle for a Comédie-Française scenery truck, the only camion big enough. The itinerary to Chambord, the destination of the picture, had been laid out to provide detours around low bridges and sharp corners, but nobody had thought of telephone wires. Medusa bogged down in the suburbs of Paris between two telephone poles. A hurry call was put in to the *Ministre des Postes, Télégraphes, et Téléphones*. After considerable irritation and discussion, he sent a squad of emergency workmen, who sped on ahead of the truck, clipping wires, then backtracked to restring them and soothe irate telephone subscribers.

The "Venus de Milo" and the "Victoire de Samothrace" were moved from their pedestals by means of levers and pulleys. They were then wrapped, boxed, and lying on their sides, slid out along the corridors and down some specially built ramps. Field Marshal Göring is such an admirer of "Venus" that he paid her a visit at Chambord, combining the call on her with some deer-shooting in the château's park. The R.A.F. tried to combine it with some Göring-shooting, and bombed at him but missed.

The third frantic Louvre trek came in May, 1940. The Germans were swarming down from the north. Most museum men were in the Army. In the confusion, even Napoleon's famous cocked hat, in flight from the Invalides, was picked up by the Germans in its hatbox on the Etampes road. Aided by the Louvre wives, the Louvre female staff did a heroic, hustling job, rushing over the countryside in trains and trucks to collect the museum's canvas treasures from the dozens of scattered châteaux which had been chosen as refuges eight months before. The ladies couldn't manage the sculpture—too heavy. With what they had collected, they headed toward a savage, mountainous region in the Unoccupied Department of Aveyron and its damp, ancient little abbatial Château du Loc-Dieu, originally known as Locus Dei, or Place of God. There, in the bedroom of a demobilized curator, "Mona Lisa" came to temporary rest. As he nervously moaned, "Since I've been sleeping with 'Mona Lisa,' I haven't closed an eye."

The fourth move came in September, 1940. Three of the curators, reassembled in the Loc-dieu, begged gasoline from what was left of the French Army, insisting that art was collateral and that the Louvre treasures were a national fortune, mildewing in the mountain mist. The collection was then sent on its way to its present home in Montauban. The museum is closed to the public. Inside, the Louvre's curators are doing more cleaning and polishing than the Louvre has had time for in the last hundred years.

The Escape of Mrs. Jeffries

MAY 22, 1943 Last September, Mrs. Ellen Jeffries, an American expatriate who had lived in France for twenty years because she was in love with it, tardily decided to leave Paris. Actually, Mrs. Jeffries is not her name, nor are any of the other names in this narrative the names of the people involved. In 1942, after two years of the German occupation, she was among the dozen or more diehards, all women, left over from that colony of about five thousand Americans to whom Paris, during the twenties and thirties, had seemed liberty itself. Since Pearl Harbor, however, detention, *résidence forcée,* or even a concentration camp looked like the inevitable expatriate American way. Or there was flight. By finally making up her mind, on September 1st, to leave, and by moving as rapidly, which in the end meant as illegally, as possible, Mrs. Jeffries managed to arrive in New York the second week of April, 1943. All things considered, including the fact that her travel problems included escapes across two French borders and that escapes are slow-moving projects demanding lots of careful talk first, Mrs. Jeffries, who is forty-five, statuesque, unmelodramatic, New Hampshire-born, a seasoned traveller, and nobody's fool, thinks she made fast time.

Certainly, by last September, it was already better, in Paris, to be conquered French than unconquered American, especially if you wanted to leave it. A trickle of Frenchmen, preferably those who were on food or collaboration business, were given German *Ausweise,* the *Kommandantur* exit visas, which allowed them to cross from Occupied into Vichy France. But no American in Paris last summer was given an exit visa for any reason whatever. The Germans had decided that all Americans were dishonorable. As proof, they pointed out that resident Americans, who before Pearl Harbor had been graciously granted passes merely to visit in the Unoccupied Zone, had from there impolitely run for the Spanish border and home. Even before Pearl Harbor, the Nazis, to keep closer tabs on those who were left in Paris and the environs, had ordered them not to set foot outside the Departments of the Seine and the Seine-et-Oise and to report once a week to their local police station to sign an alien ledger which contained their photographs and data on them. After Pearl Harbor, the ladies also had to register at the Chambre des Députés, where the Germans, ironically, had set up their alien-enemy *Büro,* and sign a new Nazi alien-enemy questionnaire which included the optimistic inquiry *"Avez-vous un cheval?"* Two entire lines were reserved for this "Have you a horse?" question. There was no need for the Germans to wonder if American men had horses to donate to the Reichswehr, because all male Americans had been crowded into detention barracks at Compiègne a week after America had entered the war.

In the two years that had passed since the Germans had officially cut France in two, the first, wild seepage of refugees, members of separated families, and soldiers' wives and children across the Armistice demarcation line had settled down into an orderly but illicit commuting, organized, for patriotism or pay, by guides who shuttled back and forth two or three times a week with passengers in tow. Right now nobody seems to know if this smuggling of human beings is still going on, since the Nazis occupy both halves of France. All that is known is that early in February, 1943, the Germans, typically, declared that the demarcation line had been erased but that identification papers or passports, which are precisely what some people either do not possess or most want to hide, must still be shown in order to cross what no longer exists. Early in the spring of 1942 the French were still crossing, for fifty or a hundred francs a head, or for nothing, if poor and in trouble. Then, in May, there was a terrible, little-publicized *rafle*, or raid, on the remaining foreign Jews in Paris, which drastically worsened the chances of anyone's crossing the border. The Nazis ordered that non-French Jewish men, women, and children be separated from one another and sent off, in a new, triple form of segregation, to different camps. When the Gestapo arrived in the Belleville Jewish quarter of Paris to enforce the order, some parents threw themselves and their children, or pushed one another, out of the windows of their homes rather than be separated. A new wild flight of Jews from the rest of Occupied France stampeded the border guides. As a result, the guide fees for everybody, Jew or non-Jew, rose in the tragic competition for flight. Also, the Nazi border patrols, an especially venal lot, boosted their bribery rates or refused to coöperate at all. Then, after the Commandos made their first big Continental raid, on August 19th, at Dieppe, the Nazi restrictions on the movements of the population, which had slackened slightly in the course of two years, suddenly tightened. For passing Jews guides were shot, passing anybody over the line became more difficult, and passing any English-speaking person became dangerous and thus even costlier. Mrs. Jeffries was automatically a bad proposition, from the guides' viewpoint, because, though a Presbyterian, she was a forty-five-year-old American female and therefore regarded as bothersome if everybody should have to cut and run from a Nazi patrol.

To start dickering for one of these crossings, the regular Parisian phrase was *"Connaissez-vous un passage?"* This was usually addressed to any of the ubiquitous, omniscient, and trusted café waiters who, since the German occupation, have performed a patriotic service and earned a little extra by purveying to Parisians certain anti-Nazi necessities, such as black-market food tips, contraband cigarettes, British radio news, and introductions to border guides. On September 1st, Mrs. Jeffries found her waiter. His first offer was an exorbitant demand for eleven thousand francs from a *type* who, upon a refusal, immediately came down to a bargain eight thousand. As was customary, this proposition was offered by a guide's Paris under-cover, or contact, man, who on an every-other-day schedule got together passage parties of a dozen or more people. The guide furnished transportation, exclusive of railroad accommodation, in the shape of hay carts or trucks for long detours on border side roads, and made arrangements for, but didn't pay for, food and lodging en route. For his aid, integrity, organization, and knowledge of the ropes, he charged an over-all service fee. Most of the guides operated in one of five or six topographically convenient crossing points, of which the eastern, being closer to Paris, were the more popular. The Nazis got around, in rotation, to each exit, for a spell methodically watched it like a cat, then went and eyed another place while the mice scurried out through the unplugged holes. During the first week in September, all the eastern passage points were suddenly reported *brûlé*, or hot. The guides got word, through their grapevines, that the Nazi patrols were searching all buses on roads approaching the eastern border crossings; at the same time the Paris Nazis had a temporary fit of checking the identity papers of all travellers leaving by the Gare de Lyon and the Gare d'Austerlitz. Mrs. Jeffries lay low and passed up the eight-thousand bargain.

By the middle of September the coast looked clear again. Through a second and better-connected waiter, Mrs. Jeffries paid a rock-bottom five-thousand-franc fee to a bold, brown-eyed, young de Gaullist named René, the contact man for a guide, a big farm-owner in the district through which she was to cross. She sent her luggage to Lyons, the first city in the Unoccupied Zone she was aiming for, by train; it is one of the anomalies of life under the Nazis that property has more right of way than people. For the crossing, René advised her to travel light, with only a rucksack on her back, in case she had to run. On September 16th, he told her to meet him at a certain railroad station the next morning at six in order to fight for a seat on the eight-o'clock train and for the love of God not to talk in public, as her American-accented French was *formidable*. At seven o'clock, by which time Mrs. Jeffries had silently struggled into her seat, René appeared and, busy with last-minute details, asked her to find an extra seat for what he called a friend, who was going with them. Largely by sign language, she wangled a seat in the next coach for the friend, who, from the brief view she had of him, looked to be French, fortyish, pale, and nervous. After the train had started and she had painfully watched the Tour Eiffel fade from her life and view, she began, irresistibly, to enjoy her journey through rural France. She had not been allowed to travel for nearly two years. Also, she had a fine shoe-box lunch with her. A French woman friend who owned a little place outside Paris had brought her, the day before, three precious fresh hard-boiled eggs, two *pâté maison* sandwiches, and a nearly ripe home-grown pear.

Well before noon and well inside the demarcation border, Mrs. Jeffries, according to plan, got off the train at a small town and walked down the main street to the foot of a hill, where René had said she would find a *bistro*. She found five and, being thirsty, chose the nicest and ordered the customary glass of bad beer. René eventually rolled up in an old Citroën, and with him was the guide. When René introduced her to the guide, Joseph, her stomach, which had turned over in terror whenever she thought about making the crossing, was quieted. Joseph was a middle-aged, bull-necked countryman, paternal, polite, and bustling. René, it developed, was in a hurry to get on to Marseilles. The two men had a confidential conversation, but she could not help overhearing some of it, and she gathered that René was on a gun-running job for de Gaulle and that Joseph planned to hide him in the back of the Citroën under some vegetables and drive him to a railway station on the other side of the border, where René would get back on the train he had just got off. The train, she knew, would be held up for hours at the border while the French and German police inspected *Ausweise* and civil papers, which René apparently never fussed with, hunted in the toilets and under the seats for refugees, and searched passengers for contraband. Contraband was anything portable, precious, and personal left after two years of German occupation; it could be love letters, family messages, trinkets, old furs, more money than your visa said you possessed, or fine jewels.

René and Joseph left on their mission, Joseph promising to return as soon as possible. As Mrs. Jeffries sat alone, drinking her beer, the pale Frenchman of that morning's journey came up and introduced himself as Monsieur Georges. Then he introduced what seemed to be the rest of Joseph's crossing party—three French provincial matrons who said they were sisters, a Jewish Frenchwoman with a sick-looking little boy, three melancholy young Dutch Jews, and a French sailor in uniform. As if France had never been defeated or divided, the sailor had spent his leave, as usual, visiting his mother in Paris and was now on his way back to his ship in Toulon. Georges begged Mrs. Jeffries, on account of her accent, not to talk, and then invited her to play *belote*, a talkative card game. Since she didn't know how, he told her the story of his recent life. He had wanted to fight on the side of noble-hearted Russia and so had volunteered to be smuggled from Paris across the border near Lyons and thence to London to join the de Gaulle army as a mechanic. She asked in a whisper whether he was an airplane or a tank mechanic. He said he was neither; he was an expert maker of frames for ladies' petit-point handbags, the sort formerly sold to the American and now to the German tourist trade. He proudly said that it cost the de Gaulle movement twenty thousand francs to smuggle a man like him from Paris to London. He had false teeth, limp gray hair, spots on his vest, and delicate, artisan's hands. Because Mrs.

Jeffries was polite, she didn't say she thought that the Fighting French had made a poor buy.

Late in the afternoon Joseph returned and moved his party to a second *bistro*, one farther up the hill and near a church. Four Gestapo agents were drinking beer at the *zinc*. Joseph claimed that he could spot them a mile off, because the Gestapo invariably wore ersatz tweeds of either a bilious brown or an unpleasant gray, apparently the only choice left to the Germans, and they always shaved their necks and carried briefcases, neither of these habits French. The waiter at the new *bistro* warned Joseph's party not to talk over their drinks and then cracked off-color jokes, which made the three Gallic matrons laugh hysterically. At five o'clock Joseph led Mrs. Jeffries around the corner to a photographer, who took her picture and made out a false French civilian's identification paper which she would get, complete with her picture, the next day on the other side of the border. He told her that the paper was made out in a Gallic version of her name and warned her not to forget that she was to become, temporarily, Madame Hélène Geoffroi.

Shortly afterward, behind the church, Joseph and Mrs. Jeffries joined the rest of the party, who were huddled against the choir door. Joseph hurriedly piled them all into a waiting butcher's camion and pulled a pair of black curtains tight across the back. Inside they found fragments of suet and dried blood and three more Jews. The camion started off. Five minutes later, Joseph, who was driving, was stopped for questioning by two German patrolmen. Behind the black curtains the three new Jews whispered nervously, which made everybody else even more nervous. Then the Germans said, *"Heil Hitler und merci,"* and the truck set off again. After an hour's drive the truck stopped, Joseph unbuttoned the curtains, and they climbed out. They were in the country, behind a building that will here be described as an old blacksmith's shop. They hurried inside and were put in a new annex, where apparently machine parts were being manufactured. This part of the shop was not yet entirely roofed over, and for the next few hours the party watched the darkening sky and then the stars. As they sat, they could hear an unseen little river frothing against boulders. Joseph had told them that the river, which marked the border, was where they were to cross into the Unoccupied Zone that night and that the rocks were what they were to cross on. No one, not even Monsieur Georges, talked much. It was better not to say anything about where you came from and it was certainly too soon to discuss where you thought you would eventually arrive. Finally they heard two members of the German night patrol approach the shop on their first round. Over the noise of the water and their own thumping hearts, the hidden party listened to the

German voices lifted in puffing, pidgin French. Apparently the two Nazis were hungry only for conversation, though Mrs. Jeffries heard Joseph offer them chocolate. He did not offer them cigarettes or money, the two other things German soldiers have an appetite for.

The party was to cross at nine. At ten minutes to nine, Joseph brought in a young peasant whom he called his nephew. He looked nothing like Joseph. He was big, stalwart, and dressed only in swimming trunks. Joseph explained that the river was no more than four feet deep and that if anyone fell in, not to scream, because his nephew, who would be standing in the middle, would come to the rescue. "We have him here to tranquillize the ladies," Joseph added gravely. Then, less confidently, he said that the Nazi patrol ought to be a quarter of a mile away by then but that one never could tell about those monsters. Everyone was instructed to crouch while crossing the river, in order to be less visible and a smaller target in case the Nazis came back and started to fire. The party was to cross rapidly and one by one.

Everybody filed out of the blacksmith shop and to the edge of the river. Mrs. Jeffries followed the French sailor. Crossing the river, she could see, on the far side, the pompon of his cap silhouetted against the stars. As she stepped, crouching, on the third boulder, she put one foot on the hem of her raincoat and almost fell in. The unlikely nephew, chest-deep in the water, laughed and whispered, *"Courage."* When Mrs. Jeffries got to the other side of the little river, she ran, still crouching, for a quarter of a mile through a field of stubble. Finally she came to a dirt road that led to a village. Then, as already instructed by Joseph, she turned to the right and knocked at the door of the second cottage. A fat, red-faced young woman opened the door. When Mrs. Jeffries asked if she were Joseph's aunt, she nodded indifferently. Falsehoods and the pounding heart of someone who had just run the line meant nothing to her. Fugitives were a business. Without being asked, she said that Mrs. Jeffries could have a bed to herself for fifty francs. Apparently Joseph, like a capitalist carefully splitting up his investments, had distributed his party all over the neighborhood.

Mrs. Jeffries inspected the bed. It looked filthy and stank in memory of other refugees who had lain on it, maybe trembling the way Mrs. Jeffries trembled now. From her rucksack she took out a bottle of perfume and sprinkled the pillow, and then tried, unsuccessfully, to eat one of the hard-boiled eggs. She went to bed with her clothes on. The combination of the bed smell and the perfume made her sick, but there was nothing in the room to be sick in, so she forced herself to go to sleep. In the morning the fat young woman gave her acorn coffee and a slice of sour gray bread. She took the fifty francs agreed upon and absorbed another fifty as tip because she had not asked Madame to sign a lodger's slip, as the law demands. For fugitives, every evasion of the law is a luxury which must be paid for extra, though unofficial kindnesses often come free of charge.

Joseph had told Mrs. Jeffries to go to the local *épicerie* after breakfast and ask the owner for her false French civilian paper. Like a prestidigitator, the grocer obligingly pulled it out of the inside of his old hat. Then he pointed down the empty road and said, "Joseph said to walk that way. You'll meet a truck." After walking a mile in the mild sun, she sat down under a tree to smoke, to wonder what had happened to the truck, and to look at herself, and her new life history, as Madame Hélène Geoffroi. The photograph was nothing like her and the paper said that she had been born in Normandy in a town she had never heard of. A truck rattled by, stopped, and backed up; it contained Joseph and the rest of his party. "You will never get to New York sitting down like that," he called, and they all laughed excitedly. Everyone, even the melancholy Jews, seemed united by a temporary sort of gaiety because of the success of what they had been through together the night before.

At noon they pulled up at one of those modest country inns famed for generations for its cuisine. The black-market luncheon proved to be finer than anything Mrs. Jeffries had sampled since France fell—multiple hors-d'œuvres, delicious local trout (it being Friday), grilled chops, two vegetables, ripe cheese, fruit compote, and a serious Burgundy. Monsieur Georges, who sat beside her, remarked how wise he had been to put his false teeth in his breast pocket before the crossing. He had been afraid that, as he jumped for the rocks, the teeth might fall out of his face. Mrs. Jeffries paid a luncheon check of seven hundred francs, or seven dollars. The waiter had regarded Georges as her husband and had put him on her bill. After the tasty barley coffee, the chef-owner of the place came in to receive compliments on his food. He said that he had run a *fin bec* restaurant at Menton until the Italians came but that he did not like macaroni cooking. Being both an artist and a patriot, he had moved away.

After lunch Mrs. Jeffries and Georges, who were bound for Lyons, said goodbye to the rest of the party. Where the others were going, or trying to go, they alone knew. On saying goodbye to Joseph, Mrs. Jeffries thanked him with real emotion. He must have been used to that. All he said was *"Ce n'est rien, Madame. À votre service."* He was going back to the *bistro* on the hill and tomorrow night he and another party would be crossing the river. A local guide named Jean, who did odd jobs for Joseph, was detailed to the Lyons contingent, which was joined by an elderly Serb underground worker. They were to sit up in the restaurant until three in the morning, walk to the nearest railway station, and catch an early train for Lyons. There Jean would introduce them in a certain café, where a patriot (as in

70

French Revolutionary times, today all the pals among *le peuple* are patriots) would tip them off to some safe rooms to live in. As Madame Hélène Geoffroi, Mrs. Jeffries tried to show her false paper to the ticket taker at the station next morning. Though under orders from the Vichy police to check up on all travellers, he didn't bother to glance at her forgery, which disappointed her.

Owing to a saboteur's wreck on the main line, their train was four hours late, and they wearily arrived at eleven in the morning at the Lyons café. There a peppery young Fighting Frenchman, Marcel, who had expected only Jean, and him on time, flew into a temper at the sight of an unexpected American woman, an unexplained old Serb, and the unwelcome Georges. As one of the local Fighting French authorities, Marcel ordered Georges back to Paris because he considered him something de Gaulle would not have as a gift. Suspicious and arrogant, Marcel then shut up like a clam, refusing aid to any of them. Apologetically, the Serb offered Mrs. Jeffries the address of a compatriot's boarding house which was reported to have nice food. With her rucksack still on her back, she took three wrong trams to the outskirts of Lyons, walked up four long, wrong streets, and finally managed to arrive, weeping with fatigue, at what turned out to be an ordinary French lodging house for men workers. "Ah, if Madame were only not a woman," the patriot proprietor wailed. He nevertheless offered to give her lunch in his barracklike dining room, where about a hundred workmen were already feeding. However, as the Serb had prophesied, the stew was excellent. While Madame was still reviving herself on it, he walked in. He apologized for intruding and said he had worried about her. It occurred to Mrs. Jeffries at that moment that for the past two years in Paris she had lived her quiet, expatriate, familiar existence without difficulties and also without anyone's help. In Lyons she was a stranger and in a bad way. It was over her stew that she realized that the war had indeed reclassified people; that to those in trouble people had now become very kind or very cruel or as indifferent as stones. At the Serb's kindness she started crying again.

Like friendly homing pigeons, Mrs. Jeffries and the Serb returned to the café. It was closed. From behind the door the owner shouted that the police were expecting an anti-Vichy riot and to get off the streets, quick. Mrs. Jeffries and the Serb ran down the street. At the first hotel they came to, he pushed her in and, still running, disappeared. When she asked for lodging, the woman at the desk calmly offered her a bathroom to sleep in. The city was jammed; the annual commercial fair, the famous Foire de Lyon, was opening that week, just as if war and riots were routine and just as if the fair would show something besides ersatz. When Mrs. Jeffries handed over her false French civilian paper, which, if she spent the night even in the bathroom, would have to be copied on a *fiche* to be presented to the police the next morning, the woman said sharply, "French? With that accent?" Mrs. Jeffries, a poor liar, lamely murmured that she had been brought up in America. "You should say that with more conviction," the woman replied, and put the *fiche* into a desk drawer. Alarmed, Mrs. Jeffries casually strolled out onto the street, then ran back to the café, where, on the deserted sidewalk, the Serb and the angry Marcel were arguing. Marcel became even angrier when she told him of the suspicion which her false French paper had aroused. He declared that since she was an American she hadn't needed such a paper in the first place, that her Parisian *carte d'identité* sufficed in Vichy France, and that if the woman squealed, all of Joseph's papers forged by that particular photographer of foreigners who did need them would become hot. While tearing up her Geoffroi paper, he forbade Mrs. Jefferies to return to the hotel. When she said that she had to sleep somewhere and that she hadn't had her clothes off for two nights, he unexpectedly apologized. Rather grudgingly, he invited her to stay the night with him, explaining that he was sleeping, *sub rosa*, in a collaborationist uncle's flat and that both he and she would have to be up and out before seven the next morning, when the uncle was returning from a big business trip. Marcel said that his family were bitterly divided; half were de Gaullists like himself and the other half were like the rich, Pétainist, avuncular swine. While they were still talking, the café reopened, and she was able to get a much-needed glass of weak beer. Apparently the riot had been called off.

That evening, after dinner, she took a Saturday-night bath in the collaborationist's luxurious bathtub. Next morning, early, she made both beds, as womanly thanks for the hospitality, and by seven Marcel had installed her in the centre of Lyons in what called itself a hotel but was really three floors of furnished rooms over a side-street shop. The hotel did not register its lodgers on any *fiche* and had no breakfasts, hot water, or closets. The clothes cupboard in her room was a length of pink cretonne stretched diagonally across one corner on a string, not nearly big enough to hold her clothes when she picked up her trunk, which had come through more easily than she had. She was to live in this room for the next eight weeks, which was the length of time it would take her to get the solemn, legal papers necessary for her to leave France illegally. The Nazis have upset the law, the logic, and the sense of humor of all Europe.

MAY 29, 1943 Lyons was Mrs. Jeffries' first stop in her homeward Paris-to-New York flight. After the dramas of German occupation which were constantly shaking Paris, she had expected to find life dull in Unoccupied Lyons, and especially in the shabby, side-street lodging house where she had settled while planning her next move. However, once she had accepted the difference between the French attitude toward recent history that she had known in Paris and the attitude that she found in Lyons, she had an undeniably stimulating sojourn. In Paris the French had been against the Germans. In Lyons, which the Germans were not to march into until nine days before she left, the French were still enjoying being against other French. Lyons proudly rated itself the most excited and exciting city in Unoccupied France. Certainly bombs in the Royalists' Action Française newspaper offices, in Pétain's Legion headquarters, and in Laval's recruiting stations, where French workmen were being enrolled for labor in Germany, were regarded as commonplaces, and so were street riots and clashes between the silk-mill hands, the brutal Darlan police (modelled on the Gestapo), the Vichy police, and the Lyons police, in all possible combinations, and so, too, were arrests, escapes, denunciations, plots, and counterplots. The Lyonnais subsisted on the violences indigenous to their city, which was the Unoccupied receiving end of whatever was shipped out of Germany on the Mulhouse express and whatever sneaked out of Paris on the P.L.M. *rapide*. For the underground anti-Nazi groups in France, Lyons was the reckless halfway house between northern France and Marseilles. In Lyons gun smugglers dictated reports to their confidential secretaries and provided the customary fifty-thousand-franc fees to complacent guards who would wink at a lucky comrade's escape from some Occupied prison, saboteurs held conferences like good businessmen, and draftsmen made blueprints for railway wrecks.

Lyons was the first Unoccupied stop for the escaping Jews, old and young, who never ceased rolling down from the north. The Cathedral's archbishop, Monseigneur Gerlier, boldly adopted a hundred of the foreign Jewish children who had been torn from their parents and sent to concentration camps after a Vichy roundup that had netted ten thousand Jews. French prisoners from Germany who had been wounded by the R.A.F. bombers arrived at the Lyons railway station in coaches which the Germans had carefully labelled *"Blessés par les avions anglais."* One day, in the station, a trainload of returned French war prisoners just arriving from Germany patriotically threw stones, with all their weak strength, at a trainload of French workmen who, with what even the non-collaborationist French at first esteemed equal patriotism, were just starting off to Germany in exchange for the incoming prisoners.

The various patriots' cafés in Lyòns functioned as forums, checkrooms, and occasionally dormitories for patriots' out-of-town friends, their suspicious-looking packages, and their girls. In one of the cafés there circulated a young patriot who was, for his underground group, the official killer of members who squealed. He was green-eyed and handsome, had been a gigolo in a well-known Montmartre *boîte* formerly enjoyed by American tourist ladies, had nervous, beautiful hands that itched at the sight of money, and was, his comrades reported, excellent at what they called serious jobs but unreliable at details of organization, which bored him. He dressed in what he thought was the perfect English manner, but he always looked a little too neat. His father was an electrician. The killer dreamed of a France of the future in which, after the Americans had won, he and his father would install expensive American radios in every house in the nation.

In the patriot groups, generosities were fantastic but not uncommon. Among those who were really working for *la patrie*, aid and money were handed around as if both were magnificently uncostly. The traditional French grip on the banknote seemed finally to have been loosed in a gesture of desperate, tardy patriotism. A thousand francs, or five or ten thousand, could always be raised to send some Frenchman on one of the many militant jobs of *les services* (which is what the underground movements are called), in which the success of a man's assignment could often be proved only by his being imprisoned or shot. Because resistance needs equipment, especially scarce in a land where the conqueror has swept the shelves bare, the cash boxes of *les services* had to be kept overflowing. Even to hire a rope long and strong enough to help a comrade escape from the third story of a prison cost twenty thousand francs, or two hundred dollars at the black-market rate of exchange. Wild and naïve schemes flourished among the patriots, and often worked. One morning Mrs. Jeffries was wakened at her rooming house by a youth who claimed to be an American and said that his father had been a Yankee soldier in the last war. And did the American lady want to go back to New York in a submarine or on a bomber? He could send her free in either one if she could leave in a half hour. She felt that she could not dress so quickly.

When the Americans finally, in the invasion of Africa, on Sunday, November 8th, took their first strategic step toward Europe, Mrs. Jeffries, who had then been in Lyons seven weeks, got the news at breakfast in her favorite patriots' café. The owner came to her table to tell her and offer his felicitations. The clients cheered her. Americans were rare in Lyons and together she and the good news made it a great occasion. "Pétain ordered us to retreat! If we'd only retreated far enough, now we would be in Africa with the Yanks!" one Frenchman shouted to her. When she took out a package of old, bootlegged Lucky Strikes, she was cheered again. To the Lyonnais the Luckies seemed positive proof that the Americans had actually arrived from across the Atlantic.

During the next two days Lyons seethed with excitement and what turned out to be mistaken preparation for its new rôle in France's history. The city, in response to a radioed appeal from General de Gaulle in London, busily prepared a reckless Fighting French street demonstration for Wednesday, which was Armistice Day. Instead, on Wednesday, the Germans marched in, en route for Marseilles and eventually Toulon. At ten o'clock that morning, when Mrs. Jeffries walked out of her rooming house to have breakfast, she found, instead of a de Gaulle parade on the Place Bellecour, Vichy police circling in a protecting ring around a dozen Germans with machine guns, ready, if necessary, for the sullen crowd which had gathered. All day the Germans poured through in camions with equipment which looked old and used and "nothing like 1940," the Lyonnais jeered with satisfaction. But the Germans continued to pour through the city all night, and what was rushed past after curfew in the dark was, as anyone who dared peer out from behind his window curtains could see, powerfully shining and new. There were miles of unscarred tanks, trucks, and troop carriers packed with jolted, drowsing Nazis, gleaming swarms of buzzing motorcycles, and lumbering contingents of immaculate, stiff-necked guns. By morning German *Kommissäre* were domiciled in requisitioned hotels, including the town's finest, the Grand-Nouvel. At first the Lyonnais would not believe their eyes and insisted that the Germans were only resting, *de passage*. Then the city realized that it was occupied. No one in Lyons had seen more than one egg a month for half a year. When the news got around that the Germans were really in residence, the black market unfroze, Lyons swarmed to its restaurants, and there was a binge of five-egg omelettes which produced a municipal bilious attack. To make sure that the Nazis wouldn't get so much as one yolk, Lyons ate its entire stock of thousands of stale eggs in twenty-four hours flat.

Mrs. Jeffries had left Paris, on September 17th, just in time. On September 24th the Paris Nazis had arrested her remaining American women friends and shipped them for detention to a hotel in the Vosges spa town of Vittel. Now Mrs. Jeffries felt that the Germans, in occupying Lyons, were catching up with her too. On November 18th, a week after they had come, she went with her American passport to the Spanish consulate and asked for a Spanish visa, the fourth and most difficult of a quartet of permits upon whose accumulation and synchronization a traveller's departure from France depended. These four legal treasures, coming in time, were wings on a refugee's feet, but late, they could be like stones around a refugee's neck, pulling him down to destruction. The first permit was dependent merely upon the possession of a *carte d'identité* and a passport, and each succeeding one upon the one before; the first, third, and fourth were good for only a month; and it could take three months to obtain the whole set, during which time, just as the fourth was granted, the first and third could expire, and the process, through a series of renewals, would have to start all over again. In despair, some refugees killed themselves after a losing race to make their *papiers* come out even, and others, who had enough money to live on through a first lengthy paper-stamping period of hope, became penniless during the second attempt and, unable to escape, eventually rotted in jails or concentration camps. In war-racked, refugee-ridden Europe, people are no longer people, they are their papers.

In the seven weeks she had been in Lyons, Mrs. Jeffries had, with diligence, accumulated and kept up to date the first three of her permits. The first was her *permis de séjour* from the Rhône prefecture, allowing her to remain in Lyons, where she had no business to be in the first place and where the Vichy police might nab her. Lyons was a refugee bottleneck, so European fugitives were denied *permis* by the hundreds every day, but Mrs. Jeffries, favored as an American by the municipal clerks, some of whom, from the Vichy viewpoint, hadn't yet got into line, obtained her *permis* after only a week of obstinate finagling. Once she had this No. 1 stamp, she could safely go to the Sûreté and ask for her stamp No. 2, a Vichy France *visa de sortie*. Vichy's visa took four weeks. Paper No. 3 was her Portuguese visa, good for only a month, which took two weeks to obtain and on the possession of which her subsequent Spanish visa, also good for only a month, depended. Spain, which is politically worried and physically undernourished, allows no foreigner to enter unless he has stamped proof that he means to hurry right out again, usually to Lisbon and its airport, Europe's last exit. On November 18th, when Mrs. Jeffries asked the Spanish consulate clerk for her visa, he informed her that (a) Spain had that day mobilized its army, (b) he had heard the the Spanish border was in consequence closed, (c) he had heard that it was open twice a week but that the trains were booked so solidly that no one could get on one for six months, (d) he had heard it was open for one hour every afternoon to pass mail and telegrams only, and (e) he knew it would take ten days for the *señora* to obtain a Spanish visa unless she wished to make him, as she had implied she would, a gracious gift of five hundred francs for the Spanish poor, in which case she could have her visa the day after tomorrow.

Mrs. Jeffries gave him the five hundred francs and two days later he gave her the visa and the official information that the border was indeed closed tighter than a trap. However, he reminded her that in Spain, as in most of contemporary Europe, her visa, paradoxically, would be honored even though she entered the country by stealth. He kindly suggested that she go and look around in the French border city of Pau. Pau, Mrs. Jeffries knew, was the trading centre for the mountaineer guides who, for a terrific price, walked their refugee clients over the Pyrenees into Spain.

On November 20th, a little over two months out of Paris, Mrs. Jeffries unhooked her rucksack from underneath the pink cretonne curtains in her Lyons rooming house and started for Pau. Her train trip from Lyons to Pau, which would have taken about sixteen hours in peacetime, took the wornout French locomotives twenty-four hours on France's dilapidated railroad tracks. Mrs. Jeffries was lucky; she had a seat for the entire journey. The late November rains, which are southern France's version of early winter, had set in. Her second-class coach was overcrowded, unheated, and damp. Whenever her feet felt congealed in her inadequate, wooden-soled sandals, which are what most women in France now have to wear, she sat on her feet, like Buddha, which most French women have of late learned how to do.

In Pau the only place she could find to sleep was a maid's room under the mansard of a third-class hotel. For two years all the first-class hotels of Pau, the capital of the Basses-Pyrénées, like those of all the so-called Unoccupied key cities, had been occupied by the German Gestapo and Armistice Commission. Now, since the Nazis had made the occupation official, the second-class hostelries had been booked for the oncoming German Army *Kommandanturen*. Her first three days in Pau, Mrs. Jeffries found no French face which she wanted to trust with her peculiarly personal question, "Pardon me, but do you know anyone who could smuggle me across the Spanish border?" After the rebellious air of Paris and the violence of Lyons, the sullen atmosphere of bourgeois, once-fashionable Pau was not encouraging. The city seemed indifferent to the war, which had never really touched it; hardened to its Germans, who had come with defeat; and annoyed at America's North African invasion, whose first military achievement, as far as Pau could see, was the cutting off of the city's best black-market green-vegetable supply.

Mrs. Jeffries hoped to avoid walking across the mountains into Spain. She had tried to find in Pau one of the local patriot *cheminots*, who, like thousands of their fellow railroad workers all over France, were helping to resist the Germans by helping anybody who hated them, and by carrying messages for underground *services*, transporting their agents, sidetracking shipments to Germany, chalking tortoises (the symbol of slowdowns) on every piece of freight, sabotaging, passing fugitives in good standing, and the like. Mrs. Jeffries hoped to arrange for a ride across the Pyrenees to

Spain in a nice freight car. But the superb, skillful patriotism of the *cheminots*, which everyone in France knew about, had finally become too familiar to the Nazis, and, in a typical, Hydra-headed plan, they had decided to kill the French railroad men's resistance movement, and further paralyze the French people's ability to move about, by inviting twelve thousand French railway workers to go to Germany, since too many German railroad men were on duty in Russia. By the time Mrs. Jeffries began to get her bearings in Pau, dozens of the district's *cheminots* were already in concentration camps for turning down the German invitation to travel, the railroad grapevine was in disorder, and the stowing away of an American woman in a box car was out of the question.

All in all, for the first twelve days Mrs. Jeffries was in Pau, it seemed impossible to find someone to smuggle her out in any way whatever. The smuggling had to be done by guides, arrangements for whom were made by contact men, and no contact man was willing to load a woman onto his unsuspecting mountaineer guide. It was a tough walking trip over the Pyrenees, the Pyrenees' passes being on the whole higher than those in the Alps, and the guides wanted no females, especially one who was forty-five and an American to boot. No one really wanted to smuggle Americans of either sex, because for two years Americans had been as rare as hen's teeth around Pau and so were material for comment. In the first week, after getting a foothold in a good assortment of cafés, high and low, Mrs. Jeffries was refused admittance to over two dozen passage parties she'd heard about. The second week she concentrated on contact men who made appointments only at night; they seemed more responsible, as they usually held respectable office jobs by day. An insurance clerk pessimistically refused to try to pass her or anybody else, because fifty Frenchmen he had helped pass the week before had been caught by the Spaniards and were already back home again and under surveillance; they were white-collar men and students who, since the American invasion, had been eager to go to North Africa, join the French forces, and *"refaire la guerre avec les frères américains."* A kindly, hard-up Swede made a contact for her, and got an offer for an immediate crossing at twenty thousand francs. He thought the fee was too high, and while he was still haggling with the contact man, the party started off for the mountains.

Finally, in a lively café which specialized in B.B.C. news broadcasts, tuned down to a whisper, Mrs. Jeffries discovered a native waiter who had escaped from a prison camp in Germany and who offered not only to seek a contact but, in his enthusiasm, to lend her the money, if necessary, for a passage, which he said ordinarily cost from two to ten thousand francs but for her would be astronomically higher. He was still looking for a passage at any price when, on November 24th, the German Army trucked in and occupied Pau. Three days later the French garrison there was demobilized. That night the waiter told her that after France fell the French soldiers had been mostly anti-British and pro-Vichy. Then, after the Dieppe Commando raid, he said, the men had turned around and wanted to *rejoindre les Alliés*, too late. The American invasion of Africa had added to their fever to fight the Germans again. As an answer to this pro-Allied sentiment, the Germans, in one swift blow delivered everywhere at once in Unoccupied France, in one day demobilized all that was left of what had once been France's army, thus scattering the men and their rebellious hopes and turning what had been men with guns into eighty thousand defenseless unemployed, ripe for shipping to Germany's labor camps. The waiter said that in Pau that morning, while some of the French officers wept, the Germans had simply ordered the French soldiers to fall in line, stack their arms, and fall out as civilians because the French Army no longer existed. Back in their barracks, where they had providently hidden a cache of pistols, the soldiers tied the weapons under their ill-fitting, baggy breeches and got away with them, prepared for the great day when the Yanks would invade France. What uniforms the demobilized soldiers did not have on their backs were gathered up by the Nazis and sent to Germany to add to the Nazi wool pile.

On her twelfth day in Pau, Mrs. Jeffries decided that at least she would be ready and properly dressed for a crossing at a moment's notice, should an offer come. She had shipped her trunk there from Lyons, and it was still at the railway station, waiting baggage-car room on a train to Spain. An amenable porter let her open it and take out the warm clothes she wanted, change into them in the dirty ladies' toilet, and pack the light clothes she had taken off. With her ski boots in her hand, she walked out of the station dressed in a tweed skirt, wool stockings, sweater, scarf, topcoat, and mittens, and nearly roasted en route to a second-hand bookshop, where, it was reported, the proprietress ran a smugglers' travel agency on the side. There she got a too prompt, overenthusiastic reply. The woman said *"Oui"* and in the same breath demanded fifty thousand francs for a crossing with a group leaving the next morning. She said that the trip would be de luxe, with donkeys to ride up the lower slopes and only two hours of what she called promenading on the peaks. Mrs. Jeffries, who had nearly forty thousand francs left in her pocketbook, declared, with equal airiness, that she had only thirty-five thousand francs on earth, and walked out. When she returned to her rooming house, the concierge whispered to her that the Gestapo had called, requesting her to appear at the *Kommissäriat* the next morning. Mrs. Jeffries ran back, sweating, to the bookshop and the woman big-heartedly accepted the thirty-five thousand francs.

JUNE 5, 1943 Mrs. Jefferies had paid a thirty-five-thousand-franc fee for the services of a guide, had packed her rucksack, had put on her warmest clothes, and was ready to set out from Pau to cross the Pyrenees into Spain. The plan for this, her second, illegal border crossing was simple. All she had to do was pick up a contact man the next morning at the Pau bookshop where she had arranged for what the proprietress had called her mountain *promenade*, go with him to the station, and board a certain southbound train, on which, before it started, the bookshop woman's husband, coming in on an earlier northbound train from border business, would find them. The husband would inform the contact man what town they were to get off at, which guide was to take the job, which taxi-man to trust, and other vital details. The husband's train was late. Mrs. Jeffries' train was about to depart and the contact man was hanging nervously out the window when the husband, from a window of his train, arriving on the next track, shouted, "Not now! Tomorrow night!" Mrs. Jeffries had checked out of her third-class hotel and it was an additional letdown for her to realize that she didn't have even the dreary maid's room she had been occupying there to spend the next thirty-six hours in. The bookshop woman warned her to keep out of the cafés, as that was where the Gestapo, who were after her, always looked first. She recommended a humble *pension* where no one asked questions or names. Mrs. Jeffries got a room that had a broken window, through which, as special preparation for the crossing, she caught cold.

Mrs. Jeffries and the contact man left Pau by another train the following evening, and in the last vestiges of daylight they got off at a way station and stepped into a waiting taxi and into the company of three men who apparently were to cross with her. All three spoke French with a slight accent and all three immediately protested that she spoke French with a heavy accent and was a woman besides. All three, furthermore, violently agreed that an American woman in the party made the crossing look like a dangerous job. After an hour's quarrelsome ride, the five of them stepped out in the dark into what smelled like a farmyard and fumbled their way into a low building. They were in a sheepfold, together with the warm sheep. The contact man departed. Ten minutes later he returned and said that the coast was clear. He led the party outdoors and, after a brief walk, into a cottage, pleasant and immaculate, which turned out to be the guide's. Their guide, a man named Boniface, who ran a speakeasy in his parlor, where he sold rum by the glass, had just said good night to his last customers. He was big, blond, and dignified. He accepted the surprise of having an American lady with taciturn calm. His young wife served the party a superb supper of black bean soup, an omelet of fresh eggs, a whole roasted baby lamb killed for them that day, goat cheese, strong mountain wine, and a warm loaf of home-made white bread. It was the first white bread Mrs. Jeffries had seen in two years and it tasted like manna.

The bookshop woman had talked of donkeys and a two-hour stroll on the peaks; at the station her husband had mentioned a truck and a four-hour walk. Now Boniface warned them that they would walk on their own legs for fifteen or twenty hours, from the time they left his front door until they slid downhill into Spain, that along the line there was an ascent of seven thousand feet, and that at least one or two nights would be passed in shepherds' huts, unoccupied because of the season of the year. Boniface himself was to take them about three-quarters of the way and then hand them over to a Spanish guide who would meet the party en route. One of the three male travellers, who before supper had formally introduced himself under a fancy French name, angrily declared that he was returning to Pau with the contact man to complain about the American woman, to complain about the distance over the mountains, and to demand his money back. After he had slammed the cottage door on his way out, one of the two remaining men, a dark little fellow, said sadly that his friend would unfortunately be back, that both his fine name and passport were false, that he was really named Fishbein and was a crooked Strasbourg Jew, and that he himself was a Polish Jew named Kowalski.

Kowalski was, he said, a watchmaker; he had become a naturalized Frenchman eighteen years ago and had spent his savings of a hundred thousand francs to get himself and his wife from Paris via Toulouse to Pau. Three days ago the Germans had literally kicked the Kowalskis out of their room in Pau, torn him from his wife, and said that she could sleep under the bridges. Madame Kowalski had a weak heart, which would not permit her to walk over the mountains. He could do nothing but leave her there, wondering if he would ever see her again. He was going to try to get to Tunisia and join up as a chauffeur for the American soldiers. The hitherto silent No. 3 of the party, a blond, blue-eyed young man, then said that he would not tell his name or nationality until they reached Spain. When Mrs. Jeffries laughed and said he was a German, he laughed, too, in self-conscious surprise. He said that he planned to tell the American consul at Madrid that he was an American and so get to Casablanca. Then, in broken English, he said to Mrs. Jeffries that his mother's sister lived in Yorkville and gave her name and address. After they had all retired for the night, Mrs. Jeffries was unable to sleep at first because there was only a thin partition between her room and the room occupied by the two men and the German kept her awake with his haranguing.

Next morning breakfast was brought up to the travellers. They ate together in Mrs. Jeffries' room, at her invitation. They were forbidden to go downstairs all day for fear the parlor grog customers, who twice daily were augmented by the Nazi patrol, would see them. Over their hot milk and grain coffee, the blond young man, who had weakened in his resolve at least to the point of calling himself Hans, was still talking. He declared that the whole thing looked like a middle-class swindle to him, that he was an anti-Nazi Socialist who had been in the Foreign Legion, that that cow of a woman in Pau had gypped them all, that he had paid her what she called a bargain price of thirty-five thousand francs because his cousin had paid the same the week before, that the two Jews, because they were Jews, had each had to pay fifty thousand francs, that God alone knew what Madame the American had had to pay, and that out of this fortune the noble Boniface, who did almost all the work and took almost all the risk, received only two thousand francs for the whole job. At noon the noble Boniface brought up a dozen fried eggs, with ham, and said that the other *monsieur*—Fishbein, or whatever his name was—had better return from Pau that day if he expected to cross into Spain before spring. A shepherd down from the uplands had just reported that snow was expected in two days; when it arrived, the pass would be closed for the winter. Fishbein, arrayed in a brand-new mountain-climbing outfit of glossy brown corduroy, turned up for a cold lamb supper.

On the following day, the party set off in the blackness just before dawn. The slopes of the foothills were steep, slippery with dried grass, and tiring. Mrs. Jeffries, who hadn't eaten as well in two years as she had during the past two days, was short of breath. Boniface vainly kept urging speed; until they reached their first stop, at a shepherd's hut, a few hours up, they would be in danger of encountering the French customs guard, a neighbor of Boniface and a law-abiding man. They came to the hut just before noon. Boniface forbade them to kindle a fire for fear his *douanier* would see the smoke. In the confused haste of departure, no one had remembered to take along water. A lunch of cheese and chocolate made them thirstier. While they rested, Boniface, who had to meet a rum-smuggling friend, walked off into the panorama of soaring granite slopes like a man going to keep a business engagement just around the corner. It was nearly dusk when he returned with a jug of icy mountain-torrent water and bad news. The Spanish guide, who was to meet them the next day, was brûlé, or hot; the Nazi patrol was after him and anyone else loose on the mountains. Boniface ordered the party to lie low and spend the night where it was.

The hut contained a shelf on which the shepherd, when he was with his flock in the summer, slept on a pallet of bracken. It was too late in the year for bracken, so Mrs. Jeffries slept on the bare boards. The four men slept on the floor.

Daybreak was magnificent in the circus-shaped valleys below, but Boniface was too familiar with the view to waste time on it and was impatient to start the big climb. That day they walked nine hours single file, stopping twice to eat chocolate and bread. All morning the men begged Mrs. Jeffries not to hold them back but to walk faster. By noon only Boniface was still striding along easily. They had left the fan-ribbed plateaus for the Pyrenees' upper reaches and were ascending the gullies that marked the next portion of their route. Once Mrs. Jeffries lit a cigarette, but she quickly found that she was too busy walking to smoke. The gullies, which were the beds of torrents in spring, became rougher and steeper and the stones they walked on rolled in little avalanches underfoot. To maintain her balance, she had to keep her eyes on the toes of her boots and on the heels of the boots in front of her; this gave her something to concentrate on and steadied her. Like a man showing off the local sights to a visiting lady, Boniface politely pointed out to her evidences of his rum runners— the charred wood of a fire under a sheltering rock and later, in a gulch, a broken cask, which it made her thirsty to look at.

A soft rain started and then turned to sleet. Fishbein, who was hung about with small luggage, entreated Mrs. Jeffries to shelter under her topcoat a cardboard box which he said contained noodles, though it felt heavier to her. By four they entered the pass, seventy-five hundred feet above sea level, which Boniface had been aiming for. On the boulders beside a waterfall at which they stopped to drink, they found whiskers of ice that were refreshing to the throat. Here Fishbein emitted a series of questions he had apparently been storing up during the plodding, single-file silence of the day. Did Boniface know if you could get good prices for Moroccan food in the black market in Marseilles? How much could you get for English gold sovereigns in Lisbon? Was it true that saccharine was selling for two thousand pesetas a kilo in Madrid, and did he know anybody on the other side of the border who had ever heard of the stuff? "We have heard enough, Monsieur," said Boniface, "to know that saccharine is so scarce in Pau, that the cafés serve it already dissolved in bottles, like sugar water. Here in the mountains, when war comes, we use honey. From father to son we have smuggled rum. *Ça, c'est notre droit.* But we never smuggled dirty things like drugs, even sweet ones." He turned to Mrs. Jeffries. "Give him back his package," he ordered. She handed it over, saying she supposed that Fishbein, after all, was not fool enough to ask her to lug noodles over the Pyrenees and that the box was too light for gold but probably heavy enough for saccharine. Fishbein didn't look at the other men, but he laughed at her and took back his box with alacrity.

At sundown, an increasingly cold wind revived Mrs. Jeffries' New Hampshire blood and gave her second strength, but it seemed to exhaust the already weary men, who begged Boniface, at whose heels she was sturdily treading, to slow down, for the lady's sake. Just before nightfall they reached a second shepherd's hut, also vacant. It proved to be comfortably large; its shelf was big enough for all four travellers to throw themselves down together to rest, close, indifferent, exhausted. A while later, after cheese and chocolate, Mrs. Jeffries uncorked a flask of armagnac she had brought with her, Hans produced a jar of jam, and Kowalski passed around a box of biscuits. There was a spring by the hut but no bucket, so they leaned over the pool and drank from their dirty hands.

At four the next morning the Spanish guide arrived with his dog and a Basque friend. The three had walked all night in contempt of the Nazi patrols, who didn't know their way around in the dark. The Spaniard, who looked like an American Indian and was a taciturn man, grunted what little he had to say in a very limited French. The dog was affectionate. The Basque spoke fluent French and carried a hunting gun, forbidden in France since the armistice. He said that he had brought it along for any game birds he might encounter but that he preferred to shoot at the Nazi patrols; in the mountains their corpses were never found. In the dark and another rainstorm, they started off on their two ways, big Boniface to go alone back home and the crossing party on toward invisible Spain. The party now included two mountaineers, but in the damp darkness Mrs. Jeffries' real guide was whatever light neck scarf was visible in front of her. The Spaniard, who led the way, was nervous and stopped to listen a lot. Just before dawn they walked past a big stone house, inside which a dog barked. No one, however, came outdoors to see what was up. Long after sunup the gullies still gleamed with the ice that had formed in the night. By noon Mrs. Jeffries' pack—her rucksack and a small overnight case strapped to it with her belt— seemed so heavy that she could scarcely breathe in the thin mountain air. Apologetically she offered the mountaineers a thousand francs each if they would carry her luggage. The Spaniard reluctantly took the money. The Basque refused at first to accept her banknote; *tout de même*, he said, he was only a friend, not a guide entitled to pay. Then he gave in.

By two o'clock the party had almost reached the Spanish border. The Spaniard then thought he heard a Nazi patrol and hastily ordered the travellers to slide down a series of gulches. The stones, as Mrs. Jeffries' skirt rolled up, cut her bare thighs. It took the party two more hours to zigzag their way up the side of a mountain to get back on the trail again.

Just before they came to the border, their route was strewn with morsels of torn paper. These were the fragments of passports which escaping Frenchmen, who probably aimed to pass themselves off as French-Canadians, had destroyed, as the last proof of their national identity. Hans was not surprised to find a piece of his cousin's forged French passport behind a rock. A tall, impressive stone monument, with "France" carved on the north side and "España" on the south, marked the border line. The party rushed a few feet into Spain and started laughing. They had arrived and felt safe. Hysterically, the German, the Pole, and the Alsatian began asking the American Mrs. Jeffries' advice and shouting their immediate plans. Hans asked if he might become her brother in Spain, since he was going to be American anyhow. It seemed to her a good idea. Fishbein and Kowalski said that they would declare themselves French-Canadians, since they spoke no English. Fishbein said that Quebec was the popular birthplace these days and Kowalski was enthusiastic, though he couldn't remember the name and kept asking Mrs. Jeffries, "Where was it that I was born?"

Their gaiety vanished when their escorts refused to go any farther. The Spaniard and his friend had walked all night, they lived over on the next ridge, and they had to bring another party across the next day, if the snow held off. Mrs. Jeffries, Kowalski, and Hans each offered first the Spaniard and then his friend a thousand francs to continue, but Fishbein wouldn't offer anything. Both escorts haughtily refused to accept any more money, but they nevertheless accompanied the party another mile to the brow of the mountain. There the guide pointed to a settlement far below. He told his party to go to a house with a wire fence and ask for the friend of José. The two mountaineers and the dog then turned on their heels toward home.

In the scattered settlement, which the crossing party reached before dusk, no one had heard of José or his friend, and the first three dwellings Mrs. Jeffries and the men came upon all had wire fences. At the third, a tall, elderly Spanish shepherd with two tall young sons hospitably took them in. His cottage consisted of a single room, without illumination except for two resin torches stuck in iron rings beside the fireplace. The room opened into a haymow. While the sons stared in embarrassment, Mrs. Jeffries took off her sweater and skirt by the fire and changed to a rumpled flannel dress. The father gave the visitors bread and two bottles of dark wine, for which he would take no money. He and his sons then sat down at a small table and ate their frugal supper of cabbage soup from one pitifully small pot. There was apparently no other food in the house. The hungry party slept in the haymow and next morning washed in a brook.

By eight o'clock, Hans and Kowalski, who had gone forth to see what sort of hamlet they were in and how they could get out of it, had already been arrested. Fishbein came running into the cottage with the news, plucked his precious cardboard box and bags from the corner in which he had placed them, and plunged into the haymow. For a few minutes Mrs. Jeffries heard him burrowing. She never laid eyes on him again.

Two youthful, smiling members of the *guardia civil*, wearing cocked hats, walked in, quite sociably, with the arrested men. Mrs. Jeffries was not arrested, because she had a passport, but she was detained for questioning. She heard Hans, in Foreign Legion Spanish, tell the police that he was her *hermano*, Frank Jeffries, of Nuevo Hampshire. Kowalski said nothing; he merely looked sad and fatalistic. Neither of them had papers to prove or disprove anything they might say. Hans claimed that their papers had been stolen. Both believed the popular French legend that there were British and American consuls at the big, nearby town of X and that these officials had the magic power of transmuting men, willingly without a country, into British and American soldiers and transporting them to fight on the North African front. There was some discussion between the young policemen of whether it would be correct to let the three foreigners hire a cart to take them to the nearest village jail, ten kilometres distant, or whether they should walk. Kowalski, the only one who had any Spanish money, paid a hundred pesetas for the use of their host's cart. They reached the jail at four.

At the jail the two men were searched for dangerous instruments and Hans's nailfile was taken from him. He stuck to his story that he was Mrs. Jeffries' brother, young Jeffries; neither he nor Mrs. Jeffries had stopped to think, though the village police chief thought of it right away, that as a Jeffries he could at best be only her brother-in-law. The chief, who seemed to be in a dither, said that he had been swamped by ninety so-called French-Canadians in five days and that his jail was full. *Sotto voce*, the two members of the *guardia civil* suggested to the *americana*, whose pocketbook they had just searched for forbidden foreign monies, that, if she wanted to rid herself of her two thousand illegal French francs, accommodations could perhaps be had in the village's crowded hotel for the night for her relative, friend, and self, and how many rooms would they want? Hans and Kowalski humbly whispered, "One room for us all would be fine." Mrs. Jeffries said oh, for the love of God, could she room alone for a change?

Mrs. Jeffries was granted the luxury of solitude. Her room contained an enlarged photograph of a young man whom the proprietress bitterly described as her last and littlest brother, shot by Franco. Three others, she said, had died as Loyalist soldiers during the Civil War. She advised Kowalski and Hans to write that night to the British and American consuls in Madrid and say that if they never turned up to look for them in the stinkhole jail in the town of X.

The bus to X the next morning contained Mrs. Jeffries, Hans, Kowalski, and eighteen arrested Frenchmen who still hoped to get to North Africa to fight alongside the Americans. Most of the eighteen were advance-guard men and had groups of followers waiting in France to start if and when the chiefs got safely through. An ex-Army officer on the seat beside Mrs. Jeffries was a de Gaullist volunteer who had been arrested in Dakar and sent to a prison camp in Pétain's France, where he had learned English and Spanish from other prisoners and, like them, lived on carrot tops. Thirteen of his comrades there had starved to death. When some food packages from home finally came through, five of the men gained enough strength to escape from the concentration camp. He said that the friends of the American lady were lucky not to have been arrested till morning; he and twelve of the others in the bus had spent the night in the village calaboose in a room with a privy in it; the room was so small that five men took turns standing up while eight men lay on the floor. They had been given no food for twenty-four hours. When the French officer discovered that Mrs. Jeffries was that rare traveller, one whose passport and papers were actually in order, she instantly became, in his eyes, a sort of emissary extraordinary. The unreasonable European conviction in a crisis that Americans are saviors who can think of everything and get anything done swept through the bus when the prisoners saw the officer start scribbling on bits of paper. As fugitives, and experienced rebels, they guessed what that meant; he was trusting her with the names and addresses of Spanish friends who might intercede for him if he was imprisoned. Immediately all the men tried to crowd around her in an eager, swaying mass, to give her their own touchstone addresses or their mothers' names. Would she write *Maman*, would she even write President Roosevelt? Most of the men were fliers. One ex-captain had five hundred pilots back in France waiting a chance to fly American fighting planes; the group in the bus included everything from two frightened students who didn't want to be sent to work in Germany to a retired artillery colonel. All the Frenchmen implicitly believed that the British and American consulates could get them through Axis Spain and over to Allied North Africa, which they admitted would be a miracle if it came off but a disgrace if it didn't.

The two amiable members of the *guardia civil* had told Mrs. Jeffries, probably to please a lady, that she was *en libertad* and that there was an American consul at X. At the X police station, which, Spanish fashion, reopened for business at ten o'clock at night, she learned that the nearest British and American consulates were at Madrid and that she certainly was not at liberty. Furthermore, as the police department's problem child, she was put at the end of the night's docket for special questioning, not because she had entered Spain illegally but because her papers were suspiciously O.K. She sat in the stationhouse till midnight, helplessly watching and hearing Hans and Kowalski and all eighteen militant Frenchmen from the bus interrogated into jail. Seventeen of the eighteen declared, while the Spanish roared with laughter, that they were born in Quebec. The retired artillery colonel, who wanted to be different, said he had been born in Winnipeg. Mrs. Jeffries felt very sad when she said good night to Kowalski, whom she promised to visit in jail next day, and to Hans, whom she kissed on both cheeks to strengthen the brother-and-sister story. The police, after studying her papers and questioning her, told her to return in the morning and sent her to a hotel, where a housekeeper was assigned to watch her closely. At 1 A.M. she took off all her clothes for the first time in four days. Her feet had bled when she was crossing the mountains and her thighs were still lacerated from sliding down gullies. Then she took her first bath since leaving Lyons.

The next morning Mrs. Jeffries discovered that though she was in Spain physically she was not there officially and that though she had money in her pocket she was penniless. She had crossed the border with exactly fifty dollars in American currency and a Banque de France draft for two hundred pesetas. No one in X would touch her greenbacks, American money being too illegal in provincial Spain even for the black market. No bank would cash her draft, which was drawn on a bank in the Spanish border town of Canfranc, across the Pyrenees from Pau. The Spanish police refused to admit that she was in Spain at all, because Canfranc, and not X, had also been put on her passport as her Spanish port of entry by the accommodating Lyons Spanish consulate clerk, who was obliged to write down some entrance town and knew that she was planning to smuggle herself across somewhere in the neighborhood of Canfranc. This clerk had also told her that her draft would be good anywhere in Spain and that she need never set foot in Canfranc. Now it looked as if she wouldn't even be allowed to, since, on top of everything else, her hotel refused to let her leave town unless she paid her bill. The police, on the other hand, wouldn't let her stay in town unless her entry visa was stamped at Canfranc first. The police unsentimentally advised her to raise some cash by selling her wedding ring, which she still wore. That noon, in the hotel corridor, a courtly, middle-aged Spaniard made her a remarkable speech in French which began, "I am not very rich." In it, he explained that he had heard of her sad case and would she permit him to lend her the money for her hotel bill and her journey to Canfranc? When, in her gratitude, she offered him her ring as security to cover his fantastic offer, he refused it. His only request was that the American *señora* post from Lisbon a love letter to his fiancée, aged thirty-five, who for ten years had lived in Rio de Janeiro. At that moment he seemed to Mrs. Jeffries the most quixotic, romantic, and kind man in the world.

Spanish trains, because of a shortage of equipment, run into a terminal point one day and out of it the next. X was such a point and this was X's out day, so Mrs. Jeffries left that night at six for the town of Saragossa, which was south, and there she had to wait from midnight till six the next morning for a train to Canfranc, which was north. Two other hotel guests, who also had port-of-entry and money complications at Canfranc, made the trip with her. They were a German-Jewish couple travelling as Catholics on false French passports, which were nothing but sheets of typewriter paper stamped with visas for which, being Jews, they had been forced to pay ten times what Mrs. Jeffries had paid. The couple were desperate because their Portuguese visas, without which their entry visas into Spain were not valid, had just lapsed and they feared, with justification, that they would be sent back to the Nazis in France. By the time Mrs. Jeffries cashed her draft and arrived at the police station in Canfranc to get her passport stamped, the couple's Spanish visas had, indeed, been invalidated and they were speechless with terror. In this state they numbly refused to act as interpreters for an even more tragic female compatriot, just picked up by the police, who could not figure her out. Through Mrs. Jeffries' questionings in halting, high-school German, it was revealed that this woman was Jewish, from Frankfort, and sixty, and had four American dollars and thirty French francs to her name, plus a sister in New Jersey and a ticket to Palestine on a ship which had sailed from Barcelona the month before. The police had temporarily saved her life by arresting her in the border hills; she was in a daze, her feet were frozen, her luggage consisted of a string shopping bag, and she claimed that she had crossed the Pyrenees alone. Her mind was still wandering. She thought that Canfranc, which is in the mountains, was Barcelona, which is on the sea. Mrs. Jeffries took her to a restaurant and fed her. In the midst of the meal she whispered reproachfully, "I have never eaten any but kosher food," and hid some morsels of broken bread in her shopping bag. After coffee she tried to pay her half of the check. Later the police said that they had no choice but to return her to France, though Mrs. Jeffries cajoled, stormed, made a scene, and prophesied that they were sending the old woman back to a very disagreeable death.

From Canfranc Mrs. Jeffries wearily took the train back to Saragossa. That evening, at the Saragossa station, where she was to catch the express for Madrid, she again met, to her surprise, the Jewish couple, shaken but hopeful. They had been able to "arrange things" with the Canfranc police. To pay for their tickets to Madrid, they were selling a heavy gold chain to the station lunch-counter woman, who really did not want to buy it; she said that this sort of jewelry only reminded her of the troubles everybody had been through.

Mrs. Jeffries, at least, was fortunate enough to have three pesetas left when she arrived in Madrid, so she was able to take a tram to the American consulate. There she found a comforting letter of credit, a Clipper reservation, and loving, questioning letters from her worried New Hampshire family. Then the troubles of the world at large and of the Spaniards in particular, with civil war behind them and poverty ahead; the nightmare, somnambulistic existence of refugees, all trying to wake up outside of the continent of Europe; the xenophobia of embittered, hungry Madrileños; the Puerta del Sol prison across the street from one of the nicest cafés in town, and the fourteen other city prisons with anxious crowds hovering nervously at the gates; the sick faces and shabby clothes of the city's poor—the whole, costly, cruel Fascist pattern of life began closing in on her again. In Madrid the penniless political prisoners were dying in rocky cells underground and up on the streets life was even more expensive than it had been under the German occupation in Paris. She spent a hundred and thirty dollars in eight days in Madrid, though all she did was pay her debt to the Quixote in the hotel in X, buy one necessary pair of bad stockings for $3.50, live *en pension* with poor meals and no butter at the second-class Hotel Nacional, and purchase food packages for the now-imprisoned middle-aged Jewish couple, who, whatever they had arranged for themselves in Canfranc, had not been able to make it stick in Madrid. She received a pathetic postal card from Hans, in a concentration camp with Kowalski at Campo de Miranda de Ebro, in the mountains. Like a man of the modern world, he said that it was not a bad concentration camp, as camps went, and that the American consul had sent him neither passport, uniform, nor food. In a faint, pencilled postscript in English he added, "I am kold. Write soonly. Your brother, Frank J."

It took a full eight days and ceaseless scurrying for Mrs. Jeffries to renew her Portuguese visa, which had lapsed, and to obtain a precious temporary extension of her Spanish visa until the new Portuguese stamp was obtained. The complications of special police papers, which the Franco administration had built up like a towering wall against foreigners, whom it was supposed to keep from staying in the country, in the end merely made it more difficult for them to leave. For forty-eight hours she stayed in her hotel because the Madrid police had taken and held her passport. In the Europe of today, to walk around without your passport buttoned in your pocket is as abnormal as it would be to walk around without your heart beating in your body.

Ignorance, revenge, and bureaucracy in all their contemporary European forms made Mrs. Jeffries' days in Madrid a seesaw of uncertainty. Until her last hour there she did not know when she would leave or why it could not have been sooner. No one in any country in Europe knows what is going on in the country next to it; international trains, whose movement formerly seemed as sure as the sun's, are now spoken of as if they could disappear off the face of the earth once they crossed a border. Officials themselves, who have people's lives, documents, and plans in their hands, know little that is exact, except that whatever they know can change by breakfast tomorrow. In place of certainty there is only a vast, tangled ball of rumor. In place of sensible, humane procedure, now destroyed by wars, revenge, suspicion, and power politics, petty official strictures have been built up against which the individual is as helpless as a caged animal. Because Mrs. Jeffries had lived in so-called Communistic France under the Front Populaire, which favored the Spanish Loyalists, a high-up Spanish Fascist official spitefully delayed signing one of her papers, which made her miss the night express she was scheduled to take to Lisbon. Because she had lived in non-interventionist France under the Radical Socialists, who had imprisoned refugee Loyalists, a lower-down Spanish Republican concierge maliciously made her miss the next night's train.

Mrs. Jeffries had been officially told that the Madrid-Libson sleeping compartments cost seventy pesetas and could be arranged for only with the porter on the train; rumor told her that the compartments actually cost thirty pesetas at the railway station but were sold there only to Spaniards. She got on the train Monday, December 21, 1942, with seventy-five pesetas in her pocket and discovered that the porter demanded eighty for a berth. Fortunately, an Englishman in the crowded day coach had the eighty and was willing to spend it, so at least she was able to get a seat. She had been officially told that she could take a hundred pesetas from Spain into Portugal. Next morning, at the Portuguese border, a Spanish customs inspector told her she could not take even her seventy-five pesetas out, that all of it had to be left behind for the poor of Spain. A jovial Spanish policeman advised her to spend her money for breakfast in the station. She spent her pesetas for her breakfast and for his, too. The policeman drank a cup of coffee and a bottle of anisette.

After the harshness of Madrid, Lisbon seemed soft. After the acute astringencies of the rest of Europe, Portugal seemed only pinched. The hotels and bars of Lisbon, the last diplomatic freehold on the Continent's all-important Atlantic coastline, were full of Turks, Americans, English,

Poles, French, Germans, Scandinavians, Swiss, Iranians, South Americans, and a medley of decorated buttonholes, uniforms, medals, spies, oil men, ambassadors, black-market agents, legation attachés, political secretaries, and Berlin *Damen* who, if they had any chic at all, were sized up as tarts doubling as *agents provocateurs*. Mrs. Jeffries passed Christmas Day in bed, reading a second-hand copy of Voltaire's "Candide," which is now having a popular revival among Lisbon's international, war-worn misanthropes, possibly because it cynically describes the city's calamitous earthquake of nearly two hundred years back as being (like Europe's new disasters?) something which was "all for the best in the best of all possible worlds."

Mrs. Jeffries had supposed that she would leave Lisbon, and all Europe, shortly after New Year's Day. However, an early January Clipper reservation was cancelled owing to the priorities of diplomats and generals. As the weeks went by, she was squeezed out again and again by diplomats' secretaries, lend-lease agents, and the military. Along with a growing crowd of patient, unimportant civilians, Mrs. Jeffries, awaiting her turn, saw the winter out and spring established in Lisbon before she was at last lucky enough to get another Clipper passage for the first week in April. Seven months after Mrs. Jeffries had left Paris, she left Europe and started flying, roundabout, toward the United States. To get to New York from Lisbon she flew to Portuguese Guinea, and from there to Fisherman's Lake in Liberia, where the passengers lunched on fried pork chops a few steps from the equator. From there she flew the South Atlantic to Natal in Brazil, then to Belém in the same country, then north to Port of Spain in Trinidad, on to San Juan in Puerto Rico, to Bermuda, and, on her fourth day in the air, to LaGuardia Field, wet but welcome in an April shower. She had never flown home before. It didn't seem quite right to land in New York without first sighting the Statue of Liberty.

Letter from Cologne

MARCH 19, 1945 Cologne-on-the-Rhine is now a model of destruction. The nearby city of Aachen died in a different way: its handsome, melancholy skeleton is left upright; behind its elegant, carved façades, it was burned out. Cologne and its heavy, medieval pomp were blown up. By its river bank, Cologne lies recumbent, without beauty, shapeless in the rubble and loneliness of complete physical defeat. Through its clogged side streets trickles what is left of its life, a dwindled population in black and with bundles—the silent German people appropriate to the silent city.

Most of the people in Cologne have little to say. Dazed by a week of defeat, three years of bombings, and twelve years of propaganda, the old men and the women and children who now inhabit the city sound as if they had lost all ability to think rationally or to tell the truth. Nor did the last orders from their departing Nazi government encourage accurate conversation. One brand-new, fragile-looking item that is seen again and again along the sodden Cologne streets, battered by weather and war, is a propaganda poster pasted on the remaining walls. In Gothic letters, and with exclamation point, the poster advises *"Schweigen siegen!"*—"To keep silent is to win." This poster was put up just before the American First Army's triumphant entrance into the city. Having lost the war of arms, defeated Germany is apparently counting again on the psychological victory she won in the last peace—the victory of silence, lies, whining, energy, devotion, and guile. Even the children seem to have been given their orders to tell the same old patriotic little Nazi fibs. Some small boys I saw who were patently wearing their Hitlerjugend caps, from which the insignia had been removed, told me, with no timidity whatever, that these were ordinary winter caps. Then, overcome by the farcical ease of their first trick on the decadent democratic foreigner, they fled, giggling, to hide behind a ruined doorway. Theirs was the only laughter I have heard in Cologne. The other day, from the nearby city of Bonn, which our troops were then entering, news came to Cologne of an extraordinary proposition. Being a university town, Bonn felt competent to offer, for our American Army's help, the city's own selected corps of interpreters, all speaking perfect Oxford English and high German, who could thus replace, in our relations with the Bonn civilians, our own Army interpreters, many of whom are German Jews.

The only Cologne German I have talked to who has made sense began with the customary subservient lies but ended, at least, with his version of Teutonic truth. He lives near the gate of the Klingelpütz Gestapo prison and for forty years was a paper bundler for the *Kölnische Zeitung*, which was the town's leading conservative Catholic newspaper. He opened our conversation by mumbling mendaciously that no Germans had ever believed Germany could win the war, then admitted that the shocking idea of losing it had come to him and everyone else only when their Army failed to capture Stalingrad. I asked him if the Germans had not been discouraged when Japan pulled the powerful, productive United States into the conflict. He said that they had, on the contrary, rejoiced and had at once intelligently declared war on us themselves. By doing that, he explained, they forced upon us that war on two fronts which had long been the German high command's formula for military defeat. He actually seemed able to accept philosophically the idea of Germany's fast-approaching defeat—on two fronts—since it proved that the German high command had been, for Germany anyhow, absolutely right. He furthermore felt that somehow England had failed to keep a date with history by not falling by 1941.

He and his patient, nervous wife, whom I also talked with, had been bombed out three times, but she had been buried alive with him only twice, since in the terrible daylight bombing of September 17, 1944, she had been away from home in a food queue and had popped into one of the available *Bunker*, as the Germans call their airraid shelters. It had never occurred to them to leave Cologne, where food was fairly easy to get. Anyway, every other place was being bombed, too, and refugees were resented. The couple showed me their cellar room, where they had been sleeping, cooking, and hoping for the past fourteen months. It looked and smelled orthodox in the circumstances—damp, dark, crowded with a mixture of bedding and skillets, family photographs, and mudstained clothes. The mud of Cologne is part wallpaper from the city's bombed homes, part window panes, part books, part slate roofs fallen from fine old buildings, and surely part blood from the two hundred thousand dead, the fourth of Cologne's population now in peace. The paper bundler and his wife were planning to sleep upstairs now that the Americans had come. "*Gott sei Dank,*" the woman said bleakly. "Anyhow, they bring an end to the war."

The power of survival of the poor apartment house in which this couple live was shared by few of the city's grand mansions. The bombs had left the paper bundler's ground-floor bedroom intact. From its single window was visible, in the rubble-strewn areaway outside, a discarded Nazi flag. It could have been tossed only from that room. Like all the Nazi flags that had been dumped, like scarlet garbage, into the corners of alleys, its arrival there was dated. It had surely lain there from precisely four-thirty of the Tuesday afternoon on which the American Army officially took over the city and began its appreciative collection of such German souvenirs as Nazi flags. Cologne was so thoroughly destroyed by bombings that the German Army did not bother to boobytrap its ruins, presumably figuring, incorrectly, that they contained nothing attractive to the American soldier.

The hundred thousand inhabitants of Cologne who lived like troglodytes in their caves during all our blitzes are now coming up from underground to present themselves, with pale servility, to the U. S. Army's Military Government, which has already got a census under way. Three hours after our Army had fought its last bleeding step in, this military government started to operate. Much of the impression we make on captive Germany and it makes on us will be formalized in our first civilian relations with Cologne, our first big conquered city. The dangerous, comfortable moment in Germany may come when the American administrators, quite naturally, find the obedient, obsequious, efficient enemy Germans easier to deal with than the scatterbrained, individualistic French have been, or the captious Belgians, or the obstinate Dutch.

Fraternization carries a heavy penalty in Cologne. What was called in Aachen, where we began our first relations with the Germans en masse, the sixty-five-dollar question—the amount of the fine, as ordered by General Eisenhower, a soldier had to pay for talking to a German *Mädchen*—has been raised in Cologne to a ten-year prison sentence. I saw a soldier take longer than necessary to discuss with a Cologne *Fräulein* the problem of getting his laundry done, in itself a permitted brief platonic dialogue. An M.P. picked him up, theoretically for ten years. Another soldier nipped by an M.P. proved to be a Pennsylvania Dutch reconnaissance man who was lost and asking his way, in bad German, along the ruined streets. Our Army captured some splendid colored *Stadtpläne*, or city maps, of Cologne, but unfortunately the streets they indicate are often no longer there. Even the city parks are plowed under. To the Germans, with their worshipful sense of iconography, it must be shocking to sit for a moment's rest in a park beneath a blasted tree and a headless statue of the beautiful old Kaiserin Louise.

Cologne contains two important chambers of horrors. It was good that a half dozen of us American journalists viewed them together, so that our eyewitness reports would be unanimous and would be believed. Sometimes it appears that Americans in general and the good-and-bad-Germans school in particular do not wish to hear about Nazi atrocities. One of the great differences between some officers and their men here is that the officers are inclined to believe, even at this late date, that German sadism is a lot of hysterical bunk, whereas their men usually know that it is an unpleasant truth. Certainly the wrecked human beings whom I saw tumbling to liberty through the grilled doorway of the Klingelpütz Gestapo prison on the cold Saturday after our Army had entered Cologne were scarred, starved, in-the-flesh proofs of the existence of very bad Germans indeed. During their first half hour's delirium of freedom and fresh air, these men and women who had been imprisoned for the adultness of their political faith acted like lunatics—sobbing, falling down on the cobblestones of the courtyard, wagging their heads, and holding their temples, where they had most often been beaten. From the nose of one French boy the blood spurted in a pale-pink, excited, pulsing jet. A tall, once strong Dutch workingman kept shouting, in German, "We must never forget!

Swear it!" A thin young Belgian, in what had once been good tweeds, stood praying over a mound of earth in the prison courtyard. His father and four other prisoners had been buried there the night before our soldiers came in. The son had made a cross by binding two bits of wood together with a frayed strap he had been using as a belt for his trousers. Then he had prayed. He apologized to me in English for not being shaved. At first he refused a cigarette—"for fear of depriving you." He and his dead father had been resistance men. The most startling member of the group was the still exquisitely pretty Brussels girl in a saintly blue rain cape who had spent nineteen months of her nineteen years in Gestapo prisons for having helped R.A.F. fliers to escape. Another surprise was a seventy-year-old Dutch grandmother, complete with dignity, four languages, gold-rimmed glasses, and a decent black fur coat. She had listened to the London B.B.C. broadcasts. There were also several blond, tubercular Russian girls, some terrified-looking, speechless Poles, and three completely crazed Germans. One liberated Frenchman was a Montmartre café waiter who had refused to go to Germany to work and had therefore been sent there and put in a concentration camp, the first of a series of nine camps. He had escaped nine times and been caught nine times. His eyes, teeth, hands, head, and feet had all been injured by the beatings the Germans had given him. In one camp, on the Vistula River, he had labored one summer, along with some starving Poles, dredging sand to make a bathing beach for the *Herrenvolk* officers.

The second horror chamber was the Gestapo office in the Apellhof Platz, across from the court of appeals it had ignored. Near the curiously undamaged office, on a mattress in the middle of a wrecked street, lay three young non-German corpses. These were the bodies of men who were being dragged by two Gestapo men to the questioning room when an American shell fell and, perhaps fortunately, killed all five men. High above them lay a sixth victim of the same shell: a well-to-do, stay-at-home old German, still wearing a nice blue suit and his wedding ring, his prosperous person caught, but still intact, underneath the staircase on the second-floor landing of his big house, half of which had been sheared away just an inch from where he lay. Below the Gestapo office was a small sub-basement cell where, the Klingelpütz prisoners said, the Gestapo had hung other prisoners six at a time by crowding them into a row, standing them on stools, dropping nooses around their necks from an overhead bar, and then kicking the stools out from beneath their feet. One Italian became a legend by kicking his stool loose himself and shouting, as his final strangled words, *"Viva l'Italia! Viva la libertà!"*

The Gestapo sub-basement smelled of a rotting haunch of horsemeat from which a hoof still dangled. Supplies, apparently, had run low as the

Americans approached the city. In the office were files containing some copies of an S.S. French-language leaflet destined for French slave-labor gangs in Germany. The leaflet said, "French comrades, conscious of the future of thy country, thou canst not remain neutral in this conflict, thou shouldst take up arms to fight at thy European brothers' sides. Thy country sinks beneath Jewish-Anglo-American bombs. Thy parents lie amid the ruins. Come avenge them. Come with us to chase these assassins from France, give thyself the honor of not leaving this task to Germans alone. Come, combat with us the true enemies of thy land, those who turn it into a vast cemetery, the Jews. France will relive, thanks to thee, and thou wilt participate with us in its arising again in the new National Socialist regime which we will set up after our victory. Offer thy services to the French Armed Elite Guard or to the French National Socialist movement, 7 Freytagstrasse, in Düsseldorf."

The buildings of architectural interest in Cologne have been seventy-five-per-cent destroyed, the Fine Arts and Monuments section of our Army reports. The Wallraf-Richartz Museum, which contained good paintings of the South German and Cologne schools of 1300–1550, including various Altdorfers, Cranachs, and Dürers, and Stephan Lochner's famous "Madonna in an Arbor of Roses," was demolished, a loss in itself because of its fine cloisters, but the paintings had been evacuated. Our art experts figure only a ten-per-cent damage to Cologne Cathedral, which typical Hohenzollern egotism put over as one of the sublimest in the world, although its pleasant Gothic nave was finished in exactly 1880 (a priest was still on hand with a throwaway historical booklet to give our tourist soldiers) and is only slightly better than Fifth Avenue's St. Patrick's. The really great loss to Cologne and the world are its eleventh-century Romanesque churches, such as the decagonal St. Gereon, which has been cut in two, and, above all, the Apostles' Church, with its twelfth-century side aisles, superb mosaics, and magnificent domed crossing. I stumbled and crawled up a nobly proportioned aisle into which the mosaic dome had crumbled in colored ruin. Overhead, four of the dome's ribs and its lantern, miraculously intact, were outlined as naked, resistant, architectural principles—nearly a thousand years old in wisdom and balance—against the dull modern sky. Across that sky flew a gaggle of nine planes. The mortar shells of the Nazis still fighting on the other side of the Rhine began dropping, a long way off, into what had once been their fine city. The air shook, and from the church's injured choir great drops of red mosaics bled down onto the altar.

It is reasonable to think that Cologne's panorama of ruin will be typical of what our rapidly advancing Army will see in city after city. Because

Germany is populous, more cities have been destroyed there than in any other country in Europe. Defeat in the last war did not cost Germany a stone. This time the destroyer of others is herself destroyed. This physical destruction of Germany is the one positive reason for thinking that this time the Allies may win the peace. However they decide to divide Germany, her cities, if they are like Cologne, are already divided into morsels of stone no bigger than your hand.

Letters from Nuremberg

DECEMBER 17, 1945 There are two sights in Germany which seem equally to give dramatic proof that the Allies won the war. One is the vast spectacle of any ruined German city, open to the skies, and the other is the small tableau of the Nazi-filled prisoners' box, beneath the floodlights, in the war-crimes courtroom in Nuremberg. Almost everything else in Germany—in the American zone, at least—seems to be some sort of sign that we Allies are at a loss in the peace. But the mere sight of Hermann Göring—for once sitting down, silent and almost slender, as a civilian and a prisoner in the same town where, during the second great *Parteitag*, ten years ago, he was baying "*Heil*" as he strutted the swastika-hung streets, fat, decorated, in uniform, and loose on society—is a stimulating, satisfying proof that at least we Allies won the war the Nazis started. When you look at the startling ruins of Nuremberg, you are looking at a result of the war. When you look at the prisoners on view in the courthouse, you are looking at twenty-two of the causes. It is an astonishing view of humanity.

Ex-Reichsmarschall Göring's twenty-one colleagues seem dominated by him in the prisoners' dock, just as they were when they were all free. By his superior supply of theatrical energy, fancy clothes, and interest in the proceedings, and by his air of participation, Göring maintains his position of Prisoner No. 1, sitting in the dock's most prominent and only comfortable seat—first row on the aisle. Behind him he has one level of the dock balustrade to rest his back against, and at his side a lower level to rest his right elbow and write upon. At this advantageous corner post, he scribbles like a busybody diarist with a perfect view of the terrible goings on. Of all the Nazis' hierarchy whose faces were already famous when they appeared at the big *Parteitag*, his has since changed the least. Then it looked like the face of an aging, fat tenor; now it looks like the face of a middle-aged, fleshy contralto (but in either case a star). Hess seems the most altered. Once the lower part of his dark countenance was heavy, not only with confidence but with a disciple's swollen sentimentality. Now his face is blanched, sharp, disillusioned, and irascible, and if he finds himself being stared at by a foreigner, he stares back with humorous hostility.

Some of the journalists have equipped themselves with mother-of-pearl opera glasses or with black Army binoculars to squint at the prisoners, fifty feet away, in an attempt to discover enlarged signs of shame, alarm, or guilt on their features. Now, in the fourth week of the trial, the twenty-two Nazi faces show nothing—at any rate to the naked eye—but occasional reflexes of strained attentiveness, as when a Nazi soldier's private movie of highlights in a Warsaw pogrom were being shown to the courtroom. Maybe the prisoners are by now so accustomed to the faint lights which illuminate their faces when the room is darkened for a film that they have learned to hide their feelings. Or maybe they have recently seen and heard so many horrible proofs of what they and theirs did that their faces, like their memories, are used to it all.

To the rest of us, this pogrom picture seemed rather special. Part of the negative had been burned, perhaps in one of the ghetto fires which, as some Nazi snapshots showed, were getting out of hand. (The snapshots also showed Jews jumping from fourth-story windows. Smoking them out had been the fun and the goal of the day's job, according to the Nazi military report read aloud at the trial.) However, enough was left of the burned movie, which was shown twice in succession and at half speed, to give a clear view of naked Jews, male and female, moving with a floating, unearthly slowness and a nightmare-like dignity among the clubs and kicks of the laughing German soldiers. One nude Jew still had his hat, which he modestly held before him. One thin young Jewess, lying on a sidewalk, was helped to her feet by an officer so that she could be knocked down again. The movies and snapshots were presented by the American prosecution as illustrations to texts read aloud from the diary of Nazi Governor General Frank of Poland. After seeing these pogrom pictures and hearing excerpts from Frank's Polish memoirs ("My attitude toward the Jews will therefore be based only on the expectation that they will disappear. They must be done away with. We must annihilate the Jews"), one might have thought that Christian prisoner Frank kept his eyes cast down because he was ashamed to look the court in the face. However, as it later turned out, his eyes were really cast down upon a note of protest he was hastily scribbling to his lawyer.

The one good result of the interruption by the lawyer when he got the note was that momentarily, anyway, it cut short the reading aloud of documents by the American prosecution. Thrice in one sitting of the fourth week, Tribunal President Sir Geoffrey Lawrence was driven to protest that the trial would never end if our lawyers continued to read aloud documents they had already read aloud twice before. Even Hess showed that he was not mad when he offered to get his memory back if it would only speed up the trial. It would seem that we Americans, prosecuting the most nebulous possible charge—crimes against humanity—have, ever since our own Chief Prosecutor Jackson's precise, idealistic, impressive opening, weakened our case, already difficult because the charge lacks precedence, by our irrelevancies and redundancies. In three and a half days the British presented their case against the Nazis for waging a war of aggression on Poland, Norway, Denmark, Belgium, Holland, Greece, and Yugoslavia—a lot of ground. We Americans took five days merely for the case of Austria and Czechoslovakia, and broke up the resultant boredom in court only with the irrelevant diversion of horror movies of Belsen, Dachau, and Buchenwald, which are not in either country. On the whole, our lawyers have succeeded in making the world's most completely planned and horribly melodramatic war dull and incoherent. And, though it may be less important, several of our legal men have evidenced an ignorance of Europe, politically and historically, which might have seemed patriotic back home but seems something else at what has been earnestly described as the greatest trial in history.

All the Allied counsel admitted to ignorance, as well as stupefaction, when, as a consequence of Frank's note to his lawyer, one of the German defense counsel rose to protest arrogantly because the German prisoners were not enjoying the benefit of what he grandiloquently called the superior "basic principle of all German law": Law No. something-or-other, which permits the defendant to have the whole truth, good as well as bad, said about him, "it being the duty of the prosecution also to present exculpating as well as inculpating evidence." After the Russian, French, English, and American judges had all declared that they had never heard of such a law, it was hunted up in the German code, translated, and transmitted through the earphones, not only in the Allied languages but also in German, just in case some of the twenty-two Nazi prisoners had also never heard of such legal kindness. A second objection raised by the German counsel as the result of Frank's protest—against the reading of documents unfavorable to him so early in the trial—was even more interesting, because it revealed the rustiness of the German legal-defense mentality, which, during the twelve years that these clients were in power, didn't have much practice. Indeed, the best that the German counsel could say for Frank (according to the interpreter's running translation) was that "the content of the testimony against him is terrible and depressing for the human spirit and civilization is justly indignant. But the consequence of such perverted testimony, until the defendants can speak for themselves later in the trial, makes truth suffer and leaves justice endangered. The highest human principle is truth and we wish to find out the truth for our children."

Some non-German experts think that if the German defense is so crazy about using truth at this late date in German history, it would serve its clients better if it would touch upon some of the bitter peacetime truths about the Allies that are now going the rounds. For instance, the news of the renaissance of Fascism, mostly in England, was carried in the South German edition of *Stars & Stripes*, hundreds of copies of which daily litter the building in which the trial is going on. The London B.B.C.'s comment that Mosley's British right to free speech could not be interfered with now that the war was over was common gossip in Nuremberg Allied offices, where bilingual German employees have good ears. From the same two news sources, von Ribbentrop's defense could have learned that at the auction in London of his Embassy furnishings, one British Fascist not only paid a fat price for a bust of Hitler but told the press that it might have an even greater value soon, and British women bid so wildly for Hitler portraits that they were taken off the sale list. In *Stars & Stripes*, the German defense could also have read reports of American discrimination against Negro soldiers as well as against Jews, and with even greater profit could have read of the trial in England in which American officers were charged with the inhuman treatment of soldier prisoners. As one German ex-professor sadly remarked, "The worst of Nazism is that parts of it are now organized, instead of unorganized, kinds of thinking, and all over the world many people still have such thoughts."

Whatever else the German population is thinking, it is not thinking much about the Nuremberg trial. The *Nürnberger Nachrichten*, which is the local newspaper licensed by our Military Government, had to be prodded by us to give the trial a bit more space and lately has been allotting it three-quarters of the second of its four pages. Its account lays typically Teutonic emphasis on the trial's occasional allusions to the Nazi war plans, such as the Barbarossa Plan, which was the full-fledged plan of attack on Russia, or the still-born Felix Plan, which was to have been the attack on Gibraltar. The same German ex-professor says that the reasons the Germans are what he calls utterly uninterested in the trial are: First, everyone has too many private troubles, such as the loss of a husband or son, no coal, no window panes, or not enough good food, and no longer cares about political characters like Göring but wants news of where his son died or about his neighbors' disasters. Second, after twelve years of propaganda, the Germans do not believe anything they read, so they don't bother to read it, but look in their papers only to see what trains are running or to study, say, the American Military Government's order that in divorce proceedings and for the reading of wedding banns, both interested parties must be present. Third, the humbler classes, which, he says, lived on their emotions and did not care for ideas, are now too dazed to learn to put their minds on an editorial. Fourth, the educated classes refuse to listen to talk of the trials. They have heard too much of those twenty-two men and now do not wish to hear even about their guilt. In any case, they think the trial is an effort at propaganda rather than at justice, a myth they have forgotten about and so no longer believe in. Fifth, the Germans of all classes are now abnormal, like people who have come out of a boiler factory and cannot hear small noises any more. They are deaf. They are apathetic. No one, not even the upper classes, has any impulse toward responsibility now. All use our Military Government as an excuse for deciding nothing and consider Germans who work with our Military Government collaborators.

In summing up, the ex-professor says that the four elements in Hitler's ideology which most affected the German mind were militarism, anti-Semitism, nationalism (or pan-Germanism), and totalitarianism, of which ideas only the first has been weakened by defeat. As for democracy, the Bavarians, at least, think it might be wonderful if anybody seemed to know exactly what it was or is. Because we Americans have authorized six Bavarian political parties to function, the Germans deduce that this must be democracy. But since five of the parties have the same program, they say it is silly. Above all, the German people, amid their rubble and their muddy memory of an orderly and cruel belief in empire, are shocked at our laissez-faire, at our uncertainty and untidiness in the face of what are to them accumulating and anguishing complications. They have only ideas to divert them from their daily dilemma. Seven out of every ten Germans, according to the ex-professor, seem to believe that the next war will come within six months, that it will obviously be the Americans and British against the barbarous Russians, and that what is left of us Anglo-Saxons will one day declare that the German fear of having Russia in Europe was indeed justified. Not one German in ten, or in ten thousand, seems to have enough grasp of recent history to recall that it was Germany which pulled Russia into the center of Europe in the first place.

A year ago, the people of Nuremberg will tell you, they began rereading their old English books—Sir Walter Scott and Oscar Wilde, both prewar favorites—in the tramcars and on the trains. The excuse was always that they needed to brush up on their vocabulary in case some *verdammte* Allied fliers were shot down in their neighborhood and they were called upon to do some skillful interrogating. Everybody knew that everybody else was relearning English because it would be the language of the victors.

FEBRUARY 27, 1946 The trial of the twenty-two criminal characters here has reached its midpoint. The Allied prosecution has rested its case. The defense of the Nazis has begun. There must be millions of people, especially the Europeans that suffered under them for years, who have wondered with bitter curiosity what in God's name the Germans could say for themselves on the reckoning day. Now they have started to say it. Since last November, when the trials began, the American, British, French, and Russian prosecutions' principal task has been to prove to the court that the Nazis did wrong. In the few hours the Germans have just taken to outline their defense, it has become clear that they are not going to try to disprove that they did wrong. They are actually and characteristically going to try to prove that they did right. Reichsmarschall Göring's defense lawyer has gone even further. One of the novelties he has offered is that it was really the Allies who had committed the original wrongs.

While the war was going on, the Allies had a threefold declared aim: to defeat the German Army, to bring the Nazi leaders to trial, and to reëducate the German mind. What the opening Nuremberg defense counsel have just offered is more than a mere display of Grade B legal talent; it is an absolutely first-rate demonstration of the still unreconstructed prewar German mind. The mental qualities the German defense has shown so far sound comical but are no laughing matter—egomania, mythomania, paranoia, superiority complex, and a general falling flat in those areas in which, in civilized men's minds, logic and morality have always been supreme.

It is significant that of the two German lawyers chosen to carry the principal presentation of the defense, one is old enough to have matured under the Kaiser, the other is young enough to have grown up under the Weimar Republic, and in defending their Nazis, they see eye to eye. The one who opened the case was Göring's lawyer, Dr. Otto Stahmer, who is in his sixties, crop-headed, and truculent, and who has none of the long-white-haired elegance which several of the other senior German bar members at the trial affect. The second major figure is von Ribbentrop's representative, young Dr. Martin Horn, who had not previously appeared because, German rumor candidly said, he wanted as little contact as possible with a courtroom so full of Jews. Horn's hair is long but black. He is remarkable for his superior air, for his ignorance of English politics, and finally, when he gets into deep water, for repeatedly having to leave the lectern to beg some quick advice from Admiral Raeder's counsel, one of the picturesque, older, long-haired set. Another, though less important and less impressive, personage is Hess's lawyer, little Dr. Alfred Seidel, whose chin barely comes up to the pulpit where the lawyers, including the stout and splendid Sir David Maxwell Fyfe, acting Allied chief prosecutor, cluster around their glasses of water, their fine legal points, and their microphone.

The first important point about the German lawyers' buildup for their clients was their inability to comprehend the difference between the relevant and the irrelevant. In their national lack of logic, anything was relevant to them if it suited their book. The oddest incident during their presentation of their fantastic list of Allied witnesses and writings whom and which they wanted to question and to cite was the long, patient, pedagogic effort, led by Court President Sir Geoffrey Lawrence (and in which the American, British, French, and Russian prosecutors all finally joined in), to din into the Göring, Ribbentrop, and Hess lawyers' heads what the word "relevant" has meant for centuries in law. As Sir Geoffrey dryly announced to the third of these, "I have amply explained it three times. I shall now make a fourth and final endeavor." The irrelevancy of some of the witnesses the Germans named was as obvious as the air of persecution with which the German lawyers fought for their inclusion. Göring's lawyer asked to have called, as a character witness who could testify to Göring's having disapproved of terror bombing, a certain Luftwaffe doctor whose relevancy consisted of his having been Göring's physician but having nevertheless refused to take part in some grisly experiments at Dachau with five hundred living Poles' brains. To prove that Ribbentrop had not desired war with France, His ex-Excellency's lawyer wanted as witnesses the French accused-collaborationist Count de Castellane and the ditto Marquis and Marquise de Polignac; to prove he had not wanted war with England, he wanted as witness a member of the Bath Club whom Ribbentrop had asked in London, in 1936, to introduce him to Premier Baldwin. The payoff was Ribbentrop's call for an English party named Professor Cornwall Evans, whom Sir David, whose job it was to check over the witness list, frankly declared he'd never heard of and who is not in *Who's Who*. (One of the trial's high moments was the blank look on the voluble Russian interpreter's little face when she found herself up against putting *Who's Who* into dialectic language.)

Of the strange list of Allied and German writings the defense wished to cite from—it wasn't clear whether to prove that the Nazis were right in trying to conquer the world or whether to prove that they hadn't tried to conquer it after all—probably the most sensible item was the Germanophile tome "Warnings and Predictions," by the late enthusiast Lord Rothermere. Other books were Sir Nevile Henderson's "Failure of a Mission," "Step by Step," by the Nazis' illustrious arch-enemy Winston Churchill, and "The Building of a Nation," signed by Hermann Göring but actually written by the faithful manager of his estate. Also listed for citation were a Philadelphia speech made by General Tasker H. Bliss in 1928 about "what really happened at the Paris peace conference of 1919"; some 1927 speeches by Joseph Paul-Boncour about the League of Nations, and by Lloyd George, who never trusted it; a captured copy of some secret reports of the French General Staff; and, as final authority, naturally, the German Foreign Office White Book.

It was Göring's Dr. Stahmer who, as a loyal German mythomaniac, or a plain international liar, took the cake. "It was a well-known fact that the war in the beginning was conducted with relative humanity," he stated, choosing to ignore the well-known fact that the German Army, in order to terrorize the Belgians into rapid submission in 1940, had shown them official films taken the autumn before that displayed the Wehrmacht's ghastly terrorization of the wretched Poles. It was only in the second, or Anglo-American, phase of the war that nastiness set in, the Doctor said smoothly. In an effort to explain away a document, signed by the Anglophile Ribbentrop, O.K.'ing the practice of shooting downed R.A.F. fliers, Stahmer declared that "retaliations justify actions which under normal circumstances might be illegal." Then he added his clearest axiom of amorality: "It is impossible to judge an action if the motive is not known." Thus, it is necessary to know the motive behind Dachau before judging on the output of corpses.

It was odd to sit in the Nuremberg court and hear young Dr. Horn, runner-up for the cake, state that it might well have been the international London Naval Conference of 1935 that drove Hitler's hypersensitive Third Reich into rearmament, obviously making the war John Bull's and not Adolf's fault. In the summer of 1936, in this then picturesque and intact city of Nuremberg, the Nazis were staging (in the great Zeppelin Stadium, now used as a football bowl by Allied soldiers) their grandiose fourth Party Day military displays. These consisted of an eight-day parading of military strength and of equipment of a blitzkrieg type then unknown in England or western Europe—the public première of Panzer divisions, of a brand-new Luftwaffe roaring overhead, of demonstrations by the ace Udet of dive-bombing, of flame-throwers in rows, of motorcycle corps in formation, of solid city blocks of whippet and giant tanks, of miles of marching, goose-stepping, uniformed men, and, above all, of hundreds of thousands of civilian German faces lifted to bay to the blue Bavarian skies, "Today Germany, tomorrow the world."

It was also odd to hear Horn demand the anti-"Nahsi" Winston Churchill as a witness, claiming that Churchill's sentiments had more than anything else to do with Germany's preparing for war because at that time he had been "somewhat of an official as the leader of His Majesty's loyal Opposition." When Sir David politely explained that the loyal opposer of that time had been Clement Attlee and that Churchill had then been merely an uninfluential back-bencher, it was the Allies' turn to smile in court. The Germans' turn had come shortly before, when their side had demanded as a witness the Nazi military attaché in Moscow at the time of the signing of the Russo-German non-aggression pact. It was a tense moment in the courtroom, except for the levity in the prisoners' box, whose occupants presumably had been tipped off to what was coming and were leaning forward eagerly, with wide smiles; Göring, who had been sitting with a G.I. blanket wrapped around him like a smart steamer rug, wriggled with delight. This inevitable, potentially troublesome, first allusion to the pact, which everyone on the Allied side had been waiting for, some with trepidation, others with blatant complacency, nevertheless left the British president and the Allied prosecution chief floundering, until Russian Prosecutor Rudenko strode to the lectern and swiftly declared that it was not the signing of the pact but its violation by the Germans that came within the scope of those criminal charges which are the exclusive concern of the Nuremberg court. It was a brilliant recovery. It even dimmed Göring's smile, temporarily.

Last on the Allied alphabetical list, the Russians dominated the trials with their brief, dramatic peroration and with their special nationalistic vocabulary, no matter in which of the four courtroom languages it was heard. Theretofore the Germans had been referred to by the Allies simply as "the Germans" or "the Nazis," without adjectives. The Russians are more literary, elaborate, and inventive. In reporting on what the war meant to them back home, they referred with angry, often hyphenated flourishes to pogrom-maker Hitler, Fascist-German conspirators, Hitlerian hordes, Hitlerite pirates, Fascist barbarians, and German-Fascist intruders, the last being their favorite. The Russians have taken under their wing the Czechs, Yugoslavs, Latvians, Lithuanians, and Estonians, and when the Soviet's Assistant Prosecutor Raginsky cried, "Your Honor, the whole world knows about the Hitlerite misdeeds at Lidice!," he produced a thrilling effect, even in translation and through earphones.

Among the few Russian witnesses brought from the Soviet Republics was the curator of the Hermitage Museum, in Leningrad, notable not only for his vast, dignified gray beard, which is practically the size of a broom, but also for having produced the one burst of unchecked laughter in court the Bench has yet permitted. Under German cross-examination (after he had told how the Germans had willfully shelled his precious museum and after he had given citations from a ninety-page document on the German destruction of Russian art in general), a German counsel imprudently asked how he knew that the destruction of the Hermitage was intentional; was he, as well as an art expert, also an authority on artillery fire? The fine, furious old man answered, with the greatest simplicity, that the Nazis had hit the neighboring bridge only once but had hit his beloved museum thirty times and that even he knew enough about artillery to figure out that the Germans weren't such bad shots as that.

Most of the Russian information was not funny, especially for the prisoners. As the other Allied prosecutors had done before them, the Russians pinned down each prisoner with copies of his own damning, signed, personal, and often secret documents, since each prisoner, whatever his pompous, ministerial title, had, during and before the war, actually worked knowingly, busily, and competently at his terrible tasks of cruelty, torture, devastation, injustice, arrogance, and death. The Russians spiked Prisoner No. 7, Governor General of Poland Frank, with a quotation from what they quaintly described as his "calico-bound diary." In it he commented on his beloved Führer's new, especially important orders to him about "my task of pacifying Warsaw—that is, razing Warsaw to the ground." And then the Russians introduced his self-congratulatory telegram to Hitler, which began, "The city of Warsaw is wreathed in flames. The burning of the houses is the most reliable method of preventing the escape of the insurgents," meaning the citizenry. Prisoner No. 4, Keitel, Chief of the High Command, was accused by the Russians of having complained, in writing, of the lack of ruthlessness toward the Russians. Even No. 14, Baldur von Schirach, though officially only the Leader of the Hitler Youth, was praised by Göring in a 1941 conference report to his Gauleiters for having had the brilliant idea of helping starve the Ukrainians by carting off their butter and eggs to a local German noodle factory for the benefit of the fat *Volk* of Berlin. Of unimportant Prisoner No. 15, Gauleiter Sauckel, Göring declared, in the same conference report, "I don't want to praise Sauckel. He doesn't need it. But what he achieved in obtaining workers from all over Europe and putting them into our industries is unique"—

which it was. Of Sauckel's eight and a half million slave laborers, whom he himself wittily declared in writing "he had not removed for pleasure or for fun," at least a million died of overwork.

Prisoner No. 1 Göring's conference report to his Gauleiters is twenty-five pages long and makes fascinating out-of-court reading in Nuremberg today. So far, it is the most disingenuous, unconsciously entertaining, and intimate account that has been given here of Göring as a vivid personality, as the Nazis' most capable planner (despite the fact that he was not interested in their precious statistics: "Don't give me five figures. They slide right out of my head"), as the Nazi Party's dominant go-getter, and as a master of barbed jollity. Though his defense, naturally, will be based on his supposed ignorance of what was going on, this report proves that he was a wise Party man. According to the Nazi stenographers' file of documents, Göring declared at the conference, "What happens to the French is a matter of complete indifference to me. I should think it a bad idea if we ourselves didn't have a fabulous restaurant in Paris. Maxim's must have the best food for us but not for the French to saunter in on. In other times this food subject was simpler. It was called plundering. Practices seem to have become more humane, but I intend to plunder, nevertheless, and profitably. There will be such inflation in France that everything will go to smash. The franc will be worth no more than a well-known type of paper used for a certain purpose. Only then will France be hit as we want her to be hit. As for the Russians, handle them in a cruel manner. Don't spoil them. Don't forget that the decisive arguments are speed and severity."

Some snapshots that were taken by sentimental, *gemütlich* German soldiers while passing through Yugoslavia and Czechoslovakia and were shown to the Nuremberg court just before the German defense had begun its paltry attempt to stack the cards made clear that Göring's Russian policy was pretty popular with the Nazis wherever they went. The snapshots, for instance, showed citizens who had been strung up in the main streets of Belgrade. For once, the Wehrmacht soldiers had been generous with their cigarettes and had given a few to the local inhabitants; the pictures showed that they had stuck cigarettes in the dead men's mouths, then posed themselves alongside and looked pleasant while the camera clicked. The snapshots also showed—in addition to a German police dog eating a living man, and a starved pig eating a living man, wife and child while bystanding Germans pointed and laughed—a child who had been decapitated and several adult heads without bodies. It must have been spring down there. Beside the heads the German soldiers had stuck signs on which they had scribbled, "Spring Fruit!"

All the German defense can do is continue to put on their tawdry sleight-of-hand performance. On the other side of the vast building, in the Tribunal document rooms, are tons of documents unwittingly furnished by the prisoner Nazis themselves, written and signed by them in their days of success. No matter what color paper the words are printed on, all these Nazi documents are really blood red.

MARCH 7, 1946 Whatever Churchill's anti-Russian speech sounded like to the outside world, it exploded over the Allied courthouse in wrecked Nuremberg like a large, postwar bombshell. The Western Allies are living closer to the Russians here than anywhere else in Europe, including Berlin. The reason for the presence of us all here—an exotic, shut-off, quadripartite community, about two thousand strong—is the Tribunal, which seems a small Allied island of hope, sanity, and justice surrounded by the sullen, Valhalla-minded Germans and their ruined town. There are a hundred and sixty journalists in Nuremberg—momentarily the world's largest news group in one place covering one event—who are mostly writing for the world's largest newspapers, from Moscow to San Francisco. We ourselves have only one daily newspaper to read, *Stars & Stripes*, which gave us the startling headline "Unite to Stop Russians, Churchill Warns." Phone calls to London are difficult, since they must go through a military switchboard to Frankfurt, to be transferred there, through another military switchboard, to England, and then through another military switchboard to the London civilian circuit, while snowstorms have broken down the lines in France. But even bad connections have made it clear that Churchill's words have started to echo. In Nuremberg, all we know is what we see and hear. In court, we saw the German lawyers hold the *Stars & Stripes* high in their hands so that Göring and their other clients in the prisoners' box could burst into smiling animation at the glorious good news. In the press-camp dining room, we saw the German waiters lingering to eavesdrop when Churchill's name came up. What we have heard is only what the Russians here say. They say that they have listened to so many harsh capitalistic words in the past that a few thousand more from Churchill can't make any difference now.

In the courtroom, the German lawyers are hustling through their defense. The longer it goes on, the more it sounds the same. When the prisoners' turn to speak for themselves comes, it is thought, Rudolf Hess is likely to vary the chorus by rising to shout that he regrets nothing and still believes in his Führer. So far, according to the lawyers' pleas, not one of the once high-and-mighty, superefficient, noisily loyal Nazi overlords has admitted knowing what he was doing when he was helping run the Reich and the war. All of them imply, however, that something must have been wrong, because they all blame someone else. Not one of them has spared the Führer who made him. Hitler is one of two guilty ghosts—Himmler is the other—now taking the rap in the courtroom.

Chief of the Gestapo Ernst Kaltenbrunner's defense has been typical. It ignores the bad deeds attributed to him and claims for him good deeds no one has ever heard of. Thus his defense states that the idea for putting a stop to Jewish persecutions in October, 1944—an idea first heard of by the rest of us in March, 1946—was Kaltenbrunner's, not Hitler's. Youth Leader Baldur von Schirach's defense is that he warned the Führer that he would never be able to hate the United States, as was apparently ordered at headquarters, and that, furthermore, he had always been against the horrible business of leading fine German youth into war. Governor General of Poland Hans Frank, whose famous diary dilates upon the thousands of corpses he created and contains his bedtime thoughts on how to exterminate more Poles tomorrow, now claims that he tried three times to resign as governor; that the Polish massacres and pogroms shocked him, too, and were ordered by his enemy, Himmler, who accused him of being treacherously pro-Polish; and that, most important of all, he never wrote his diary. It seems that it was written by his secretary, one Helene Kraffczyk. President of the Reichsbank Hjalmar Schacht's defense is that though he raised billions for what was palpably rearmament, he didn't know that it would lead to war, in which he has never believed, having always been a pacifist, as Hitler well knew.

The defense of Alfred Rosenberg, prewar Minister of Weltanschau (the word for the Nazis' ideological way of viewing the world) and Commissioner for Eastern Occupied Territories, was the only one which gave a good time to everybody in court, except possibly the translators. Rosenberg's notion of defense was to offer twenty-two books—mostly on philosophy and mostly written by German college professors—including one called "Creative Stupidity," by a Dr. Hellpach, of the University of Heidelberg; Rosenberg's own *magnum opus*, "Mythus"; "The Passing of the Great Race," by the late Madison Grant, described as Curator of the American Museum of Natural History, in New York (he was a trustee); and even "The Introduction to Metaphysics," by the noted French-Jewish philosopher Henri Bergson. All these tomes were adduced to prove, in Rosenberg's own words (by the time the American translator got through with them), that his "intuitive method of perception and irrational [*sic*] philosophy had a predecessor in the French romantic movement and that the German neo-romantic movement took the German spiritual life with elemental force and was also represented by recognized scientists of the universities. And that it has been proved by historic-philosophic realizations that every historical appearance becomes degenerate against its will." The morbid German sensitiveness, in spots, to outside opinion was revealed in the umbrage taken by Rosenberg's counsel when his client's race-hatred philosophy was referred to in court as "disgusting teachings" by the Russians and as "a throw-back to demoniacal barbarism" by the French. His lawyer replied crisply, "He cannot be held responsible for the over-theorizing [i.e., the physical extension] of his doctrine."

Since Rosenberg, an early convert to Hitler, was chiefly responsible for the anti-Semitic, Aryan, *Herrenvolk* ideologies that the subsequent Nazis so bloodily believed in, the explanation offered by his defense counsel of his anti-Semitic position is of interest. The defense simply claims that he "imagined the Jewish question would be solved for Germany and Europe without force [and that] remarks had been made from the Jewish side which understandably had very much hurt the feelings of National [Socialist] and Christian circles." It winds up: "As proof that no guilt should be attached to him because of the physical extermination of the Jews, [it should be realized that] he did not participate in a psychological preparation for war or in the conspiracy for the enslavement of German culture [but that] in his capacity of missionary over all the mental and world ideological education of the Nazi Party . . . he especially worked toward a peaceful settlement of nations under the four big European powers [Italy, France, Germany, England]." Before very long, judges from two of those big European powers will, in all likelihood, order Missionary Rosenberg to be hanged.

MARCH 15, 1946 In one way, at least, the Germans on trial for their lives in the Nuremberg Tribunal have the same aim we Allies have. They, too, want to leave for history a record of their side of the story. Until Reichsmarschall Hermann Göring spoke from the witness stand, they had left an unexpected, astonishing, complete, and simple record of nothing but cowardice and treachery. For twelve years they had manifested their fanatical devotion to the Nazi trinity—their leader, their Greater Germany, and their cult of manly bravery. Until Göring presented the opening chapter of his political autobiography, however, not one Nazi prisoner had lifted a loyal word for any of these; every man's defense plea, including the one offered by Göring's own counsel, had blamed the next Nazi above him, with the result that, as a terrible tribute to the *Führerprinzip*, it was only dead Hitler, at the top, who could be guilty in the end. Neither their witnesses nor their documents once mentioned the word "*Vaterland*." French adolescents in the Resistance had the pluck to sing the "Marseillaise" to S.S.

firing squads. There seemed to be no "Horst Wessel" choral spirit in the prisoner's box. It is a fact that the twenty-two Nazis there helped put millions of people to death, quickly or slowly, by torture, murder, or starvation. But not one of them seemed to want to die for the thing they killed the millions for. Nobody said he would be proud to hang for his belief in the bloodthirsty ideology that cost the millions their lives. Never before in modern history had the entire upper hierarchy of an impassioned and successful regime literally and voluntarily disappeared in defeat like the Nazis, leaving no chiefs or believers standing, no well-known martyrs in sight, no ambitious pretenders willing to carry on. For the twelve years—and especially the last, terrible six—that these men in the box were in power, the world thought that they meant it. Then, as this trial went on, it became clear that they didn't mean anything except their desire to fight for their skins. It's no exaggeration to say that the Nuremberg courthouse is the scene of the Nazis' last big battle.

More and more the German lawyers have built their fight around the bastion of the Reichsmarschall himself, and their system of camouflage for him became increasingly clear. As might have been expected, two completely different German versions of the Nazi story are being unfolded here. The first is what the German witnesses choose to say about the German prisoners, and the second is what our Allied prosecution pulls out of the witnesses by cross-examination. You would never know that these two stories were about the same people or the same incidents. Probably in no other court record have the words "humane" and "benevolent" appeared as often as they have here, especially in connection with Göring. Never before, surely, have all witnesses in a trial lied so openly, so persistently, or so freely. For example, Field Marshal General Erhardt Milch, who, of the many witnesses up to now, has the shiftiest look and speaks the most beautiful German, declared jesuitically that he wished to believe that Germany's declaration of war in 1939 was a real surprise to all the prisoners. He added that he thought Germany had been less prepared for war then than either France or Poland, because both these enemies had had more time to prepare; and that his and Göring's air force had had only thirty-seven light little planes in it in 1938, and that even when it whizzed over Poland in 1939 it still was only on the defensive. Milch gave the appearance of being Göring's *porte-parole*. It could be inferred from what he said that Göring's final defense would be based on Milch's careful statements that Göring opposed Hitler's attack on Russia as creating one of those two-front wars which "Mein Kampf" had sensibly argued couldn't be won; that the decline in Göring's closeness to Hitler dated from that summer; and, above all, that after the crashing victory in France, Hitler's conduct was abnormal, in the light of what he had formerly preached about two fronts. These are the items which Milch, Göring's most important witness, volunteered.

Cross-examination pulled out of Milch that once the Russian war was on, he had found it, as he indiscreetly wrote someone, "amusing" to have his air force compel Russian prisoners to man German guns against Allied fliers. Chief Prosecutor Robert Jackson squeezed out of him the fact that he had forced his mother to declare him illegitimate—because her husband's family had Jewish blood—so that he might, as a full, fake Aryan, join the Nazi Party. That was in the early days of the Party, which, according to Milch's testimony, was, from the moment Hitler seized power, an S.S. spy nest within which everybody, even bold Göring, walked in fear and trembling. Milch also added, as a sample of German humor, that you had to separate words and deeds when considering whether a country should live up to its treaties; and, as a sample of naïveté, that when, as an inquiring citizen, he had visited Dachau in the early thirties (Göring was then in charge of it), it was so well run that it had its own slaughterhouse. This produced a spate of hysterical laughter in court which the bench instantly silenced.

The only defense testimony that had a damaging effect on Göring's case was in part the result of the stupidity of a theretofore unheard-of but important Nazi character, Adjutant Karl Bodenschatz, and in part of Chief Prosecutor Jackson's ability to wrench things out of him. Bodenschatz, Göring's former adjutant, declared that in 1936, when the Nazis sent thousands of German volunteers into Franco's Spain as "observers," Göring made some solemn historical comments on this opening gambit: "It is as if the great war had started, though we have not yet fired a shot. It would be better if we could keep quiet until 1941, but we may not be able to manage that." At this time, Göring also said that his air force was mobilized as though it were at war. The next year, he continued, all German industry had to produce as though the country were at war. One has to be at the trial in Nuremberg to realize that the foregoing is regarded by the Germans not as evidence of a national conspiracy to launch an aggressive war but as a good, Nazi proof that Hermann Göring personally did not want any war—until 1941, that is. To build up Göring as a pro-Semite, the devoted adjutant further declared that the Reichsmarschall had ordered him to save numerous Jews, who turned out, under Jackson's cross-examination, to number ten or twenty, including an old couple who had sheltered Göring and dressed his wound when he was hiding from the police after Hitler's Munich beer-hall putsch. Bodenschatz's proof that Göring was against torture, as practiced in the concentration camps of 1940 (which Göring, one must remember, didn't know existed), was that in 1933, at the Krupp gun works, Göring had made a speech against vivisection. Jackson's triumph was in brutally forcing Bodenschatz to admit, step by step, that he and Göring knew that there were places for Jews which they both politely called "collection camps"; that collection camps were places where state enemies were winnowed for shipment to places which they both called "work camps"; and that "a work camp was a camp where people worked *but* were not mistreated—" "Whereas," Jackson interrupted, "a concentration camp was a camp where people worked *and* were mistreated. Thank you."

Under the court's floodlights, turned on for the purpose of taking motion pictures of such high points in the trial, the sweat could be seen pouring off the middle-aged Bodenschatz's bony face. His eyes could be marked in their frightened flight back and forth from Göring in the prisoners' box to Jackson in the prosecution pulpit. Then, like a slow echo repeating what counsel and devotion had told him not to forget to say, the adjutant added, in a low voice, that exactly one year ago Göring had confided to him, in distress, "Many Jews have perished and we must pay dear." The victorious liberating Allies had just captured Göring in Austria and had informed him that concentration camps existed in Germany.

Shortly before Göring himself stepped to the witness stand, he had been described by his sinister four-year-plan economic expert, a one-star S.S. general, as "the last great figure from the Renaissance." When Göring stood up to take his oath, he undeniably looked the bravura personality in his vast, sagging, dove-colored jacket and his matching voluminous breeches, with his fine, high, maroon boots and his maroon neckerchief, and above it his hard, blue eyes and what is left of the familiar fleshiness of his mobile, theatrical face. Then, in an agreeable, reedy baritone voice that never halted but merely swerved to follow the movement of his memories, he began the story of his political life. "I was against the Republic," he said. "In November of the year 1922, on a Sunday in Munich, I attended a protest meeting. Toward the end, Adolf Hitler appeared. I had heard his name mentioned briefly and wanted to hear what he had to say. He refused to speak. But he spoke the next day on the Peace of Versailles. He said that until Germany was strong it was useless to protest. This was my thought in the depth of my soul. We spoke together of things dear to our hearts. I told him he could dispose of me and of my person as he saw fit. Later, I joined his Party." That was the way it all started.

During the next three days, as Göring narrated his and his Führer's extraordinary past together, building it up again from his powerful memory and with the agile intelligence that had aided in its construction in the first place, into the courtroom came the repeated muffled boom of dynamite clearing the wreckage of Nuremberg. Göring's recital was an astonishing performance. It was the greatest success story of a failure in modern times. A narrative delivered ad lib but with the vocabulary and coherence of a high-class serial, it developed into a dramatic study of two men's minds and their planned effect on the body of Europe. Göring's stream of words swept away all the Germans' legal efforts and false pleas to save him, and themselves, which had preceded him in court. What he offered his judges was no *mea culpa* but a dissertation on the technique of power. On the witness stand, he didn't wait to be asked questions by the Allied prosecution; he told them the German answers first. The Reichsmarschall made Machiavelli's Prince look like a dull apologist; Göring was decidedly more amoral, and funnier. The horrifying weakness in everything he said was that it took no account of the destruction it had caused in other men's or nations' lives. What he offered, essentially, was the Teutonic fallacy that the divine right of kings, which used to be limited to one individual, had been bestowed upon the entire German nation, which was therefore free to do anything to anybody.

Everybody in court had suffered, one way or another, from Göring's mind, but few had ever before sat and listened to it work. There was considerable surprise, though there should not have been, that behind his fancy tailoring, his fat, and his medals he had one of the best brains of a period in history when good brains were rare. On the stand, he was malicious and disturbing. He pointed out that only rich nations could afford the luxury of democracy, with its wasteful political squabbles and parliamentary inefficiencies, so he and his Führer, as he constantly called him, had aimed at the economy of single power for poor Germany. He said he probably didn't understand freedom, but he nevertheless had freed German workers from both the strikes and the lockouts that bother the democracies in their liberty. He cited the Communist Party and the Catholic Church as two flourishing institutions that operate on his theory of one-man, totalitarian power. He spoke candidly of having sent his young fliers in rotation to Franco's war so that they could try their wings in a sort of rehearsal. To pique the British, he said that the American Air Forces had assured the Allied victory, and to annoy America, he said he had hoped to develop a bomber strong enough to go to the States and back. He recounted that he had once apologized to the German Communist Ernst Thaelmann for his having been hit on the head by the Gestapo and had added that if the Communists and not the Nazis had won, he, Göring, wouldn't have been hit on the head but would have had it cut off by the G.P.U. To which the Communist "agreed in the friendliest fashion."

Then Göring began on the sellout of Europe, country by country. The Anschluss had been a walkover; earlier, France and England had been prepared to offer him a free hand in Austria if Germany had been willing to swap it for sanctions in Spain. Czechoslovakia was more dangerous; he had hobnobbed with some English at San Remo and afterward was able to tell the Führer that the British had swallowed the Anschluss but might be upset by Czechoslovakia, and that he didn't want to "have to bomb beautiful Prague," and that, anyway, those Britishers might toss out useful Chamberlain and bring in anti-Nazi Churchill. The night of the Anschluss, at a ball in Berlin, Göring had given his word of honor to the frightened Czech ambassador that Germany was only marching into Austria, not into Czechoslovakia. "But I did not give my word of honor that we *never* would march in," Göring said stiffly. Yes, the Nazis had subsidized Quisling. They knew that the Russians and British had been pouring bribes into Norway. Unfortunately, Göring left the bribing of Quisling to the Nazi foreign office and he frankly thought they had been niggardly. "I always remember the trouble we had in the first war," he reminisced genially, "because we didn't give Rumania enough." He was sorry about Poland; he had formerly had pleasant times there. He did not say if he was sorry about ruined Germany. Göring insisted throughout on taking his share of the responsibilities: the Anschluss and Munich were his doing; Danzig was the Führer's. Apparently, like partners in power, they divided the jobs up, as in any office. Göring had been furious about the march into Norway, but only because somebody forgot to tell him about it in advance. When asked by his counsel if the High Command had been consulted about starting the war, he said, "German generals are never asked to vote on war. One way to prevent war might be to ask the generals if they want to fight or go home." There was strained laughter in the court at this want-to-go-home jibe at the Americans.

Aside from its pungent flashes of humor, which were like footnotes, Göring's twenty-one hours on the witness stand amounted to an alarmingly serious lecture given by an active, if captive, historian on the most cynical military period in Europe's history. What his lecture featured was economic warfare, in the modern manner, which marks the difference between military murder in the nineteenth century and the twentieth. The court transcript of Göring's speech is a bibliographic item for future historians to collect. It was the complicated narrative of a brain without a conscience. Except for the constant reference to airplanes, it did indeed sound like something read from a family parchment in the Renaissance. Within its own framework, the story had veracity. None of the diplomatic observers in court thought he told any lies. They agreed that he had been, in fact, illuminating.

There were not more than a few hundred people in the courtroom. They had the awful privilege of listening to the personal recital of a man who helped tear apart millions of lives, as if with those large, white hands that gestured as he sat on the Nuremberg witness stand.

MARCH 22, 1946 On a recent visit to Nuremberg, a noted British lawyer optimistically wrote to a colleague, "I expect you feel, as I do, that the first really great and dramatic moment of this trial will come when Göring is cross-examined by the American prosecutor, Jackson. It will be a duel to the death between the representative of all that is worth while in civilization and the last important surviving protagonist of all that was evil. In a sense, the whole result of the trial depends upon the outcome of that duel, and whilst the world could see the importance of the great and decisive battles fought out between the armed forces arrayed against each other, I hope that they may see the immense importance of the decisive battle of ideas to be fought out that day in the courtroom. It will color this trial from now on and it may very well color the thoughts of men for generations to come."

The future thoughts of democratic men will have to take their hue from other, rosier episodes in the trial, for in that extremely important Göring-Jackson duel it was, unhappily, Prosecutor Jackson who lost. When the former Reichsmarschall strode from the witness stand to the prisoners' box after his last session with Mr. Jackson, he was congratulated and smiled upon by his fellow-Nazis there, like a gladiator who has just won his fight. He had even won it noisily, which added to the blaring, triumphal note. He had successfully shouted at Prosecutor Jackson, who back home is a Justice of the Supreme Court. There had been no "battle of ideas," because Jackson seemed not to be able to think of any. There had been nothing more—and that much was bad enough—than an important struggle between two opposing men's brains and personalities, and Göring showed more of both. He displayed, besides, a phenomenal memory and a remarkable gift for casuistic maneuver, and he was naturally more knowledgeable about Nazi and other European history. Also, he showed a diabolical skill in drawing on American and English history for familiar paradoxes and damaging precedents. As a fantastic and formidable personality, he temporarily produced an even greater confusion in the sensible legal minds at Nuremberg than Laval did in Paris at the trial of Pétain.

As the trial moved out of its preparatory period of massive, static documentation and entered its period of skirmishing and battle in the open, where the brains and personalities of the opponents were what counted, Jackson began to show inadequacies as the leading Allied man. Up to then his main contribution to this very special legal scene had been the high humanitarianism which marked his fine opening address in November. Beneath that humanitarianism there lies his burning private conviction that the Nazi prisoners are mere common criminals. This, too logically, led to his treating them in a blustering police-court manner, which was successful with the craven small fry but disastrous for him in cross-examining that uncommon criminal, Göring, himself accustomed to blustering in a grander way. Even physically, Jackson cut a poor figure. He unbuttoned his coat, whisked it back over his hips, and, with his hands in his back pockets, spraddled and teetered like a country lawyer. Not only did he seem to lack the background and wisdom of our Justice Holmes tradition, but his prepared European foreground was full of holes, which he fell into en route to setting traps for Göring.

In view of the fact that the Russian Chief Prosecutor, Roman Andreyevich Rudenko, and the British Chief Prosecutor, Sir David Maxwell Fyfe, had to be sent in as cross-examiners to master Göring and to obtain what amounted to the first confession from him, perhaps the American domination of the court will from now on decline. As the Court sees it, the Nuremberg trial is a Yalta Conference idea of President Roosevelt's, and though the Russians, British, and French gravely and fully have joined in, they have modestly regarded what goes on in the courthouse as mostly an American show. For this reason, the opening cross-examination of Göring was left, as a compliment, to what it was hoped would be typical Yankee shrewdness. The French know nothing of cross-examining, the Russians supposedly knew nothing, and the British know so much that, even belatedly, they were able to save the day. Of the four charges brought against the Nazis—conspiracy (which includes breaking treaties), crimes against peace, war crimes, and crimes against humanity—the British have concentrated on the charge of breaking treaties. And while the Russians and French addressed themselves to the charges of war of aggression (crimes against peace) and war crimes, the Americans took on the over-all charge of crimes against humanity. We seem to have overlooked the importance of choosing men who could carry the heavy burden we volunteered for. For instance, among the early minor figures on the American legal team there was an unfortunately memorable young captain who opened his court speech to and about a troubled world with the peculiarly personal confidence that if the microphone recorded any special disturbances, they would be the quaking of his knees, shaking as they had not shaken since his wedding day. Then Sidney S. Alderman, a member of the American prosecuting staff, may be a noted expert on American railroads, but he certainly was lost in Nuremberg among the terrible documents whose relative values in the timetable of Europe's ruin he couldn't be expected to make head or tail of. On the whole, the American team has consisted of simple Davids sent in against Nazi Goliaths on faith rather than with equipment—Davids entitled, symbolically, to their small stature because their cause was great.

The French influence in the court has been almost non-existent, even though in the Nazi war of aggression, France was the greatest to fall. Of the eight judges, the two French ones are hardly ever consulted in any crisis on court procedure; sometimes an American or British judge glances at them and there are weary nods of assent by the two French heads. Until a fortnight ago, the Cartesian spirit of yesterday was at a disadvantage in relation to the muddled Teutonic metaphysics now being expensively brought to trial; owing to bureaucratic confusion back in Paris, the French representatives here had not been paid their salaries since October, which could shake any man's faith in logic.

The militant attitude of the Russians has had a visibly strengthening effect on the Court, even when the Russian officials sit watchfully silent. Of the judges, only the Russians are in khaki; of the prosecuting lawyers, only the Russians wear a kind of regimental dress—chocolate-brown uniforms with green trimmings. Even the Russian female interpreters and typists can easily be identified, in court or out of it, if only by a rear view of their military-looking frocks. Each of the four Allied prosecutions has brought to this international tribunal its special flavor. The Russian contribution has been mostly emotional—a swift heartbeat of anger and anguish which Chief Prosecutor Rudenko has made audible to the listening Court, as if his microphone were a sort of stethoscope. When it looked, because of the weakness of the American cross-examination, as if Göring had fixed his legend to live forever, it was the Russian reminders of Nazi rottenness that aided the British in dealing, yesterday, what can be regarded as the death blow.

In the end, it is probably the British who will dominate this Allied gathering, as they did the last time, over a hundred years ago, punishment was meted out to a modern European man mad enough to think he could conquer the Continent—and Russia. After Waterloo, the English were satisfied to exile Napoleon to one of their islands, where it was intended that the world should forget him. With that kind of experience behind them, it is natural that certain of the British in Nuremberg have been more worried than their Allied colleagues about the great length of the trial and the fact that the wily and seemingly uncontrollable Göring was taking the opportunity to offer the Germans far too much to remember. It is not only the British worldliness and sense of history that give them a special place in the trial; it is their legal prestige, exemplified in the person of the Court President, Sir Geoffrey Lawrence. The mere sight of his bald, wise, Dickensian head sets the tone of the bench. His courtesy to the German lawyers has been cutting; a sample, shown to Göring's Dr. Stahmer: "What you have just said seems to me the acme of irrelevance." One of the sights outside the courthouse is the glorious daily arrival of Sir Geoffrey in a magnificent black limousine, glistening against the dusty ruins of the bombed walls. Attired in a long, blue broadcloth coat and a bowler, he passes through the courthouse door while the Allied guards of the day— the Russians with medals or the French with berets or the Tommies with battle ribbons or the Americans in snow-white helmets—stiffly present arms. In the courtroom itself, the same physical dignity and sartorial elegance of Prosecutor Sir David Maxwell Fyfe, impeccable in his Foreign Office attire, have unquestionably affected the Nazis, hypersensitive to formality and chic in the male.

As the cross-examiner who forced a weary Göring to admit that, by deduction, at least, Hitler had been a murderer, Sir David was polished, courteous, and artful. His strength lay in conducting the cross-examination in a manner that clearly kept Göring guessing about what was coming next, and each question made his line of thought more baffling. During this vital cross-examination, Sir David's professional affability disappeared. The pitying patience with which he had politely referred to "our young friend," when von Ribbentrop's youthful Dr. Horn made a bloomer, and his handsome way of referring to our Justice Biddle, on the bench, as "the learned American judge"—these easy verbal gestures were gone. With his excellent mind, his vast legal knowledge, and the added passion of a just inquisition, he stood behind his lectern and prosecuted the seated Göring into at least a partial state of destruction. He succeeded in doing what had not yet been done: he forced Göring to separate himself intellectually from the Nazi myth, he forced him to admit the difference between the glorified Nazi plan and the ghastly human results.

The German lawyers have been mentally mediocre and politically mixed —Nazis and anti-Nazis. The Allies permitted Nazis to be chosen lest the German people think that anti-Nazis were halfhearted defenders and justice was not being done. The German lawyer best known to Americans is

Professor Herbert Kraus, who is Schacht's white-haired associate counsel and who held the chair of International Law at Göttingen until 1937, when the Nazis dismissed him for being philosophically pro-Semitic. Kraus looks like a Dürer drawing, wears a borrowed red-caped university robe because his own was destroyed in last year's bombing of Nuremberg (along with a nearly completed legal treatise he had been working on for thirteen years), and before the war had been a lecturer at Columbia, the University of Chicago, and Princeton. He is amiable, describes himself as a wild smoker of American cigarettes when he can get them, and declares that the main German legal incomprehension of the Nuremberg trial is based on the fact that the Allies have charged the Nazis with conspiracy, a charge, the Germans claim, that cannot be made against a legal government, which the Nazi regime was. That a legal German government might have conspired against another legal government was a notion which seemed not to have occurred to the Professor or the other defense lawyers.

Because the victorious Allied world considered the Nazis so palpably guilty of the ruin of Europe that the Nuremberg trial was to serve merely as a legal demonstration of their culpability, there has been, outside Nuremberg, the easy conclusion that since we had enough on them to hang them, they would certainly hang. As a matter of fact, since we chose the law as our medium of vengeance, it has been necessary to satisfy the law, to furnish it with proof. Conspiracy was the Allies' primary charge, and conspiracy is one of the most difficult crimes to prove. And since we set up a bench of judges, who naturally must have legal proof, the Allied prosecution's task has been more difficult than any except lawyers could know. Hitler's absence from the courtroom has been scarcely less troubling than his presence would have been. Absent, he has been, in a sense, both the murderer and the murdered. He has been the alibi and the corpse. He has furthermore been the martyr and the guilty party. But had Göring accepted his Führer's order last year to kill himself, the task of the prosecution would have been less complex. Apparently even the Germans had no idea how formidable a mind and personality Göring still has. Until Göring—the last important surviving Nazi brain, its dishonest processes arrogantly alive in the still proud, corpulent body of the smiling, gray-uniformed man— was legally brought low before the Court, it could not be said that the Allies had established their case in law.

As for the twenty-one minor compatriots surrounding Göring in the prisoners' box, they seem already waxen and posthumous, like museum figures of the members of some nefarious long-ago regime which had failed. Whatever the sentences the twenty-two men will ultimately receive, it will be less what the French, the Russian, the American, and the British lawycrs have said in the Nuremberg court than the documents the Nazis themselves, with typical German orderliness, wrote and signed in their destructive years that will condemn them.

Letter from Amsterdam

FEBRUARY 6, 1947 Before the Nazi war, there were a hundred thousand Jews living in Amsterdam. Today, there are five thousand. Catching Jews here was easy. The Gestapo merely cut the bridges of the canals leading to the Jewish neighborhoods they called ghettos, flushed the inmates out of their little eighteenth-century houses, shot those who tried to swim the canals to escape from what had suddenly become fatal racial islands, tagged the marooned remainder with yellow Stars of David, and carted them off in cattle cars to the Fatherland's concentration camps. Of Holland's hundred and forty thousand Jews, a hundred and fourteen thousand perished under the Germans, as did more than fifty thousand of the three hundred and fifty thousand Dutch Christians deported as slave labor. In addition, twenty-five thousand Dutch starved to death at home, three thousand in Amsterdam during the unexpectedly melodramatic, awful last eight months of the war; eighteen thousand civilians were killed here and there over the Lowlands, half by friends in the air and half by foes on the ground, as happens in up-to-date war; and thirty thousand Dutch colonials from the East Indies government ranks and tea-and-coffee trade died in Japanese prison camps. In the light of these statistics and of the natural Dutch habit of industriousness, plus the presence in an addled, raddled postwar world of much pressing work to be done, it is easy to understand why there is no unemployment in Holland.

The Amsterdam canals being filled with snow, ice, and skaters instead of with busy boats, in this coldest winter in years, householders consider themselves lucky to have a coal ration that will keep one room warm all season. The city's black-market restaurants feature loaded hors-d'œuvre tables, fresh soles a foot and a half long, partridge, boar steaks, and the best French wines, but the Dutch workingman, sitting in his single cozy room, is entitled, according to his ration cards, to only the equivalent of three meatballs and two eggs a week, one new suit a year, and no Holland gin ever. By government decision, Dutch hens, sheep, and distillers are working for the export trade and foreign exchange. The Dutch of all classes have always been heavy eaters. The war and its resulting shortages have pulled their equalitarianism askew. There is a greater difference today between the diets of the middle class and the laboring class than at any other time since before the days of the sixteenth-century Breughel, on whose museum canvases the humble are still feasting in magnificent colors on beef haunches that now only the *nouveaux riches* can afford.

Of the six big western Dutch business centers—Amsterdam, Haarlem, Leiden, Delft, The Hague, and Rotterdam, which lie as close together as Long Island towns—only The Hague and Rotterdam show scars of war. The center of Rotterdam, where in 1940 the Nazis bragged that they had bombed thirty-five thousand inhabitants to death in seven minutes flat, is still unreconstructed. The Rotterdammers declare, surprisingly, that only nine hundred were killed. The Dutch think that since the city had already capitulated, the air raid was a little Nazi mistake, which was artfully converted into terror propaganda. The wealthy Hague residential district of Bezuidenhout is also in ruins. The bombing that caused them was, without any doubt, a British error; the Dutch say that the R.A.F. pilots simply read their maps backward, that their real target was the opposite side of town, where the Germans were firing their V-2s, supposedly on London. Most of them rocketed up all right, but some of them, instead of heading for England, dropped back on The Hague. They always managed to miss the famous Hague Peace Palace, which is still foolishly intact.

Most of Holland's war injuries have resulted in semi-paralysis rather than scars. Train service has been slowed down, because the Nazis sent Holland's Diesel engines to the Rumanians, who were the only members of the Axis with enough oil to run them. The Nazis also borrowed most of the Netherlands' telephone equipment, so a priority system has had to be set up for calls between the six big western cities. Third-grade calls, which are the lowest in priority, the cheapest, and the slowest to be put through, are what an ordinary letter is for the post office; second-grade calls are like special-delivery letters; and first-grade calls, which cost five times as much as third-grade, are handled speedily, like telegrams. Whereas France got the best occupation treatment in the west, the Dutch got the worst. They were occupied and robbed not by the so-called *korrekt* German military but by the civilian Gestapo. Since Holland was scheduled geopolitically for incorporation into the Reich, the Germans treated it brutally—just like one of the family.

The English are openly grim and melancholy about their colonial-empire troubles, which the British newspapers are full of. Holland, with the third-biggest colonial empire, has the same kind of troubles, but most of the Dutch talk little about them and the papers diplomatically print only obscurities about the rebellion, or armed truce, in the East Indies. There the Dutch have for centuries fostered a fantastically rich trade in spices, tin, rubber, coffee, tea, and so on. About a fifth of Holland's income depends on her colonies, where, the Dutch bluntly say, between a fifth and sixth of the investments is in the hands of British and Americans, who do nothing to help. Colonies seem and smell closer in Amsterdam than they do anywhere in London except on what is left of the old East India Docks. Amsterdam's finest canal, with the town's richest antique brick mansions and the grandest carved-mahogany interiors, is the Heerengracht, or Gentleman Merchant's Canal. The Keizersgracht and Prinsengracht, or Emperor's and Prince's Canals, rank distinctly second and third. The offices of Amsterdam's merchants, at least, still smell of exotic riches, of black-market Sumatra cigars, and of well-sugared, aromatic Java coffee, which is served all day long. Beside the canals, there are Javanese students snowballing Dutch boys; in hotel lobbies, there are graceful, spice-scented half-caste ladies.

Former colonial officials say that they dug worms and ate them to avoid starvation in their Japanese prison camps. Apparently, their wives, in the women's camps, ate nothing worse than boiled snails and weeds. The camp guards, having heard that white ladies needed carbohydrates and fresh air, fed them the powdered sago once used to starch their husbands' white linen suits and for nearly four years kept them busy out of doors moving stones from one spot to another and then back again—stones the size of a loaf of bread if the guards felt good and stones the size of watermelons if they felt bad. Today, the rebel Indonesian Republic and its nationalist native leader, President Soekarno, hold all of Sumatra and Java except five Dutch footholds (and the surrounding countryside): Medan, Semarang, the lovely mountain towns of Bandoeng and Soerabaja, both jammed with military-protected whites waiting to return to their wasted tea gardens and coffee plantations, and Batavia, where the Dutch government sits, having been driven out of the nearby Governor's Palace, at Buitenzorg. Reactionary Hollanders suspect that Soekarno plans to sell out his Republic three ways—to the Russians, the Americans, and the British—all at once. Moderate Hollanders think that the main difference between the rebel and the loyal Indonesians is that the former want to be free of the Dutch and the latter want to be free under the Dutch.

Holland is now somewhat Anglophobe, because the British had to commandeer aid from the defeated Japanese in order to support the Dutch against the rebellious Javanese—a paradoxical situation in which everybody lost face except the wonderful little Japs. With the exception of her helpless five-day fight against the Germans in 1940, Holland has not been at war officially since the Belgian secession, in 1830–39. Raw recruits, wearing surplus British battle dress, complete with khaki tam-o'-shanters, now swarm the railway stations en route for the Dutch Indies and its peculiar armed truce, in which other recruits are being killed. What is going on in Indonesia is, perhaps, the normal struggle of our time between capital and labor, made more exotic by capital's being white and labor a pretty brown. Holland's future will be shaped by the outcome.

Dutch resistance during the war against Germany centered in Amsterdam and was called *de Illegaliteit,* or the Illegality. Holland's geography provides no heaths or hills to resist in, hide among, or fight from. A Dutch mouse sitting on a Gestapo chief's carpet would have been no more visible than a Dutch patriot operating from his land's flat, unprotected, treeless plains. The Illegality forged papers and ration cards, operated a secret Holland-to-England radio station in the basement of Amsterdam's handsome eighteenth-century orphan asylum, and founded three clandestine political newspapers—the *Word* (Socialist), the *Truth* (Communist), and *Loyalty* (Right Wing)—which are coming out, aboveground and influentially, today. The Gestapo punished the Illegality with mounting savagery during the last, desperate months of the war, dragging its members from prison to shoot them in the streets and forcing passersby to crowd about and watch.

The Battle of Arnhem, which dominated the closing phase of the war for the Dutch, did Holland harm in several ways. From the railway station, Arnhem looks like any lucky, untouched eastern Dutch town. Only when you walk down the streets, which uselessly lead through wasteland along the Rhine, do you see where half a big town once lay, now so neatly reduced to nothing that what is left of its outline is lost in a mere few inches of snow. To the Allies, the dramatic, dangerous delay at Arnhem is remembered only as the last hitch but one—at Bastogne—in the final, concentrated push to Berlin. To Amsterdammers, informed over the Illegality Dutch radio that Arnhem was the beginning of liberation for all Holland, the battle still means Mad Tuesday—the first Tuesday in September, 1944, when, the Nazis having fled, Amsterdammers began celebrating their freedom. (By Friday, the Nazis were back, shooting the celebrators.) On Mad Tuesday, all Dutch railway men struck, to impede Nazi operations. From then until May 6th of the next year, when the war ended in such international excitement that only the Dutch seemed to notice that their entire country was finally free, not a Dutch train moved, not a letter was legally delivered, and, in the cities, eight months of isolation and starvation had to be endured. As a Dutch painter later said, "By March, our faces were pale green, like imitation van Goghs." Women's ankles and wrists were so swollen from starvation that they could hardly walk to the distant fields and dig the sugar beets to feed their families; all the young men grew beards to try to look more than forty, the age limit for last-minute Nazi labor gangs. The Concertgebeouw's head porter recently said that it normally takes six of his men to move a concert grand piano but that by April of 1944 the average weight of his assistants had dropped to around ninety pounds and it took ten of them to move a piano. When the other hungry western Europeans were liberated, newspaper headlines pictured them as starving. Only the Dutch were really starving, and the only headline they got was one to the inaccurate effect that their inundated lands would be unfertile because of the salt water for twenty-five years. Heavy rains rinsed the topsoil sweet for replanting. The worst inundation caused by the Allied bombing of dikes occurred on the wheat-bearing southern island of Walcheren, where the Dutch had to suffer along with the Germans to permit Allied supply ships free passage in to Antwerp. The Nazis' cruelest blow, delivered just before they fled, was against the cattle lands of northern Wieringen, where they wantonly blew up the dikes on the old Zuyder Zee.

The very names of the Dutch political parties described a government that contains elements from the twentieth, nineteenth, eighteenth, seventeenth, and even sixteenth centuries. This government is an oddity in Protestant Holland's modern history. Of the hundred seats in Parliament, thirty-two were won by the *Katholieke Volkspartij* in the first postwar elections, last May. This gave the Catholics first place. Holland has been Calvinist and anti-Pope ever since the soul-shaking Reformation divided Europe into two quarreling Christian camps. Today, the Dutch say that the two faiths are about equal in power, because a few post-Reformation Catholic families have built themselves up into the present big party by having more children than the Protestants felt they could afford and because the Church has taken the extra mouths into the priesthood and nunneries. Last May, the priest, nuns, and lay Catholics here were better organized than the Protestant voters. The fear that the two Christian sects once had of each other is now submerged in their common fear of Communism. The winning Catholics were hailed by the Protestants as the "savior of our freedom" and a bulwark against the Communists, who came in fourth, with ten seats. Second strongest is the Labor Party, significantly made up of Socialists, Left Wing Papists, ex-Illegalists, members of the professional class, and even high officials, such as Amsterdam's present burgomaster. Third comes the Calvinist Anti-Revolutionary Party, which was founded to demonstrate Christ and the Revelation of the Bible in protest against the eighteenth-century French Revolution's Goddess of Reason and Wicked Atheism. A fifth group, which ran but won nothing, is the Bellamy Party. The Dutch seem surprised that we Americans never heard of our own Mr. Bellamy, the nineteenth-century utopian. He has eleven thousand followers here—reformers, theosophists, vegetarians, and members of the Dutch Jack London Society, which is against circuses and the training or killing of animals. The Bellamy–Jack Londoners recently wrote a stiff note to Princess Elizabeth of England after she attended her first foxhunt.

Queen Wilhelmina, being a constitutional monarch, is supposed to have no party, but everyone knows that she has and that it is the Christian Historical Party, which has one of the oldest democratic political platforms in Europe. This platform evolved from Holland's suffering in the Eighty Years' War, during which the Dutch developed the Theory of the Rights of Man, which they proudly claim was the ideological forebear of the American Revolution and even that awful French Revolution. The Christian Historicals, who always stick with the old nineteenth-century liberals and ran last among the important parties, are ultraconservative, under the Queen's influence, and have been described by some observers as the core of the nation. The Queen, incidentally, still permits no low-necked dresses at her court. Amsterdam law demands that the tops and bottoms of women's bathing suits be attached to each other, preventing midriff exposure. And, in case Hollywood press agents are interested, none of the bathing-beauty pictures they send to Holland are ever printed in the papers.

Many of the Dutch will have to go to the commercial tulip fields this spring if they want to see tulips bloom. In the interest of foreign exchange, Holland's postwar tulip-bulb crop will largely flower in the United States. People have not been permitted to buy bulbs to replace those they ate from their own little gardens. They say that boiled tulip bulbs tasted sweetish —like boiled chestnuts—and caused poisoning and retching if you ate more than three or four at a sitting. For the last eight months of the war, the Dutch lived on them. They were usually made into *tulpen pannekoeken*, or tulip pancakes, fried and browned in cabbage-seed oil. They were sickening, unnourishing, but filling, and they were swallowed with gratitude.

The Vienna Opera

MAY 10, 1947   When, in 1938, the Nazis were talking Anschluss, they shouted that the German and the Austrian *Kultur* were sacredly one and indivisible. But in defeat, in 1945, one of the fleeing Germans' last acts was to set fire to Vienna's beautiful Saint Stephen's Cathedral and its revered Burgtheater—both of them now empty architectural shells—as if the perfect Rhineland Gothic of the first one and the classic Teutonic repertory of the other had suddenly become alien, after all. Vienna's elegant Opera House, on the other hand, was turned into a shell by American bombers. In the spring warmth, the city's opera troupe, transplanted after the liberation to the historic Theater an der Wien of Beethoven's day, is thriving. This past winter season, however, was tough. Each performance depended on the day's conditions: Was there enough coal for enough power for a few trams to run? Was the snow too deep for audience and singers to walk? How many sopranos and tenors would arrive late and hoarse? Would there be enough electricity to light the show, assuming that singers and ticket holders got there? As a matter of record, the Opera never skipped a performance. In the bombing of the Opera House, eighty thousand costumes were turned to ashes. To aid the denuded singers, the state recently chipped in part of the *Volksoper* wardrobe. Wearing these hand-me-downs, the singers look fine in the current repertory, which includes an excellent "Don Giovanni"; the morbidly popular "Salome"; the racially popular "Walküre," splendidly conducted by Knappertsbusch; and a worldly, typically Viennese "Der Rosenkavalier," always the world's best, since only in Vienna is such sad sophistication indigenous. According to the opera's Herr Direktor, Professor Franz Salmhofer, his chief problem right now is to continue getting double food rations for his stars, who he insists cannot remain plump enough to sing well on the ration of fifteen hundred and fifty calories a day. Like most of the older European theatre men, Professor Salmhofer finds that his intimate prewar world has grown smaller: more than thirty of his friends disappeared in concentration camps, his wife's parents died in a deportation train, and his grandparents became euthanasia victims merely because they were too old to be worth feeding.

Vienna Night Life

JULY 19, 1947 The internationalism of Vienna's theatre is normal for a civilized capital city that was long isolated by war and ideology. The majority of the plays are French, British, or American, of which the most important, as intellectual fare, are Cocteau's "Die Höllische maschine" ("La Machine Infernale"), Coward's "Intimitäten" ("Private Lives"), and Thornton Wilder's "Wir Sind Noch Einmal Davon Gekommen" ("The Skin of Our Teeth"), which the Viennese find mad and fascinating. The only successful native play is "Das Heilige Experiment" ("The Holy Experiment"), which is about eighteenth-century Jesuits in Paraguay. The plot concerns some good Fathers who, finding they cannot convert the natives, compromise by giving them a more humane standard of living, for which the Church castigates them, with the reminder that their duty is to save souls, not to make human beings more comfortable. Though the theme seems to the foreign visitor an obvious refurbishing of the Nazi dogma that doctrinal belief is more important than kindness to one's fellow-men, the Viennese, who should know, assure foreigners that the play is merely an interesting historical one about Jesuits and Paraguayans. The gayest musical running in Vienna is the *Volksoper*'s revival of Offenbach's "Orpheus in der Unterwelt," which had been banned by the Nazis because the composer was a Jew. The shortened and modernized production of this broad, farcical *opéra bouffe* is by Willi Forst, who is memorable for his acting in the charming film "Zwei Herzen im Dreivierteltakt." His most popular scenic touch is a four-language traffic sign, exactly like a corner traffic sign in occupied Vienna, whose arrow says in German, English, French, and Russian, "Hell." It brings down the house.

Of the four German-language newspapers that the Allies license, direct, and censor, the American-controlled *Wiener Kurier* and the British-controlled *Welt Presse* sell best among the Viennese, a large majority of whom hope that the democratic Anglo-Saxon version of events is the one that is finally going to turn out to be true. The French control the weekly *Welt am Montag* and the Russians the daily *Österreiche Zeitung*. The Russians also offer weekly magazines, a monthly periodical for youth, and superior propaganda setup that directs undeviating, well-worked-out editorial attacks against the Americans. In an effort to check the natural Austrian talent for complaining, which could be politically troublesome now, each Ally has announced in its paper—with varying degrees of emphasis, depending upon its Home Office's foreign policy—that the conditions in Germany should make the Austrians feel blessed. But the Viennese continue to sigh and disbelieve. Frank about their own character, they are certain that the Germans organize everything better, even defeat.

Though the Russians have more officers here than any other Ally, they maintain only one officers' club—in a garden suite in the Hofburg, the former imperial palace. The American officers have so many clubs that they issue a book of bar chits, good in half a dozen of them. These places have made them indifferent to the existence of all but one of the native night clubs, and that one is now off limits for them. It is the Oriental, which functions in an exotically decorated cellar; during the war it was a basement bordello, run for Gestapo bigwigs and other Nazi V.I.P.s by an obliging, well-known character named Achmid Bey, an Egyptian who operated a chain of brothels throughout eastern Europe and shipped his girls around among them, like trained seals. The Oriental has kept its name but changed its program, now being merely the hottest night spot in town; it offers strip-tease dancers, a type never known in Vienna's waltz days. The Kaiserbar, off Kärntnerstrasse, is still elegant and international, with atmosphere, a dance band, and drinks as close to de luxe as the times permit. It was sideswiped by a Russian shell during the siege of Vienna and so lost its famous, lovely little windows cut from white alabaster— rarities usually found in a Romanesque church. The most interesting night club, the Schiefe Laterne (the Tilted Lantern), near the Opera, is seldom noticed by foreigners. It is frequented by eastern Europe's theatre, vaudeville, and film people, and by local night-club entertainers, who gather there, after their own shows have ended, to try out new numbers, sing old ones, poke fun at the Allies, and eat and drink black market. It is not spectacular, but it has lots of character. Except in such nocturnal corners, there is little but beer for the Viennese to drink, though Vienna's pleasant suburban wine crop is reported to have been plentiful last year. According to waiters now passing out *dunkles* or *helles Bier* instead of wine, all the Gumpoldskirchener, formerly a favorite wine of workmen on Saturday nights, has disappeared into the black market, from which it reappears at about thirty-five schillings a bottle, a tenth of what a workingman earns a month.

Letter from Warsaw

MAY 22, 1947 Warsaw is the most conscientiously achieved big ruin in Europe. This peculiar distinction was acquired in the summer and fall of 1944, when the city was blown up carefully, block by block and house by house, by the Germans as punishment for its insurrection. Up to that time, the blitzkrieg and the subsequent Stukas had inflicted injuries equal only to London's. Most of Warsaw's ruins visible today are the result of that businesslike wrecking job done by the mile by the vindictive Nazis, who lacked neither method nor dynamite.

The Warsovians have suffered more in the way of war, rebellion, deportation, destruction, and political revolution than the population of any other Continental capital city. The lives of the people in Warsaw have been dilated by extraordinary dramas, and the scene they still live in fits what they have been through. Everywhere you look, there is an air of large-scale unreality. During the recent sunny weekends, from the cavernous, wrecked façades of nice apartment houses have emerged troops of decently dressed families, like bourgeois troglodytes out for a Sunday stroll. The spring heat has also brought up disquieting smells from yawning basements. (No one here has the consolation of thinking that all of Warsaw's quarter-million dead were properly buried.) Behind ruined building fronts, in courtyards all over town, there are fragments of flats or patched-up parlors or kitchens in which whole families manage to live and even keep clean. Middle-aged, well-educated matrons, whose only previous work was raising their children, now killed, housekeep together in clusters of two or three to a battered room, having learned to earn their living by day in offices and to endure that great hardship, lack of privacy. The only relief in the monotony of the city's red-brick ruins—Warsaw has always lacked building stone—is the white ribbon of new, one-story stucco shops trimming the edge of the business district. Because of the hit-or-miss rebuilding that is now going on, a reconditioned luxury flat may be sandwiched between floors that are swarming tenements, complete with sweetmeat sellers squatting at the building's front door. A once wealthy countess —Warsaw is fairly full of them—is living in a dirt-floored home that started as a double bed for herself and her husband in a lean-to built

131

against a wall of a demolished building. It has been expanded to afford corners for plumbing, cooking, sleeping, and entertaining, and has been decorated with retrieved oddments of fine furnishings. Building materials are scarce and high. In one flat recently reconstructed for a large family, there are no doors. They cost too much. Still, having whole walls and windows seems wonderful enough.

In all this physical confusion, people's dramatic histories are their identification tags. In one household of five children, two belong to one woman and the others belong to two of her sisters, who were both killed in the insurrection. A young woman who regrets that she cannot show you her father's excellent library can't show it because he and it were bombed. The two prettiest stenographers working in a government office have labor-camp numbers tattooed on their arms. The white-haired old man you met last night knows that his wife is buried somewhere under the ruins of their house.

On the midtown Sikorski Avenue, rebuilt cafés offer luscious ice cream, a favorite Polish dish. On the other hand, much of the milk here is tubercular. In the fine restaurants, the country's plentiful beet sugar is still served in the grand Polish manner—from a square, antique silver box that looks like a jewel case. In a restaurant such as the Canalleto, there are little carafes of *wodka*; the famous cold crayfish soup concocted with dill, beets, cream, and cucumbers; fresh salmon; meat three times a week, and always dripping with butter; and wonderful chocolate cakes. Lunch for three is about two thousand zloty, or twenty dollars at the legal rate of exchange. An office worker earns six thousand zloty a month; the director of an art museum earns seven thousand. It costs a married couple twenty thousand zloty a month to live just modestly; it costs fifteen hundred zloty a day to feed a *dorozka* horse. The few Poles who can afford it still eat enough at their classic 3 P.M. dinner to last them a week; the regular poor are, as they always have been, undernourished; and, in between, the thousands of new poor manage to get along some way, no one can tell exactly how. People who had never been shopkeepers have opened shops. Everyone who can has to earn, and the new amateurs have replaced the trained business people who were killed. This makes for revived commerce and general inefficiency. Destruction has created new trades. There is, for instance, a brisk business in reburnishing table silver tarnished in the war's fires.

The biggest business here, logically, is rebuilding, or planning to rebuild, the city. Humanists consider the government's plans too doctrinal. In the new Warsaw, now only on paper, there will be specified places for everybody and everything, with a center for labor, commerce, factories, recreation, and government workers, and with green belts and restricted sections for people in government-approved work and an outside area for the others. At present, anybody who wants to is encouraged to build a house, even of one story, on any approved residential street, provided the foundation will support five more stories someday, six stories being the prescribed, planned limit. There are few takers for this proposition. It is generally assumed that the government may soon seize such useful property and that the political future will not be one in which a landlord will be protected, or even thanked.

Of the several revolutionary reforms decreed by the Lublin Communist government late in 1944, only the first still affects everybody's life. To deflate the war-weakened currency, Lublin called in all the country's money, issued new bank notes, credited each citizen with one zloty for every two he turned in, and then permitted him actually to take home exactly five hundred zloty—at that time about enough for a week's food—and froze the balance. Everybody supposedly was levelled off and had to start at scratch. There was chaos. Factories and businesses closed. Housewives did better; they bartered miniatures, shoes, tables, and rings for food. A sort of normality was restored, at least for some, when the Lublin black market in foreign money began quietly functioning: on trains, bicycles, and peasant carts, Poles of all sorts arrived in town with all kinds of hoarded foreign money. The Lublin currency reform has entrenched the dollar and sterling black market, which the present Communist-dominated government is, of course, bitterly against. It has forced everybody who has nothing left to sell to go to work; it has not abolished capitalism. Poles are spiritedly encouraged to open savings accounts with their new money, because the stability of the citizenry is vital to the country's recovery.

The fact that there are practically no Russians behind Poland's iron curtain comes as a considerable surprise. Attachés in the American, British, and French Embassies have grown tired of repeating this piece of information to visitors here and to their governments at home, which seem to keep regarding it as incredible news. Russia operates a sort of absentee government in Poland. There are Russian soldiers on the Polish-German border. The Russians have their own communications system between Poland and Moscow. But there are no Russians in Poland's state hierarchy, and rarely are any seen on Warsaw's streets. Being former conquerors, they are as unpopular as the Germans, and they are feared even more, because many Poles think the Russians aim to conquer again. Scratch a Pole and you find a Pole, even if he is a Communist. What is happening in Poland is an example of the new Politburo foreign policy; i.e., Polish Communists—though they may have to phone Moscow daily, like a boy reporting to his father—are free to create a Polish type of Communism, and it is their job to make it popular with both the Poles and the Kremlin. Unofficially, the Polish Communists admit that the recent elections that put them in were rigged. Unofficially, their colleagues the Socialists admit that if the elections had not been rigged, the conservative Polish Peasant Party would have won, and then the Russians might have reoccupied Poland and run it themselves. The Peasant Party now admits that the prewar, anti-Left Pilsudski elections were crooked, too. The tragedy of the Poles is that they are always talking about freedom from someone else but are afraid to give it to one another. The Polish Communists are governing with a light hand, with relatively little Communism, and with few Communists (the Party is frankly a sub-minority), of whom even fewer are politically trained. They are also governing with undeniable success. Foreign observers think that most of the credit for the success belongs to Hilary Minc, a former statistical clerk who went to Moscow before the war and stayed there until 1944 (probably while he was being trained in the Five-Year Plan office), when he turned up in the Lublin group as Industrial Minister, a post he still holds. Dividing industry into fourteen branches, each headed by a Vice-Minister, he has set up a tightly knit structure, with himself sitting on top, and makes it run at a remarkable tempo. It is he who sets the pace for all Poland.

The Communist Party's great, sinister achievement is the Urząd Bezpieczeństwa—the hundred and seventy thousand Security Police, all Poles, in uniform and out, who are the Party's spies. In public, Poles, especially if they are with foreigners, are careful of what they say. The specialty of the Bezpieczeństwa—disrespectfully called the Betsy Boys by foreigners, whom they may not touch—are "blockades," which are less prevalent now than they were last year. A blockade is a method of finding out whom So-and-So, considered to be suspect, is seeing. Everyone who calls at his flat—the milk girl, his old aunt, or even some one who has just knocked at the wrong door—is popped inside and held incommunicado. After several days of this, So-and-So's flat may be jammed with people, while their families go crazy. Last year, one wit, hearing that a pal of his was blockaded, put an ad in the paper announcing that the pal's flat was for rent. Within an hour, five hundred flat-hungry Warsovians stormed the door, and the blockade was broken by sheer ridicule. Poles are afraid that a new restriction will soon be imposed upon them: that they will no longer be able to listen to the Polish-language B.B.C. broadcasts from London. The prewar wireless sets, already selling second-hand at the high price of thirty-five thousand zloty, are wearing out, and the government plans to manufacture only a Russian model, nicknamed Eat What I Give You, which is no more than an outlet of a master receiving set that will be set up in the concierge's flat. If the concierge is wise, he will select for his tenants only government-approved programs, of which B.B.C. is not one.

Warsaw's tragic sixty-three-day insurrection, which began in August, 1944, was a spontaneous combustion. The British and American command gave the Poles the go-ahead signal simply because they were already at the bursting point anyway, as the Germans had surmised. The revolt could have been effective only if the advancing Russians had, as expected, crossed the Vistula on the outer edge of town and hurried in to give the Germans the coup de grâce. Momentarily held up by some surprise Panzer divisions, the Russians halted on the far side of the river and waited, in plain sight, while the Poles and Germans conveniently killed each other. Warsaw will never forgive the Russians. Under Stuka bombing and machine-gun fire, the insurrectionists' only system of communications was the city's sewers. It took about twelve hours, wading hip deep in sewage, to zigzag from the market square to the town's center, three kilometres away, through the sewers, which were hung with little electric lights. Many fainted and drowned and are still there. In their sixty-three days of fighting, the Poles starved. One woman recently said that once a butcher offered her a dog's leg. She ran away, because she was so hungry she was afraid she would buy and eat it. After the Warsaw insurrection was crushed, the Nazis devoted three months to their systematic task of blowing the city to bits. The Russians walked in, easily, in January, 1945.

When the Nazi Governor-General of Poland, Hans Frank, was being tried at Nuremberg, he complained that the Warsaw Jewry had risen against him and said that the severe measures he had taken were retaliatory. It is true that in the spring of 1943 the martyrized Jews, certain that they were doomed to the crematories, bravely turned, themselves, to the Mosaic law—an eye for an eye. With guns bought from venal Nazi soldiers, they rose and killed all the Germans they could. Frank then fired the Jews' houses, burning them alive, or stripped them naked on the streets and had them potshot as they ran. He literally levelled the ghetto. Today, it is merely an undulating heath of crushed red bricks.

Most of the foreign-embassy people are now squeezed into the dilapidated old Hotel Polonia, on Pilsudski Avenue. A Polish woman not long ago recalled the time, early in the Nazi occupation, when she saw a German soldier, stiffly on guard before the Polonia's door, suddenly scoop up a passing little Jewish girl, lift a manhole cover in the street, toss her down out of sight, close the manhole, and resume his impeccable stance as sentry of civilization.

Letter from the Ghetto

WARSAW, JUNE 10, 1947 The Polish Jews who are left say that living in Poland is like walking around in a cemetery. There were three and a half million Jews when the Germans came, and fewer than seventy-five thousand when the war ended. Between two and three hundred thousand have since been repatriated, but so many, also, have emigrated that the total number of Jews now in Poland is probably no more than a hundred thousand. For nearly two years, Polish Jews have been fleeing from their homeland, principally funnelling out through the southern border town of Kladzko, crossing Czechoslovakia, and aiming either for the Holy Land or, second best, for Munich, in the American Zone. Seven weeks ago, the United States Army European Command shut our zone against any more displaced persons. Polish Jews were not specifically mentioned in the orders, but since they were the only national group still flowing into our D.P. camps in large numbers, they were the most affected. The Polish border has just been closed to Jews without papers, too, and its guards, according to report, have been instructed to shoot. Aside from guns, a closed border means merely that to cross it legally an emigrating Jew must have a passport—a one-way paper, for going out only. There is no thought of returning. Last year's open frontier, or "green border"—meaning that Jews could cross illegally and without passports anywhere in the unpatrolled country-side—was intelligently condoned by the government, then unable to protect its Jews, who were therefore considered safer anywhere else. Today's strictly guarded frontier, over which only a dozen Jews a week cross, all legally, is just one indication that the government has been somewhat strengthened. Polish Jews preferred to go over the green border quickly as stateless human beings and without legal identity rather than waste any time waiting for Polish papers. Most of them—wherever they have gone or may go, legally or illegally, and whether Zionists or non-Zionists—hope eventually to reach Palestine. Many would go anywhere on earth if they could only leave the scene of the tortures and murder of their families.

The Jews have more than their memories to run away from. Anti-

Semitism did not disappear with the Germans. Only a few weeks ago, some Jewish houses were burned down in an anti-Jewish demonstration in Stettin. During the German occupation, Polish anti-Semitism was largely in abeyance, and even a certain amount of pro-Semitism was practiced, as a form of anti-Germanism and thus patriotic. German excesses—their cattle cars packed with doomed Jews and their gas chambers for thousands —made the principle of anti-Semitism untenable, especially to the older generation of Poles. When the Germans left, anti-Semitism became patriotic again among certain inflammable younger nationals. A recent report on last summer's pogrom at Kielce, a town south of Warsaw, revealed that the Christian boy who it was claimed had witnessed the imaginary ritual sacrifices that incited the killings was at the specified time out picking cherries with an aunt. In the first month after the Kielce pogrom, thirty-two thousand Jews stampeded toward the frontier, cramming the passenger trains and even piling themselves onto flatcars, as though they were goods for export. The trains were raided en route, and the Jews removed and killed, by the reactionary National Armed Forces, which were known during the insurrection against the German conquerors as the Boys of the Forest. The anti-Semitism that is going on now has been rather accurately described as "sporadic and unorganized," but it is not negligible.

Since the Jews of Poland endured, simply because they were Jews, the absolute extremities of suffering under the Germans, they now can look on their lesser miseries under the Poles with a certain objectivity. Many intellectual Jews think that Poland's ages-long anti-Semitism is rooted in the medievalism of her Church and the fanatical Catholicism of the Polish people, to which the sartorial medievalism of Poland's bearded and ringleted orthodox Jewry and its conservative religious doctrines must have been the tragically ideal irritant. Polish Catholics, however, give three other reasons for the recent revival of anti-Semitism. (1) Courageous, compassionate Catholics—apparently there were many—who began by hiding one Jew early in the war ended up by hiding several of his uncles or cousins who crept in during the five years of terror, and the Christians' noble impulses wore thin. (2) In cities where Jews were torn from their homes and greedy Christians—apparently there were many of these, too— moved into them, occasional Jewish owners have turned up again, during the acute housing shortage, and these Christians are afraid they may be ousted, hence are resentful. (3) Jews are associated in Catholic minds with the detested Communist Party. As a matter of fact, the Jews are a small minority in the Communist government and in the leadership of the Party, and, anomalously, Poland's Communist Party is strictly Catholic in its ideology, though, naturally, anticlerical and on the outs with the Vatican, having broken the sacred Concordat. Whatever Lenin thought of religion as an opiate, neither his party nor any other could gain any headway in pious Poland without the Holy Family.

The Communist government has certainly made special and logical efforts to aid the uprooted Jews; it has been planting thousands of them in the western "recovered lands," formerly German, where they are supposed to become farmers. The Ministry of Public Administration has also set up an Office of Repatriation to help expedite the return from Russia and Germany of Polish Jews; many of those in Russia have wanted to come back because they have figured that their chances of getting to Palestine— the only country where they feel they can be happy, provided, of course, that they can get in—would be better from Poland.

The Jews in Poland say that before the Polish and American Zone borders were closed, the emigration problem had already become so complex that it involved sectarianism, local political maneuvers, international strategy, and even the belief in a just God. The Polish Jewish leaders bitterly accept the fact that, since their Promised Land is only one element in the broader question of who is going to have control of the Suez Canal and the Golden Horn, the foreign policies of certain nations are the primary Palestine issue—not for Polish Jews but for those great outsiders, England, Russia, and the United States, all jockeying for power in the eastern Mediterranean. Another of Palestine's pressing issues is simply local in Poland—the confusions and divisions among the various factions of Jews. The orthodox congregations are led by the Jewish Religious Community Council, which, in accordance with Israel's ancient tradition, regards Palestine as home but is purely religious, and does not demand a political state of Zion. The Jewish Central Committee, whose main purpose is to organize Jewish farm and industrial coöperatives in Poland, is supported by modern, mostly non-practicing Jews, and though some of these are non-Zionist Communists and Socialists, many are Zionists, and therefore take a stand at variance with the Community Council's. Most of the orthodox Jews are non-Communist, often anti-Russian, and sometimes even confusedly pro-British, being old-fashioned believers in capitalism. Many of the Central Committee followers are pro-Communist, pro-Russian, and definitely against the British Empire. To complete the circle, many orthodox Polish Jews are obviously as shocked as Polish Catholics by Jewish Communism. And to confound everything further, the Central Committee is backed by the Communist government, which nevertheless has not so far flatly supported Zion.

The Polish Jewish leaders agree that when our Army closed our German zone against further D.P.s, the emigration problem became so much worse that it may actually be resolved more quickly than it would have been otherwise. One optimistic rabbi thinks that our ruling might force England to let the Jews into Palestine, after all; or, better, that England might let them into England; or, best, that the American ruling might force America herself into letting them into the U.S.A. The question the Polish Jews most often ask of Americans is: Why won't we give them the unused immigration quotas of Germany and Austria that accumulated during those war years when both their armies were killing Jews? Poland's quota is precisely 6,524 Polish nationals a year. The would-be Polish immigrants are divided by American law into a preferred and a non-preferred group. The former, who are allotted fifty per cent of the small quota, are the approximately forty thousand parents of prewar-naturalized Poles in the States, husbands of citizens, and skilled agriculturists. Of these, our consulates have already registered twenty-six thousand, or eight years' worth, so far held up mostly by lack of ships and Polish passports and United States visas. In the non-preferred group come—if they so elect—almost all the hundred thousand Jews in Poland and the approximately hundred thousand Polish Jewish D.P.s still in our camps in Germany, who together could fill the immigration quota for sixty years. The situation will be little relieved, naturally, until we expand the Polish national quota or until we have a special quota either borrowed from the unused wartime German and Austrian quotas or boldly created expressly to help those who are left of Poland's Jews.

The standard prewar complaint of Polish Christendom against Polish Jewry was that the Jews were especially good traders. But the Polish Christians are not doing too badly by and for themselves now. Because of the Poles' rather elegant lack of efficiency and the absence of experience among the thousands of aristocratic and bourgeois new poor now in trade, foreign observers are astonished at seeing how well business, both legal and illegal, rattles along without the Jews. According to recent government statistics, thirty-three thousand Jews are working in the country's heavy and light industries, which, considering the number of Jews left, is a high figure. For people waiting to leave and planning to travel light anyway, a job in a factory is more easily dropped and forgotten than a nice, newly set-up shop. The Germans destroyed all the old Jewish shops. There are no new ones.

Until the Germans occupied Warsaw, there was only a voluntary ghetto —a neighborhood of principally six-story apartment houses (near the medieval gilt-and-frescoed cottages on the Old City Market Square), in which three-quarters of the inhabitants were Jews who chose to live close to each other. The Germans created a compulsory ghetto by driving out of the district all but the Jews and then walling them in. It was behind this ghetto wall, in the insurgent summer of 1943, that the Germans exterminated sixty thousand Warsaw Jews. Two Nazi prisoners who were mixed up in the Polish pogroms have just arrived in Warsaw. Both have already been tried for other crimes—one of them was condemned to death, the other sentenced to life imprisonment—but will be tried again, and certainly condemned to death, in the country where the greatest of their crimes against humanity were committed. One prisoner is aristocratic General Jürgen von Stroop, of the S.S., who was Warsaw's Chief of Police. His most interesting memento of the city, displayed at the Nuremberg Tribunal, was his luxurious, hand-bound red leather photograph album, with its gold-tooled title, "The Razing of Warsaw's Ghetto," and fine photographic illustrations of his success. His travelling companion, a proletarian S.S., is Erich Mussfeldt, chief operator of the crematorium at Maidanek. He was given his job there because of his civilian training; he had been a baker in Berlin. Upon their arrival in Poland, the General had nothing to say to the National Tribunal guards who took charge of them. Mussfeldt, however, told them of his nice treatment in the American prison at Lansberg. There he had received three thousand calories of food daily, including white bread and butter, as well as twenty American cigarettes, a package of American tobacco twice a week, and every other week a box of cookies.

Letter from Berlin

JULY 12, 1947 The Unter den Linden section of Berlin is like a coffin a mile long, with two dead Germanys inside. When the Kaiser lost Germany's war of European conquest, his empire died in the now gutted Unter den Linden Palace. When Hitler lost his war of world conquest, his Third Reich died in the now equally gutted Wilhelmstrasse Chancellery, just around the corner from the mortuary thoroughfare. This is the symbolic mile of Berlin that millions of Russian, British, and American armed men fought against. There is still a kind of awful majesty about it—spacious, wrecked, and historical, with nothing left but its name, not even its old linden trees. The meaning of its devastation has not yet grown stale. It looks like what it was meant to be—the greatest, most humiliating example of punishment to fit the crime that the modern Germans have suffered. Most Germans regard it and the other of their country's ruins not as punishment but as a sort of martyrdom.

The new Germany is only what is left of Hitler's dead Germany. Three and a half million of his Nazis important enough to be judged by a Denazification court have been, or still are being, tried in our American Zone alone. But the bulk of a country's population cannot be put in jail. The bulk of Germany, as the Germans themselves phrase it, still "thinks brown," meaning *Braunhaus*, or Nazi. The exceptions belong to that infinitesimal group of anti-Fascists who survived the war in Germany or who have returned from exile. They usually hold political or editorial posts, but their number is so small that they are more critics than leaders of today's Germany. The new Germany is bitter against everyone else on earth, and curiously self-satisfied. Bursting with complaints of her hunger, lost homes, and other sufferings, she considers without interest or compassion the pains and losses she imposed on others, and she expects and takes, usually with carping rather than thanks, charity from those nations she tried to destroy. Naturally, no hungry *Hausfrau* will admit that she wanted a war that brought her nothing but food queues. The Nuremberg Trials put the spotlight on the brilliant, foul complexities of the big Nazis' master plans, but the average German can truthfully state that such remarkable ideas certainly never occurred to him. The significant Berlin catch-all phrase is "That was the war, but this is the peace." This cryptic remark means, in free translation, that the people feel no responsibility for the war, which they regard as an act of history, and that they consider the troubles and confusions of the peace the Allies' fault. People here never mention Hitler's name any more. They just say darkly, *"Früher war es besser* [Things were better before]," meaning under Hitler. Only a few Germans seem to remember that, beginning with the occupations of 1940, some of them had the sense to launch the slogan "Enjoy the war. The peace will be terrible." It is.

During the May and June food shortage, Berliners lost so much weight that three of them can now sit in the Untergrund seats designed for two. The first evidence they show of hunger edema is a swelling over and under the eyes, then comes vertigo, and then swelling around the joints, especially the knees. On Berlin's streets, you see old men sitting on the curb or among the ruins, holding their heads until the dizzy spells pass, and old women whose spindly shanks bulge like melons at the knees. According to one Berlin doctor, hunger edema is a low-blood-pressure condition in which the heart and other organs lack the necessary energy to do their work. The blood pressure of middle-aged edematous Berliners averages somewhere between eighty and ninety. The cure—aside from eating, of course—lies in doses of real coffee, at six hundred marks a pound on the black market, and of a German drug called symptol, both of which lift blood pressure; and in a drug called strophantine, for the kidneys. The same doctor says that quadripartite zoning has paralyzed the distribution of medicines in Germany. Berlin doctors have petitioned for a change in Paragraph 218 of the German penal code, which makes abortion a crime. They want it altered temporarily to permit legal abortion in hospitals, during the first three months of pregnancy, in the case of what they elaborately describe as "women in a desolate condition, with no windowpanes or adequate furniture in bombed-out living quarters, and unlikely to be able to nurse their infants."

The first thing we Americans were going to do when we got our German zone and Berlin sector running was give a good, rousing democratic education, especially in history, to those crazy young Nazis. Germans are still laughing at what some of them call our six-day-bicycle-race notion of teaching Hitler *Jugend* how to become democrats. At the end of twenty-four months, the achievements of our military government's educational program are, according to several of our disheartened experts in that line, pretty sad. Certainly one big hitch is that no history at all is being taught in most Berlin schools, because it was agreed that any version of history taught in any sector of Berlin must first be approved by all four of the Allied *Kommandatura*, whose dissensions even over the history they themselves are making is itself a chapter of history. The events that led up to the history-teaching impasse seem to have been: (1) last year the Russians offered their official version in a pamphlet accenting, naturally, the materialistic concept of history; (2) unwilling to accept this, we Americans painstakingly put together a pamphlet of our own, accenting our broader view of history, which we finally handed to the Russians in May; and (3) by that time, according to German professorial gossip, the impatient Russians had published several editions of their original pamphlet and the German teachers in their sector were busy teaching it. In addition, the French have prepared a lively history of nineteenth-century libertarian movements, illustrated by topical paintings by Delacroix and others. This volume, however, is called chauvinistic by the three other Allies. The British have produced a weighty, two-volume world history, the first volume of which ends with man's discovery, in the middle sixteen-hundreds, of the principle of the pendulum. We Americans have finally published a very brief selection of world-history dates, prepared by German teachers, which begins with Greece in 500 B.C. and ends in 1939 with the discovery of how to produce atomic fission by, among others, two German scientists, both refugees from Nazi Germany.

Whether the Western three of the Berlin *Kommandatura* know it or not, five courses in history are now being taught in Berlin University, which is in the Russian sector. According to a philosophy professor there—who is himself teaching a heavily attended course called Political and Social Problems Today, all of them viewed in accordance with the materialistic concept of history—a favorite course is the History of the Constitutions, Beginning with the French Revolution. At the Fachschule für Tischler und Innen Architekten, Berlin's trade school in the Russian Friederichshain district, present-day materialistic history is being lived, if not taught. Of three technical books the seniors need most, few possess more than two, owing to the scarcity of the books, their price, and the students' poverty. In the school black market, each book costs a hundred and fifty marks, half a white-collar worker's monthly salary. Most of the students are young war veterans—manually skillful chaps who were machine-gunners, sappers, signal-corps technicians, and such. The majority of them have to skip classes at least two days a week to work their black-market connections, from which they obtain the Swiss sunglasses, American cold cream, and ersatz French perfumes that are this summer's fastest-moving items and that enable them to live. Many student veterans of the fighting in Russia who saw Communism at close range say, "*Ich bin vom Kommunismus satt* [I have had my bellyful of Communism]." Others, who only helped wreck Europe and know its misery to the full, say, "Communism is the natural hope now of everyone to whom it offers a gain, not a loss, a loss being what it offers to the rich Americans." A third group of students say that they are sick of politics and all parties and want only "to be individualists for the first time in our lives." Almost none of them thinks that Germany has a chance of developing "the luxury of a democracy."

Which way Germany will lean—East or West—is obviously the vital question. Or will there be two Germanys—a Russian one with Berlin as her capital, and a Western one with Frankfurt as her capital? The school of thought that assumes Germany will lean toward the West believes that Germany will function as a neo-Fascist European wing of an increasingly reactionary United States—a sort of foreign legion for us, in case of trouble with Russia. They think that there is no chance of Germany's going Communist, because millions of Germans are still such good Nazis that they regard Moscow as Hell and Stalin as the Devil. The school of thought that assumes Germany will go Communist gives the following arguments: Only the pontifical positivism of Communism will suit the authoritarian German mind; Russia is now next door on the East, and the pull from the East on Germany is the magnetism of adjoining territories, whereas the appeal from the West, which really means the U.S.A., is interrupted and almost drowned by the Atlantic Ocean; and above all, in the historical cycle, Russia is on her way up and moving on the world, whereas the democracies have passed their peak of power and are in a state of flux. Germany has twice recently lost her chance to be great on her own. The megalomaniac Germans may well opt, as their last chance to be great, to go Communist and thus be great not under Russia but with Russia—if they have their way.

According to both schools of thought, England and France are merely holdovers from their own pasts, not influences in the future. Indeed, it is possible that the old European civilization, which they largely created and balanced, has been destroyed by Germany's two wars. It would seem that Europe's future shape will be determined by what are, in the strict, classic sense of the word, the three least civilized nations—the United States, Russia, and Germany, or what the first two make of Germany, the barbarian of the Continent.

Most Berliners with anything good and unbroken, such as Biedermeier furniture or fine white Meissen porcelain, are selling it, piece by piece, to live. The buyers are those who still have remnants of their fortunes, and they are buying mostly art, as an investment. In marks at least, if not in cigarettes, prices are very high. Germans have been selling Germans a lot of rather nice old Japanese ivories left over from the friendly days of the Berlin-Tokyo entente. Among the modern art works best liked are those of Germany's two most noted anti-Nazi woman artists, the lithographer Käthe Kollwitz, who died during the war and whose work, such as her "The Prisoners," now fetches around ten thousand marks apiece; and Renée Sintenis, still handsome and working, and still Europe's most gifted *animalier*. Casts of her prewar three-inch-high bronze "Young Donkey" sell for around thirty-five hundred marks, and her rarer, hand-high nudes bring fifty-five hundred marks and up. Frau Sintenis's studio in the Nollendorf Platz quarter was repeatedly bombed, and she was finally burned out. In the fire, she suffered an injury that resulted in the amputation of one of her right fingers, though in no loss in her ability to sculpt. Her new works, especially her horses, which have the romantic beauty of dwarf Remingtons, are collectors' items.

Germany has hardly been in a condition, physical or mental, to produce many new books, but ninety-seven recently published books by German anti-Nazi resistance writers were shown not long ago at the Charlottenburg Palace book fair. Unquestionably, the most important is "Der S.S. Staat," a book about the German system of running concentration camps, by

Eugen Kogon, who was a prisoner for seven years at Dachau. This enormous, highly documented tome is written with a historian's sobriety. It details how those horrible S.S. cities functioned—organization, labor turnover, postal service, uniforms, feeding, finances, punishments, crematories, and S.S. management psychology. The final chapter, "The German People and the Concentration Camps," is subtitled "'We Did Not Know.'" They still claim they do not know. This book could tell them. It will doubtless be the least purchased new book in Germany.

It would sometimes seem that the only people who really want war between Russia and the United States are the Germans. Back on Decoration Day, our Berlin Command staged a small morning parade at Tempelhof Field, accompanied by a modest fly-by of planes, which afterward buzzed over Berlin. By evening, the city was seething with the rumor that the war had started at last—whether in the Arctic Circle or in the Dardanelles, nobody seemed quite sure.

The G.I.s here say that the war after the atomic-bomb war will be fought with spears.

Trial in Königstein

SEPTEMBER 8, 1948 Königstein is a typical, tidy, picturesque little German spa, of three thousand inhabitants, not counting the visiting invalids, in the province of Hesse-Nassau. High-busted, beamed old houses ornament Königstein's main street. Perched on a crag outside the village are the customary castle ruins. Königstein's waters are fancied by sufferers from heart trouble. The most distinguished cardiac case there just now is the elderly Fritz Thyssen, formerly one of Germany's greatest industrialists, at present dwelling in the nicest sanatorium, which is on the main street, and being tried by the village *Spruchkammer* as an alleged major Nazi.

Königstein's *Spruchkammer* is sitting in what used to be the dining room of the Parkhotel-Bender, which also is on the main street. The dining room still has its prewar wallpaper of faded, optimistic pink flowers. This prandial note dominates the courtroom, the principals being a group of nine men sitting on dining-room chairs at dining-room tables. The *Vorsitzender,* or chairman, who acts as judge, is Hans Albrecht, a dark man of cold intelligence and explosive temperament. He was a violent early anti-Nazi, is a member of the German Demo-Christian Party, or C.D.V., and, by profession, is an engineer. (There are not enough real magistrates to go around, because too few of them resisted the corruptions of justice demanded by the Nazis.) Four townsmen, each a member of one of the four leading local political parties, also sit in the court, to see that no political injustice is done. At their left sits the prosecutor, Gunther Knust, who acts increasingly like the prisoner's comforter rather than his bloodhound. At their right sits the attorney for the defense, Dr. H. Elschied, an able, conceited, paunchy young giant, who is a member of the German Economic Council. His assistant, a silent man, is Ferdinand La Fontaine, who has a profile as handsome as his name and a habit of grimacing abstractedly, like a man suffering from battle shock. Facing the Judge sits Thyssen, in an old, elegant brown suit. His bent back is turned to a group of spectators at the rear of the room. He recently suffered a stroke, and his head shakes in a trembling gesture of negation, as if in denial of all that is brought up against him. His voice sounds hollow but equable, with the almost genial fatalism of a polite, destroyed old man. His diction is indistinct, owing to the indignity of many missing teeth. Behind him, the audience in the dining room swells and ebbs; the men of Königstein settle down to listen all morning— there are no afternoon sessions—and the women tiptoe in and out on their way to or from the shops.

On the opening day of the trial, August 16th, the three-hundred-page indictment was read. It charged Thyssen with, among other things, having provided money for Hitler's Munich putsch of 1923 and, later, with having given a million marks to his party. The book "I Paid Hitler," printed during the war and purporting to be Thyssen's political apologia, written by him in collaboration with a French publisher, was submitted as evidence. Luckily for him, the court finally decided to reject "I Paid Hitler," whose title alone was incriminating enough. Thyssen had declared the volume to be inaccurate and unauthorized, and said that he had seen and corrected only the first few pages of the manuscript. He had not even known it was published until, while he was a prisoner in the concentration camp of Oranienburg, a Gestapo agent angrily wagged the book under his nose; he thought then that the cursed book would be the end of him. On the ninth day of the trial, the Judge, surprisingly, began reading aloud, in fairly good English, from *Life*, which in 1940 published some Thyssen letters of protest to Göring and Hitler. The prisoner declared that these were authentic.

Throughout the trial, Thyssen's contentions have sounded candid and as simple as water. He said that in 1922 he had become a follower of old

Ludendorff and his *Freikorps* resistance against the French occupation of the Ruhr. (The medieval castle outside Königstein was ruined by Napoleon's artillery. As late as 1925, the Parkhotel-Bender was a billet for the French army of occupation. All the Rhineland district, of which Hesse-Nassau is a part, devoutly hates the French.) In 1923, when Ludendorff backed Hitler, Thyssen backed Ludendorff with money, some of which he knew went to the new National Socialist Party. "I admit I was pro-Nazi for a year then, and for another year, between 1932 and 1933," Thyssen said. "But I no longer believed after Hitler broke his promises to me." Thyssen had understood that Hitler would fulfill Thyssen's four purely personal demands: a concordat with the Vatican (he was an ardent Catholic), a treaty with Poland, a treaty with England, and the restoration of the Hohenzollerns. The naïve fatuity of this last notion, as recalled by him in court, had an air of confessional sincerity. "But I never gave a million marks, or any money, to Hitler's party after it came into power," he said. "There was a man named Schwartz who was the party treasurer. Ask him. Maybe he is alive somewhere. Or in prison."

A Spruchkammer trial develops its evidence out of the infinitesimal testimonies of witnesses who have travelled miles to say almost nothing. A bad witness for Thyssen was an ex-mayor of Hamborn, where, from 1871, the Thyssen family operated its great smelting works and steel mills. In 1932, the ex-mayor heard Thyssen introduce Hitler, as a speaker, at Cologne's "most exclusive club." "That was the last time I talked to Hitler," mused Thyssen. "The last time I ever saw him was at a distance at the Olympic Games in Berlin. Hitler was sitting with the British Ambassadress as his guest of honor." Thyssen said this with sad humor, as if merely commenting on how the world turns.

A witness who was very nearly too good for him was his wife's former personal maid. She wore a formidable blue Tyrolian huntress hat and sounded coached, and twice the explosive anti-Nazi Judge shouted at her. She said that around the house the master had always been complaining about Hitler. The day before war was declared, the family were all at Bad Gastein, in Austria. There the master received a telegram from Göring ordering him to return to Berlin to vote, in the Reichstag, for war. Thyssen, whatever he thought of the Nazis by then, was a superannuated Nazi-*cum*-Stahlhelm deputy left over from the earlier parliamentary days. The maid sent Göring Thyssen's telegram of refusal, which denounced the war, especially if Germany was in cahoots with Russia, on which Germany would become dependent for raw materials. He also, according to the maid, refused to take the advice of his son-in-law, referred to as Count

Zichy—now living in the Argentine—to flee that day to Switzerland (though he did flee the next day). "The master was always as obstinate as a billy goat," the maid testified, then added, in a respectful aside to Thyssen, "If I may say so, sir." The courtroom tittered. The maid did return to Germany, and, in Heidelberg, sent another telegram for him, this time to Hitler, saying that Thyssen would tell the world what Hitler had done to the German people. Then the scandalized Gestapo arrested her.

The funniest testimony was Thyssen's own, given when the Judge asked him if he had ever protested against the Nazi treatment of Catholics and Jews. "Oh, yes," he said. "Once, Göring asked me up for deer hunting in his East Prussia shooting box and—" The Judge, dazed, broke in to ask what deer had to do with religious persecution. Well, it seems that Göring had cavalierly sent him out to hunt deer accompanied merely by a forester. When the two men got into the woods, a deer walked by, on a path before them, "exactly as if on Göring's orders." Thyssen banged and missed. A second tame deer was lured up, by the forester's beating on a biscuit box, and again Thyssen missed. The third pet deer the forester, with apologies, shot for him, because the Marshal raged so loudly if guests returned empty-handed. Göring deigned to appear for dinner, at which Thyssen spoke his piece against the persecution of Catholics and Jews. The next morning, Göring did not come down to breakfast—"and it was skimpy, too." "Was that all?" asked the Judge, evidently determined not to laugh. "It was sufficient," Thyssen replied comfortably. The breakfast situation proved he was out of favor on account of his protest the night before. The words "favor" and "disfavor" recur constantly in *Spruchkammern*. The anguish that disfavor caused some men then must have been no less than the utility it possesses now.

Thyssen's handsomest witness—they had met in Nuremberg Prison—was Fritz Wiedemann, the tall, attractive, ambitious buccaneer who had been Hitler's captain in the Sixteenth Bavarian Infantry Reserve in the first World War and who by 1934 was a Nazi brigadier general and the Führer's adjutant. His testimony was brief: One night in 1935, when he was dining with his Führer, Göring rushed in to complain that Thyssen was carping at them again.

Of his own life, Wiedemann said that in 1939 he, too, fell from favor and was exiled, as consul in San Francisco. "And that really was exile," he murmured, truckling to the Germans' anti-American emotions. He did not mention the fact that our government later forced him to be withdrawn, as a spy. Ever deeper in disfavor, he was then promoted to consul general in Tientsin. In private conversation with the writer later, Wiedemann described Hitler, in the first World War, as "quiet, modest, brave, and reliable"—one of his three best dispatch-carriers. One of the two others is also dead, and the third is a bricklayer in Wasserburg. In 1919, on the wall of the Circus Krone, in Munich, Wiedemann saw a poster announcing that Adolf Hitler would speak that night. "That can't be our little Adolf," he said to a regimental friend. "Oh, yes, it is," the friend replied. "He has changed a lot. You ought to go hear him."

In private talk, Thyssen, who speaks excellent English, reveals a re- markable memory, the relics of conversational grace, and the bewildered philosophy of an old Catholic millionaire who has often been helpless in the hands of younger, stronger men. He has been an inmate of a lunatic asylum and four concentration camps. He was in Cannes when France fell, and the French promised him protection. But in 1941 Vichy traded him to the Germans for two French generals, and he was sent to a Potsdam asylum, where he spent two years in solitary confinement. Then there were two years at Oranienburg, and two months at Buchenwald, where he met Léon Blum—"a delightful man, though perhaps too idealistic. Pray give him my greetings"—and two weeks at Dachau. He was captured by Amer icans in a Tyrol concentration camp a day before he was, on Himmler's orders, to be shot. He thinks that the Germans are incapable of democracy and that they need a British-type constitutional monarchy, perhaps headed by the Wittelsbach Ruprecht of Bavaria. Once, when he and Hitler were still speaking, he asked Hitler how he managed to mesmerize the crowds. Hitler said, "When I start making a speech, I work and think hard for the first ten minutes. From then on I could talk nonsense and it would make no difference," and he gave his barking laugh.

As the trial moves toward its close, which will probably be next week, it seems clear that the court intends at least to confiscate Thyssen's personal fortune, figured at three hundred million marks, and to socialize the family steelworks. The betting is that, aside from that, he will get off free.

After the court's morning sessions, a fantastic claque of German dow- agers loyally awaits Thyssen in the hotel corridor. They wear aristocratic, prewar tailored suits, rather like riding jackets, and carry gold lorgnons, through which they glance at nobody. One of them wears exquisite oyster- colored glacé-kid laced high shoes, which were the style under the late Kaiser. On school holidays, the dining-room court crowd always includes a dozen or more tall, barelegged, earnest adolescents from Königstein's *Gymnasium*. These boys are very interested in the trial. They say they want to find out what the past was like and who the men were behind all the historic things they hear about.

Displaced Persons

ASCHAFFENBURG, OCTOBER 20, 1948 After more than three years of peace, three-quarters of a million uprooted European human beings are still living in the American Zone of Germany, all of them willing to go anywhere on earth except home. In the course of this suspended period of time, these people have turned into statistics and initials. Five hundred and ninety-eight thousand of them have been formally metamorphosed into D.P.s, or Displaced Persons, and are living in some three hundred International Refugee Organization camps. (The remaining hundred and fifty thousand, because of their hazy D.P. status, are not entitled to full camp care, or, because of their realism or energy, have merged with the Germans—who guiltily hate them—and are struggling for jobs in the midst of German unemployment and weathering the dog-eat-dog existence of Germany's present-day economy.) What the camp D.P.s are really living in is three hundred limbos—chiefly former Wehrmacht garrisons, now ironically housing what is left of the expatriate nationals whom the Nazis maneuvered around Europe as doomed inferiors. One of the camps is outside the town of Aschaffenburg, in Bavaria, in a quadrangle of barracks on a hill. Another camp is in Würzburg, where there are two garrisons, one on each side of the Main River, near the bombed remains of the famous fifteenth-century statue-inhabited bridge. Wherever these camps are, they tend to be monotonously alike—modern, German, military establishments. Typically, a camp is a quarter-mile square of harsh, four-story green stucco buildings that show signs of Allied bombings and D.P. repairs. According to I.R.O. rules, each building must house a minimum of three hundred D.P.s, in rows of communal bedrooms, all furnished out of salvaged materials and all smelling of smeared cleanliness, hall-room cooking, and cramped decencies. Every D.P. is theoretically entitled to forty-five square feet of living space. Sometimes a honeymoon pair is allowed to enjoy it. Otherwise, there may be in one room a couple, two children, and a mother-in-law, or three unrelated adults, with maybe a curtain for privacy. The beds are cots, and a packing case is likely to serve as a table. In such circumstances, the D.P.s dwell, eat, breed, wait, and ponder their futures, living a simulacrum of life that has no connection with the world outside except through the world's callousness and charity.

Like a well-functioning imitation of a town, each camp has its D.P.

mayor, police chief, rival political leaders, teachers, and garbage collectors, and one socially superior barracks, where the bourgeois remnants maintain the familiar notion of a select neighborhood, and where they cling together among fewer odors and try to keep up their French. Each camp is a microcosm of capitalistic society outside; D.P. shoemakers, tailors, and carpenters ply their trades, participating in financial transactions for which the medium of exchange is now the Deutsche Mark but for which American baby foods, cigarettes, and canned goods, black-marketed by our occupying Army, provided the currency at the beginning.

Each of the three hundred limbos also enjoys the Old World ingredient of arrogant nationalisms and religions. At Camp Wildflecken, a former training school for Hitler's S.S., there are ten thousand Roman Catholic Poles; at Giebelstadt, a former Luftwaffe airfield, there are seventeen hundred Jews, mainly Polish; at Aschaffenburg, six thousand Orthodox Catholic Ukrainians; at Würzburg, a colony of Protestant Estonians; at Schweinfurt, two thousand Catholic Lithuanians. In the Orthodox Catholic camps, a church is usually set up in a barracks attic, on the ecclesiastical principle that no human activity in a building may take place on a higher level than the service to God does. On Sundays, the Aschaffenburg garret church is currently decked with gaudy dahlias from the camp gardens, a magnificent choir of twenty-four young males sings, and the altar, constructed of embroidery-covered American canned-food boxes, is piously served.

To maintain peace and cut down the number of fist fights, the I.R.O. tries to arrange matters so that each camp—or, at a minimum, each barracks—houses only one religion or nationality. There is a ferocious patriotic dreg that still bubbles up in jealousy and pride as to which nationals have suffered most in the war. The numerically dominating Polish D.P.s, some Jewish and some Catholic, point out that they are the only nationals who engaged in forced labor for the Nazis and who resisted Germans and Russians alike. The Balts, who mostly resisted only the Russians, brag least. The bouncy Ukrainians, who are the second-largest national group, claim that serving in Hitler's Army, which they did on a big scale, was merely a smart way of being anti-Russian. The Ukrainians are the most obstreperously nationalistic of the lot. Recently grown contemptuous of the Saturday-night folk dancing with which other groups keep their national memories warm, the Ukrainian D.P. Scientific Society of Aschaffenburg gave six soirée lectures on Tripilla Culture, and its prehistoric fishing habits and pottery. The Society handed out a pamphlet explaining, in English, that "Tripilla is a peculiar rich culture five thousand years before our times in the Don River town of Tripilla by Kiev. Tripilla

Culture, we admit, constituted for the coming into existence of Ukraini-ans." The D.P. Ukrainians snoozed through the lectures, and loved them.

Reality is further drained from D.P. camp life by the fact that many of the dulled, amiable-looking inhabitants have been through hegiras and immeasurable tragedies that in ordinary existence could prove heroism or lift morale but that in D.P. circles have merely levelled everyone to the cruel, flat surface of commonplace destiny. Some of them have smelled their families burning in crematories, have borne children in beet fields, or have been castrated like calves. Some have walked halfway across Europe on feet that became splayed, have suffered tortures like martyrs, have been beaten like slaves, have been tattooed with serial numbers. Almost all of them have not only survived their frightful experience but have physically recovered. Now the one remaining drama is the hope of emigration tomor-row or, as part of yesterday, of finding that some of their family is still alive, in another D.P. camp, and painstakingly getting their relatives, after months of red tape, into their camp, their barracks, the bed beside their own. Among the Slavs, especially, the family is precious flesh, to be re-united even unto the most remote, broken-down cousinship. This spring, a mysterious, fierce, silent little Polish girl, aged about thirteen, was picked up in Berlin by the German police and sent to an I.R.O. children's camp near Heidelberg. She disappeared, to hunt for somebody who turned out to be a D.P. great-aunt. By last month, the girl had fished out seven more apparently legitimate remote relatives, from camps all over the American Zone; she now has them with her at Aschaffenburg. She refuses to tell how she travelled or got her clues. The D.P. grapevine is the best and most alert underground communication system in Western Europe today.

Of all those now homeless in this foreign land, the Jews are the cheeriest —a situation without precedent in the Jewish people's sad, roving history. Ninety per cent of the Jewish D.P.s in the American Zone have signed up to go to Israel. Their leaders squabble, as a matter of principle, with the I.R.O., because it has a policy of not sending anyone to a war zone. The Jewish Agency for Palestine is sending the D.P.s out anyway, and with particular speed if they are healthy and under forty-five, the military age limit. Many of the Jewish camps are clustered near Bayreuth, with its operatic echoes of Hitler's favorite, Aryan composer. The swellest Jewish camp is made up of Luftwaffe officers' homes at the Giebelstadt Airdrome. Like the inmates of several other Jewish camps, the Giebelstadt D.P.s are being supplied with various raw materials, for manufacture, by the Ameri-can Jewish Joint Distribution Committee. In a bombed-out airfield ma-chine shop, they are turning out jaunty caps and warm overcoats, and what are probably Europe's finest work shoes, of superb brown leather, with decorative steel brads and a slice of thin steel in the heels. The workers are careful to say that they do not know where these goods go, but the coats could be useful against Jerusalem's winter chill and the sturdy shoes are suited to Palestine's rocky fields. Some Giebelstadt D.P.s are earning enough money to pay German villagers to cut their wood and do their chores—a bitterly pleasant change.

The hardest blows to D.P. morale have been the long delay by the United States in passing a refugee-immigration bill and then the nature of the act recently passed. The D.P.s know that America has generously fed their stomachs. They feel that its immigration bill starves their hopes. The act disfavors the predominating D.P. Polish Catholics and Jews; favors the minority Protestant Balts, as a weak insult to Russia; demands almost a Thomas Committee screening of D.P. convictions, characters, bodies, and literacies; and requires, for those accepted, assurance, from sponsors, of jobs, and "safe and sanitary housing without displacing some other person from such housing"—maybe brand-new mansions in the skies. The I.R.O., which views itself as self-liquidating, figures that, with today's limited shipping, it can get seventy-five thousand D.P.s to our welcoming shores by midsummer next year. Those of the two hundred and five thousand allowed under the bill who fail to enter by July, 1950, can mildew to death in the camps, unless our congressmen think again.

As the London *Times* has noted, there is a whiff of the slave market in the invitations to D.P.s to enter most countries—including England, which cheerfully calls her D.P. immigration scheme Westward Ho! The D.P.s say cynically, "What is wanted is the pounds of flesh—young, strong, male, and single." Few countries want wives, children, or old begetters. In fact, only Belgium has put into practice a humane scheme—she is admitting twenty thousand D.P. miners and, after three months' work, their entire families. Iraq's recent request for ten doctors without wives is merely the smallest and most candid national project. During the I.R.O.'s last fiscal year, which ended in July, it was able to settle all over the world only the equal of what the United States can legally admit in the next two years, idealist America having up to now admitted fewer D.P.s, proportionately, than any other large power. After all the humanitarian talk, the world's offers to save the D.P.s have been mean.

Most of the D.P.s now in camps have, through delay, lost their sense of choice in regard to what remains of life. From U.N.R.R.A., they attained their peak of "relief and rehabilitation" three years ago. Except for the Jews, whose faces are finally turned again toward Israel, the D.P.s are indeed unconnected with reality. Their favorite reading matter is the pictures in the advertisements in old Army copies of the *Saturday Evening Post*, which they naïvely believe are photographs of miracles of human comfort, justice, and liberty, probably obtained by pressing an electric button. They want to go to the America of their dreams; they fear that the Argentine is too far, Morocco too hot, Canada too cold, England too harsh, Australia too full of horned toads—which it is, according to a startled convoy of D.P. Lithuanians who lately arrived there. And Sweden is too close to Moscow. A psychoanalyst's recent report on certain D.P.s in this district should qualify them for immediate American citizenship. What these D.P.s most fear is insecurity and Russia.

Letter from the Schwarzwald

AUGUST 14, 1950 To anyone who has known Germany before, the Germans today can be quite a shock. Right now, they are acting not like themselves, as Europe was forced to know them during and between the two World Wars, but just about like everybody else in Western Europe, or—too late, of course—like normal human beings, with mixed worries and successes and without any special tribal aims, interpretations, credos, pretensions, or metaphysics. In brief, they are acting in a way that would have been abnormal, and probably treasonable, under Hitler or the Kaiser. The Germans Europe knew only too well for the last two generations were specially constructed, were Germans whose every act and thought was directed (first to a chorus of *"Hoch!"s*, then to a chorus of *"Heil!"s*) toward the enhancement of the *Vaterland*. Today, the Germans are leaderless, and for five years Germany has been a four-compartment, four-language nation —zoned into American, French, British, and Russian Germanys. Maybe this is what has effected in the Germans the psychological change that at least three out of four of the former Allies once naïvely hoped would benefit us all.

This summer, especially, the Schwarzwald district has had more success than worry. The Schwarzwald is in Baden, which in turn is in the lower half of the dumbbell-shaped French Zone; the Saar is in the top part. The Schwarzwald takes its name from what still magnificently covers part of it—the ancient Black Forest, for centuries the richest, tallest, most redolent, most spectacular, most sombre stand of timber in Western Europe. Below the lofty forests, the lesser Schwarzwald hills modestly carry on its perpendicular pattern with miles of vineyards in neat uphill rows. In the valleys between, there are small yellow wheatfields. The Schwarzwald has been bossed by the French ever since Germany was partitioned. In January of last year, the French occupation chief, General

Pierre Koenig, ruled that most business operations in Baden were to be turned back to the Germans, thus freeing commerce from French priorities and certain other controls. What this release indicated was that in four years of peace the French had got what they came for—a modicum of material recompense and a symbolic revenge, both precious to them. Only the French, in contrast to the two other Western Allies, have been able suavely to state that their occupation has paid out—in contrast, especially, to the American occupation, which has been as costly to the United States taxpayer as it would have been to send all our boys over to be educated at Heidelberg or Munich. After the Nazi occupation of France, which lasted five years, and after five years of the Allied occupation of Germany, no realistic French officials here (or in Paris, either) pretend that occupation is anything but calamitous to the business of the occupied and ruinous to the morale of the occupier. Following the French release of Baden business affairs, prosperity has sprung up in the Schwarzwald district like the *Pfifferling* mushrooms in its Black Forest glades.

Naturally, what the French were principally after, and what the Baden citizens again have the use of, was the Black Forest timber. This was God's gift and is one of the few things here that anyone, French or German, particularly wants. Ever since the time of Bismarck, who early took trees seriously, these forest tracts have belonged in large part not to individuals but to communities. Though the Germans are confirmed dendrophiles and the Nazi pagan program gave the inspiring Black Forest a semi-sacred value, it was Hitler himself, preparing for war, who for three years regularly cut twenty per cent more than the forest's annual conservation-policy maximum of 1,800,000 cubic metres of wood from its 420,000 hectares of timber. He also annually cut a hundred per cent more than the conservation-policy maximum of the East Prussian forests, which, the anti-Communist Baden foresters now say, with heavy humor, used to keep the dangerous wind from the Russian steppes out of Berlin—"*und nun schau es mal an* [and look at it now]." French experts claim that the Führer cut many millions of cubic metres of French wood during the war. In exchange for this, the French demanded four million cubic metres from the Black Forest in four years and by the summer of 1948 had got it, cutting it, when necessary, along the roadsides. That is bad forestry, but the Germans who were obliged to cut it lacked the wagons requisite for deep-woods work. Part of France's success with her occupation policy is her ability to say, "You did it to me first." Though the German mind has always lacked the Gallic comprehension of logic, even the Hegelian, anti-Semitic Teutons could understand this application of the Mosaic law of an eye for an eye. During the first three years of wood-chopping, the French also took the Schwarzwald's milk, cheese, butter, and meat, on the same principle. They ignored the Baden wines, which are as undistinguished as they are copious.

The Black Forest woodworkers' association, the Holzverarbeitende Industrie, now has its headquarters in a repaired, pompous former private house in the city of Freiburg. The Holzverarbeitende represents two hundred firms that, among them, are willing to manufacture from wood anything that will sell. Less wood is going into cloth than did in the first years after the war. If German cloth is to be labelled as wool, it must now be one-third wool, which shows how standards here have risen. The Germans have lost one of their best postwar jokes: "We don't have moths in our clothes, we have woodworms." Woodworking firms are making a candid twelve-per-cent profit, though two-fifths of their prewar national market has been cut off by the closing of the Russian Zone. The association, which earlier in the occupation obtained for its members varnish, nails, paint, and the like from France, on which they got their postwar start (though the French carted off most of their fancier wood-cutting machines), now defends them from both French and German government officials and acts as a clearing house for technical, legal, and other problems.

It is the wartime ruining of Germany as a whole that is providing the Schwarzwald with its market and prosperity. What was not destroyed by bombings deteriorated through lack of repairs and has had to be fixed up or replaced. In this region, lavender or pink paint brightens the outsides of old village inns, blending with the inevitable petunias in the flower boxes. The interiors of many of the inns are brand-new. Near Freiburg, an inn-keeper whose specialties are *truite au bleu* and *Kirschwasser* completely renovated his *Weinstube* in seventeen days flat, with fine Black Forest pine panels, benches, tables, and other furnishings, and is doing a roaring business with the local German gentry and tradesmen, who are spending money as well as making it. Only those who saw the German cities after the war, smashed like teacups, can realize that everything, down to teacups, had to be replaced and can know to what an extent the Germans have mended and rebuilt. The newness of everything adds a gleam to the Germans' air of prosperity in the French Zone—new buses, new circus vans, even new wagons for gypsy caravans, new bikes for the *Kinder*, new toys, new frying pans, new electric shops filled with new electric percolators, new sports clothes for men, new summer dresses for women. At a recent Schwarzwald village funeral, all the women wore new deep mourning that would have made the French bereaved, in their rusty weeds, weep with jealousy. The German chimney sweep, still traditionally sooty-faced, wearing his black top hat and carrying his long brushes over his shoulder, now travels between chimneys on his new motorcycle.

The French Army never engaged in any black-market activity here, the soldiers having had nothing to sell. Cigarettes were never confused with currency, as they were in the American Zone. The real beginning of the Germans' renaissance in Baden, as elsewhere, was, of course, the revaluation of the Deutsche Mark, now called the DM, in June of 1948. The French franc is officially pegged at eighty-three to one DM. In two years, the DM has hardened on German energy and performance. All food was off ration by last December. In its prosperity, German living is perhaps a fraction dearer than French, but Germany is at least a year ahead of France in rebuilding. Of course, one must remember that it was only the cities of Germany that were destroyed; the countryside was scarcely touched. Here, as everywhere else in Germany, the countryside is like a pretty picture.

There has been a secondary business revival in the spa resorts. Their mildly curative waters were also God's gift, and were appreciated as long ago as the time of the Roman conquest. The Germans have big investments in hotels at Badenweiler, Freudenstadt, Bühlerhöhe, St. Blasien, and other towns. Since the end of the war, the hotels have been successively occupied and dilapidated by French troops and by German refugees from Poland, Czechoslovakia, the Russian Zone, and, especially, Schleswig-Holstein (overcrowded with refugees from the Russian Zone), all of whom the local Germans disdain; by tubercular French children and other civilians, sent here for a change of air; and, finally, by French soldiers wounded in the Indo-China war. The most popular and stylish resort place this season is Badenweiler, a fairly picturesque little South Baden hill town. Its large, luxurious Römerbad Hotel has been outfitted with everything from water taps, beds, and draperies to garden chairs. In the chairs sit the crowds of guests, mostly of the type who "wash their hands only twice a day," as the snob Germans say, meaning that they are unused to such accommodations. In the nearby Kurpark, they loll about during their convalescence or their holiday, beside bandstands and the outdoor swimming pools, putting big servings of whipped cream on their afternoon coffee ice cream. There are taxes on everything: There is a fifty-five-per-cent profits tax on German business to cover French occupation costs; in restaurants and hotels there are taxes on service, on wine, on inexplicables which, with breakfast, overnight double the cost of one's room; there is even a ten-per-cent tax on ice cream.

Along the perimeter of the bourgeois and agrarian prosperity is a Badenweiler fringe composed of refugee aristocrats from East Prussia and Pomerania who have lost all they ever had to the Russians and hence speak authoritatively about what a Russian invasion of Western Europe would be like. Some of them have settled in Badenweiler because it is only a few miles from the Swiss frontier, and they fear war. These are mostly the female aristocrats. Their husbands—if they are still alive—declare, being veterans of the Russian campaign and good Junkers, that the wives had better stop their silly female *Quatsch*, since in the next war, if it comes, there will be no neutrality, not even for comfortable Switzerland. The aristocratic refugee ladies' stories are usually terrifying and are related politely to foreigners in perfect French or English. The skeleton of one such, told by a blond, well-brought-up lady of forty, is as follows: Her father, who was from Hanover, had inherited, after the First World War, the three-million-gold-mark family fortune, represented by the family country mansion and its rich farms. In 1939, the Nazis claimed the estate, for use as a munitions depot. The compensatory payment was low, but with it the father was able to buy a vast East Prussian estate, with a fine classic white country house, built in the eighteenth century by Frederick the Great as one of several for his Junker intelligentsia. The father also bought a nearby model grain and potato farm, with excellent buildings and three thousand hectares of good land. The farm and buildings were taken by the Nazis in 1940, for use as a training camp for troops who later went to Russia. When the Russians were approaching, en route to Berlin, the family was not permitted to escape. S.S. soldiers had orders to shoot all fleeing estate-owners as un-Prussian traitors. The Russians half ruined the house. Then they took away two of her second cousins, boys, as carpenter apprentices. Some old aunts were sent to labor camps in Russia. Her seventy-year-old grandmother hanged herself. That narrator was not herself a witness to these events. Before the war, she had married and settled in Switzerland. By mid-war, she was widowed. Being sensible, she had not spent all of a sum of money she had received from her father as a wedding present. With what remained, she left Switzerland just after the war and bought an eight-room house on the outskirts of Badenweiler, which was cheaper to live in than Switzerland. Then she married a German businessman who in the war had been turned into a tank officer. Six rooms of her new house were instantly requisitioned by French occupation authorities for a French officer and his family. The husband and wife still live in the two other rooms. Her house today is worth about seven thousand dollars. It is the poor and perhaps final descendant of a Hanoverian fortune of three million gold marks and a series of fine family dwellings.

With world affairs as they are now, what the Germans do, are, or think seems immaterial. Eleven years ago this summer—an equally hot, fertile summer, with equally good wheat crops, for possible Army bread—they had all our hearts in our throats with fear of a world war, but their having launched that war does not make them reliable prophets about whether another one is coming. For what it is worth, the Germans feel that they are in a no man's land in a bogus peace. Probably out of a leftover sense of their former mighty importance, they think that Stalin must be too intelligent to start a European war now, when the west half of Germany is practically a non-Communist vacuum. They think that if there is to be another world war, it will be as different from their second one as their second one was from their first one. It is beginning to dawn on the Germans that by first conniving with and then attacking the Russians, they fatally led them—and then the Americans, too—into Europe, the glass house of Western civilization.

Letter from Munich

SEPTEMBER 6, 1950 The extra tragedy of whatever survives of midtown Munich's architecture is this: The bomb-struck false Greek pillars of its theatres and museums, the broken curves of its bogus Roman victory arches, and even the dishevelled Florentine loggia called the Feldherrnhalle, sacred to the memory of Hitler's ludicrous, abortive 1923 Munich *Putsch*, which now seems historical ages ago, all look more legitimate and handsome as patched and melancholy classic ruins than they did before the war, when they were intact, pretentious, and *echt deutsch*. Munich was never the beautiful city its inhabitants, who are sentimental rather than artistic, fondly fancied, but now, like any great urban ruin, it has a certain grandeur. Sixty per cent of it was destroyed by bombs. A fifth of that has been rebuilt or repaired since the money revaluation in June, 1948, which was the beginning of West Germany's new postwar world. "Just give us another five years of peace and we can rebuild Munich so you will never know what hit us," a cheerful local architect recently said, apparently without recalling that the word "Munich" symbolizes the failure to obtain more than one year of peace for the rest of the world in 1938. Today, it is the third most rebuilt city in the Western Zone. The second is Stuttgart, which was the model city for municipal administration under the Nazis and is upholding that reputation. Hamburg is first. And Berlin is last, the Bavarians state with satisfaction, for they have always hated, while being led by, Prussia.

It is in the evening that Munich's twelve-per-cent reconstruction is particularly noticeable, when bright lights are turned on in new shopwindows. Above the brilliant rectangles of the shop fronts there usually looms the jagged emptiness of gutted upper stories. Not many new sidewalks have yet been laid, and the strolling citizenry teeters on the hillocks of the present footpaths or scuffs in their dust, absorbed by the glowing windows, filled once more with things for sale—things of every sort, all desirable, plentiful, and consoling. Many of the shopwindows are populated by handsome male dummies in ready-made tweeds (selling for sixty dollars), accompanied by female torsos in chic pale-blue corsets. More conspicuous by day are the temporary midget business huts that hedge the razed midtown blocks. The huts are, for convenience, termed taxpayers, but their function is something more. On them their owners are supposed to accumulate enough profit in a few years to erect permanent big buildings, in line with the city's ambitious plans.

With some help from E.C.A. funds, granted because Munich is theoretically a tourist center, its bombed-out hotels have been made to look utterly unlike their elegant old prewar selves, having been wisely reorganized according to a kind of coral-reef system of accretion. The Continental opened last year with a dozen ultra-up-to-date rooms. With the profit from these, new rooms, furnishings, and stories are to be added, until eventually the structure is complete. The front of the Bayerischer Hof, on the bombed and rebuilt Promenadeplatz, is mostly a little blue-lighted bar, frequented by the razzle-dazzle German and international set. It is expected that, with the fortune it is making, the hotel can rebuild itself next year. Munich's fine restaurants have returned to their rich, two-page menus of Kaisertum and Hitler days. Caviar has become one symbol of rehabilitation. The famous, dignified Schwarzwälder offers a daily blue-plate special of North Sea lobster, chicken salad, and a jar of so-called Emperor Malossol Soviet caviar, at an over-all price of around five dollars.

Munich didn't draw much of a tourist crowd this summer. One deterrent was the hard German currency, which cut down anybody's chances of finding any bargains. Thus, Munich's traditional Mozart-Wagner-Strauss *Festspiel*, revived this summer after a hiatus of eleven years, was enjoyed for the most part by *Münchner*, and especially by those who were able to pay the high prices for the Munich Première of Richard Strauss's "Daphne," the keystone of the Bayerische Staatsoper Opera Festival. It was written by the old genius shortly before the war, is in one act (it lasts an hour and three quarters, without a pause), has beauty in it, almost no "Rosenkavalier," some "Elektra," and a lot of "Liebestod." The set was better than the singing, and more artful. When the soprano Daphne, punished for her chastity by the tenor Apollo, turned into a laurel tree, the tree slowly sprouted and grew on one stage elevator, going up, while the Greek maid behind it sadly disappeared on another, going down—no mean trick, considering the size of Fräulein Annelies Kupper, who sang the title role.

In what is left of the residential districts, life is cramped and distorted. Living space is allocated officially. Those who by luck retained an unbombed apartment now, by logic, have strangers living with them, probably sleeping in their parlor and certainly sharing their kitchen and bath. A married couple is entitled to one room, plus maybe part of another for offspring. One middle-aged couple are now commuting from nearby Nymphenburg, where they are legally enjoying six rooms. Room 1 they are entitled to because they are married, Room 2 because the husband is an intellectual and entitled to one room for his brain, Room 3 because the original tenant, from whom they sublease, sub rosa, was entitled to it as a premium for rebuilding after bombing, Rooms 4 and 5 because the kitchen was large enough to partition and make a place for the cook to bed down; Room 6 is the bath.

Few people have that sort of comfort except the very rich, who either never lost their money and privileges or have regained them. In the old days, Bavaria was famous for its green meadows, its mountain yodelling, and its agriculture. Today, industrialization is the thing, and an industrial élite has grown up, with earnings from chemicals, steel, motors, etc. Its members were useful to Hitler and have been almost as useful to the American Zone authorities. Last summer, the new, exciting luxury here was bicycles. This year, it is automobiles. About twenty-five new cars a day are bought in Munich and flash their way among the ruins. The modest ex-Nazi *Volkswagen* costs around eleven hundred dollars, and the Taunus around fifteen hundred; the popular imported Chevrolet and the Borgward, made in Bremen but given the American look, cost around eighteen hundred. Taxes and gasoline average forty-five dollars a month, even for a *Volkswagen*. Gasoline, strictly rationed, costs about twelve cents a litre, or approximately half as much as a nice white wine.

There is a fashionable set in Munich, led by Herzeleide Biron von Curland, a daughter of Prince Oskar, the Kaiser's fifth son. In conformity with the usual Bismarckian mixture of aristocracy and big money, the smart set's leading man is an official of the Bavarian State Bank. The outstanding German industrialist and money men, whose lives and fortunes came safely through the war, are tougher than ever and surer than ever of Germany's importance to the world. What some of them say runs like this: We know that the Germans are hated, but Europe cannot live without Germany's dominant production potential; we would heartily favor the French Schuman steel-and-coal plan, and Churchill's Western Union, too, if the other *verdammten* English would help them function. For these men, Düsseldorf, as manufacturing center of the Ruhr, is the real vital heart of Germany, compared to which Bonn is a haggling political market place and Berlin an ideological football field, where fatal accidents could happen. The only possible American propaganda that would impress Germans, the big-money men say, would be the news that the United States Army could protect the Germans from the Russians; everything else is *quatsch*. These Germans think that if another war should come, neither the French nor the Italians would fight, except in preliminary civil wars. On the other hand, they think the Germans *would* fight. They think that German rearmament is inevitable, and suggest that a sort of Foreign Legion—*"wie die Franzosen haben,"* they graciously add—be activated immediately, in which all West European men willing to go to war against Communism could volunteer and be counted now, and, if need be, battle under the flag of the United Nations. Some of these industrialists believe that if Russia were to win, they and Germany as a whole, as valuable individuals and a valuable nation, would be given favorable terms, under which they could do *kolossal* big business with the Soviets. They visualize a vast super-production mating of the greatest demand and the greatest answering efficiency. Despite these optimistic visions, in most of the serious German talk there is an undertone of gloom about Germany's fate, a remarkable reversal of the old faith in Germany's triumphant destiny. As one of Hitler's earliest Munich converts recently stated, from his present rural seclusion, "Germany today is a state of organized disappointment. German youth has nothing to follow except its libido."

In the cool Hofbräuhaus and Hofbräuhauskeller, where for years *Münchner* gathered in vast congregations to sing and drink fine beer, there now gather only small groups, mostly of quiet, youngish workingmen—ex-soldiers who went to war in their teens. The German soldiers constituted the most travelled European army of modern times, and therefore now constitute the most internationally experienced working class, for whatever this fact is worth, considering the conditions under which the experience was gathered—with guns in hand to kill, or with harsh orders to seize and occupy, or as prisoners of war, or as defeated men in rout. Travel showed the German the faces of other peoples, at last vaguely visible behind the mirror in which he had always seen his own Narcissan blond face. Defeat took some of the Nazi ferment out of him. At the mention of foreign place names, the Hofbräuhaus drinkers' eyes brighten, though the recollections can be unhappy (an arm lost in the desert with Rommel or a foot frozen in the Pripet Marshes) as well as lovely (swims in the Danube, siestas in

Rome, visits to the Tour Eiffel in Paris—"*très choli*"). The ex-soldiers seem to be the only Bavarians who don't complain about the American occupation; they were occupiers themselves. Most of the Hofbräuhaus men would like to emigrate to North or South America. They do not say so with hope or affection. It seems to them that they are merely making a statement that any sensible European would make today.

Politically the most explosive and socially the most dissatisfied Germans in Bavaria (pop. 9,340,000, by last year's census) are two and a half million foreign-born Germans. They are the expellees, or *Neubürger*—new (and unwilling) citizens of the Western Zone. They are not officially D.P.s, who are equally dissatisfied refugees. Mostly, the expellees are from the part of Poland that the Kaisers and Hitler ruled and that Stalin now uses, or Sudetendeutsche from the portion of Czechoslovakia that Hitler annexed in 1938, in perhaps his most gigantically fatuous gesture, that of "bringing the Sudetendeutschen home to the Reich." That is just where they—and a few million others like them, from other lands—now are. They find themselves unwanted, even hated, and their only wish is to go back where they came from, and whence they were ejected in revenge by the Czechs. These two and a half million *Neubürger* worry Bavaria, for all Bavarians must bear the burden of their support, principally by paying *Neubürger* doles out of their taxes or, on demand of the Wohnungsbehörde (a housing bureau), squeezing *Neubürger* into their homes. In the Bavarian villages, one person in four is an expellee. After all, if the *Neubürger* were unaided and unhoused, a couple of million of them, homeless, penniless, and unemployed, would starve and die on the roadsides, and their corpses would rot there, like the corpses of Jews who died during the Nazi deportations. The old, characteristic, shifty lack of logic seems to prevent the home Germans from seeing any irony in their getting brother-refugees thrown back on them, the Nazi enthusiasts who set going the most horrifying, inhuman upheaval of hegiras and refugees in modern history.

Most Germans treat the *Neubürger* like dirt, or at any rate like something they wish they could brush off. It is chiefly the *Neubürger* the Germans whine about. The expellees also whine. Some live in camps. Some are in Dachau—which is ironic, too—where they have erected a pretty birdhouse on the site of the old crematory. Some live in barns or sheds, or several families live in one room or, at best, with one native German family, which regards them as parasites. Bavarian *Neubürger* account for more than half the state's unemployment; they are the last to be hired and the first to be fired. (It is possible that the government finds the big labor pool useful in keeping down wages, so that West Germany can undercut other Europeans on export prices.) A few *Neubürger* have built prosperous little businesses on small government loans—mostly for the manufacture of glass or musical instruments. Like all refugees for whom responsibility must be laid at the Nazi door, the *Neubürger* have a hard lot. This month, the vice-chancellor of the Bonn government raised a cheer from a hundred and fifty thousand of them meeting impatiently in Stuttgart when he slyly suggested that their plight was the fault of the Allies. It is true that at the Potsdam Conference the Allies officially classified as "ethnic transfers" forced flights that were already an irrevocable *fait accompli*. When the Nazi Army began its retreat from the Eastern and Central European lands it had overrun, these ethnic Germans—who were mostly wholehearted Nazis—were hurled out on the heels of the troops.

The *Neubürger* have a political party, called the League of the Homeless, which last July made a strong showing in a Schleswig-Holstein election. Voting en bloc, the expellees could perhaps hold the balance of power in any future German federal government. The expellees are violent nationalists, Pan-Germanists, and Irredentists. They are already demanding that all those dangerously disputable ethnic German territories that border the Baltic states or lie east of the Oder-Neisse line, in Poland and Czechoslovakia, where their forefathers prospered for centuries and they themselves heiled Hitler, be returned to Germany. Some of them think that the land that should be given to them right now is the million and a quarter acres in the American Zone that were owned by seven hundred rich German individuals or organizations—land that, according to a land-reform law passed three years ago, was to be divided up among the expellees and native German small landholders and workers. So far, only seventy thousand acres have been distributed.

What the life of the *Neubürger* has been for the last five years is unpleasant, if logical. What they have done to the Bavarian economy is tersely summed up in a paragraph from an August report on the little village of Uffing, which has nine hundred and ninety-nine native Germans, each of whom pays nearly forty dollars a month in taxes to maintain the town's four hundred and ninety-six unwelcome *Neubürger*. Among these *Neubürger* are three hundred and eleven from Czechoslovakia, a hundred and three from Poland, and scatterings from East Prussia, Pomerania, Austria, Rumania, Yugoslavia, Hungary, and Lithuania. The paragraph ends with this comment, gravely entitled "The Political Problem": "There is great tension here as a result of Korean events. The peoples ask if Europe will be protected or become a second Korea. Who will care for the *Neubürger* in case of conflict? Can American Europe really give mass support and will it give it or will it only give Germany away?"

II

৶

Goethe in Hollywood: Thomas Mann

DECEMBER 13, 1941 For forty years, Thomas Mann has endured the singular experience of being regularly described, while still alive, in terms usually reserved for the exceptional dead. In a half-dozen languages he has been called a genius, a modern classic, Germany's noblest novelist, and, occasionally, one of the immortal literary figures of all countries, of all time. In the King's English of the book critics of London, the only literate capital where he has never caught on, he has also been described, less conventionally, as heavy weather. Before Hitler ordered Mann's political books to be burned, German spokesmen, with their special racial passion for altitude, had solemnly lifted Mann's major fictional works to the rank of "Faust," "Pilgrim's Progress," "The Divine Comedy," and, as a final tribute, Beethoven's ninth symphony. A couple of months ago a Nazi radio commentator simply pegged him under the head of "degenerate Western literature." By his New York publisher, Alfred Knopf, Mann is professionally presented as "the greatest living man of letters," a carefully composed selling slogan with a fine, chiselled touch applicable to a public statue. By Mann's few friends, less numerous than the members of his own large family, it has been stated as a natural law that "one speaks of him with the reverence he deserves." Thus they speak of him reverently, though they also call him Tommy. His children, of whom there are six, cheerfully refer to him, beyond his hearing, as the Master.

Thomas Mann, now sixty-six years old and on his thirty-first book, began being exactly what he is today when he was twenty-five and had just completed his first novel. Mann's youth and age, gauged by the interior and the exterior of his impressive head, seem peculiarly interchangeable, because both his work and his physiognomy started by being mature and have remained perfectly preserved. Mann's first opus, "Buddenbrooks," a quarter-million-word, two-volume biographical account of the melancholy decline of three earlier generations of very rich merchant Manns, was written by the young author as a private performance, to read aloud to his less opulent family to amuse them after dinner. However, it was the Buddenbrook family's sad, sure sense of social insecurity, felt as Europe's newly industrialized eighteen-hundreds ended, which made the novel, when published, Germany's first disturbing national classic of the nineteen-hundreds. Its sales eventually reached 1,300,000 copies, making it the biggest best-seller, next to Remarque's "All Quiet on the Western Front," of pre-Hitler Europe. "It was fame," as Mann himself commented a few years ago in his privately printed "A Sketch of My Life," employing that lenslike literary manner he invented as a young man in order to view himself with magnified detachment. "I was snatched up into a whirl of success. My mailbag was swollen, money flowed in streams, my picture appeared in the papers, a hundred pens made copy of the product of my secluded hours, the world embraced me amid congratulations and shouts of praise. . . . Society took me up—in so far as I let it, for in this respect society has never been very successful."

Certainly, Mann is a recluse, though an elegant one. Even his children, when little, rarely saw him. To them he was the invisible smell of glue from the fine bookbindings in his study and the smoke of his expensive light cigars. In the midst of the ample life he was born in, married into, and writes about, he has always remained comfortably cloistered. He has never made an appreciable use of his select social position but has been careful to take it for granted. He was born to the bourgeois purple. In the seventeen-hundreds, the Mann family, prosperous, prolific woolen drapers in Nürnberg, moved to Lübeck, where they eventually became even more flourishing grain merchants. For a precious hundred years they inhabited mansions, ate rich, stately dinners, and became senators and consuls. They finally attained the climax of their commercial disintegration not only by losing their business but also by producing Thomas and his elder brother, Heinrich, a pair of purely literary scions. From this biological break with family precedent, Heinrich, who took after their mother, a lady with Latin blood, has derived less fame but possibly a lot more pleasure than the more Mannlike Thomas has. Thomas Mann, as shocked by his talent as if he were one of his own conservative Hanseatic ancestors, from the very first regarded his or anybody's creative temperament as a suspicious, unhealthy crack in the ideal, solid *Bürgertum* norm, and has always thought the perfect artist—Goethe or Wagner or himself, each of whom he has spent years of his life conscientiously analyzing—a singular cross between a social pariah and a savior of civilization, with a dash of the charlatan thrown in. To the aesthetic refinement of this blend he has devoted his career.

In appearance, Thomas Mann is *démodé* in the grand style. A disrespectful press photographer once said Mann looks like a well-carved, old-fashioned walking stick. His face has the ligneous angles of a museum woodcut. Beneath his properly tailored tweeds, he moves with the correct, erect, salon stiffness of an older Teutonic generation. His manners are a model. Strangers whom his poise alarms consider him a monster of politeness. He presents a kindly yet intimidating supercivilized surface which is partly the product of his native character and partly a deliberate construction of his own. Beneath this lies his air of inner preoccupation, illuminated by intermittent flashes of outward interest, and enlivened by the occasional, gentle boom of his Nordic baritone voice. In conversation (he doesn't talk much, but at times he discourses) he contributes, at rare moments, a tardy, three-toned laugh, like an indulgent, superior spectre who has heard a delayed overtone of humor which the rest of the company's duller ears have missed. For those he knows well, behind his courtly gestures and silences there are festooned affections and loyalties. When necessary, he goes out of his way very handsomely. There appears to be nothing even remotely casual in the whole complex Mann personality. In spirit, he is melancholy, ironic, weighty, and serene. He is used to his instinctive pessimism by now and it doesn't upset him. He has no deistic conviction, but lately he has put a veneer of Christianity upon the lectures he has been giving on tour. With his profound interest in the fate of humanity, he might have become a religious writer if he had had any faith. Mentally, he is the perfect man of integrity; he is cautious, conservative, egocentric, and explorative. He moves slowly in a circle, or even consciously sidewise, toward a decision, does not bother to think of anything that he is not going to ponder recurrently, has the past on his mind, and suffers, profitably, from total recall. Socially, both as an upper-class European and a sensitive individual, he is skeptical of but not indifferent to this world's gauds. He'll usually choose the pure-silk people, a yard wide. As a young intellectual, he saw no reason a poet's trousers and coat shouldn't match, disliked bohemianism because he thought it disorderly, and was a daydreamer, idle, vain, irritable, and scornful; he was impressionable and assimilative rather than ardent or generous. Today, no bad qualities show. This gives Mann an awesome psychological shape, like a large, unfamiliar figure seen from a distance.

Though Mann has spent forty years as a novelist creating characters in print, on the whole he is devoid of interest in flesh-and-blood people. He views them as models rather than as mortals. He forgets both names and faces; he politely asks the dinner guest once again if she is married but will recall a curious ring she wore on her right hand a year before. He himself has noticeably well-sculptured hands; his books contain frequent descriptions of shapely fingernails. Of a handsome young woman, lunching for the first time at his Munich family table, he remarked to one of his daughters, with the abstract detachment of an author discussing a snag in a plot, "Strange. If your friend were a boy, she would be very beautiful." A person's appearance may fill Mann's eye, but the suitable psychology to accompany this appearance he himself supplies, often in a subsequent short story. Like his rich mercantile forebears, he is less an inventor than a wise and thrifty manipulator. As a young author, his skill at borrowing his acquaintances as material for his writings led to his being accused not only of incorporating a certain neighbor in an acid short story called "Tristan" but also of peeking at him from a window with opera glasses. Mann declared that, as usual with his characters, he himself was mostly the Tristan in question, but he admitted using and enjoying the opera glasses. Indubitably, Mann's lack of intimate interest in others has been compensated for by his conscientious and fecund concentration on himself as material for ten or more of his famous and varied characterizations. Whereas the narcissism of most romantic writers leads them to use themselves as heroes, Mann's has led him to use himself as almost everything— as a hunchback, a swindler, a dilettante, as at least two overbred bourgeois youths, named Hanno and Hans, and as a regular bevy of authors, including Dr. Gustave Aschenbach, hero of "Death in Venice," whom Mann describes as a European writer so great that "his antithetic eloquence led serious critics to rank it" with Schiller's. (This is usually cited as one of Mann's characteristic bits of humor, the joke, of course, being that Mann isn't like Schiller but like Goethe.) Mann has recently even endowed the Biblical character of the young Joseph in "Joseph in Egypt" with some of his own psychology as a Nordic youth. It is no joke to say that the greatest study of Mann is Mann. One of his children has said it is difficult not to see his writings as "a complex of family allusions." Unconsciously, the Mann children speak of their father as if he were an edition.

Though friendly, Mann has no intimate friends. He says he can count on the fingers of one hand the persons he has addressed with the familiar German *Du*. In America he has two old acquaintances—Bruno Frank, the German writer, and Alfred Knopf. As the patrician Mann likes a good glass of wine, so he also likes a good financial contract. No publisher, in his estimation, could overpay him. Mann usually writes an inscription to Knopf in a copy of each new book as it comes from the Borzoi press. Two, written in Mann's quaint English, are to his "splendig publisher." The dedication for "Joseph and His Brothers" fills a page and is in one sentence that runs to seventy-seven words in German. It is worthy of translation:

As a most felicitous result of this visit so rich in impressions and happy moments, I regard, dear Mr. Knopf, the human deepening and strengthening of the relationship between you, my American publisher, and myself—a relationship which I now ought to beg you to call friendship and to which I want to give expression when from my heart I dedicate to you this copy of your elegant edition of my most recent work as a remembrance of my first visit to New York, which you transformed into a unique celebration.

Because Mann can't say no (though he doesn't say yes), he often consents to receive important newly arrived German émigrés here, just as in Germany he used to give all young German writers, even those without talent, notes to his publishers. In Hollywood he is a lustrous acquisition to the speakers' tables of some of the most recherché public political dinners. At a British War Relief function recently he made his appearance with Lotte Lehmann, Bruno Walter, Basil Rathbone, and other celebrities. When in the East, he ordinarily sees only three Americans, the trio being headed by his translator, Mrs. H. T. Lowe-Porter. The second is Miss Caroline Newton, daughter of the bibliophile A. Edward Newton. Until recently, when she gave the project up, Miss Newton, who is a psychoanalyst, was preparing, under Mann's own aegis, a psychoanalytical interpretation of him and his work. It was she who introduced him to the works of Freud, on whom he later wrote a long essay. The third is Mrs. Eugene Meyer, wife of the publisher of the Washington *Post* and a specialist in doing lengthy Mann book reviews for the Sunday *Times*. On occasion, when Mann must see or simply wishes to see someone important, Mrs. Meyer entertains for him on her spacious estate at Mount Kisco, where, spared the trials of being a host, he can function merely as the honored guest. All these ladies are useful to him and are proud elements in the secretive and swirling domestic nimbus that surrounds the novelist, himself quiet, quizzical, usually invisible, and probably behind a closed door in the exact centre of it all. Each of these ladies is a bluestocking, all are joined together in a cult of admiration for Mann, and each separately (or so it is said) sometimes wonders what the other two are doing there. Mrs. Meyer, in quoting from Mann's works in her book reviews, pointedly uses her own personal, not Mrs. Lowe-Porter's official, translation.

Mann's private life is more of an open book than any he has written. Though he is himself a studious post-Bismarckian humanist with a lofty moral style, his novels and short stories contain many characters who, beneath the complicated, noble dressing of the author's style, are flatly morbid and unmoral. Indeed, he has a *fin-de-siècle* literary interest in unhappiness, deformity, disease, decadence, abnormality, suicide, and death that has practically become a majestic Mann trademark. His novel "The Magic Mountain," while it is ranked primarily as his major philosophical production, has as its setting a tuberculosis sanatorium in Switzerland. Although the sanatorium is supposed to symbolize unhealthy European capitalistic society just before the first World War and though one of the most attractive male characters, who dies of snake poisoning, is supposed to symbolize the sensuous life, there is a great deal about lungs which is purely physiological. The short story "Tristan" involves a young matron with tuberculosis of the trachea. As a demonstration of Mann's extraordinarily professional bedside manner, there is a remarkable chapter in "Buddenbrooks" which begins, "Cases of typhoid fever take the following course," and then for three pages pursues it. Mann denies he ever wanted to be a doctor, yet as a writer he is indubitably drawn to characters who run a temperature.

The short novel "Royal Highness" concerns a princeling with a withered arm, "Little Herr Friedemann" is a short story about a hunchback suicide, and "Little Lizzy" concerns a fat cuckold's fatal heart attack. As their author says, he has, in the classic tradition, the creative artist's natural bias toward death. "The Blood of the Walsungs" is a short story of Jewish twin-brother-and-sister incest in the *moderne Kunst* Munich manner. "Death in Venice," which many critics consider one of the most nearly perfect short stories of our time and Mann's most romantic tale of love, relates the tragic attraction of a middle-aged literary German widower to a beautiful thirteen-year-old Polish boy. Death, in the Venetian manner, from the plague of cholera, resolves the elderly, helpless passion. With touching surprise, Mann admits that "Death in Venice" turned out to be "perverse in more than the sense" he had planned.

Because the German Thomas Mann and the French André Gide have acquired similar cultlike followings, because each is the most conspicuous literary talent of his nation, but, above all, because both have shown a certain interest in the same *morbidezza*, comparisons between the two have been inevitable. When, a few years ago, translations of "Buddenbrooks" and "The Magic Mountain" appeared in France, many readers were of two minds about Mann. Some Parisians thought he was simply bad Gide, while others merely thought he was as bad as Gide. Gide himself thought Mann was like no one else. Of "The Magic Mountain," he said, *"Cette œuvre considérable n'est vraiment comparable à rien."* This remains Mann's favorite compliment of all time. In England, where Mann has been little read or esteemed, the writing crowd considered him opaque, unlike Gide, the wicked, translucent crystal. Viewing them as two intellectual European leaders, the English intelligentsia seemed to think that Gide made a path and Mann made a mosaic. One famous German anti-

English critic thought Mann wrote "without love" for his characters and seemed like Thackeray. In this country, where Mann is far and away the most read and the most influential foreign author alive, he not only is not compared to Gide but is regarded as a kind of new Tolstoy. Mann never thinks of his work in terms of any other writer, living or dead.

Ever since Thomas Mann began to write, he has written each morning from nine-thirty till noon. To his labors he says he gives "zealous preparation" and writes "with the patience which my native slowness laid upon me, a phlegm perhaps better described as restrained nervousness." He writes about forty lines a day. His concentration is prodigious. He can work anywhere, under any conditions, in any environment. He has done his writing in his summer houses, his winter town homes, in trains, in hotels, on shipboard, in strange cities, in Italian fishing ports, in a beach chair on a Baltic dune, or as a weekend guest in an American garden—a man who will be "writing probably on his way to his own funeral," as one astonished Connecticut host noted in his private correspondence, "and while being very much part of the world around him, in his quiet, courteous ways, writing as if that world did not exist." Only once in Mann's long career of writing has his habit of the daily stint been interrupted. That was in 1933, in Switzerland, when he realized that what had begun as a casual, pleasant holiday from Germany must continue as a painful exile. Here at last, for this deeply racial Teuton, was tragical material for motionless thought and grief rather than for some ever-growing manuscript.

He has no control over his literary mileage. The most popular of his works in America, "The Magic Mountain," started out to be a *novella* and ended up as an enormous two-volume novel that took twelve years to complete. "The Beloved Returns," last year's full-length *vie romanciée* about Goethe, started as a short sketch. "Joseph in Egypt," which has already run into a trilogy of novels and may become a tetralogy, since it is already going backward into the story of Jacob, began as a little preface he was asked to write for a folio of Biblical drawings by an artist friend of Frau Mann's.

Mann writes his works in school notebooks, in longhand. His small, tight script is so difficult to read that he makes it an excuse for never writing anyone letters. His wife is his expert decoder. As part of her métier of devotion, built around his career of writing, she learned typing, and on their travels she carries a portable typewriter in order to keep abreast of his voluminous manuscripts. Frau Mann, the family manager and businessman, is a small, volatile, articulate, personable lady with short gray hair and considerable worldly experience. It is unquestionably a tribute to her that there have been moments when publishers felt that Thomas Mann as a bachelor would have been easier to handle as an author.

Frau Mann was born Katja Pringsheim, of a rich, highly cultivated Jewish family, originally from Oels in Silesia. Her grandfather built the railroads in the Upper Silesian industrial area and his Wilhelmstrasse mansion was notable as the Haus Pringsheim. Her father, Alfred Pringsheim, assembled a famous collection of Italian trecento and quatrocento majolicas which ranked as the finest in existence outside a museum and ran to four hundred items, supplemented by a two-volume illustrated catalogue. Frau Mann's father was also a member of the Bavarian Academy of Science, a brilliant mathematician and lecturer, an acquaintance of Richard Wagner, a musicologue, a bibliophile, and an art-lover in general. He abandoned the faith of his fathers, married a Christian, Fräulein Hedwig Dohm, of a Berlin literary family, and made of their Munich home in Arcisstrasse a centre of the Bavarian capital's social and artistic life during the reign of Ludwig II and the Regency. As a child, Fräulein Katja, like her four brothers, one of whom was her twin, possessed a private library of beautifully bound books and was brought up in the double luxury of an atmosphere that was both rich and brainy. Though Mann's family had been well educated rather than intellectual, the author and his wife, who first met in Munich when he was in his late twenties, had much in common—mainly in elegance of background that was still traditional in big German mercantile and industrial families. To set against the Pringsheims' gilded Renaissance salons, Mann possessed, at least in memory, the parquetry ballroom of his childhood, where, before the family lost its money, "officers of the garrison," as he later contentedly wrote, "courted the daughters of the patriciate." Against the imposing public funeral of the celebrated Munich artist Lembach, who had painted Fräulein Katja's portrait and whose interment the very cultivated Pringsheims attended almost as though it were an artistic event, Mann could match the funeral of his father, "which in size and pomp," as he later specified in his memoirs, "surpassed anything that had been seen in Lübeck for years," his father having been so important a grandee that the Hanseatic troops dipped their colors to him as he passed them on the street.

Thomas Mann was thirty years old when, as he still sentimentally recorded twenty-five years later, "I exchanged rings with my fairy bride." He had first seen her, and been attracted to her, in a more realistic vein, on a Munich tramcar, while she was having a victorious argument with the conductor. From this highly successful marriage have come six children and about two dozen volumes.

Mann's own family, whose decadence he even as a boy proudly accepted as evidence of its aristocracy, did indeed rank as tiptop. His great-grandfather established the clan in Lübeck, which, from the thirteenth through the seventeenth century, was head of the Hanseatic League, that shrewd alliance of rich traders controlling the maritime commerce of northern Europe. The great-grandfather wore powdered wigs and lace frills and was a Voltairian freethinker. Mann's grandfather, who was Consul to the Netherlands, wore leg-o'-mutton sleeves and linen chokers, and ranked as a pillar in the family's strict Protestant Church. He was what was then called, politically, a liberal, which at that moment in German history meant he considered the democratizing of the Lübeck Senate only a piece of bad taste. He spoke French and Low German around the house, where the family motto, "Work, Pray, Save," was carved over the great front door, and he once drove his coach-and-four to south Germany, where he did a nice bit of business in wheat for the Prussian Army, which was just then preparing for Napoleon and Waterloo. Mann's father was a senator of Lübeck and was also twice mayor; he died at an early age of blood poisoning, when his son was fifteen. Thomas's mother, a pure exotic in this northern family, was Julia Da Silva-Bruhns, who was born in Brazil, the daughter of a resident German planter and his South American wife, who was in turn the offspring of a Portuguese-Indian union. This foreign Frau Mann was beautiful and musical. Thomas Mann had two sisters, both of whom died by their own hand. With his startling genius for appreciating every dramatic scrap of family material and also for invariably publishing it, he relates in his autobiography that his sister Clara was an untalented actress, unconventional, macabre, and refined, that she kept a skull and poison in her room, that she was betrothed to an Alsatian industrialist, that a doctor "used his power over her for his own gratification," that the fiancé discovered he had been deceived, and that she then "took her cyanide, enough to kill a whole regiment of soldiers. The last that was heard from her," Mann adds with fraternal clinical accuracy, "was the sound of the gargling with which she tried to cool the burning of her corroded throat." He has not yet set down the subsequent sad case of his other sister, Julia. "Her grave is too new," he has written. "I will leave the story to a later narrative in a larger frame," in all probability to be furnished by his publisher.

As a child, little Thomas had a happy, privileged, sheltered life. As a boy, he loathed school. As a youth in his late teens, upon the sale, after his father's death, of the family mansion and the father's share of the Mann grain business, which had long been running downhill, Mann moved with his mother to Munich, where he became an insurance clerk. Working at his job by day, at night he began to try his hand at short stories and, on having the first accepted, gave up business forever and entered the University of Munich, where he remained briefly. He afterward spent a scant year in

Italy with his brother Heinrich, who, though he was later to become an author, was then studying to be a painter. Thomas, the young northerner, didn't like the south; as he said, all that *bellezza* made him nervous. To stabilize himself amid the glories of Rome, he devoured Scandinavian and Russian literature in translation. The brothers spent much of their time playing dominoes in cafés and carefully made no friends.

Back in Munich, Mann, then in his early twenties, was taken on the staff of *Simplicissimus*, the weightiest, wittiest satiric magazine in Europe. When he was a book-loving child, his first literary stimulation had been received from Hans Andersen; when he was a boy, he had devoured Schiller, along with his afternoon plate of bread and butter. In his Munich twenties, he was subjected to two profoundly maturing influences. The first was the works of Nietzsche, from whom Mann, though disdaining the philosopher's blond-beast doctrine, absorbed the dogma of victory over self. The second influence was Schopenhauer, a set of whose works he bought at a sale, for months left uncut, and then suddenly absorbed, reading day and night, as one reads only once in a lifetime. What Mann derived from Schopenhauer was, oddly enough, he has stated, "the element of eroticism and mystic unity" in the great pessimist's philosophy.

In 1899, at the age of twenty-four, Mann sent the manuscript of "Buddenbrooks" to Berlin's most distinguished publishing house, S. Fischer Verlag. It is a wonder that the publishers ever read, let alone accepted, "Buddenbrooks." It was written in longhand and on both sides of the paper. When Mann mailed it at the post office, he carefully insured it for a thousand marks, because it was the only copy on earth, and the post-office clerk smiled. The serious young author had drastically underestimated himself. In the next twenty-five years, the book went through a hundred and fifty-nine editions, founded his fame, and started his fortune. "Buddenbrooks" was published in 1900. It thus came into the European world two years before Samuel Butler's posthumous novel, "The Way of All Flesh," had been heard of. In their separate ways, these were the key German and English books about unhappy fathers and sons, about family fights between members of a decadent nineteenth-century class, fights which were in miniature prophetic of the twentieth-century wars between nations, which were to kill a way of life.

Mann's first visit to America, made in 1934 at the invitation of his publisher, was tied up to the celebration of his fifty-ninth birthday, and was turned into quite a New York literary event, with local literati, including Mayor LaGuardia, attending a dinner in his honor at the Plaza Hotel. Mann, who was trying to learn English, made a speech in which, as a compliment, he meant to call Alfred Knopf a creator and called him a creature. Mann later said that this constituted his début in the English language. After two other visits, one of which was for the purpose of making a lecture tour, Mann returned here, with his wife, in 1938 to be welcomed as his country's leading literary anti-Nazi. Upon his arrival, he announced to the astonished New York ship reporters, "Where I am, there is Germany." The next year he applied for his naturalization papers. At first the Manns lived in Princeton, where the university had invited him to give some public lectures on the humanities. These lectures proved difficult. They had to be written in German and translated, and the English had to be annotated with diacritical markings and little private cabalistic signs to guide his pronunciation. Last year he resigned his post and the family moved to Pacific Palisades, one of Los Angeles' elegant scenic suburbs, near Hollywood. Mann likes living in a small town surrounded by scenery which pleases him on his occasional motor rides. He enjoys few diversions unless they figure in his orderly routine. After his morning's work, he takes a brisk walk with Niko, his poodle, before lunch. There have been a series of dearly loved dogs in his life; indeed, the only story he ever wrote with a happy ending was one about a dog. Mann also cares about eating, in a controlled way. He likes rich and childish dishes. He also likes the beginnings and the ends of his dinners, favoring tasty soups and American ice cream.

One of Mann's few recreations has been his interest in the occult. While he states in his essay "An Experience in the Occult" that "spiritualism is a kind of backstairs metaphysics," he still declares that at one séance he saw—and "may lightning strike me if I lie"—a handkerchief levitated thrice from the floor and "on my honor" a typewriter which clicked without being touched by human stenographic hands. The séance, at any rate, led to a remarkably interesting chapter in "The Magic Mountain," in which, what with Mann's economical habit of utilizing the last bit of substance in his private life, the séance turns up in some detail. He is still titillated by parlor demonstrations. As he says, dryly, "I should like once more to crane my neck, and with the nerves of my digestive apparatus all on edge with the fantasticality of it, once more, just once, see the impossible come to pass."

Though Hollywood is now the German intellectual émigrés' accepted centre, Mann's interest in settling there was not altogether social. Apparently he has recently played with the idea of writing a Hollywood novel as a parallel to "The Magic Mountain" and its special theme of sickness. He thinks there is a psychological condition peculiar to Hollywood which makes of it an island not unlike his island of Davos, on its Swiss mountaintop. Mann also has a tiny Achilles' heel; he would love to have a movie made of one of his novels. In the *Times'* critique of his "Joseph in Egypt," his reviewer, Mrs. Meyer, who often speaks as Mann's Delphic oracle, stated that the book contained drama such as even Hollywood had never approached. Among members of the book trade this was taken to mean that Mann, a master psychologist, hoped that Hollywood, piqued, would say that it could indeed approach anything, even the subject of a contract. A nibble was actually made by one of the film companies, but the scheme fell through, supposedly because the officials felt that only David Wark Griffith in his heyday could have dared tackle such a situation.

Albert Einstein is considered by American experts on refugees to be the ideal émigré, since he does and says too little ever to get into trouble. The Manns, more expansive, have occasionally been in mild and comical hot water. Just as Mann has a literary habit of writing in symbols, in private life he is secretive, in a dignified way. Accordingly, he and his wife never seek advice until it is too late, and during the opinion-asking stage they will ask for twelve opinions, then settle on a thirteenth of their own, usually erroneous. They appear to be influenced by whoever has had the last ten thousand words with them, but actually they can't be steered. As one of their patient, devoted, and admiring friends says, getting the Manns out of trouble is like unravelling an onion. Mann trouble always shapes up into two separate mysteries: first, how they got into it, which they are reticent about explaining; and second, how to get them out, since they have probably thrown away relevant letters, mislaid telephone numbers, or thought that somebody involved was somebody else in the first place. For instance, he once had homonym trouble with an Angell of Yale University, who wrote him asking for some original Mann manuscripts and inviting him to lunch. By the time Mann found out that his Angell, whom he had supposed to be President James Rowland Angell, was a mere graduate student, he had accepted the invitation and sent along some manuscripts. Soon afterward he received an invitation from the official Angell to deliver an address at Yale. Mann politely went through with the lunch at the student's home and, killing two birds with one stone, that same afternoon delivered his address amid considerable fanfare. Pulling himself together, Mann then presented Yale with an imposing collection not only of his manuscripts but of photographs, letters, and memorabilia in general, to form what became the university's Thomas Mann Archive.

Just two months ago, taking advantage of an international convention forbidding the distribution of propaganda to prisoners of war, the Germans suddenly put a ban on the circulation of Mann's books among German prisoners in England. In the last war, Mann was exempted from military service because the Imperial German Army doctor who examined him was a reverent admirer of his writings. As Mann says in his autobiography, "He laid his hand on my bare shoulder and said, 'You shall be left alone.' "

DECEMBER 20, 1941 The fact that Thomas Mann today is a political refugee and the circumstance that he is living in exile in our democracy constitute a pair of the more illuminating personal paradoxes involved in this present war. When the last war ended, Mann was still ignorant of politics, he disliked the democratic form of government, and he published, in 1918, a much-discussed essay, "The Reflections of a Non-Political Man" to prove both. Mann was still an ivory-tower German aesthete interested in liberty for the artist, not the polloi; he was a humanist concerned with the brain, not the body politic. In his so aptly named essay, Mann blamed Bismarck for teaching romantic Germany about politics in the first place; he further wrote, "Democracy is an empty frame of life," declared his mistrust of the citizen type, whom he dubbed *Herr Omnes* ("Mr. Everybody"), and added, "I want neither parliamentarianism nor party administration. I want no politics at all. I want objectivity, order, and dignity." He also wanted to polish off, with dignity, his novel-writing brother, Heinrich, who was pro-democrat, pro-politics, pro-French, and, what was apparently worse, against the German bourgeoisie. In Heinrich's realistic social novel, "The Poor," published the year before, he had attacked the Wilhelmenian middle class as a soulless, greedy, ambitious lot. To Thomas, the younger but more famous literary Mann, who was still wrapped elegantly, as in a démodé, brocaded house robe, in the nineteenth-century family glamour of the Mann (or Buddenbrooks) *Bürgertum*, this was doubtless *lèse-majesté*.

This bitter ideological feud between the two Manns led postwar Germany's agitated political circles to nickname them *die feindlichen Brüder* ("the enemy brothers"), a reference to two medieval robber-baron brothers who had built neighboring castles on the Rhone because they hated each other so much they could not let each other out of sight. The feud also led to Heinrich Mann's becoming one of the most beloved leaders of the young German intellectuals, who, impatient with the old bourgeoisie, disgusted by the now-collapsed monarchy, and alarmed by the notion that revolution was brewing, were ardently gathering in support of the democratic ideals of the new Weimar Republic. As little boys, the *feindlichen* brothers Mann shared the same bedroom but often did not talk to each other; when they grew up, they failed to speak even the same language. Heinrich, who took after their Latin mother, was Gallic-minded, in a pinkish, liberal way was still cheering for the French Revolution, held Flaubert and Zola as his gods, had aimed in his half-dozen unappreciated books at being a European rather than a Germanic writer, and liked

Bordeaux wine. Thomas drank Rhine wine and, in his own special fashion, Wagner, Martin Luther, and deep drafts of Goethe. In 1918, in his non-political essay, he described Heinrich (without actually naming him, of course, for it was a well-bred feud) as a *Zivilisationsliterat*. By this, Thomas, who thought French *Zivilisation* inferior to German *Kultur*, apparently meant that his brother was a Frenchified scribbler.

Thomas Mann, like most proud men of his class, was violently partisan in the last war. In Germany's first victorious year, he published a patriotic polemic extolling Frederick the Great that included a famous preface, which, like "The Reflections of a Non-Political Man," has never been published in English. In this preface, properly called "Thoughts in War" and written in September, 1914, he said:

That conquering warring principle of today—organization—is the first principle, the very essence of art. . . . The Germans have never been as enamored of the word civilization as their western neighbors. . . . Germans have always preferred *Kultur* . . . because the word has a human content, whereas in the other we sense a political implication that fails to impress us. . . . This is because the Germans, this most inwardly directed of all peoples, this people of metaphysics, pedagogy, and music, is not politically but morally inclined. In Germany's political progress, it has shown itself more hesitant and uninterested in democracy than the other countries. . . . As if Luther and Kant did not more than compensate for the French Revolution! As if the emancipation of the individual before God and as if "The Critique of Pure Reason" were not a far more radical revolution than the proclamation of the rights of man! . . . Our soldiering spirit is related to our morality. Whereas other cultures, even in their art, incline toward a civilian pattern of ethics [*Gesittung*], German militarism remains a matter of German morals. The German soul is too deep to find in civilization its highest conception. . . . And with the same instinctive aversion it approaches the pacifist ideals of civilization, for is not peace the element of civil corruption which the German soul despises? . . . Germany's full virtue and beauty unfold only in wartime. . . . The political form of our civil freedom . . . can only be completed . . . now after certain victory, a victory in tune with the forces of history, and in the German sense, not in the Gallic, revolutionary sense. A defeated Germany would mean demoralization, ours and Europe's. After such a defeat, Europe would never be safe from Germany's militarism; Germany's victory, on the contrary, would assure Europe's peace. . . . It is not easy to be a German, not as comfortable as being an Englishman or as being a Frenchman and living with brilliance and gaiety. Our race has great trouble with itself . . . it is nauseated by itself. However, those who suffer the most are worth the most. . . . There is something deep and irrational in the German soul which presents it to more superficial people as disturbing, savage, and repulsive. This something is Germany's militarism, its moral conservatism, and soldierly morality, which refuses to acknowledge as the highest human goal the civilian spirit. . . . The Germans are great in the realm of civilian morality but do not want to be submerged by it. . . . Germany is the least known of all European peoples. . . . But it must be recognized. Life and history insist upon it, and the Germans will prove how unfeasible it is to deny, from sheer ignorance, the calling and character of this nation. You expect to isolate, encircle, and exterminate us, but Germany will defend its most hated and innermost "I" like a lion and the result of your attack will be that much to your amazement you will one day be forced to study us.

Thus ends the 1914 "Thoughts in War," perhaps the most extraordinarily accurate exposition of the German racial psychology which Mann, that noted German analyst of men and women, ever penned.

It took Mann exactly twenty-three years, starting from this political attitude, to become the militant liberal and profound hater of the German concept of racial domination that he is today. To his heavy devotion to the past and his scrupulous, weighty, literary slowness, he was gradually forced to add the burden of his long-drawn-out ideological metamorphosis. In 1923, five years after the Weimar Republic had been founded (and his brother Heinrich had successfully started leading German youth), Thomas Mann, in a Goethe Memorial Day speech to the students of the University of Frankfort-am-Main, finally advised the young folk to rally to the Republic idea, to which, with meticulous truthfulness, he admitted he was not yet converted. However, he said, the Republic offered "the climate of humanity," in which soul could speak to soul rather than citizen to citizen. It was this literary mixture of metaphysics, formal non-democracy, and old-fashioned Prussian nationalism that made Mann seem a chauvinist to the French intelligentsia, still nervous in victory across the Rhine, and led the Institut de France in 1924 to describe him as a dangerous pan-Germanist of the *d'après-guerre* variety. In 1924, Mann's major opus, the 400,000-word novel called "The Magic Mountain," which he had taken twelve years to write, was published. Its European success was immense. It was translated into Hungarian, Dutch, and Swedish, and in four years sold over a hundred thousand copies even in an impoverished Germany where the sixteen-mark price of the novel could buy a dozen dinners. Mann seems to have hoped that the educated German classes would be influenced by the book's metaphysical-social European symbolism, in which a character who is a Jew with a Jesuit education represents Communism, plus medievalism, mysticism, and the Catholic Church; an Italian dialectic democrat is satirized as an organ-grinder; and a Russian seductress represents Asia and is unsuccessfully loved by the well-bred German bourgeois hero Hans, "simple-minded though pleasing." Mann was especially confident that the Teutonic reader would recognize himself in this typical German Hans and, as he later wrote in his autobiography, "could and would be guided by him." Unfortunately, it was the Austrian Adolf who soon did the guiding, and after the 1930 elections, which gave the Nazis their first big political victory, Mann made an alarmed speech of intellectual warning in Berlin during which Nazi rowdies rioted. His suddenly taking a stand vaguely disturbed the German nationalists, who ever since his early essay on the non-political man had supposed him safely on the anti-democratic side of the fence. As Germany's leading intellectual, Mann, had he remained complacent, would have been valuable to the Nazis at the moment. Furthermore, the year before, he had won the Nobel Prize for Literature, and for both national and international propaganda reasons the Nazis wanted to muscle in on his honor. In 1932 Mann addressed a lengthier, impassioned appeal to the German intelligentsia and made his first public reference to the working class, whom he praised.

In March, 1933, two weeks after the Reichstag fire and two months after Hitler had assumed power as *Reichskanzler*, Mann and his wife, who were concluding a holiday in Switzerland, received a cryptic warning from their eldest son and daughter, Klaus and Erika, telephoning from the family house in Munich. These modern young Manns, already politically prescient, begged their parents not to come home because the weather was bad. Mann naïvely replied that the weather was bad in Switzerland, too. Erika then alluded to some terrible house-cleaning ahead. It was probably Frau Mann who realized that the weather the young Manns had described was political and that the house-cleaning might be a purging of anti-Nazis. Mann and his wife never set foot in Germany again. The next day their six sons and daughters made preparations to join them and the voluntary exile of the Mann family began. When, a short time afterward, Mann's passport expired and he asked the local German consulate to have it renewed, he was politely assured this would be done immediately if he returned to Munich. It was his refusal to go back home that made his anti-Nazi attitude official in Nazi eyes.

By the end of the year, Mann's Munich house, library, and bank account had been seized by the Nazis. Late in 1936 the Nazi government deprived Mann and his family, who had remained in Switzerland, of their German nationality. It is characteristic of Mann that only in 1937, after the University of Bonn revoked the honorary degree of Doctor of Philosophy it had conferred upon him, did he break the four-year silence that marked the first stage of his exile. He had thought silence "would enable me to preserve something dear to my heart—the contact with my public in Germany;" that is, the continued circulation of his books there and what he steadfastly hoped would be their influence on German minds. On New Years' Day, 1937, Mann addressed to the dean of the philosophical faculty of the University of Bonn his first public political words of excoriation of the Nazi regime—an indignant three-thousand-word letter, since reprinted in a pamphlet called "An Exchange of Letters," which has been ranked as the noblest of Mann's political statements. His other confessions of democratic faith are "The Coming Victory of Democracy," hopefully written in the spring of 1938; "This Peace," which appeared after Munich; and, a tragical third, "This War," published early in 1940.

When Mann and his family lost their nationality, they were given honorary citizenship, by the Czecho-Slovakian Republic, as an anti-Nazi gesture. Actually, they never lived in Czecho-Slovakia; when they left Switzerland, they lived for a while in Le Lavandou and neighboring towns in the French Midi, and then settled down at Küsnacht, on the Lake of Zurich. Early in 1938, Mann received an offer from an American lecture bureau to visit the United States and go on tour. He accepted the invitation. As he had written to the dean of the University of Bonn, "I am more suited to represent [Germany's cultural] traditions than to become a martyr to them."

In the latest stage of his political evolution, Mann is now discussed in certain foreign diplomatic circles of Washington as the ideal president of the Fourth Reich, once the Nazis are defeated.

Of Mann's sons and daughters, a family friend has succinctly remarked, "The vagaries of his children have at times occupied more place in the public's mind than the distinction of their father." In a strange, literary way, the Mann children seem like fantastic illustrations of their father's books, illustrations he begot himself rather than trust some mere artist to draw. The Mann children came in what their father called rhymed couplets, or in three sets of mixed masculine and feminine endings. The best-known couplet is unquestionably the first, comprised of Erika and Klaus. Erika, born in 1906 in the comfortable family home on Poschingerstrasse, in Munich, where all the children were brought up, is considered to have the sharpest mind and the most rounded personality of the half-dozen; if Frau Mann is family manager, Erika is its superintendent. Her father relies on her judgments. She is credited with having given two years to persuading him that, in the twentieth century, to take a political stand in life was not a necessity for professional politicians alone. Her convictions about anything are always one hundred per cent, leaving no room for argument. Erika and Klaus wrote, directed, and played in "The Pepper Mill," a lively satiric review which opened in Munich just before Hitler came to power and enjoyed a thousand or more performances in Germany and five other European countries. She had studied for the German stage with Max Reinhardt, played leads in the works of Shaw and other moderns at the Munich Staatstheater and Kammerspiel, and married and divorced the actor Gustaf Gründgens, then Germany's best Left Wing Hamlet and today an important salvaged theatrical protégé of Field Marshal Göring. Several years later she married her present husband, W. H. Auden, the English poet. While she was living in Switzerland after her flight from Munich, the police had to protect her against a Nazi plot to kidnap her and take her back into Germany. Hearing that her life was endangered, Auden, who had never set eyes on her, proposed by telegram, in a gallant political gesture, in order to provide her with the British passport which marriage could confer. She joined him in England, where they were married. Before leaving Switzerland, she returned to Germany once, at night, disguised as a peasant (with fashionable smoked glasses) and entered the old home in Munich to get her father's unfinished manuscript of "Joseph and His Brothers," which he had not taken with him on what he thought was his Swiss holiday. She safely recrossed the border with the manuscript hidden under the seat of her Ford. This car was a keepsake, a first prize presented to her by Henry Ford after she had won a ten-day, 6,000-kilometre motor race around Europe.

Since Erika's arrival in America (she led the family trek in 1936 and has been living here since), she has written three books—"School for Barbarians," a bitter survey of Nazi education today; "The Lights Go Down," an account of the decline of freedom in Europe; and, in collaboration with Klaus, "Escape to Life," a story of the family containing an excellent portrait of their father. She recently returned from London, where she did some anti-Nazi German broadcasts for the B.B.C. and special correspondence for *PM*. Klaus, the most distrait and disarming of the Manns, has since youth been an enthusiastic writer in that minor way fate imposes on the sons of major writers. Klaus is now editor of *Decision*, the first of the monthly magazines to specialize in the work of foreign writers now assembled on our shores. Klaus and Erika have cut the widest swathe of all the Mann children, are the most travelled, and have been the most talked about, the most sought after, and the busiest sister-and-brother émigré unit here or in Europe. In all ways their tastes are strictly modern. In Paris, they were in the Cocteau group and entertained an almost guilty filial admiration, considering that they were Manns, for Mann's international rival, André Gide, as an intellectual foster father. Klaus and Erika always know everybody everywhere and are always active in whatever country they may find themselves. In America, they are considered to have the German-émigré situation well in hand. Among the refugees here there is a standing joke that unless you are O.K.'d by Klaus and Erika you aren't a real refugee.

Angelus Gottfried, who calls himself by his early nickname of Golo, second son and senior of the second couplet, is the family conservative and looks like a dark, agrarian edition of his urbane father. Stocky and silent, he was educated at Heidelberg and, after Hitler, at the University of Rennes. He early decided to be a historian, since it was one of the few things his father was not. Golo specializes in the anti-Napoleonic aspects of the Napoleonic period and is preparing a book on that central but little-appreciated figure Friedrich von Genz, who was secretary to the Congress of Vienna and lover of the toe-dancer Fanny Elssler. When this war broke out, Golo left Switzerland, where he was living, and went to France to be a volunteer Red Cross ambulance-driver, was thrown into a concentration camp, and reached New York only this year.

Monika, the sister of the second couplet, simplest of the eccentric sextet and even as a child always referred to as "poor Monika," has indeed had the saddest life. Her Hungarian journalist husband, Jenoe Lányi, was drowned before her eyes in the torpedoing of the City of Benares and she herself was rescued only after twenty hours of drifting in the sea. The youngest daughter, Elizabeth, now twenty-three, two years ago made an ultra-romantic marriage with the fifty-seven-year-old Giuseppe Borgese, Italy's distinguished anti-Fascist historian, poet, and novelist. He was once professor of German literature at the University of Rome and is now on the faculty of the University of Chicago. Most of the family calls Elizabeth Medi, but her father called her Lorchen and "the nearest my heart" in "Disorder and Early Sorrow." She figured as the childish heroine in this famous short story about the postwar German jazz generation for the characters of which all his children and their slangy friends served as models. Michael, nicknamed Bibi, the youngest child, is twenty-one. He plans to be a violinist. The family considers him the mother's favorite, though she tells each of her six children that he or she is her favorite in his or her individual way; the five others say this is one of her more comforting jokes. All the Manns, including Thomas's brother Heinrich, who recently arrived from France, are now in the United States. Heinrich and Thomas, whose political differences have long since been resolved in their mutual hatred of the Nazis, are now reunited in California. Recently, in a lecture, Erika said dryly that she represented the mass immigration movement called the Mann family.

Thomas Mann is a problem to his children. As nearly as can be made out, they feel for him a mixture of worship and respect and that blasé something usually found in the offspring of a famous parent. When he says anything special, his children think it must be saved for posterity and hurry to their rooms to write it down. To them he is still as much the great author as the father. One of the older sons, who no longer lives at home, decides in advance, whenever he is planning to meet his father, on a specific, intellectual topic to talk to him about. The Mann children were brought up with three privileges rare in the European bourgeois home. They were given the libertarian privilege of making or breaking their own lives, they were taught to work for the muses rather than for money, and even their maddest friends were always welcome in the home. When Mann's children were little, they were allowed as a treat after dinner to hear him read aloud from his work in hand (he is of the tradition of authors who read manuscripts aloud to family and friends) and were encouraged to read aloud their own childish compositions, to which their distinguished parent gave his kind critical attention. There was a less formal period, during the revolution and inflation following the last war, when the Mann children ran barefoot in the summer because of Germany's leather shortage and were always a little hungry because of the scarcity of food. At that time, since the summer place they had once owned at Bad Tölz had been sold to buy war bonds, the children put on their bathing suits and enjoyed ersatz water sports in their garden in Munich, with their father animatedly squirting them with a hose. Even in this he set his own high standard. To this day they remember that he delighted in calling his fanciest sprinkling an art. When he dramatically read Grimm's Fairy Tales aloud to them, they thought he should have been an actor; when he drew bizarre pictures for them, they thought he should have been an artist. (As a matter of fact, as a young man, he had contributed some drawings, principally of unorthodox monsters, to *Simplicissimus*.) When he whistled alto for his children's Christmas carols, they thought he should have been an orchestra conductor, which he also thought he would have liked to be. His own childhood, spent in Lübeck, had been more severely classic. He named his rocking horse Achilles and his paper dolls Zeus, Hermes, and Helios; with them he played an Olympian game in which he waged battles against the castles of the gods. He ran his own puppet show, was his own singer, pianist, and violinist, and produced nothing but operas. He continued his fiddling until he was a young man, then resigned himself, he says, to mere listening.

Mann's musical knowledge is as remarkable as his visual sensibility is limited. There are no descriptions of great paintings in his books, and about the only thing he liked in Rome as a young tourist was Michelangelo's "Last Judgment," principally because it looked like the apotheosis of his own pessimism. His relation to music is a special combination of deep love, knowledge, and an amazing aural memory; his books are resonant with such musical interpolations as Schubert's "Der Lindenbaum" (sung during a scene at the Battle of Verdun), an aria from Bizet played in a sanatorium, and multiple citations from Wagner, usually as a prelude to death in the Bayreuth motif manner. Music for Mann is summed up in

Wagner, and to Wagner he gives hero worship tinged with criticism. As Mann says in his famous and witty essay on Wagner, "Wagner's texts are not literature—but the music is." Mann's American friends say that the only times they ever see him seem to lose himself are when he is listening to "Tristan" or "Parsifal" on the phonograph, that travelling friend of exiles. In general, Mann's taste in music begins and ends with the romantics, from Beethoven through Richard Strauss; for Bach he has more esteem than affection. He has nearly no use for modern atonal music, though he finds Stravinsky interesting if not lovable. Mann has taken music more seriously than most writers and he has a theory that he has written his major novels in a symphonic form. Thus he is always most pleased with book reviews in which he is treated as if he were a concert.

As current events have made him feel increasingly remote from life, Mann, since his arrival in America, has gone out little, either to social functions, concerts, the movies (though movies fascinate him as something new under the sun), or the theatre. He was much interested in Robert Sherwood's "There Shall Be No Night" last year and went to see it because he had heard he was the model for the character of the Finnish neurologist. If this were true, he said, he was much honored, but he thought the resemblance slight. He has read some American writers, is especially impressed by John Dos Passos and the early Ernest Hemingway, has recently enjoyed Frederic Prokosch, James M. Cain's "Serenade," John Steinbeck's "Of Mice and Men," and was at one time excited by Sinclair Lewis's "It Can't Happen Here," considered as a document rather than as a literary production. Mann says he is glad his sons and daughters are in an English-speaking country because he thinks that English will be the only literary language that will remain free in the immediate future. Since it was not a language he learned to read with ease when he was young, as he did French, which interests him less, Mann is today driven to revert, for his regular afternoon reading after his nap, to his favorites, the German classics. He reread Goethe's "Faust" five times hand running to get himself into what he considered the correct modern equivalent of the eighteenth-century mood in which to start writing his three novels about Joseph of the Old Testament days.

This trilogy, begun in 1926 and planned as a single book to be called "Joseph and His Brothers," as time went on overflowed into "Young Joseph" and then into "Joseph in Egypt," which itself ran into two volumes, and is now spreading into a tetralogy with a volume devoted to Jacob, on which Mann is working in California, where he now lives. The Joseph series (an elaboration, with symbolic commentary, of the familiar Biblical story, plus additional scholarly incidents Mann has culled from the Talmud) has, for the first time in Mann's career, put his American devotees into two frames of mind. Some say it reminds them of Shakespeare's "King Lear" and some merely say they can't read it. The nub of the argument seems to be the lengthy episode involving Potiphar's wife, treated by Mann with a candor which makes of it either the "Three Weeks" of the Old Testament or a remarkable study in Teutonic good-and-evil symbolism, depending on how the reader takes it. Some Mann readers also deplore his characteristic humorous effort in making Potiphar's wife lisp during the major seduction scene, owing to her having symbolically bitten her tongue in a preliminary attempt not to declare her passion. However, most readers, even the uncritical, agree that Potiphar's wife finally saying (in the English translation) "Thleep with me" is definitely funny.

Among European writers of intellectual stature, Mann has outsold the field in America. "Joseph in Egypt" was a Book of the Month Club dividend in 1938, and over 210,000 copies were distributed apart from its bookstore sale of about 47,000. "Buddenbrooks" has sold about 48,000 copies in America and has just been put on phonograph records for the blind and placed in the twenty-seven regional libraries for the blind by the Library of Congress. "The Magic Mountain," best known of his books among Americans, has sold more than 125,000 copies. "Death in Venice," possibly the most beloved of his stories in this country, nevertheless had an original sale (accounted for, apparently, by only his most steadfast followers) of less than 20,000. However, it was included in "Stories of Three Decades," which was also a Book of the Month Club dividend in 1936 and which sold 92,000 altogether. Even before this war, Mann's largest group of readers was, owing to the Nazis' suppression of his work, already concentrated in the United States; the Scandinavians ranked next. He has been alternately admired and suppressed by official Moscow. When the Revolution broke out he was unprintable because he was a bourgeois. After the rise of the Popular Front in France, the Soviet State publishing house brought him out in a handsome cheap edition. Just before the Berlin-Moscow pact was signed, his books began to be attacked again.

It is impossible to estimate how large a fortune Mann had assembled from his writings when the Nazis seized his worldly goods. Before the exile of the Mann family, they lived in a pleasantly prosperous manner (a country summer cottage in Memelland, the town house in Munich, automobiles, travel, six children, and vacations), a state of ease to which few German intellectuals, or even businessmen, could attain. For his American residence, Mann is now building a comfortable California type of house in a section called the Riviera, near Hollywood. His attitude toward his royalties is influenced by the fact that he believes he has a message to give to the world. Thus he has always given the sales of his books the dignified consideration which a prophet, say, would bestow upon his converts. Last year, after his *vie romanciée* about Goethe had been announced to bookshops under the title of "The Beloved Returns," Mann became uneasy and decided that he preferred to go back to the original, less sentimental title, "Lotte in Weimar." To this Mann's publisher, Alfred Knopf, agreed, but pointed out that many American Mann readers would lack the courage to ask a clerk for a book whose three-word title contained two words they wouldn't be sure how to pronounce, whereas all would know how to ask for "The Beloved Returns" without embarrassment. After a dignified family parley of several days, Mann announced that he had decided he owed those readers waiting for his new book the courtesy of a title they would be sure of. The book was published under the title "The Beloved Returns," with the subtitle "Lotte in Weimar." Everyone, presumably including his readers, was happy.

Perhaps because of his weighty personality, which, like an old-fashioned, heavily corniced library wall, rises solidly and protectingly behind the unfrivolous print of his thirty carefully written books, Thomas Mann now occupies a unique position in our country, superior to that of all the thousands of other German émigrés, intellectual or once monied, gathered here today. This position, which in three years has become legendary, he acquired partly because he takes his symbolic eminence for granted and partly because his proud racial character has served as a magnet to a company of compatriot refugees who, sick of being ashamed of their nationality, take comfort from the pride of this German gentleman whom they may never have seen, from this German author whose books they may never have read. Mann is also symbolic of those stay-at-home German generations which so carefully, unconsciously, and fatally helped bring about his own logical exile from his fatherland. As he recently wrote to his eldest daughter and son, "German freedom and the Weimar Republic have been destroyed; we, you and I, are not altogether guiltless in that matter." Maybe Weimar's Goethe, Mann's mirror, should also have been included in his roomy *mea culpa*. There is no question but that Mann successfully managed to do what most authors would have tried to avoid —he projected himself backward into history as part of his literary progress in life. Already, by his blood inheritance, bred to look like a medieval portrait of a merchant by Holbein, Mann, because of a nineteenth-century literary affectation, concentrated his young writer's mind on the eighteenth-century Goethe. With the coming of the twentieth century and its hesitant political notions, Mann, as the result of his tardy taste for politics, derived his ideological shape from the bourgeois epoch, the *Grundjahre* of Bismarck, from which the world had just emerged and which the anti-Wilhelmenian young Germans were already trying to shed. Even in his choice of physical residence, Mann, as a domestic character, was equally elegant and démodé, selecting for his marriage and his home the soothing pleasures and academic intellectualities of Munich, capital of delicious old rococo and witty neo-baroque, a city busy with sentimental dreams, devoid of factories, and miles south of the colder industrial atmosphere of brutal Berlin. It is probable that exile alone has finally imposed on Thomas Mann the tragedy of being up to date.

Friends say that Mann suffers deeply from being an émigré, cut off from his country, his people, and his language. Wherever history has moved him, from Munich to Zurich, to Le Lavandou, to Stockton Street in Princeton, to the coast of California, he has tried, with civilized design, to go on living as himself. Some refugees are chameleons, taking their color from what lies around them; Mann is of the snail type, with his self-formed dwelling firm upon his head wherever he may be forced to roam. "I shall always go home," one refugee friend of his has said, "to the house of Thomas Mann in whatever land. There our sadness as aliens is admitted; our homesickness is admitted, our sometimes outbursting love for German language and music—these are admitted. He is our most important, consoling figure. His writing, his art, his wisdom, his life have not been doomed by human circumstances."

Whatever the circumstances, Mann himself, now in his middle sixties, does not think he will endure them long. Accustomed to deciding the destinies of characters in ink, he has decided what will be for him (in the phrase he always places at the end of each of his manuscripts) the *finis operis*. In his autobiographical "Sketch of My Life" he states, without comment, "I have a feeling that I shall die at the same age as my mother, in 1945."

Cotton-Dress Girl: Bette Davis

FEBRUARY 20, 1943 Bette Davis's career as a cinema star began with her studio representative's failure to identify her on her maiden arrival at the Los Angeles railway station thirteen years ago because she didn't look to him like an actress. If today the estimated sixty million movie habitués did not know her by sight, they too might think she doesn't look like an actress. Miss Davis's success has been constructed on her tendency not to be recognized. She arrived in Hollywood with nothing positive but her intelligence, and that was against her. Negatively, Hollywood said that her smile was crooked, her cranium the wrong shape, her mouth too small, her eyes too large, her neck too long, and her erotic appeal devoid of any dimensions whatever. Furthermore, her figure was mandolin rather than guitar. Universal Studios, which had the misfortune to hold her first contract and not renew it, thought her a tense young woman who would never get anywhere. Their Carl Laemmle, Jr., dismissed her as "a cotton-dress girl," satin sweethearts then being, sociologically speaking, box-office. Samuel Goldwyn, the first producer ever to order a screen test of her, reportedly moaned, when he looked at the film, "Whom did that to me?" She did something to him again some years later when he had to pay her a fortune to star in his "The Little Foxes." In 1930, the only person who thought that she ought to be in Hollywood was her theatrical agent, and he was in New York and of two minds. When he had signed a contract with her back East, he said she was the biggest gamble he'd ever exported. Today she has the prestige of the boss woman star of Hollywood, a quarter of a million dollars a year (gross), and a long memory.

Miss Davis was born on April 5, 1908, in Lowell, Massachusetts, in a gray clapboard house built on Chester Street by her grandfather Favor, who was descended from fighting Huguenots and was himself a belligerent abolitionist. She says that the only relation between her blood and her career is battle. In her Hollywood history she has fought her way from the bottom to the top and more than once part way back again. She is a militant, lively New England character with portable principles, which she has enjoyed scrapping for on Western studio soil. She has an alert, educated mind, a tempestuous vocabulary, and far-sighted judgments. She is the cerebral type, though never calm; she may be wrong about something, but she will have thought the whole thing out splendidly. A stagehand, seeing her for the first time on the set during the recent filming of "Watch on the Rhine," said she looked to him like a Down East schoolma'am who had turned into a hell of a fine actress. She is disciplined but unpredictable, is mettlesome, is creative, and hates monotony. She is truthful, and as candid as glass. She is an individualist, and Hollywood, which once coarsely summed up this quality as a headache, now with much refinement calls her forthright. Anyone who tries to drive her gets into trouble, though she can usually be led. Her energy puts her under the necessity of feeling strongly about everything and saying how she feels. Playing a hussy's rôle, she is the type, Hollywood says, who would argue a man into a seduction but not tempt him. Her almost regal power in Hollywood still startles her, and she makes no use of it. It probably doesn't make any sense to her. Merely playing the rôle of Queen Elizabeth a few seasons ago so inflamed her democratic Massachusetts mind that she swore (rather like the Queen) at having to sit, even in Warner Brothers' studio, on a damned throne.

Miss Davis was a fledgling Broadway actress when she went to California with the irrelevant superstition that rain brought her luck. For the next three years, in the customary sunshine, she took a cruel beating. She had been brought out to be made a star in Universal's "Strictly Dishonorable," but after she arrived she was judged not to have sufficient sex appeal. In an attempt to find out what she did have enough of, and at the same time to introduce her to Hollywood dramatic standards, Universal requested that what it called her gams be photographed, that her name be changed to Bettina Dawes, which it considered a natural, and that she be test-kissed before the camera by fifteen leading men in one afternoon. After all that the studio heads cast her as the good sister in Booth Tarkington's "The Flirt," filmed as "Bad Sister." She thought that she was as much of a flop as everyone else said she was. Immediately afterward, as the result of her performance in a film which somebody manufactured in eight days flat and called "Hell's House," the management decided she had no appeal of any sort and for the rest of her first year lent her to other studios, which put wigs and false eyelashes on her and occasionally let her fall on her face for laughs. In her second year there came at last a day when it rained and when, already enjoying an oblique sort of good luck, Miss Davis was packing her bags to return to New York as a Hollywood failure. Unexpectedly, George Arliss, at that time one of the few old-fashioned local literates from the legitimate stage, telephoned to ask her to be his leading lady in "The Man Who Played God." The engagement with Arliss changed things, insofar as it gave her some momentary standing and made the disappointments of the rest of her second year even harder to bear. Her third year was running into her fourth when, despite six months of devious resistance by Warner Brothers, for whom she was working, and finally because no other actress would touch the job, she was allowed to play the great rôle of Mildred, the waitress, in the R.K.O. production of Somerset Maugham's "Of Human Bondage." It was a cotton-dress part, but it enabled her to establish herself as a new kind of star.

Playing Mildred was what made Bette Davis in Hollywood and in the world outside. Her characteristic misfortunes, once private matters that added up to failure, became public matters that led to success. Her critical faculty at low ebb because of the ravages her ego had suffered for three years, Miss Davis never entertained any idea that her Mildred ought to have received the annual feminine best-performance award, or Oscar, of the Academy of Motion Picture Arts and Sciences, the winning of which is to a Hollywood player what winning the Kentucky Derby is to a horse.

However, the idea occurred to a number of argumentative New York and California critics after the Oscar had been given to the indubitably excellent Claudette Colbert for "It Happened One Night," which was a bigger hit than the Maugham film. So next year Miss Davis received the Oscar, tardy but sincere, which was aimed in retrospect at her Mildred but which was at least nominally for her less remarkable Joyce Heath in "Dangerous." Then, two years later, the Selznick Studio began such mammoth preparations for "Gone with the Wind" that Warner Brothers hastily whipped up a Civil War opus of their own called "Jezebel" and put Miss Davis in the title rôle. Though Miss Davis had audibly hoped to be lent to Selznick to play Scarlett, the director of the picture had decided that as a New Englander she lacked the Southern sex appeal which he subsequently found in the British Vivien Leigh. So Miss Davis not only played Jezebel but also won her second Academy award for it, which in a way turned out to be worse than not playing Scarlett, because the next year, when she gave, in "Dark Victory," what critics still rank her top performance, Miss Leigh almost automatically won the season's award for her work in "Gone with the Wind." As Hollywood abbreviates the paradoxes, in "Victory," which was Davis's tops, she had to lose the Oscar to Leigh, who got it on "The Wind" because Davis had just got it on "Jezebel" because she hadn't got it on her next-to-tops "Bondage" because she had to lose it to Colbert in "One Night," which was why Davis had got her original Oscar on "Dangerous" in the first place. By way of extra irony, the nickname of Oscar for the Academy's bronze statuette was her own invention. At the time she was married to Harmon Nelson, whose middle name is Oscar.

One of Miss Davis's favorite possessions is a present from her family, a gold bracelet hung with little golden eggs. It is a token of appreciation for the talented goose who laid them. Her family—which now consists only of her mother, Mrs. Ruth Davis, who intelligently shaped Bette's life and has been her sagacious seeing eye, and Bette's younger, brunette sister, Barbara, now Mrs. Robert Pelgram—has always been an integral part of her life. She has been especially close to them ever since her parents were divorced. Her father, the late Harlow Morell Davis, was a patent lawyer. Until the feminine Davis trio settled down together (they are now, of course, separated) in California, they lived in approximately seventy-five houses in fifteen years—in Lowell, Somerville, Newton, Boston, Norwalk, Worcester, Rochester, and so on—at first because Mrs. Davis became a roving photographer in order to support herself and her daughters and later because of Bette's peripatetic beginnings in stock companies. The girls received the first four years of their education at a country-estate school in the Berkshires and their next four more realistically—when the family moved to a dark flat on the upper West Side of New York—at P.S. 186, where Bette was a zealous Girl Scout and won the All–New York grade-school prize for cookie-baking. Bette started high school in East Orange and finished it at Cushing Academy at Ashburnham, Massachusetts, where, as a sophomore of sixteen, she had a schoolgirl crush on the student she was later to marry, Harmon Nelson, and where she waited on table to help with her school expenses, an experience which she says was even more maturing than falling in love.

That summer Mrs. Davis, who was in debt, optimistically took her cameras and daughters to Peterborough, New Hampshire, which, full of actors and theatre movement, had just lost its local photographer. There Bette, aesthetically excited by the recitals of Roshanara, the Anglo-Indian dancer, who was then holding classes in the village, was invited to become a free pupil and to train to be a professional dancer. Roshanara's sudden death and a chance conversation which Mrs. Davis had with the actor Frank Conroy, who said that for once in his life he was advising a mother to put her daughter on the stage, altered everything. Bette had been inside a theatre only twice, the first time to see "The Easiest Way," the second time to see Ibsen's "The Wild Duck." She thought the gloomy Hedvig would be a wonderful part to play. Mrs. Davis, who has always doubled as mentor and prophetess in the home, predicted that her daughter was as good as signed up for the rôle.

There followed three years which Miss Davis puts under the heading of "There is no stopping a girl when she really decides to be an actress." The first attempt to stop her was made by Eva Le Gallienne, who let her read the part of a seventy-year-old Dutch character and quickly shooed her off as a "frivolous little girl." Mrs. Davis then told John Murray Anderson that she wasn't sure how soon she could pay for it but that her daughter ought to be studying in his dramatic school. This Bette did for the next two years. Her best friend there was Rosebud (afterward Joan) Blondell. Miss Davis got her first job in George Cukor's winter stock company in Rochester, where she opened in 1928 with one line in "Broadway." The prophetic Mrs. Davis, however, had told Bette she had better learn the fatter rôle of a character named Pearl, since the actress assigned to it was fated to sprain her ankle. She did, and Bette became Pearl. The next summer Bette thought she was engaged, along with Peggy Wood, Basil Rathbone, and Romney Brent, for the Cape Playhouse at Dennis, Massachusetts, but upon her arrival she discovered that there had been a misunderstanding. She could, though, stay on and usher if she wished. Miss Davis ushered and, without being asked, learned all the ingénue rôles. She got her chance, closing week, to play Dinah in "Mr. Pim Passes By." She made her New York début early in 1929 at the Provincetown Theatre, playing the rôle of

Floy, the farmer's daughter, in James Light's production of a rural drama called "The Earth Between." Next morning Brooks Atkinson remarked in the *Times* that a certain newcomer, Miss Bette Davis, "is an entrancing creature." That season her mother's earlier prediction came true. In Blanche Yurka's road company of "The Wild Duck," Miss Davis played the rôle of Hedvig, after nearly missing the part because of an attack of measles which Mrs. Davis had failed to previse. When the Broadway season of 1929 opened, Miss Davis was part of it, as the ingénue in a farce called "Broken Dishes," at the Ritz Theatre. The play ran for a hundred and seventy-eight performances. Miss Davis was getting $300 a week by the end of the run and considered that she had arrived. When Goldwyn wired from California to order his Paramount studio at Astoria to make a test of Miss Davis and it turned out to be dreadful, she was not surprised. As a New York actress, she didn't think much of anything Hollywood did; neither, in all probability, did Clark Gable, Humphrey Bogart, and Franchot Tone, who were then contented fixtures on Broadway. In 1929, on Broadway, it was Hollywood which had not yet arrived.

So far as she has been permitted, Miss Davis has molded her film career on her motto, "I love tragedy." She wisely aimed to be Hollywood's unique female expert at playing tragic, or at least miserable, heroines. Until Pearl Harbor she was the American favorite of the Japanese movie-goers because, they said, she represented the admirable principle of sad self-sacrifice. An adult-minded New Englander, atavistically suspicious of happy endings, she was so convinced by her early Hollywood parts that a floppy feminine hat was a symbol of celluloid sappiness that she later had written into her contract a clause permitting her to refuse to carry a hat in her hand like a damned basket of rosebuds. Her directors say that for Davis to get going at her best she needs to play an intelligent female who is either wrong or wronged—a cerebral skirt, preferably with a black conscience and somehow entangled with fate—against a background of earthquake, upper-class murder, or historical crisis.

Considering the dramas her talent has led her into and which she has played out to the bitter end as characters appropriately named Gabrielle Maple, Judith Traherne, Charlotte Lovell, or Henriette Deluzy-Desportes, Miss Davis has led a comparatively quiet life. In 1932, in Yuma, Arizona, with her mother and sister as witnesses, she married Harmon Nelson, then a dance-band pianist. Nelson soon became the leader of his own night-club orchestra at the Colony Club in Hollywood. The marriage lasted only six years. "He was too honorable to trade upon my position in pictures. The gulf between our earnings discouraged him. That, more than anything else, licked him," Miss Davis later bluntly wrote in the *Ladies' Home Journal*, as if forced to read aloud from some crisp, up-to-date, unhappy feminist script.

Miss Davis is now married to Arthur Farnsworth, a native of Rutland, Vermont, where his father is a doctor. Farnsworth is a handsome, ruddy-faced, laconic New Englander, formerly a professional flier and still a Quiet Birdman. He works for the Minneapolis-Honeywell Regulator Company, which now manufactures thermostats and other instruments for aircraft; temporarily, as a representative of the firm, he is working on aviation-training shorts for the Army at the Disney studio. They met in Rutland early in 1939. When Farnsworth suddenly appeared in California, late that year, gossip columnists hinted that Miss Davis was going to elope with him. "Whom should I elope from—my cook?" Miss Davis inquired sharply, and sneaked away with Farnsworth on New Year's Eve to a friend's ranch, where the marriage took place.

The Farnsworths live in a sparsely settled section of unfashionable Glendale, in what is probably the only two-bedroom, two-acre estate in the film colony. Their one-story, six-room, peak-roofed "Hansel and Gretel" house is surrounded by small, neat grounds, every inch of which is used to accommodate the California essentials—swimming pool, herbaceous borders, garden, garden fireplace for barbecues, and a small paddock and stables containing four horses, including one Palomino, a pastel breed that is now the Hollywood style. Miss Davis swims so well that she was once a member of an otherwise male lifeguard crew at Ogunquit, Maine, and rides horseback daringly, having learned on fractious studio steeds she was warned against but nevertheless tried early in her film career. The Davis place is called Riverbottom because it is in the bottom lands of the Los Angeles River. The house, for which she reportedly paid $50,000, was built so solidly that it lived through the flood of 1938, which swept away nearby dwellings, to become a white elephant on the real-estate market, since nobody, until Miss Davis turned up a couple of years later, was willing to trust the district again. She bought the place on the assumption that acts of God are rare, though she could get no local insurance company to agree with her. Riverbottom was finally insured by Lloyd's.

Her New England sense of thrift having early been shocked by the periodic auctions of the possessions of cinema stars who had flown too high, Miss Davis used to declare that she would own nothing in California which she couldn't take back East with her in a trunk. Psychologically, she led up to buying her little Western estate by buying a big New Hampshire barn and a few acres of surrounding land. The place is called Butternut Hill and is in the White Mountains. For two years, between pictures, she and her mother have been making it livable by furnishing it with American antiques they have collected. Farnsworth and the Davis ladies get along well in the community; the neighboring town of Littleton, on the Ammonoosuc River, gave Miss Davis a party on her thirty-third birthday, at which she and the governor of the state led the grand march.

When in exile in California, which is about nine months in the year, the Farnsworths, who like no fuss, live quietly. They subscribe to Alexander cocktails before their outdoor fireplace and to practical jokes, such as folding spoons and other surprises, but they serve excellent food and wine. Riverbottom's furnishings are in good taste, are mixed in period, and are apparently moved a lot. Miss Davis is the moving man's dream girl, because she is always taking things out of or putting them into storage, on the assumption that she's going somewhere else to live. Last summer, when a New York acquaintance was invited for the first time to dine in what would have been a half-empty house, Miss Davis told the mystified moving men that the guest was an intellectual who loved furniture and to hurry and bring back the absentee pieces from storage, no matter how late. The moving men turned up with their last load at 10 P.M., along with the after-dinner coffee.

Miss Davis is also the book publisher's delight. She reads just about everything as soon as it's printed, especially novels, since, as she points out, story-telling is her trade. She once took a whirl at Proust but quickly gave him up. She never reads on the set, though many stars do if they read. Since, when she is working, she has to get up at half past five in Glendale in order to be in the Warners' makeup building in Burbank by seven, and since she usually does not come home till seven in the evening, she has to do most of her reading in bed. Among her professional friends are Kay Francis, Olivia de Havilland, and Geraldine Fitzgerald, all three of whom are intelligent women. The Farnsworths also see a lot of Farnsworth's flying friends from the nearby airfields, old friends from back East, and Miss Davis's mother, sister, and brother-in-law. On the Warner lot Miss Davis's chum is Miss Margaret Donovan, who is head of the coiffure section of the makeup department and fixes her hair. The two girls are constantly bequeathing to each other new pieces of favorite costume jewelry in their wills. Miss Donovan was Miss Davis's witness at her marriage to Farnsworth. A behind-the-scenes influence is Mrs. Bridget Price, a tall, intaglio-faced English lady, an old friend of Mrs. Davis who now is officially in charge of handling the star's fan mail. There is more, however, to the connection than that; Mrs. Price is their general adviser and catalyst.

Becoming a big star often addles a human being, usually in one of three ways; the victim becomes a superior, lonely ego and stays home, or becomes a public character and goes out constantly, or becomes glamorous, no matter where he or she happens to be. Miss Davis was glamorous, years ago, for about a month. This period ended when, backed up by a smart town car containing a white poodle and liveried chauffeur, and attired in moody black velvet slacks and jacket, she met her mother, who had been on a trip East, at the Los Angeles railway station. Mrs. Davis was unable to believe her own eyes and flatly said so. The glamour was dropped later that day.

For years, before she was successful, Miss Davis sneaked off to neighborhood movies to see herself and suffer. Of her first big Hollywood première, given to her film "All This and Heaven, Too," she has said that all the ham in her was thrilled at seeing the waiting crowds and her name in lights and that there was, far more than she had imagined, excitement in sniffing the gala air and listening to the whispers and applause. She had waited a long time for it and had supposed it would never come.

Last summer Miss Davis founded the Hollywood Canteen, with, for once, the arguing not being done by her. Her idea that it should be, though independent, affiliated with the New York Stage Door Canteen, which she took as a model, outraged the motion-picture chauvinists and the Hollywood trade papers, quick to resent any compliment to Broadway. After a lot of talk and work the canteen opened in an abandoned night club on Cahuenga Boulevard. There, just as in New York, the stars wash dishes and wait on table, and patronage flourishes. The day before the opening, when Miss Davis was sweeping the floor, a soldier, attracted by a certain amount of commotion, dropped in. "Say, you look like you were Bette Davis," he observed. She said yes, she was. "Well, lady, your pictures certainly stink, but you look like sweetness and light now," he said.

In real life, as it is called, Miss Davis acts exactly as you would think from seeing her on the screen. Face to face, she is vital, arresting, restless, and informal. She gestures a great deal, as in "The Little Foxes," and has a nervous tic of tossing her head, as in "The Old Maid." She also has a woodwind laugh. Her conversation is pertinent, stimulating, and personal; it is animated by sudden ideas, reactions, and asides, almost as if she were talking to herself (which, as a matter of fact, she says she does), and these serve for her as temporary conclusions. Her vocabulary is a mixture of slang and polysyllables. It used to be rather like a Restoration comedy until some cameramen made a film of one of her heated studio arguments. As she watched the picture, she remarked, "My damns seem monotonous," and started breaking the habit. She still smokes a lot, that always having been her second vice. In the flesh she looks smaller than she does on the screen; she is five feet three and a half, and she tries not to let her weight fall below her normal hundred and ten. As Queen Elizabeth, she weighed ninety pounds and the regal robes weighed seventy-five. She likes buttermilk between meals and is loyal at any time to New England clam chowder. Like many women who work, she detests cooking, and she says that a husband who won't fry an egg for his wife when she comes home tired doesn't love her.

Miss Davis wishes that she had been born beautiful. Her magnificent plantation of ash-blonde hair is the only thing about her appearance that satisfies her. When she went into films, her first director made her bleach it, which outraged her. Letting it resume its own lambent lightness was one of her early victories. When a cinema critic admiringly referred to her as Pop Eye the Magnificent, she shrieked, alternately, with indignation and laughter. "Oh, that same old face!" she recently shouted at herself and to an open-mouthed interviewer in her dressing room. "Imagine having to look at it fifty times a day on a job like this!" It is her notably large eyes, disliked at first by both Hollywood and herself, which finally accelerated her ascent in pictures. When Hollywood at last got around to making analyses, it discovered that eighty per cent of screen acting is concentrated in the eyes. In "Dark Victory" Miss Davis made it one hundred per cent. Since her rôle was that of a woman threatened with insanity, her director wanted her to indicate her disorder by crazed motions of the hands. She decided to use only her eyes. Old cameramen say she has the most beautiful shoulder line in the business since Elsie Ferguson. Even the quantity of her erotic appeal, which so worried the studios at the beginning, has been recomputed. When, twelve years ago, a producer said she had no more sex appeal than Slim Summerville, she said he went too far. Now producers go even farther; they say she is solid, ice-cold, Puritan sex, of the type against which the Sunday blue laws had to be passed.

Directors claim that as an interesting instrument to work with there's no one within ten miles of her once the preliminary discussion of what is to be done has died down. As a matter of integrity, she won't even cross to the coffee table, centre-left, unless she has a conviction about it. Her disagreements with directors usually arise from the fact that she is still more theatre-minded than movie-minded. She instinctively favors stage realism over camera aesthetics and the customer-catering of the movies. In "Watch on the Rhine," playing the repatriated American wife of an impoverished anti-Nazi refugee, she went to bat for cotton stockings on her legs instead of silk, which photograph better. Her first row with Warner Brothers came, with customary promptness, when she was doing her first major part for them in "Bordertown," in which she was supposed to be roused out of bed in the middle of the night and insisted on realistically smearing her face with cold cream. This debate was lengthy and costly; it lasted, and held up production, for an entire day. Directors say that they never know what sort of interpretation they'll get from her, though they can bank on its being different from the different thing they expected and on its being absolutely sound. They mostly agree that her psychological diagnosis of a rôle can stabilize a whole picture; that she never throws a good line away; that her talent and technique never dry up, which in movie-making means that the final take, which may be the fiftieth repetition, done at sundown, is as fresh and careful as the first, just after breakfast; and that once she has read and digested a script, the manuscript could be lost and she could still act her rôle just as the author had intended. She loves to work, and she has endless energy for it. When the director asks people to take their places on a scene, nobody, not even child actors, can beat her onto the set. Because of what she regards as her invaluable grounding in stock, she is a remarkably quick study and is always letter perfect. Many of her arguments in the studio are with producers and directors in defense of carpenters, props, or electricians. She enjoys a good fight that doesn't even concern her, more or less as her ancestors enjoyed a good hellfire sermon.

Her long-drawn-out, bitter, running quarrel with Warner Brothers, for the past ten years her producers, has left the company and herself help-lessly united by the very furies, and profits, they have shared. As Warners were the first powerful unit to see talking pictures coming and to make ready, so they were the first to see something heterodox and useful in Miss Davis. A new style in stars can mean new millions. Warners took on Davis as a leading lady at the end of 1932. By the end of 1933 they were so sick of the bargain that they didn't even want to go to the legal bother of getting rid of her temporarily by lending her to R.K.O. for "Of Human Bondage." As Warners reportedly figured it, if she laid an egg in "Bondage," she would be even more of a dead loss to them, but if she ten-struck, she'd be harder than ever to manage, what with Warners being already groggy from exhaustion. Miss Davis says now that Warners must have thought she carried on like an ungrateful young Duse; she says she certainly thought of herself then as "a girl who was fascinated by the cultural and dramatic possibilities of the screen," with the ability, given a chance, to help make the screen adult. Warners have never said what they thought either of them thought. The Davis-Warner quarrel was basically over the difference be-tween her conviction (a result of her stage training) that the play's the thing, and that what she called "contrived parts" were really so much tripe, and the Warners' supposition that they could (as they did) give her leading-lady rôles in such peculiar concoctions as "The Fashions of 1934" and "Jimmy the Gent." When she refused pictures and parts she didn't like, as was her contractual right, they suspended her without salary, as was their right.

In 1936, while under both contract and suspension, she sailed for En-gland, where she rebelliously agreed to make a picture for Toeplitz Productions for $60,000 and was, as she expected when the London morning newspapers carried the story, promptly sued from California before nightfall. The mordant-tongued Sir Patrick Hastings opened for the distant Warner Brothers by remarking, "I think this is the action of a very naughty young lady," with which the white-wigged judge must have concurred, judging by the verdict. Being under suspension, Miss Davis lost $68,000 in Warners salary. Besides, she lost twenty-five pounds in flesh, and fifty-six hundred pounds in English monies were assessed against her as costs. She returned to California thin and broke. Warner Brothers opened their arms and Miss Davis fell into them, and they made her a present of half of the costs, granted her full-fledged stardom, and prepared to give her good pictures at last. Both had won, both had lost, both had spent a lot of money, and both were so enervated by each other that they didn't have the strength left to do anything but stay together. A recent news clipping says that Warners are now dickering for the movie rights to Miss Davis's autobiography, with the idea that she would play herself on the screen. More than any other producers, they would know how to deal with the story of her agitated career. They helped make it up.

To date, Miss Davis has done fifty-two pictures. Her contract, like most Hollywood star contracts, is for forty working weeks a year. She is paid $5,500 a week and makes four pictures annually. Her radio work probably brings in another $50,000, which takes her up to the quarter-million mark. No one knows what picture stars will do if the $25,000 salary ceiling holds good. They might make one picture a year for that sum or produce for themselves. Miss Davis would like, these being sober times, to make Edith Wharton's "Ethan Frome," as what Miss Davis terms "a New England memorial." She has also always wanted to return to Broadway for a serious fling.

If you ask the Hollywood trade who is the best actress in the business right now, the unanimous, indeed the only fashionable, answer is Davis. The trade adds, *sotto voce*, that her box-office is enormous because men fans are convinced that she is feminine, though she is really only maternal, and because she fascinates most women fans and those she doesn't fascinate she frightens. On a recent War Bond selling tour in the Ozarks and other rural districts, Miss Davis made the perturbing discovery that she scared lots of simple Americans of both sexes. This in turn alarmed her. Some metropolitan theatre critics claim that she seems complex in her rôles because she herself is an unresolved character. On the other hand, émigrés from Europe feel that she should be the dominant member of a great national stock company, like France's Comédie-Française, rather than be allowed to beat out her talent and wings in the movies. Her own idea of an ideal program would be, as she puts it, "to play one good play a winter on Broadway and then photograph it that summer in Hollywood." She will probably always think of the stage when she thinks of a good play, and to her the cinema will undoubtedly remain something done with improved lantern slides. "A movie," she once said, "is not even a dress rehearsal."

A Woman in the House: Cheryl Crawford

MAY 8, 1948 Miss Cheryl Crawford, producer of the Scotch-plaid musical comedy "Brigadoon," now in its second year on Broadway, is a small, scholarly Middle Westerner of austerely chiselled character and countenance who likes serious books, can recite all of Keats' odes from memory, and talks as little as possible. She is also a Smith College graduate, *cum laude*, class of 1925. During the first performance of "Brigadoon" at the Colonial Theatre in Boston, on its tryout tour, she insulated herself from first-night strain by shutting herself up in the theatre's office and reading an old pamphlet on Ralph Waldo Emerson she had unearthed that afternoon in a bookstall. The day before, on a literary pilgrimage, she had taxied out to Walden Pond. For the first fifteen of the twenty-two years of her theatre career, she worked mostly in the literate upper reaches of drama, with the Theatre Guild or the Group Theatre, and her studious preoccupations seemed natural enough. In the musical-comedy landscape in which she has been operating for the past seven years, her bookish interests create a startling effect, like an Act I library backdrop askew behind an Act III Maypole finale. The cast and chorus of "Brigadoon" made her a Christmas present last December of a bibliophile copy of the 1860–61 edition of Walt Whitman's "Leaves of Grass." The young people of the chorus, to whom her backstage conversation, especially during rehearsals, had seemed to have the prose simplicity of Hemingway, were astounded when they were told by a friend of hers that she was a poetry fancier and that for a Christmas present a little book of verse would be right up her alley. Miss Crawford, who has a library of two thousand high-toned volumes in her East Fifty-second Street flat, already owned a good copy of the 1880–81 edition of Whitman, but her "Brigadoon" one topped it. It was a copy inscribed on the flyleaf "To McW.," McW. having been a friend, George McWaters. Furthermore, the book contained some old newspaper clippings on the poet, such as an 1879 *Times* editorial that said, in part, "We are not among those who rank Whitman as the most original and remarkable poet of the country," and a book review by a New Englander who called his poems "picturesque ulcers." Since Miss Crawford can easily be provoked into long, tremolo quotations from Whitman's works or into denunciations of his detractors, even when they are defunct *Times* editorial writers, the "Brigadoon" Whitman has given her great satisfaction.

The Christmas presents Miss Crawford gave Alan Jay Lerner, author of "Brigadoon's" book and lyrics, were also on an academic plane. In a wholesale fashion, she gave him a copy of Ben Jonson's poems, a folio of Giotto prints, "the Elizabethan Reader," William Ellery Sedgwick's "Herman Melville: The Tragedy of Mind" (which concerns one of her favorite Americans), two volumes of Isherwood, and one of Freud. The first musical-comedy beneficiary of Miss Crawford's edifying generosities was Mary Martin, when Miss Martin was starring in an earlier Crawford musical, "One Touch of Venus," in 1943. After a year's run here, Miss Martin went on the road in the show, and when she left she was accompanied by a book trunk full of books, a surprise from Miss Crawford. It featured two biographies of Sarah Bernhardt, some Shaw, a treatise on the genius of Eleanora Duse, one on the Moscow Art Theatre, and essays on the art of acting by Henry Irving and Francisque Sarcey, a dusty old authority on the Comédie-Française. Miss Martin says that it took her two years to wade through them.

For the past seventeen years, Miss Crawford has been one of Broadway's two unintermittent woman producers—the other being Theresa Helburn, administrative director of the Theatre Guild—and no man has had a longer list of intelligent, interesting box-office failures. By and large, she devoted those years to superior plays, people, theories, and projects, which helped make distinguished theatrical history but usually omitted to make much, enough, or even any money. She became an expert at combining high aspirations with rock-bottom costs. In March, 1947, when "Brigadoon" came into the Ziegfeld Theatre with a half-million-dollar box-office advance, it also came in at the season's lowest cost for a musical. To stage it, her backers had given her two hundred thousand dollars, a fair example of what it costs nowadays to gamble on such an enterprise; she brought the production in at a cost of a hundred and sixty thousand dollars. Show business is apparently the only big business that takes failure for granted. The theatrical ledger would scare the average businessman out of his wits. A really lush musical comedy can cost three hundred thousand to produce, and a straight drama runs to sixty thousand dollars. Producing anything is a ten-to-one shot on Broadway; nine shows fail for one that succeeds. Miss

Crawford, who in her earlier days was usually associated with the nine, has produced three successes in a row since she switched to musicals. This record is so impressive that on Broadway she is almost superstitiously credited with having some special feminine formula for making them pay. An average of four unsolicited musical-show manuscripts a week come to her office, on West Forty-fifty Street. She has six musicals in the works, one of them, "A Dish for the Gods," all ready for fall production. The feminine formula she used on "Brigadoon" included the elimination of a lot of customary, costly, masculine waste. This she achieved, like millions of women before her, merely by cutting things down with a paring knife and by keeping her eyes fixed on every dollar. A rival, gentleman producer recently said, with awe, "In business, she's hair-raising about money." Most musicals involve at least eight costume changes for the female chorus. All "Brigadoon's" girls except the dancers are rigged up with a basic skirt and blouse over which tartan kilts, scarves, aprons, and the like are draped to effect changes. There was big talk of importing costly tartan kilts from Scotland; Miss Crawford bought her tartans at Gimbel's and Bloomingdale's, and the only imported items were a couple of dozen pairs of tartan stockings. "Brigadoon's" sets consist of romantic canvas drops instead of realistic wooden constructions; in a household, this would be the difference, roughly, between paying for a nice new curtain to divide a room and paying for a new wall. Furthermore, instead of following the ordinary procedure, Miss Crawford worked out the show's physical details before it went into rehearsal. It was all a result of her familiarity with what can be accomplished by a planned economy. Ever since her college days, she has been a persistent reader of the succeeding civilizations' contributions to economics, from contemporary contributions back to antique literary items, such as the seventeenth-century Mandeville's opus "The Fable of the Bees," of which she has a good early edition. Miss Crawford is especially interested in a song in her forthcoming "A Dish for the Gods," called "That's Good Economics But Awful Bad for Love."

According to a Broadway cynic, one explanation of Miss Crawford's low production costs is her ability to give her cast "the lowest salary possible and still keep up her reputation as a philanthropist." Miss Crawford is a woman with a strong social conscience. A liberal Left Winger when she was in college, she still thinks that it is only just to make the prosperous class less prosperous and give the difference to the little fellows at the bottom. When "Brigadoon" opened in New York, she was paying her chorus girls sixty-five dollars a week, as against the minimum, at that time, of fifty dollars, and she has given them three raises. The minimum is now sixty dollars; the members of her chorus get eighty. She also took out hospitalization insurance for the whole company at her own expense and gave everybody a two-week holiday with pay. Most Broadway producers regard such practices as pampering.

Miss Crawford is supposed to run Broadway's second most orderly theatrical enterprise, the first being Katharine Cornell's and Guthrie McClintic's. Her methods with her company are oddly calm. She never panics. She is always courteous and succinct. She never makes scenes or rises to them when they are made by others. This frustrates actors at first and they think that she is not paying attention to them. After they get used to it, they usually like it. When she hires an expert for a technical stage job, she offers what suggestions she has, which he can take or leave, and then lets him do the job she hired him for—a liberty that many producers, more nervous, can't bear to give, it seems. She stands by her guns; when a backer who had agreed to put forty thousand dollars into "Brigadoon" wanted the ending changed at the last minute, she simply said, "Over my dead body," which it practically would have been if the forty thousand dollars had been withdrawn at that late date. She is not as good a gambler as she thinks she is, but she is an enduring gambler. She indulges in the gambler's typical lavish generosities, followed by incongruous small gestures of economy.

"Brigadoon" had been turned down by an impressive succession of male producers, among them Billy Rose, John C. Wilson, George Abbott, Herman Shumlin, and Rodgers and Hammerstein, before Miss Crawford admired and took it. The theme is as romantic as any cry of Keats to a nightingale. The story is that love, for a young man, is worth giving up the world for, in the last act. The gentleman producers feared that this romanticism might not pay. So did many potential male backers. Seventeen of the show's thirty-eight angels are women, among them Miss Florence Vandamm, a theatrical photographer; Miss Wendy Barrie, the former film actress; Miss Margot Johnson, the literary agent; and Miss Bea Lawrence, herself a co-producer, this season, of Gielgud's "Crime and Punishment." "Brigadoon's" angels were paid back their entire investment in the record-breaking time of sixteen weeks; backers of more costly musicals sometimes wait from forty to fifty weeks, and, of course, often wait forever. Since then, Miss Crawford's backers have been receiving a monthly total of forty thousand dollars. So far, the show has made well over half a million. What the taciturn Miss Crawford has received from her Scottish gold mine, she does not say. She merely remarks dryly that she waited for it more than fifteen years.

Miss Crawford was born in 1902, in Akron, Ohio, of comfortably well-off parents who were college-educated and churchgoing. She was the eldest child. There were three brothers. Her name, Cheryl, was suggested to her mother by a friend, and Mrs. Crawford thought it a pretty one. Cheryl's father, Robert Kingsley Crawford, who at the age of seventy-six is still running a real-estate business, attended Northwestern University, and one of his brothers, now dead, was president of Allegheny College, in Meadville, Pennsylvania. Cheryl's mother, born Lu Elizabeth Parker, graduated from Buchtel College, in Akron. The Parkers were Virginians who migrated to Kentucky; Miss Lu's grandfather had served with the Northerners in the Civil War, had been disowned by his kin, and had felt that he had better move out. The Crawfords were Scots. Grandfather Crawford had moved to County Fermanagh; in Ireland, and then turned up as an American pioneer in Willow Center, Illinois. In Downers Grove, a suburb of Chicago, Cheryl's Grandmother Crawford was a power in the Woman's Christian Temperance Union and in Methodist-church circles.

At Smith, which she entered in 1921, when she was nineteen, Miss Crawford read Plato and Nietzsche and lost her religion, was a star in Professor Samuel Atkins Eliot, Jr.'s, drama class, and then took a playwriting course, in which she received an A. The summer after her junior year, instead of going home to Akron, she went to Provincetown, because of what she had heard of its famous summer playhouse, which, she belatedly discovered, had burned down seven years before. Its spirit, however, was still functioning, in a barn that had been converted into a theatre workshop, where Susan Glaspell, Harry Kemp, and others were operating under the wing of a wealthy summer visitor, Mrs. Mary Aldis, of Chicago. Mrs. Aldis hired Cheryl as technical director and paid her in board. That summer, the group put on, as the season's big and final offering, some one-act plays about the sea by Eugene O'Neill, the recently discovered American dramatist.

The autumn after her graduation, and against her family's advice, Cheryl, now twenty-two, took twenty-five hundred dollars left her by her Grandmother Parker and set off for New York and the Theatre Guild School, then the focal point for young, stage-struck intelligentsia. (The importance of this twenty-five hundred dollars' worth of free choice so impressed Miss Crawford that she not long ago arranged in her will for similar liberation funds for her brothers' children—one boy and two girls —so they, too, if necessary, may one day ignore their parents' earnest counsel.) The following summer, Miss Crawford, now a Guild School graduate, was living in Greenwich Village and trying to get a start as a stage manager on Broadway, where, with a few exceptions, females were then actresses or nothing. After the light and gas had been turned off in her apartment for non-payment, she took up poker, a game which she had never seen played at home but for which she had the nerve and the perfect inscrutable face. She often won as high as fifteen dollars an evening. And to her poker companions—artists, poets, and the like—she was soon, as she enjoys recalling, selling bathtub gin she had brewed herself. From this disgraceful life, she was saved by Theresa Helburn, who, because of her own Guild record, was willing to give a girl a chance. She offered Cheryl a part-time thirty-five-dollar-a-week job as casting secretary, and Cheryl begged permission to throw in her services as third assistant stage manager in a forthcoming show, Werfel's "Juarez and Maximilian," starring Alfred Lunt and Clare Eames. In one scene of this show, Third Assistant Stage Manager Crawford played a court lady and in another a Mexican peasant woman; she also directed an offstage nine-piece orchestra and shot off a cannon in the basement. Next year, she was head stage manager, at a hundred and fifty dollars a week, of the Guild's secondary theatre, the Garrick, and a few years later she became casting director for all Guild plays. This meant casting six shows a year, usually working, when one was in process of being assembled, from ten in the morning until the curtain went down at night, and sometimes, for big productions, interviewing two hundred and fifty actors a day. For Rouben Mamoulian's production of the Southwestern drama "Green Grow the Lilacs" (now converted into the Guild's musical state institution, "Oklahoma!"), she hired cowboys from a rodeo just closing at Madison Square Garden. She hired extras for "Roar China" in Chinatown, where she also, mistakenly, hired a Jap, whom the Chinese threw out. She cast "Porgy" in Harlem. She selected Henry Fonda as a walk-on; she chose Clifford Odets for a two-line bit in a Guild road company; and she recommended Bette Davis for a minor role, but the Guild turned her down.

In her third year with the Guild, Miss Crawford was asked to take its Negro "Porgy" cast to London. Neither she nor they had been in England before, or even on an ocean liner. They sailed on the Columbus, in second class, which was like a seasick Harlem night club all the way over. "Porgy" was booked into His Majesty's Theatre, operated by the elegant Charles Cochrane, the most impressive and important theatre man in the British Empire. An hour before curtain time on the first night, Miss Crawford noted that the program blandly announced that Mr. Cochrane was the producer of the show, with no mention at all of the New York Theatre Guild—an omission that she had observed the day before on the program proofs and that he had courteously promised to remedy. Their opening-night dialogue on the topic ran something like this: She said that he would please make an announcement before the curtain, giving the Guild credit as "Porgy's" producer. He said that he had never made a curtain announcement in his life. She said that if he didn't, her cast would remain in their dressing rooms, to which she had ordered them to retire. He said he'd be damned. At twenty-five minutes past curtain time, when the pit was whistling and lords and ladies were murmuring, Cochrane stepped before the curtain, which Miss Crawford held firmly closed against his manly back, and elegantly made his announcement. Afterward, he hissed to her, "I hope you are satisfied, Miss," and never spoke to her again during the three months the play ran in his house. "Porgy" was of interest to London largely as an etymological curiosity. The British, it appeared, were never able to understand what the cast was saying.

For the young Miss Crawford, who was already consecrated to the theatre and whose brain and imagination were by then at home only in a theatre, lighted or dark, the five seasons she spent with the Guild were the happiest years of her life. Coincidentally, they were also the most active years of the Guild's life up to then, and probably the last big days of Broadway. In the middle nineteen-twenties, there were sometimes five new openings on one night, and over three hundred new productions, counting revivals, a year (as against perhaps eighty today). The Guild had a galaxy of new stars coming up, and its ripe stars were still firmly in place—an assemblage that included the Lunts, Clare Eames, Morris Carnovsky, Edward G. Robinson, Margalo Gillmore, Pauline Lord, Helen Westley, and Dudley Digges. The scene was bright with playwrights such as O'Neill, Anderson, Behrman, Howard, Sherwood, Molnar, and Pirandello. In 1928, Miss Crawford had become an assistant director on the Guild's board, with a salary of nine thousand dollars a year, then large money indeed for a miss of twenty-six. In 1931, Miss Crawford, who was only twenty-nine, could probably have moved into the Guild's inner circle as one of the managing directors, but she chose to leave, with two other Guild members—stage manager Lee Strasberg and play reader Harold Clurman —to found what they called the Group Theatre. Strasberg says they must all three have been crazy, since they had well-paying, artistic jobs in a good, liberal organization. During the Group's eight-year existence, it earned fame and satisfaction for itself but little money, especially for the founders. They paid themselves fifty dollars weekly, often only in theory. The leading actors were paid about four times what Miss Crawford and her colleagues got. Miss Crawford, acting as the Group's manager, co-director, and principal money-raiser, set herself up in an infinitesimal office, donated by a Broadway friend and situated on top of the Forty-eighth Street Theatre, at the head of an eighty-nine-step staircase. When the group got going, it played anywhere it could find an empty house, and Miss Crawford's office naturally moved around with it.

The Group was frankly run on fanaticism, and while idealism, talent, and often brilliance were projected over the footlights, there was usually comic misery lying behind them. It was supported, spasmodically, by millionaires, writers, poets, actors, rivals, and friends; by hat-passings, by Lee Shubert, by Hollywood, and, in a way, by the depression, which in the early nineteen-thirties gave the Group's new, realistic style of plays their legitimate due as hard but nourishing slices of contemporary life. Among its backers were John Hay Whitney, who gave twelve thousand dollars; Maxwell Anderson, who gave a few thousands and a play in verse about the Russian Revolution that was never produced; Herman Shumlin, who happily gave a thousand dollars toward a play he thought was so fine that he was sure it would never make a cent. Eugene O'Neill gave some backing, and Franchot Tone (who himself had been given to the Group by the Guild, along with its blessing and a thousand dollars in backing) gave many thousands over the years, especially after he had abandoned the Group for Hollywood and could well afford it. Miss Crawford contributed her Group salary and got along on money she had saved while working for the Guild.

From the beginning, the Group members lived a communal, al-fresco summer life. Their first hegira took them to Brookfield Center, Connecticut, where they used a big barn as a workshop. Here they were idealistic indeed, with crackers and milk as their midnight supper and enthusiastic talk till dawn after evening rehearsals. The *Times* that summer reported that the Group included "twenty-one victrolas, three radios, fourteen motor cars, a complete library of symphony records, a lot of books on the theatre, four colored waiters, and Alexander Kirkland's dog." Subsequent summers were grim. In order to stay together to rehearse and theorize, the Group earned its board and keep at vacation camps, where it gave weekly bills of playlets and vaudeville sketches. It summered at places like Dover Furnace, in Dutchess County; Green Mansions, in Warrensburg, New York; and Pinebrook Club Camp, in Nichols, Connecticut. Some of its summer jobs were at kosher vacation camps, and it also did one stint at a children's Christian Science school on Long Island. In winter, back in Manhattan, many of the Group lived in what they nicknamed the Groupstroï, a poorly heated old brownstone in the West Fifties near Tenth Avenue. The Group had three aims, and it was moral about them all. It wanted to do contemporary plays of social significance; it wanted to try out the famous theories about actor training laid down by Constantin Stanislavsky, of the Moscow Art Theatre; and it wanted to establish a permanent acting company, like the Abbey Theatre, or Copeau's Théâtre du Vieux-Colombier in Paris. According to Harold Clurman, in his book on the Group, "The Fervent Years," the Group did lots of preaching at first about "inner experience, rehearsal psychology, significant contemporaneity," dynamism, creative form, and the like, and thought the commercial theatre had "no more dimension than a bordello." As for the

Stanislavsky theory of acting, he says, "its aim is to enable the actor to use himself more consciously as an instrument for the attainment of truth on the stage." In a nutshell, this truth attainment consisted of the Group actors' having to practice acting the way ballet dancers, pianists, and singers practice their arts. They had to do exercises in recall, drawn from their private lives, something like séances on a psychoanalyst's couch. In other exercises the actors played a scene by paraphrasing, ad lib, the author's words, and in others they spoke not at all but had to pantomime words such as "America," "Liberty," and "Truth." The exercises were so esoteric that in no time confused outsiders were saying that the Group actors prayed before going onstage and, much worse, that the Group itself was a cult for free love, or maybe only anarchy. The exercises, however, led Manhattan drama critics, as time went on, to admire increasingly the Group's work, which one critic called "superlative acting." Possibly the most important young talents the Group discovered were John Garfield, who for weeks had sat at the bottom of Miss Crawford's eighty-nine steps and tackled her every day for an acting job; Elia Kazan, a recent Yale graduate, who walked up the steps to ask her if he could be a Group sceneshifter, or, indeed, anything; and Clifford Odets, whom the Group transformed from a bit actor into a leading playwright.

The Group produced a half-dozen great successes that did not make a fortune and over a dozen plays that made even less. On moral principle, the top price of Group theatre seats was two dollars and a half, so even when it had a hit the box office was not a great help. The successes included the opening play, "The House of Connelly," by Paul Green, put on in 1931. It was the Yankee North's first play about the disintegrating South and got extravagantly enthusiastic reviews. Another successful play, by John Howard Lawson, was "Success Story," which Noel Coward, at least, admired so much that he saw it five times. The first major hit was the Pulitzer Prize play "Men in White," by Sidney Kingsley. It featured Alexander Kirkland, as a surgeon, and was largely backed by Doris Warner, of the Hollywood Warners. It had been discovered by Miss Crawford in a woodpile of play manuscripts in the office of Lee Shubert, who had shrewdly given her permission to poke around among them, with, of course, the understanding that he would take a slice of any profits. After "Men in White," she turned down a Hollywood offer of a thousand dollars a week. Then came Paul Green's "Johnny Johnson," a pacifist play about the first World War. It was partly backed by John Hay Whitney and contained the first music written here by Kurt Weill, already famous in Europe for his "Dreigroschenoper" score. "Johnny Johnson" was Miss Crawford's favorite, and she put it on nearly singlehanded. "Waiting for Lefty" and "Awake and Sing," the Group's most discussed and influential

successes, by the new playwright Odets, appeared next, almost simultane-
ously, and though they are still talked of admiringly by playgoers and
critics, they did not attract big crowds. "Waiting for Lefty" had to do with
a New York taxi strike, with Kazan playing a taxi-man; "Awake and Sing"
dealt with the social drama of a Jewish family in the Bronx. Both plays
were considered Leftist by the Rightist press, but the *Daily Worker* called
the second "a comedown for the Group Theatre, an unimportant play."
Two hits Miss Crawford wanted to produce were turned down in 1937 by
the rest of the Group, a circumstance that helped persuade her to walk out
of the organization. They were Maxwell Anderson's "Winterset" and
Kingsley's "Dead End." After she left, the Group also vetoed William
Saroyan's "The Time of Your Life" and made its only big profit, fifty
thousand dollars, on Odets' "Golden Boy." It was sold to the movies, and
the Group in triumph sent the play, with the New York cast, to London,
where James Agate, critic of the London *Times*, said that "the acting
attains a level which is something we know nothing at all about."

The Group had had internal difficulties even before Miss Crawford's
departure. It had almost fallen apart in 1933, because of dissension and
hard times; it was still managing to hang together when, in 1935, Clurman's wife, the Group actress Stella Adler, returning from Moscow and an
interview with Stanislavsky, reported that the Group was using his sacred
method all wrong, which put a crimp in the founders' authority. Then, in
1937, just before Miss Crawford left, there was a rebellion among the
Group actors, their complaint being that the organization was not well
directed. The Group collapsed in 1941, shortly after giving Irwin Shaw's
"Retreat to Pleasure" and just after being called by one critic "the best
acting organization in this country." Turning its back on its ideals, a large
segment of the ex-Group set out in a body for Hollywood.

As a producer on her own, Miss Crawford went along much as she had
with the Group, but with less argument. She produced several flops, including one by Dorothy Thompson, one by Marc Connelly, and one by Sir
James M. Barrie—her revival of "A Kiss for Cinderella." Once, when she
wasn't sure of a new show, she had a New York preview, at which she
distributed pencils and paper among the members of the audience, so that
they could write down yes or no. The majority wrote no, and she dropped
the play. She produced a distinguished and bold minor success about Jesus
Christ's mother and brothers, called "Family Portrait" and starring Judith
Anderson, as Mary. Miss Crawford's most interesting failure was "All the
Living," a play about insulin treatment for the insane. She thinks that it
might be a hit today. As she grimly says, "Insanity has become much more
popular." She was ten thousand dollars in debt in 1940, when she entered

upon a new and desperate, and successful, summer producing adventure in Maplewood, New Jersey, at the Maplewood Theatre. The idea, which was Miss Crawford's, was to bring over from New York, for a week apiece, Barrymore, Bankhead, Hayes, *e tutti quanti*. All these New York stars would, after they had closed on Broadway and before they went on the road, stop off at Maplewood, where New Jersey citizens could see them, possibly with their companies intact, for a dollar and fifty cents instead of the four-dollar Manhattan price. The suggestion of Maplewood as a place to try the plan was made by John Wildberg, who had been the Group's lawyer. He and Miss Crawford became associate producers in Maplewood, where, in addition to presenting a number of importations from Manhattan, they put on a revival of "Porgy and Bess." (Their association came to an end after the metropolitan production "One Touch of Venus.") The Maplewood project made money almost from the moment it started, in June, 1940. The season lasted twenty-six weeks that year, to around Thanksgiving, and twenty-three weeks in 1941, but only five weeks in 1942, because of wartime gasoline rationing. Miss Crawford was very happy in Maplewood, where, to provide an intimate, friendly touch, she forced herself to give neighborly talks and even, no matter what anguish it cost her, to tell jokes before the curtain between acts.

"Porgy and Bess," an adaptation of "Porgy" with music by George Gershwin, had been produced by the Guild in 1935. It had not been a big success. But in the next six years its tunes had swept the country, practically establishing themselves as folk songs. Miss Crawford was an ardent believer in Gershwin as a genius of popular music. Engaging Alexander Smallens, the conductor, to look through the score with her and help her excise some of the dull, purely recitative passages in favor of accenting the folk songs, she lovingly and hopefully brought "Porgy and Bess," equipped with many members of the original cast, to the Majestic Theatre in New York. It ran, off and on, for four years, in New York and on the road. Music seemed to have changed her luck.

With a lucky feeling and with Kurt Weill's "Johnny Johnson" and "Dreigroschenoper" scores in mind, she got together with Weill in the summer of 1942 to work on a new musical show, for which he had an idea. Back in 1936, the German-born Weill, a newly arrived refugee, had spent much of his time in the New York Public Library, reading to learn English. There he had come across a short story called "The Tinted Venus," by F. Anstey, the nom de plume of Thomas Anstey Guthrie, a former contributor to *Punch*. Turned into a libretto by S. J. Perelman, with lyrics by Ogden Nash—both of them new to the theatre—and with music by Weill, it became "One Touch of Venus." The show was written with both eyes on Marlene Dietrich as the amorous goddess. She got as far as coming to New York to discuss it, trekked up to the Metropolitan Museum of Art, at Miss Crawford's thoughtful suggestion, to look the Venuses over, and even signed a contract for the show, but the deal eventually fell through. When Miss Crawford approached Mary Martin with the idea of becoming Venus, Miss Martin said she was afraid not, because the Venus de Milo (the first one to come to her thoughts) was fatter than she wanted to be. She accepted the role, however, after the standard Metropolitan Museum trip, on which she discovered Venuses of all sizes.

"One Touch of Venus," which opened at the Imperial Theatre in October, 1943, ran for five hundred and sixty-seven performances here and was a hit on the road, too. It established Miss Martin as a star and it made a profit of two hundred thousand dollars. Not being the sole producer, Miss Crawford did not get all of this, but she got enough to prove that her luck had changed spectacularly. She bought a fine car, rented a fine midtown apartment, and acquired packets of fine books. As she likes the fleshpots and enjoys rich food and a glass of whiskey as well as the next man, she put on a full-time basis her talented colored cook, Rosa, who had worked for her rather irregularly for fourteen years. She also gave Rosa a share in John Wildberg's production of "Anna Lucasta," in which she had an interest. Rosa made almost four thousand dollars on it, but she did not give up cooking. Miss Crawford also bought some fine clothes with her "Venus" money. Though given to wearing tailored suits in sky or field colors, she ordered a smart black dress from Valentina and bought six costly hats on Fifth Avenue. She wore the dress once, looked imposing in it, and retired it to a closet. Detaching herself from the hats took longer. She never wore any of them; she simply went about carrying one at a time in her hand until she forgot them all in taxicabs.

Miss Crawford's new and luxurious flat gave her, for the first time in many years, enough room for her old books as well as for new ones. A college friend recalls that in Miss Crawford's early New York days her customary invitation was "Come on over to dinner and bring a book to read." She has no love for dinner chitchat, and she has an almost uncontrollable appetite for reading at any time. Few adults read as hungrily, as appreciatively, and as wonderingly as she does, as if she were still in school and enjoying it. In her reading, she shows a respect for the creative minds. She has a phenomenal memory, and she stores up culture the way some women put on weight. She would have made an excellent pedagogue or social worker, the first because of her knowledge and the second because she is forever searching among the nobler records of man for some way out of the mess man is in. Whatever book she reads—she wants no "muck of mystery stories or silly fiction"—the theory involved in its theme is what she is after, because she is a theorist. She is also an optimist, a reformer, a humanist, and even a sentimentalist. She buys all the books on nations and their problems, and on new ways of running the world. With friends, she often sits in silence, because her silence does not embarrass her. She joins only in conversations on ideas or human hopes. Then she talks expansively, warmly, and pungently, with a large vocabulary and odd, enriching allusions culled from the library of her mind.

In a bookshop, Miss Crawford is a pushover for anything at all on Jefferson, Lincoln, Melville, Emerson, and Thoreau, who are her chief American heroes. She has engravings of all five hanging in her bedroom. Aside from this quintet, she says, the men who have most influenced her thinking are Rostovtzeff, with his "Social and Economic History of the Roman Empire;" Frazer, with "The Golden Bough;" Plato, whose "Dialogues" she possesses in a handsome red leather edition of the Jowett translation; the behaviorist Pavlov, with "Conditioned Reflexes;" and Freud. Her living room has two big shelves of books on psychoanalysis; her American-history section contains some Revolutionary diaries; she owns one of the three known copies in this country of "England's Helicon, a Collection of Lyrical and Pastoral Poems Published in 1600," in an edition of 1887. There are few English poets, no matter how long dead or how recently published, that she doesn't know something about. Her memory for poetry, most of which she learned at college, is astounding. In addition to being able to recite by heart the Keats odes, she can quote great swatches of Whitman, Shelley, and Eliot. She is a considerable collector of modern Broadway Americana; she has three thousand copies of sheet-music song hits dating as far back as 1900. She used to sing them and accompany herself, left-handed, on a ukulele (she is left-handed at everything but writing, the orthodoxy having been imposed on her by Akron schoolteachers), and can still accompany herself on the piano if she practices first. She carries a tune with a solemn, quavering flute of a voice, which is nothing like the calm contralto of her ordinary speech—when she speaks.

Miss Crawford's intimate friends, of whom she seems to have several hundred, among them the more important theatrical and musical figures of her generation, think that sheer tenacity put her where she is today but that pure faith is the keynote of her character. They point out that she has the touching and melancholy eyes of the true reformer. Like many other American idealists, she is a born supporter of causes and she sits through endless committee meetings. She has a profound compassion for the oppressed, the mistreated, and the unfortunate, and believes that if there are enough energetic members on any given committee, conditions will improve. She has been a conspicuous fighter for equal rights for Negro actors in the theatre. Her managing of the "Porgy and Bess" company, an almost solidly Negro cast, was rated a triumph. In the American Repertory Company, which she launched, quite unsuccessfully, four years ago (it has since been revived, under other auspices), she featured the talented Negro Canada Lee, as Caliban, in Shakespeare's "The Tempest," along with the Norwegian Zorina as Ariel, an Italian as Ferdinand, and a Miranda from Oklahoma. The American Repertory Company, which was organized to star Eva Le Gallienne and Margaret Webster, was another of her disastrous attempts to bring an idealistic ray of light to Broadway. It is still Miss Crawford's conviction that only a subsidized repertory organization can take the theatre and actors out of mere show business and put them into a cultural haven they deserve, like the Comédie-Française of Paris or London's Old Vic, both of which are state-supported houses. Her subsequent comforting substitute for the American Repertory is the Experimental Theatre, of which she is a director and leading spirit and which operates under the sponsorship of the American National Theatre and Academy, an organization that at least has a charter from Congress. The Experimental caused considerable talk this season with its "Galileo," by Bertold Brecht and with Charles Laughton, and its recent "Skipper Next to God," by Jan de Hartog, with the former Group acolyte John Garfield. This last made enough of a hit to justify a commercial run at the Maxine Elliott Theatre. The Actors' Studio is her latest idealistic scheme. It is managed by her, Elia Kazan, and "Brigadoon's" stage director, Robert Lewis—all former Group Theatre salvationists who seemingly will never say die. The Studio is a study setup—until a few weeks ago operating above a church on West Forty-eighth Street but now in a better place, at 1697 Broadway—where talented young professionals, like David Wayne, of "Mr. Roberts;" Marlon Brando and Karl Malden, both of "A Streetcar Named Desire;" and about forty less well-known young people on Broadway work, study, train, and are rehearsed by or lectured to by friends of Miss Crawford, topnotchers of the theatre such as Thornton Wilder, Maxwell Anderson, Robert Edmond Jones, Moss Hart, and Jerome Robbins.

Although Broadway respects Miss Crawford much more in her present success, it respected her even in her lean days. Whenever she has failed, the feeling has been that she failed on the right idea. As an idealist, however, she has had to be a supersalesman. As one of her friends says, "She can sell you an egg you know is rotten, but she honestly doesn't think it is. She thinks it's a dream." In her studious, ungarrulous way, Miss Crawford seems quite content to go on, if possible, producing successful, high-class, not too costly musical comedies, but some of her friends feel that this is not good enough for her. "In this musical-comedy business," one of them said not long ago, "she's a painted horse on a merry-go-round. In the old days, it was different. She was a war horse. She looked more natural then."

Letter from Prades: Casals

JUNE 7, 1950 Until now, doubtless the only earthly connection between this remote Pyrenees village of Prades and the United States has been sculptural, and tied up with a popular Riverside Drive bus ride. The Cloisters, in Fort Tryon Park, owes its name and fine Romanesque atmosphere in part to its possession of the biggest existing slice of the once famous cloister of the Abbey of St.-Michel-de-Cuxa, situated on a hill outside Prades. The people of Prades—there is no one left in the abbey—wish that history had not removed their treasure such an exceptionally long distance from home. A new aesthetic connection between Prades and America is the Prades Bach Festival, just opened here, which is being sponsored and mainly attended by American Bach-lovers, come all the way across the seas to this rather inaccessible valley. The Festival celebrates, first, the two-hundredth anniversary of the composer's death and, second, and more locally, the reëmergence of probably his greatest living exponent, Pablo Casals, who is certainly the world's greatest cello player and since 1939 has been the village's most noted Catalan émigré from Franco's Spain.

For the occasion, Casals is playing in public for the first time since 1947, when he decided that since the democratic governments had finally accepted the dictatorship of Franco, he, as a Spaniard, must make it clear that he did not accept it. So he gave up his concert career as a protest against what he considered a morally shabby postwar world. He is performing now because some of the leading younger musicians in America sent word to him last year that his premature silence had, along with the war and postwar travel difficulties, prevented them from ever hearing him play, and also because they declared that they wanted to come over to Prades and organize a festival of homage to Bach and to him as a politico-musical idealist who had refused to compromise for them or anybody else, or even for his own pocketbook's sake. This gives a notion of the almost Chautauqua-like fervor—the hero worship, the confusion, the practicing, the rehearsing, and the great expectations—that has been rocking this simple, inexperienced old village. Its streets are now filled with a mixture of garrulous international music-loving visitors and silent old local women dressed in black, of motorcars and donkey carts. Dominating it all has been the recrudescent figure of Casals. At seventy-three, he is stout, vigorous, indefatigable, and completely bald.

On the opening night, the scene was impressive, both inside and outside the handsome big Church of St. Pierre, where the concerts are taking place. From the church square, floodlights blazed on the cream-colored thirteenth-century church tower for the first time in its existence. A peanut-and-ice-cream booth had been set up close by, as if for a county fair. The square's buildings were hung, in a sparse, economical way, with the red-and-yellow striped flag of Catalonia. Like most of this border region, Prades was Catalan until France conquered it, in the seventeenth century, and it has gone on uninterruptedly speaking and feeling Catalan, which is unquestionably why refugees like Casals have the split satisfaction of feeling both at home and in exile here. By nine o'clock, what looked like the village's entire population (about five thousand) was massed in two watchful lines, between which eight hundred concertgoers, more than half of them American, self-consciously marched up to the church door. Some of the women concertgoers wore mantillas or veils on their heads, because they were going to listen in a church. Among the members of the orchestra inside were some women, and they wore little black caps, because they were playing in a church. A request was made in the program that there be no applause in the church, so the audience rose in welcome to the Maestro and thereafter rose whenever it wished to indicate applause. The Bishop of Perpignan, over for the great event in his red cape, cap, and stockings, blessed the occasion, Casals, and the composer, whom he referred to as "Botch." The performers sat on a stage in front of the altar, in the shallow choir.

The church, whose interior is gray-stone Gothic, with Romanesque chapels and lavish baroque décor, was built for religion, not concerts. To aid the acoustics, fishlines have been stretched parallel overhead and attached to the lofty clerestory balcony, and fishlines weighted with hooks and sinkers hang down from the chapel arches in a fringe. Behind the altar, the half-hundred gold, blue, or pink cherubim, saints, and angels that populate the ceiling-high Spanish carved retable certainly pocket some of the music's clarity.

Casals opened with the first Bach Suite in G Major for Unaccompanied Cello, and in spite of the poor acoustics, a glorious volume of sound rose from his strings. The stroke of his bow was like heavy silk; his vibrato was strong and rapid as that in the throat of a young man. What Casals gave was the culmination of a life devoted to technique, enriched by recent sad years of seclusion and freed once more for pleasure. Conducting the "Brandenburg" No. 2, he made Bach sound popular, in a new, noble, fast way, instead of traditional, boring, and dull. Being a cellist, he leaned especially on the big stringed instruments for support, instead of putting the customary Teutonic reliance upon sweet violins. And, being Latin, he gave the Second "Brandenburg" an un-Germanized, southern, joyful rhythm that made it sound like the most well-tempered dance music of the ages.

It was in the morning of the day the Festival opened, however, that the really great performance of the Second "Brandenburg" was played. It was done twice—in rehearsal and, again, for a Columbia recording in the refectory of the village girls' school. Those of us who were fortunate enough to be smuggled into the refectory that forenoon heard what may have been the best performance of the entire Prades cycle. After fifty days of rehearsals, on that last great day the orchestra had a few perfect hours of mellifluous ripeness, like that of a peach or a plum; the playing was just right, and the musicians themselves were just right—slightly intoxicated by work, by June heat, by Bach, and by enthusiasm. The recording made that morning should, with luck, be a beauty.

According to reports, Columbia Records contributed fifteen thousand dollars to the purse that made the Prades Festival possible. (The purse was also contributed to by wealthy women music patrons, like Mrs. Elizabeth Sprague Coolidge and Mrs. Rosaline Leventritt, as well as by prosperous orchestras, like the Boston Symphony.) Columbia ought to get a lot of its money back on its recordings of the Festival's six chamber-music concerts and its six orchestral concerts, which include all six of the "Brandenburg" concertos, on an estimated twenty-seven platters. It is reported that Casals is to get a ten-percent royalty on everything. In addition, several visiting soloists have turned their royalties over to him for his lifetime, as a safeguard for him when he can no longer teach. But the greatest generosity was shown by the thirty-five members of the orchestra, who have given their time—about seventy days of it, by the time the nineteen days of the Festival are finished, on June 20th. Round-trip boat passages were paid for those in the orchestra—just over half—who came from the States, and the railroad fares for all the others, who came from France and Switzerland. Each member was given, in addition, three hundred dollars for other expenses. All the Americans, at least, have lost money, because of engagements elsewhere that they refused, but they are glad they came; they find Prades worth it.

Life is cheap here, and plumbing primitive. As many musicians as possible are crowded into the twenty Spartan rooms that constitute the village's Grand Hotel, its present social center. Others are rooming with hospitable villagers, or at inns in neighboring towns; often, they must bicycle home, and uphill, after each concert. On such sporting jaunts, Miss Madeline Foley, the New York cellist, who is living at the neighboring Vernet-les-Bains, carries her instrument strapped across her handle bars. All the orchestra members are top-flight, successful professionals, and most of them are young. The list includes Miss June Rotenberg, of the St. Louis Orchestra, who is one of the rare lady bull-fiddlers; Leopold Teraspulsky, the cellist; and the oboe expert Marcel Tabuteau, of the Philadelphia Orchestra. Among the visiting soloists are Leopold Mannes, Rudolf Serkin, Isaac Stern, Joseph Szigeti, Eugene Istomin, and Doda Conrad. The concertmaster is the concert violinist Alexander Schneider. For the past few years, he has been coming here to study musical interpretation with Casals.

Schneider was the leading impassioned spirit in, and inventor of, the Prades Festival. He is also leader of the fanaticism about Casals, which marks the American group particularly. At night, they sit in the Grand Hotel's modestly equipped main-street café—the Grand refused to believe that foreigners would actually cross the Atlantic to attend any Prades shindig, even if it included elephants, and so failed to lay in whiskey and gin—and argue about the psychoanalytical definitions for words like "soul," "inspiration," and "purity;" that is, when they are not discussing the Maestro. Even those who were skeptical about the legend of the Maestro and came to Prades only to polish up their technique seem now to regard him as a musical messiah. At rehearsals, and on the altar's stage, they all play with the burning attention of fanatics, and when he plays, they lean out from their places to watch his every move, like disciples who want to remember how it all looked. This attitude is a secondary characteristic of the Prades Festival, just as the secondary characteristic of the Salzburg Festival, underlying Toscanini's great direction, was chichi and clothes.

The Roussillon valley in which Prades sits is one of the richest in France. The orange earth lying between the clumsy blue mountains and, to the east, the opaque salt marshes by the Mediterranean is planted thick with orchards and lush grapevines. The latter produce a sweetish table wine from which apéritifs like Byrrh are manufactured. These are the fertile fields that the Catalonians fleeing over the mountains when Barcelona fell in 1939 camped on, destroying the tender vines, along with the French welcome, as they desperately hunted up families and friends in the dark of night, cut down fruit trees to keep warm in the chill spring rains, and lost track of the thousands of horses that they had brought with them and that took to the roads and vineyards in destructive herds. At Amélie-les-Bains, a football field was turned into a refugee field, without water supply, for thousands of dirty, thirsty men. Farther from Prades, on the Mediterranean beach of Argelès-sur-Mer, was a camp watched over by France's Moroccan soldiers, mounted on brisk little stallions, and by Senegalese troops. At Argelès, the refugees slept in holes filled with seeping sea water, caught colic, and died in great numbers, literally sick to death of the reception offered by Republican France. It was a bitter time for both Spaniards and French. Prades people say that most of the Spaniards who fled to their region were spread out northward over France by the government in order that they might find work, that some later returned to Spain and the acceptance of defeat, and that most of those who remained joined the French Communist Party.

Enrique Casals, the Maestro's brother, himself maestro of the Barcelona Symphony and here as chief of the Festival's second-violin section, says that there are two Spains today—the one imagined by Catalan refugees in France and the one seen by Spaniards who live in it. The brothers joined the Republican cause belatedly, when Franco destroyed Catalonia's new autonomy, which its patriots had dreamed of for centuries. Enrique Casals says that if there were a free election in Spain today, only about eight percent would vote for Franco. But if there were a plebiscite on doing away with him, eighty percent would vote to keep him, because they fear the disorder of Communism as they remember it even more than they do his regime. He says that you can stand on any street in Spain and say what you think about the government but you cannot print it anywhere; that while Catalan refugees here are convinced that the Franco prisons are filled with Republican patriots, the Spanish in Spain are convinced that the prisons are filled with ordinary criminals, the patriots undoubtedly having perished long since. He adds that Franco's system is bad, but at present it is not being cruelly applied.

The Maestro lives in a gardener's old-fashioned cottage at the gate of a pretentious villa, on the edge of town, that belongs to a well-to-do non-refugee Catalan family named Marty-Roy. Young musicians who have been invited to Casals' sanctum to talk or play or listen say, almost with admiration, that he lacks absolute pitch, that his piano is tuned half a tone too low, that his cello, which is an eighteenth-century Goffriller, looks as if it had not been cleaned for a hundred years, that a piece of paper is stuck under the bridge to steady it, and that a broken matchstick is wedged under a string on the fiddle head to keep it taut. One of Casals' recent visitors was Burl Ives, who serenaded him outside his window one evening with "I Know Where I'm Going." The Maestro invited him in for more ballads and returned the compliment by playing some Bach for Ives. The Maestro's closest local friend is his physician, the Catalan Dr. René Puig, who serves on the Comité d'Action of Prades—leading citizens whose dazed but efficacious devotion to the cause of having their town turned upside down, mostly for visiting foreigners, is the basis on which the Festival really functions, outside of Bach. The Action Committee organized the housing in, and transportation to and from, the hotels for miles around, all of them grander than the Grand at Prades—spa hotels at Molitg-les-Bains and Thuès-les-Bains, and, for visitors with their own cars, Font-Romeu, which is forty kilometres distant, and even Collioure, the fishing port and artist colony over on the Mediterranean. Under this pressure of tourism, the local fishermen of mountain trout, which abound in the little River Têt, have jumped their prices from seven hundred francs a kilo to twelve hundred francs.

In the Prades locality, there is one resident, Frère Louis, an elderly monk, who has been particularly interested in conversing with visitors from New York. Having heard that the section of his cloister at Fort Tryon Park is splitting its friable stone under the extreme New York temperatures, he is worried and wants news. He dwells in a modern monastery beside the antique, ruined Abbey of St.-Michel-de-Cuxa, is toothless, polite, and ruddy-faced above his patched, well-tailored white wool habit, and acts as guide now that the unhappy cloister, which till recently had no pillar *in situ*, is being partially restored. Masons lately removed ten of its magnificently preserved pink marble columns, topped with white capitals of acanthus leaves and monster heads, from the façade of Prades's St. Pierre Church, where they were stuck in the last century. These columns are now mostly in place on the site of the old cloister, and around them will be reconstructed one of its four sides. The adjacent tenth-century abbey, now a great, gutted, roofless shell of thick walls and arches, became dilapidated, Frère Louis says, during the French Revolution; the hulk and cloister were then abandoned by the monks, and were eventually acquired by some French antiquarian. In 1913, the wrecked abbey was bought, and returned as a gift to the monks, by the American sculptor George Grey Barnard, who had located thirty-seven of the cloister's columns. These a Rockefeller fund purchased for the Metropolitan Museum in 1925, and the cloister at Fort Tryon Park was subsequently constructed around them. Frère Louis says that somebody once sent him a postcard of the Cloisters, which he still treasures, showing the columns in position in Manhattan, but he asks, please, for some other postcard, showing, perhaps, the herb garden they surround (he has a garden of sorts near the abbey), and he would also like a postcard of the Hudson River, which has been reported to him as so big that he cannot visualize it. Frère Louis also politely asks if the people of New York are likely to mind his praying that someday St.-Michel-de-Cuxa's thirty-seven columns will be returned.

III

꠷

Come Down, Giuseppe!

ROME, JANUARY 17, 1942 Rome, that great antique, is now the capital of Germany's newest province, Italy. To judge by information which reached here before Mussolini bustlingly declared war on the United States on December 11th, this latest war will change nothing; it will merely intensify everything that has been going on in Italy during the past six months. For years, Il Duce has been adjuring his subjects to "live like lions." In Italy, lions customarily live in cages. The Italians are now living like lions. In the nineteenth century, Italy went through bloody revolution, civil war, and other republicanisms, preliminary to founding a united, constitutional, modern kingdom specifically created to drive its German-speaking overlords back to their home in Vienna. Now, in 1942, Italy must listen to the new gentlemen from Berlin. At the close of the first World War, Il Duce invented Fascism as a twentieth-century, neoclassical imperial machine. Now, in the second World War, he is paying royalties on his own patent to Der Führer, who perfected the idea under Nazism.

Within the past six months, in many Italian public buildings, the portraits of King Emmanuel have been replaced by photographs of Adolf Hitler. According to recent and angrily informative correspondence, written before December by Italians to some of their five million relatives and friends living in our country, the German soldiery has been riding free in Italian tramcars while the Italian private has paid his own fare. The German Army rides first-class in Italian trains, with dining-car and sleeping accommodations, and in Italian stations Italian porters carry the German luggage exactly as if the visitors were foreign ladies. Meanwhile, the Italian soldiers eat, sleep, and travel in freight cars and tote their own kit, lighter now that there aren't enough extra boots or blankets to go around. In Germany, returned Italian workmen report, the *Hausfrau* serves to her family three times as much bread, five times as much meat, and seven times as much fat and oil as the Italian *mamma mia* is allowed for her rations, owing to the fact that the Nazis are importing—the polite old economic word is still used—at least eighty-five per cent of everything the Italian farmer raises on his lovely land. In some categories, the Nazi take is even higher. Last summer Germany absorbed four hundred and eighty per cent more Italian tomatoes than the year before. Italians love their tomatoes so much that they call them *pomidoro*, or golden apples, and, indeed, they cost Italians sixty cents a pound last July. There is little Napoletana sauce this winter to put on Italian spaghetti, since there is nearly no *pomidoro* paste. Neatly proportioned to the sauce is the weekly ration of three ounces of meat—a morsel of beef as big as two fingers. Furthermore, there is only a third as much spaghetti, that Italian staff of life, as is normal to the Italian plate. As the Italians soon learned to lament after the first World War, no matter who wins, Italy loses. Being a co-partner of what has been, up to now, the winner, Italy has so far lost enough to put her in a spot somewhere just above that of conquered France. The German system of occupation in both countries has been similar, the wording different, and the result practically the same, but the realization of what it means has been slower to take shape in and to shape the increasingly disillusioned Italian stomachs, ears, eyes, and minds.

According to letters received here—many in amateur code and many candid ones complacently passed by an inefficient censor—the Italian people, just before the Italo-American war broke out, apparently already revealed three important, clear-cut dissatisfactions, racial, political, and material, with their lot. The gravest and most incurable of these is the first, the Italian people's historic dislike of the German peoples. Whether Austrian or Prussian, they are all *Tedeschi*, so far as Italians are concerned, and suspect. To hate is part of the theoretical Fascist political stimuli, but so far the easy-going Italians have been failures at it. Though during the past few years the Italians haven't exactly loved their ideological enemies (the British blockaders; the French Popular Frontists, who contemptuously called even proud Romans *les macaronis*; and the godless, anti-Catholic Soviets), today the only race most Italians have learned to hate is their allies, the Germans. Not long before our Civil War began, Venice, plus about three-fourths of inland Italy, was still suffering under the harsh Austrian conqueror, and even Italian women, if too patriotic, were being given the bastinado by the Viennese *Gauleiters*. These bitter memories are still alive. Now, the Italians say, they are having to take orders in German for the first time since their national hero, red-shirted Giuseppe Garibaldi, led Italy and the Risorgimento to freedom from the Hapsburg yoke. Last spring, after the Italian defeat in the African campaign, three hundred thousand German soldiers suddenly began swarming into Italy in what was grimly called a gesture of fraternal solidarity. Shortly afterward, on the pedestals of the hundreds of statues of Garibaldi which animate Italy, one morning there appeared, scrawled in chalk, an appeal to their savior: *"Giuseppe, scendi! Ci sono i Tedeschi!"* ("Come down, Giuseppe! The Germans are here!")

Rome seems convinced that for every two high-up Italian Fascists in the government ministries there is at least one not even very high-up Nazi who successfully throws his weight about. Every Italian businessman knows that since last July the Nazis have taken over the management of the telephone exchanges, the post offices, the electric-power plants, the railroads, the bus, air, and shipping lines, and the radio stations.

Even though it is unlikely that many Italian women yearn to wed members of the occupying German Army, such a marriage is forbidden by the blond intruders in an Army decree, which, since it implicitly puts the black-headed Italians in a position of sub-Aryan inferiority, they find insulting. Even fraternization is forbidden to German soldiers, though probably not so much for fear of race pollution as to avoid street fights. Wherever German garrisons are stationed, Germans behave like aristocratic conquerors, take over the town's best restaurants, post signs saying "For Germans Only," and bring in their own German waiters. The German officers have already had experiences in ordinary Italian restaurants with Italian waiters, who, by pretending not to understand what the *Tedeschi* order, are able to bring them the worst dish on the menu. What with macaroni already reduced by ersatz flour to a nasty brownish color and taste, there are lots of bad dishes for waiters to choose from.

The second thing most Italians don't like in their own country is their politics. The main economic point of Fascism in the first place was that Italy was a poor country without enough colonies and the Italians were a poor people without enough hope, and that Fascism was going to provide a supply of both. Since the day that Axis politics pushed Italy into the war, Italian soldiers have been in a humiliating position to note that she has lost about three-quarters of her colonies to the British, that the Australians and Germans are fighting it out for possession of Italy's Libya, and that, though the pallid King of Italy is still theoretically Emperor of Ethiopia, Haile Selassie is the emperor who is physically sitting once more on the Ethiopian throne.

Among the inefficient Fascist War Council's bitterest critics are Italian parents whose sons froze to death on Greek mountains in cotton uniforms intended for other parents' sons fighting in Libya, where they probably received winter overcoats. Most Italian mothers and fathers also know that thousands of sons have been dying with the Germans in the disastrous Russian campaign in which, even if the Germans were not losing, the Italians would gain no province. Nor do the Italian soldiers expect to make a much better showing to the world now that they've been dragged into war with the United States—a war which, as Italians' letters to their American cousins made clear, many Italians were dreading as a sort of strange, unlucky civil war in which they would be fighting their far-away, foreign blood relatives.

Because Fascism is a nationalist ideology, much of its early strength and appeal came from its exalting of militant patriotism, which, as older citizens' enthusiasm cynically waned, still served to inspire the younger males. Now even they ask sadly, "Where is the patriotism of *il Fascismo?* It has handed unhappy Italy over to the Germans." And the university students, who from the beginning of Fascism until the entrance of Italy into Germany's war were the trained chalice-bearers and cheer-leaders of the Fascist regime, have finally defaulted. In the Universities of Naples and Padua last June, the students who were asked to form volunteer battalions as a spur to Italy's lagging military spirit bluntly demanded, in exchange, to be given passing marks in their examinations; furthermore, they threw paper wads, scribbled over with scandalous references to Il Duce, into Il Duce's visiting officials' faces. At the University of Rome, the students, rather than join up, chose to dunk their university president into a rococo fountain. From all the universities combined, exactly forty undergraduates enrolled for the voluntary battalions. As punishment for the students' attitude and because they were no longer to be trusted as young Fascist leaders, they are today drafted into the Army as common soldiers, though previously a student entered automatically as what used to be known as an officer and a gentleman.

Italy's third dissatisfaction—which is with material conditions, meaning principally insufficient food and fuel—is the most important of the trio of grievances, because the Italian population blames the shortages on the objects of the two other grievances, the hated Germans and the unpopular Fascist regime, so quite a cumulative effect is achieved. The food shortage in Italy, as in all parts of Europe except Germany, is unquestionably acute. Italian doctors say that the public health has actually improved because people are eating less starchy, oil-soaked *pasta.* The people say that they feel underfed and school children are usually sleepy from malnutrition. The dread pellagra has reappeared in the valley of the Po. What seems to be undeniable is that Italy is reduced to living on fifteen per cent of the food she used to consume. Even middle-class wives who have had enough time to stand interminably in food queues and enough money to patronize the black market on the side have said in letters received here that the preoccupation with food fills their days and nights. Poor city people, who have no extra time or money, merely take their regular rationed quantities of food, principally cheese, though it's low in fat content; vegetables, though oil to cook them in is often lacking; and bread, though sixty per cent of its contents is several things other than wheat. Some school children were recently asked to state in class what a good Italian's patriotic duty was in wartime. One little miss, daughter of a high Fascist official, gave as her definition "In wartime every good Italian should hoard food, like my dear mamma." Hoarding can be punished by heavy fines or death.

Because of the increased impatient grumbling of these Italian masses, the Fascist Party has recently threatened what it dialectically calls "a return to the origins." Evidently this phrase refers to the brutal repressive acts on which Fascism based its difficult rise to power. The Fascists are still in power, and, perhaps because of the dissatisfaction they give, will probably be held there, if only by their Machiavellian German ally.

The second material shortage, that of fuel, falls more equally than the food scarcity on rich and poor alike. Nature failed to endow Italy with coal, war with England cut off English anthracite, and Germany is now the coal baron of Europe. This winter she made Italy pay in advance for a ration of household coal for a normal one hundred and twenty-five days of winter heating, then sent enough for only forty days of seven hours a day, at a total cost to the householder of about $24 per room. Italy, being out of luck generally, is now enduring the coldest winter she has known in twenty years. To keep warm in their apartments, smart young Roman matrons wear their chilly ersatz woollen slacks, which a recent edict forbids them to wear on the street. (Slacks were popularized among chic Italian women by Contessa Edda Ciano, Mussolini's daughter.) Peasants, to keep warm and cook their noontime dinners, have been cutting down their magnificent old olive and mulberry trees for fuel. This has scandalized the Germans, who say they need the olives for oil and the mulberry leaves for silkworms, which in turn are needed to make silk for German parachutes. Doubtless, however, no German could be as shocked at the necessity for these destructive rural deeds as the classic-souled, landscape-loving Italian, axe in hand.

These short coal rations which Germany is sending to Italy seem to some seasoned observers not so much proof of a scarcity caused by war and transportation difficulties as evidence of a German industrial plan to destroy partner Italy as well as everybody else in Europe. Certainly it is noteworthy that in the past twelve months Germany has sent only thirty per cent of the commercial coal which Italy needs for her vital domestic and war industries. Because of this shortage, many of the biggest factories

225

of Milan and Turin are losing one out of every six work hours. As a result, impatient German suggestions have already been made to Italian capitalists that, since Italians don't seem to get much done anyhow, they should ship their factory machinery to the Rhineland, where men are blonds. Furthermore, as for labor, Germany since August has been demanding that ten per cent of Italy's skilled workmen should volunteer, as the Germans call it, to work in Germany. The volunteering is arranged by a Nazi official's conscripting every tenth man on the Fascists' lists of skilled laborers and bundling him off to Germany. There, curiously enough, these Italians, whose delicate fingers have been trained in the tradition of a nation that produced the wonderworks of the Renaissance and who today are still rated as the most dexterous and talented artisans of Europe, are put to work as laborers in the fields or are sent down with a pick and shovel into the mines. Reports smuggled out by these men to their families back home declare that in the bombed districts the Germans, whenever it is possible, are decentralizing their factories by installing the machinery in the laborers' cottages. The men also mention queer, repellent Nazi foods. These included ersatzes which they had heard of but had never had to taste before and something which the Nazis described as artificial blood. This horrified the drafted Italian workmen, who have always been too poor to have much taste for meat but who, when they get it, like it well done.

Small businessmen are now also angry as the government and the war push them to the wall. Though one of Fascism's earliest popular planks was a promise to save the little businessman at the expense of the big, rich combines, today the Italian state grants to the great corporations the exclusive right to buy and sell materials vital to the conduct of the war. The result is a series of big-business Fascist oligarchies, busy supplying the tools to fight what they call other countries' plutocracies. As for the Italian poor, they angrily say that the only people who could ever have hoped to grow rich on Fascism are the Party Fascists. Even the government newspapers, in a nervous attempt to regain the people's favor and trust, last autumn indignantly reported prosecutions of Fascist Party men (usually small fry) for trafficking in the black food market at terrific prices and profits. Three months ago the black market went out of business, not because of reform but because there was no longer sufficient food to supply it. One of the things kept out of the papers is all news of the wave of robberies which, because of poverty, is sweeping through the cities. For years after Mussolini came to power he was praised as the man who made Italian trains run on time and suppressed Italy's bands of thieves. Today workmen waste hours on slow street cars, and throughout Italy second-story men have been so busy at night that some large insurance companies refuse to insure householders against robbery.

In higher commercial circles, the venality which is spreading like a plague over all Europe as a result of gross or petty tyrannies, business restrictions, and the thousands of permits that must be signed before contracts can be undertaken has forced bribery onto most Italian businessmen as a bureaucratic expedient. The businessman has found he can speed things up only by giving fat presents to Fascist Party officials, to their lobbying henchmen, or to Fascist Party officials' lady friends, who, as members of an old, influential European profession, seem to be coming into their own again. Even men now prefer bribes of jewelry to money. In September, the sale of jewelry was forbidden, but there is still no law against giving it away. The Fascist government's October announcement that the forthcoming annual budget would take three-quarters of the Italian national income, the consequent crack on the Rome stock market, the soaring of prices of necessities, which in some cases cost five times what they did a year ago, and an increase of about twenty-five per cent in the volume of paper currency have demoralized any remaining civilized esteem for money per se, even as graft.

There is no banner for anything like open rebellion in Italy and no chief to wave it. There is a bitter joke in Rome today that everybody is anti-Fascist, including the Fascists. Certainly the diehard Fascists now follow Nazi Germany rather than Mussolini. Their bellwether is Roberto Farinacci, owner of the Cremona newspaper *Regime Fascista*. He is described as being Italy's own Darlan, a critic and German-manipulated puppet rival of Mussolini, and thus sponsor for the greater-collaboration-with-Germany movement. The lukewarm anti-German Fascists say that if Germany wins, Hitler will get rid of Mussolini, and if Germany loses, Italy will get rid of Mussolini, and in either case they, the moderates, will swing into power. A Leftish movement, if not revolution, is more likely. Many upper-class, unpolitical Italians hope that Italy is the weak point in Germany's empire that will cause Germany to lose the war. Many Army men have lately begun to feel that a defeated Italy could be part of Germany's morbid, metaphysical world plan. Few Italians have any faith in their royal house; they call it *un pesce in barile,* which means a fish in a barrel, or, in our own terms, someone who carries water on both shoulders.

For centuries Italians have had a talent for secret, subversive societies. The strange trials just ended at Trieste, involving so-called anti-Italian activities dated 1938, are interpreted as being the government's belated acknowledgement of the anti-Fascist movements now rapidly gaining in popularity in Italy. The underground societies, upon which some people, especially in England and America, perhaps put too much hope, employ elaborate codes and precautions. The leaders organize sabotage, such as slowdowns in factories engaged in war work, or help foment unrest, such as the violent bread strikes which took place in Turin and Milan last June. Society members boycott newspapers every Thursday. Since all papers are owned by Party leaders, this buying strike hits some Fascist pocketbook. By their grapevine method, the societies distribute endless pamphlets and, what is more valuable, pass on news heard through the forbidden American and English shortwave broadcasts, though the punishment for listening to any foreign station not controlled by the Nazis has just been trebled to eighteen months' imprisonment.

The general tendency of these societies is so far not revolutionary but purely republican, on the Mazzini or Garibaldi model. There is a republican pirate radio station, called La Voce della Libertà, operated by a democratic group brave enough to risk death, or at least *confino*, the Italian version of the concentration camp. Among some younger workingmen, especially since Russia came into the war, there has been a reanimation of the Communist groups, which for the past twenty years have been so well organized that now the other societies are copying their cellular framework. The young Communists in Italy employ an odd dialectic device called *vittimismo*, or victimization, which consists of getting themselves put in prison in order to focus the anti-Fascist attention and faith of the Italian working classes, supposedly easily impressed by martyrdom. On the whole, though, the fight against godless Russia has been more popular in Catholic Italy than any other campaign in this unpopular war. Among the young intellectuals the great movement is the Movimento Universitario Rivoluzionario Italiano, which began last June with the anti-war demonstrations of the students at the University of Rome and has since spread to all the colleges. Their program is simple: no dictatorship, no Germans. Their propaganda is poetic; the students go about reciting the verses of the noted Risorgimento poets.

There is also a unique, mysterious Roman group, called the Organization of the Lost Sheep (Organizzazione delle Pecorelle Smarrite), which is probably anti-Fascist, though it may be only pro-profit. At any rate, Italians who have thousand-lire notes in their pockets and are willing to be driven in a car with its curtains drawn, so they cannot identify the neighborhood or house where the Lost Sheep operate, can usually obtain from them passports to flee the country or other vital papers.

Against all the anti-Fascist secret societies in Italy are arrayed thirteen governmental spy organizations, each of which is empowered to make arrests and which spies concentratedly in its own field—Army, Navy, government offices, or whatever. The most feared and hated are the Ovra, which is Italy's Gestapo, and Mussolini's private spy troop, the Informatori Privati del Duce.

Letters from Italy written to known anti-Fascists here just before December were carefully censored by Italian authorities, whole portions being neatly snipped out by a razor blade or blacked out with India ink. Most of the poor Italian families here continued to receive their news untouched and couched in simple domestic code. As one November letter forcefully phrased it, "Papa's [Mussolini's] house [Italy] is infested with bedbugs [Germans.] It is useless to try insecticide [rebellion] on this kind of hard-shelled vermin. As long as poor Papa lives he is our master and we must wait. We really wish he were dead. He is full of diseases."

A more elegant and pensive letter of revelation from a young upper-middle-class Roman matron painfully paints her family's tableau as an illustration of what is happening to the life she once knew. "No one makes plans," she writes. "We all live from day to day. There is little gay news. Cousin Maria has announced her marriage, but there is little hope for happiness in times like these. Uncle Carlo has just given Aunt Teresina a 200,000-lire sable coat and bought himself a string of race horses. What with and what for?" The letter goes on to say that Uncle Carlo's factory in Turin had some new government contracts, which probably paid more than they should. Business was like that in war-torn Europe and everyone first bought things and then sold things in a circle of confusion. The food shortage had affected Aunt Luisa's liver; there was a great deal of liver trouble, even among the young. Aunt Luisa's older son's feet had been frozen in the Greek mountain campaign and one, perhaps both, had been amputated. The younger boy, Luigi, had been sent to the Russian front; no news, of course. The writer's favorite brother, Ernesto, was a test pilot of planes to be sent to Africa.

"It breaks my heart. He won't last long," she wrote. "Our shortage of good materials makes plane-testing even more dangerous than being a sailor"—a sly reference to the sinkings of the poorly armored Italian warships. If you could believe it, Cousin Rosetta, who always used to be going to Mass, now had a lover, a *nouveau riche* who had given her an appalling emerald bracelet. The breakdown in morale among their old school friends was absolutely frightening. Her sister-in-law had given up bridge for poker and run up huge gambling debts. The writer's own little daughter, Bianca, was well but underweight, like everybody, and was having calcium and vitamin injections as long as they could afford them and medical supplies held out. Doctors had no gasoline for their cars and therefore could make no calls on distant patients; everyone was terrified of falling ill. Servants, *grazie a Dio*, were still cheap, though her last two maids had been called back to work on their families' farms. Oh, yes, Aunt Teresina's eldest sister, the sweet, unmarried one, had nearly no money, kept to her room, refused to look at any newspapers, and read nothing but Dante.

"The deformed economics we are living in are unbalancing many people's minds," the last paragraph added. "I am finishing this letter while waiting to make what we call a 'deal' with a peasant for a sack of potatoes and one of beans. It is the big business of the week. Supplies are so precious that we keep everything locked up against thieves and even against the cook. My cupboard keys hang at my belt and when I walk around the house I rattle like the chatelaine of a medieval fortress. I don't think we will die of hunger, but my husband says business will starve. We are still in love; married couples who are happy are rare now. We lack moral and intellectual satisfactions to keep us going. Foreign novels are forbidden. Theatres and movies are zero. In Rome, music has been good. Berlin sends us Furtwängler and Gieseking, and in exchange we send Berlin our De Sabata and Molinari, maestro of our Augusteo symphony orchestra. No one thinks the good old life can ever come back. Despite bombs in Naples and Genoa and lack of food everywhere, existence is still relatively bearable if you have some money. I think we Italians are confused by the war and its many meanings and developments. In this super-civilization, materialism has become of supreme importance and realism has seized us, and they have both come on the scene only in time to destroy, as they did in France."

Apparently the sole consolation of millions of thoughtful Italians, rich or humble, is that after twenty years Italians still make poor Fascists, that *mamma mia*, home, the Virgin Mary, a sense of the ridiculous, solo songs, laughter, individualism, and meridional dispositions are possessions that cannot be regimented.

This last autumn the season at Salsomaggiore, which ranks socially as Italy's White Sulphur Springs, was feverishly brilliant. Because of the war in the Mediterranean, all seaside resorts had been closed during the summer, and this fashionable Lombardy thermal station profited. At the leading hotel, since Italy's youth was away on one front or another, there were no men under forty. The male guests, however, were at least solid millionaires, Party bigwigs, great industrialists, men on the make, and royalty. The women guests dressed dashingly for dinner, orchids were as common as daisies, and the display of jewels was astonishing even for Cellini-loving Italy. The bracelets and cabochons exchanged for weekend favors were a feature of the Monday lunch. According to one shrewd, worldly widow present, the hedonism, the gems, the frenetic, rich nocturnal scene behind the lighted windows and the long, black vista stretching to the peasant poor in the country outside were like a mistake in history, as if Italy had suddenly slipped and fallen back into the conscienceless time of some medieval de' Medici.

There will be no more letters from Italy, except those smuggled out, until the war comes to an end. The last ones to arrive describe *la patria* as a country caught in its own Latin variety of Europe's Nordic turmoil—an Italy filled with people who were losing the hope and the habit of their lives, of men frantically making money or laboriously going without it, of ersatz morals growing as shoddy as ersatz clothes, of the soul of a classical people focussed on a mere dish of food, and, over an antique landscape and its architecture, an intimation of bad weather, like a cloud of melancholy.

In Rome, in November, there was a story going the rounds which ran as follows: a man fishing in the Tiber caught a very small minnow. To the minnow, which he lifted from his line and took in his hand, he apostrophized, "O little fish, what can I do with thee? I cannot fry thee; I have no olive oil. I cannot roast thee; I have no butter. I cannot bake thee; I have no flour. Indeed, I cannot cook thee at all, since I have no fuel for my hearthstone. There remains naught I can do with thee but toss thee back into the Tiber." This he did. A moment later the minnow rose to the surface, lifted his fin in the familiar salute and cried, *"Viva Il Duce!"* This fish was the last Fascist.

Letter from Rome

NOVEMBER 21, 1945 There is, paradoxically, more Latin vitality in Rome, capital city of Italian defeat, than in Paris, which was on the winning side. France lost her prestige in her fateful fall in 1940 and her psyche still suffers. The Italians, who haven't had a chance to bother about prestige since Julius Caesar and the Renaissance de' Medici, and who have the philosophic habit of being losers even when they're among the victors, actually won something this time, though they had to lose the war to do it. They won the fall of Fascism. This triumph, along with the people's instinct for survival as a classic race, makes Rome seem animate to a degree that is rare among what is left of Europe's capital cities today.

The Via Condotti, the most elegant shopping street south of the Alps, offers the amazing postwar spectacle of beautiful things to buy, though they are scarce. The Nazis would be outraged if they could see the fine leathers, wools, and silks which their Axis ally sensibly and disloyally hid—ladies' handbags, lingerie, and men's fine suitings at forty thousand lire a suit. Even the black-market *nouveaux riches* are beginning to find the prices they themselves set too steep. Jewellers or silversmiths who buy, sell, or reset family heirlooms are about the only people doing a big business. Families with valuable objects, and without the five hundred lire it can cost one person to eat decently for one day, slowly sell their belongings on their way downhill. People with cash don't trust it, with the lire at three hundred and fifty-one to the black-market dollar, so they buy emeralds or *ottocento* chairs. Rome's auction rooms are bustling and sad. The black market, which in France is modestly hidden, in Rome is as visible as a naked marble statue in a public piazza. It is everywhere—at the Porta Pinciana, where handsome girls sell battered, single American cigarettes; at the Campo de' Fiori, among the succulent still lifes of the cheese shops; and on the sunny corners where the hawkers' carts stand. So many elegant Romans are wearing black-market British and American Army blankets made up into overcoats—dyed all the darker colors—that there is a popular verse in Roman dialect, sung to the tune of "Pistol Packin' Mamma," which declares that the blanket wearers hide when an Allied general walks by. *Il Globo*, Rome's leading financial daily, solemnly quotes the black-market prices for foreign monies and domestic foods; British gold is quoted right next to meat either with bones or (at a hundred lire higher) without.

The disparity between what Rome's rich and poor eat is not much greater now than it has often been in her cruel and backward past, but the sense of injustice is larger, angrier, and more dangerous. Under Fascism, even the poorest folk had steaming spaghetti and olive oil. Oil is now six hundred and thirty lire a litre. Coal is so costly that the poor bitterly say it would be cheaper to burn their paper money in the kitchen stove. Landlords are among the new poor. They have been allowed only a slight boost in rents in ten years. One pet-loving landlord of a midtown nine-room flat gets eight hundred lire a month in rent, which just pays the food bill for his two cats. In Milan, a city that was half bombed out, anyone who will move out of a furnished room, which generally rents for fifteen thousand a month, can get a set price of six hundred thousand lire. In Turin, where the northern fogs have been followed by freezing weather, schools are closing for lack of windowpanes and heat, and postmen are refusing to deliver letters because they have no shoes. Because they sabotaged the electric plants, Turin patriots, as well as other citizens, now eat a cold dinner by candlelight. The war has apparently exhausted even the Italian rains. The summer drought left the land so hard that peasants have not been able to plow in order to sow their winter wheat.

Italy's present is painful, and to most Italians the future looks precarious. Yet the habit of history and the drama of change have once more vitalized Rome.

Certainly government here is full of troubles. As the Italians piously cry, "Christ on earth couldn't govern in such conditions." Ex-schoolmaster Premier Ferruccio Parri and his Ministers have proved themselves to be anti-Fascist, intelligent, honest, and inexperienced, and by conscientiously representing all six parties of the National Resistance, from Communist Left to Liberal Right, they neutralized themselves to begin with and then were pompously paralyzed by the Allies. By backing the Right all over Europe and the King and Badoglio in Rome, by claiming that the Parri democratic, partisan government lacks strength (what it most lacks, under the Allied armistice terms, is trade treaties to provide work and food, and what it lacks almost as badly is enough police to keep burglars, let alone hungry political rioters, in order), and by miscellaneous other acts of commission and omission, the Americans and British have seen to it that the first fine fervor of anti-Fascist, pro-democratic feeling is dying. The British in Italy take a colonial attitude toward the natives. As for America's attitude, the Italians think that it is exemplified by President Truman's and Secretary Byrnes' statements that they had never even read the belatedly announced terms of the armistice granted by the Allies.

The young Italian generation, educated in Fascism, is disoriented but more than anything else reactionary. The city's twenty-three newspapers, which were all ready to boost democracy, especially after the assassination of that talkative tyrant in Milan, are now sensitively sliding toward a reactionary Right. Even the dwindling Italian Communist Party declares that all it now desires is mere democracy. In Italy's groping confusion there is a fantastic popular movement called the Forty-niners, the purpose of which is to have Italy added to our own forty-eight states. Another, less naïve national movement, Qualunquismo—named after the weekly *Uomo Qualunque*, or *Any Man*—has been gaining influence among anti-Leftists in the boot provinces of the country. This movement, which has no constructive program, merely stands for discontentment. The paper, which has a circulation of half a million, was founded last January as a possible money-making freak by a red-faced, middle-aged blond Neapolitan named Guglielmo Giannini, a former tenth-rate writer of killer-diller movie thrillers. The idea was that southern Italians might be amused to read about their general complaints on postwar life in addition to voicing them. Qualunquismo soon became an abscess. The Roman Socialist paper *Avanti* claimed that the movement was being backed by the Scalera brothers, once prominent and Fascist, and probably still reactionary and rich, but in any case now in jail.

Italian Films

DECEMBER 1, 1945 The best film in Europe is Italian, and it has not been presented at Santa Cecilia's festival. It is called "Città Aperta" ("Open City") and is a story of resistance Roman shoeshine ragamuffins and their priest, who is shot by the Germans, and of parents who are separated from their children by death or imprisonment. It is a moving, inspiring, living tragedy of young and aged fraternity and of family devotion, and it is the first great resistance film to come out of Europe— perhaps the best picture Italy has ever made. It is the fourth picture of a young cinematographer, Roberto Rossellini, and was made during the difficult winter of 1944–1945 without a permit, without studio lights, often without any electricity at all, on five-year-old remnants of film, in a deserted ballroom off the Via del Tritone. Vito, the star bootblack of the film, is now back bootblacking on the piazzas as the breadwinner for his mother and five younger brothers and sisters; his father died in one of the bombings of Rome.

NOVEMBER 9, 1946 A remarkably fine new Italian film, "Paisan" ("Buddy"), directed by the gifted newcomer Rossellini, who made the extraordinary "Open City," has just been given a gala preview. It was shown in an exquisite eighteenth-century baroque private theatre—made into a projection room—in one of the grandiose old palaces now comfortably occupied by the Roman film industry. The picture is made up of a half-dozen unrelated human incidents, or short stories, some tragic, some humorous, all of them separated geographically and yet all part of the

Italian panorama and those patches of its population that became involved with Partisanship and with the invading Anglo-Saxons during the war. With one or two exceptions, the film is acted not by professional actors but by peasants, by ex-Partisans or their widows and children, by our G.I.s, and by monks. The dialogue is a mixture of Italian and English. In time, the film runs from the Sicilian landings through the stalemate at the Gothic Line to the battles in the Po Valley. The first episode has to do with the language difficulties of war: a Sicilian peasant girl tries unsuccessfully to save a G.I. on a lonely outpost from being shot by German snipers and then is herself shot by other G.I.s, simply because she isn't able to explain what it's all about. Then there is a wonderful, typically jovial Neapolitan incident in which an enormous, drunken Negro M.P. on a binge is bought for a few lira, practically like a slave, by a little ragamuffin who wants to steal his shoes. A brilliant recreation of the liberation of Florence shows street fighting between Partisans and Fascists as the dangerous sidewalk civil war it must have been. In this episode an English nurse searches for her Italian lover in the front-line streets and ends up in a doorway holding someone else's lover, dead, whom she never saw before. The most amazing acting in the movie is done by some old monks in a Gothic Line monastery, who had never seen a movie and didn't know they were being filmed. The episode they figure in is like a chapter in Rabelais. Three American Army chaplains—a Catholic, a Protestant, and a Jew—beg a night's hospitality among the monks, who, when they discover that the last two visitors are not Catholic, start fasting in an effort to convert them to the only true faith. The final, and longest, episode, which takes place in the rice paddies and marshes of the Po Valley, is concerned with the hopeless fight of two secret-service officers, an American and a Briton, who are parachuted into that watery waste, where the ill-equipped Partisans are losing their fight against the well-equipped Germans and against drowning. In this last episode, everything but courage itself is drowned.

MAY 15, 1948 There was a private showing of an extraordinary new film, "Germania—Anno Zero," made in Berlin, and in German, by the master Italian film director, Rossellini, creator of "Open City" and "Paisan." His detractors claim that again he has turned out nothing more than a superb documentary. The truth is that, as in his other postwar films, he has used contemporary history as a documented background for his human drama. The hero of this opus is played by a blond boy of thirteen, Edmund Menschke, a Berliner and, like the rest of the cast, an amateur. The drama unrolled in the film is tragic, simple, and devoid of sentimentality. It details, amid the Berlin ruins, the sad development and end of Edmund, young and shapeless enough to be forced into the rotten Berlin black-market struggle by his bourgeois family—his old-fashioned, bedridden father, his pro-Nazi hero of a brother, and his refined sister, who nobly refuses to become a prostitute. In the boy's confusion over his growing burdens, and at the amoral advice of friends, he poisons his father to eliminate one hungry mouth, and, after having been slapped by a teacher for his crime (since he is so young a murderer), hurls himself to his death from his family's bombed-out apartment into the bombed-out street below.

Once again, Rossellini has worked out a theme that ranks with those of the great novelists. Once again, he has followed his procedure of directing and photographing a film without a script, relying only on his imagination and an idea, which he develops as he goes along. The German dialogue of the film is diffuse, probably because Rossellini does not know the language. Technically, the film shows some of the earmarks of its director's sudden success. It is loosely put together and needs emphasis and cutting. Nevertheless, it is still the most remarkable European film of this year.

Rossellini, Zampa, De Sica

JANUARY 28, 1949 After the war, three youngish Italian cinema directors—Roberto Rossellini, Luigi Zampa, and Vittorio De Sica—began separately to experiment with a new, naturalistic type of film, based on a special blend of disorganization, penury, realism, and imagination. For plots, they took the unused dramas that postwar history was writing around their own people's lives. Their films have become internationally famous; four of them—Rossellini's "Open City" and "Paisan," De Sica's "Shoe-Shine," and Zampa's "To Live in Peace"—have won major American awards. These men have founded a literary-celluloid Italian style of realistic storytelling. The latest example has just made its appearance here —De Sica's "Ladri di Biciclette," or "Bicycle Thieves." Even the commercial cinema people regard it as a *capo lavoro*. It was produced last summer and cost eighty million lire, which at the time amounted to $133,000. It deals with a Roman father who is out of work and the effect of this circumstance upon his child, one of those competent, symbolic little Italian boys who in the films stand for the overpopulation that is part of every poor Italian family's drama. The film offers fat streaks of humor and long, lean strips of sadness. It was acted by non-professionals. The leading characters are an unemployed mechanic and his spry young son. Papà is offered a job as billposter, provided he can get his bicycle out of hock, it being requisite for transporting him and the tools of his new trade. He and his wife retrieve the bicycle by pawning their bed linen. While he is slapping up his first advertising poster—it happens to be one showing Rita Hayworth—on a Roman wall, his bicycle is stolen. The major part of the picture is the vain chase of father and son through the streets of Rome, through a church, through a bordello (its door is respectably slammed in the little boy's face), and through the crowds at a junk fair to find the bike, or at least the thief. In the end, the desperate father steals somebody else's bicycle, is instantly caught by the owner, and is beaten but not turned over to the police. This is the quasi-happy ending.

Neither this nor any other of these films has been very popular with the Italian critics or the Italian moviegoers, though Zampa enjoyed a certain success with "The Honorable Angelina," starring the magnificent Anna Magnani—a comedy about the useless rebellion of some poor Roman matrons against the housing shortage. The pictures are, however, a great success in the United States, France, Brazil, Argentina, and Chile. "Angelina" was the film hit of last year in Buenos Aires, where it pushed even the North American films into a back seat. Another, Alessandro Blasetti's "Four Steps in the Clouds," the story of a henpecked candy salesman, made a hit in Paris a year and a half ago, and more recently in New York. It was an unusually flat failure in Rome. It was made from an early script by a young Florentine named Piero Tellini, who is the most gifted transcriber of life for the Italian films. He wrote the scripts for "To Live in Peace," "The Honorable Angelina," "One of a Crowd," and "Many Dreams Along the Way," and for Zampa's new film "The Tocsin," made last summer on the island of Ischia and to be released here next month. Tellini's private intellectual interest is the study of metaphysics, especially the Pythagorean mysteries. Rossellini uses no script writer; he simply starts out with an idea and a camera and makes up the plot as he goes along, a practice that drives his company mad. To date, none of this group of directors has developed the Hollywood touch.

Yet Hollywood's output is what the Italian filmgoers and critics prefer. Miss Hayworth, or Tyrone Power, dubbed, is a hot favorite over any bicycle thief. The flickering genius of these Italian films, with their mixture of realism and fine, voluble acting, their classic pathos and fleshy humor, their background of poverty and the picturesque, and, above all, their new technique, which turns them into documentaries of postwar history, of neighborhoods, or of human hearts and pocketbooks—all this, which is rare novelty to the rest of us, is too familiar to the Italians. Such films are bits of their own lives. The Italians would rather look at things strange, rich, and unreal, like the lives invented in Hollywood. That is probably the biggest backhanded compliment in the movie business.

Letter from Capri

OCTOBER 15, 1946 In the three years since the Fifth Army landed on Salerno beach, a quarter of a million American soldiers and officers have come to spend their leave on this year-round resort island of Capri, and they are still coming, a few hundred a month. It was the first rest center our armed forces had in all Europe. A mountain of rock that has weathered centuries of males cutting didos on it, beginning with the time of the hedonistic Emperor Tiberius, Capri has withstood the American visitation better than some of the more modern leave spots, such as Paris and Cannes. In the summer of 1945, when Americans were still pouring into the island's infinitesimal port at the rate of a thousand a week, the American military governor felt it his duty to requisition one of the grandest villas above Saracena Beach just for the convenience of brass-hat bathers. At that time, a house belonging to Gracie Fields was being used as an American officers' snack bar, and a hideous mansion belonging to Countess Edda Ciano was still, though situated high on a peak, a pilgrimage center for our more energetic souvenir hunters, who admired her majolica bathroom tiles. During this period, too, the flocks of jeeps careening down the precipitous curves of the island's roads nearly scared the one-horse *carrozzelle* out of business. The Capri boatman's favorite new American expression in those days was "hubba hubba." These unhurried days, the visiting American soldier's favorite expression is *"aspet',"* Neapolitan dialect for "wait." The Widow Ciano's villa is now reserved for honeymooning officers and brides. Miss Fields has recently been in brief residence on what is once more her private property. Mrs. Harrison Williams, arriving by yacht not long ago, spent four days in her pink villa. There remains only one jeep—with trailer. It takes our military bathers to the Marina Piccola every day at noon and returns at sundown to pick them up. (The azure waters are so tepid that the bathing season continues into November.) The only major establishments still requisitioned are the Hotel Tiberio, for our soldiers, and the Hotel Quisisana, for our officers.

In their hotels, the conquerors have been consuming their Spam, canned peas, and canned compote of California fruit, and have been squirting their canned lemon juice into their drinks, on an island where lemon trees abound, where the modest *trattorie* on the Piazza give off the scent of fresh lamb cooking in olive oil and rosemary, where the doorways of cavernous shops are brightened by the brilliant, spectacular fresh fruits and vegetables of southern Italy—giant red and yellow pimientos, super-giant, two-pound, pink-cheeked Roman peaches, albino or mauve eggplants, almond-shaped melons, gold-flecked muscat grapes, and white or Paisley-purple figs. It's safe to say that our officers and men here have eaten worse than any peasant on the island—a real tribute to what is now the one strictly enforced commissary rule of an army whose soldiers' black-marketeering of cigarettes and supplies still sets the unofficial rate of exchange in occupied, inflated Europe. They eat rigorously, respectably, and dully the chow sent from home, and not like locusts, as did their German predecessors. Because a night-club setting is regarded as the only appropriate one for our Army messes in Europe, the Quisisana Spam has, at least, been served to the ceaseless strains of music. Until two in the morning over the weekends, there have lately wafted through the palms and porticoes of the hotel garden the insistent trumpetings of an Italian orchestra, perhaps competent at "O Sole Mio" but ordered to try to tootle "In the Mood," while from balcony bedrooms have come the squeals of officers' infants longing for sleep. The Army's glorious, unbridled, carefree days on leave are over; the nice wives have arrived from the Middle West, and breakfast at the Quisisana is no longer a hangover but a baby parade.

Despite Capri's uniquely uncomfortable rocky beaches and its loin-straining hills, it attracted, during the twenties and the first half of the thirties, an ease-loving, semi-intelligentsia international crowd of Romans, Neapolitans, Anglo-Saxons, and Parisians, who, by preferring the island's sophisticated rusticities to the more worldly beauties of the Lido, revived its antique popularity. It was not until the war in Ethiopia, when Fascism really began strutting, that the Ciano group suddenly infested Capri and with its xenophobia drove out the internationals. Lenin had once visited the island in exile, to think. Now the vaporous Italian royalties came, and the heavy-chic Nazis (such as the late Reichsmarschall Göring), the Mussolini hierarchy, its gilded sycophants from the Roman *palazzi*, and its steely-eyed followers among the Milanese industrialists—Europe's new power group, some now long in their graves, others just finished dying. Today, when Capri has been mostly given back to the Italians, the island is a small financial thermometer that shows which vacationing classes have been most affected by the fevers of inflation. Certainly the Capri holiday class least touched, of those that date back to the pre-Ciano days, is the wealthy Neapolitan nobles—buxom duchesses and handsome young counts whose vast, rich farmlands have been under their escutcheons since feudal times and whose agrarian attitude is still medieval. (It is on their estates that the politically fermenting peasants have recently been squatting, claiming that the acreage is theirs by human right, because their sweat has watered it for generations.) The wheat and olive crops on the Neapolitan nobles' farms are wonderful this year, and their anti-Republic and pro-Monarchy wailings are shrill, while the government ration of spaghetti and olive oil continues to be hardly enough to keep a Neapolitan ragamuffin alive, apparently because he represents the lowest form of Italian life. Another well-off holiday class on Capri is at the other end of the social scale—newcomers nobody knows and everybody recognizes at a glance as the flashy, fat Neapolitan black-marketeers and their plump females.

The hardest-hit class among the old visitors, judging by its almost total absence, is the small intellectuals—the artists and minor poets—whose modest incomes were often hardly enough for existence, let alone holidays. Inflation prices have made these incomes almost derisory. Enrico Prampolini, one of the early Italian Futurists, who goes back in international art history to the *Little Review* days, was doyen of this past summer's art colony, and Alberto Moravia, perhaps Italy's most talented and unpredictable novelist, was naturally the leader of the literary group on the island. His new novel, written here and named "Agostino" because he finished it in August, will soon be published in translation in America. He has also been working on the scenario of Jean-Paul Sartre's play "Huis Clos," which is soon to be filmed in Italy. But the most noticeable vacuum in Capri has probably been caused by travel difficulties rather than financial ones: the absence of those famous foreign eccentrics—usually British and artistic, literary, or rich—who used to superanimate the island. This summer, this group's sole representative was Norman Douglas, who, at the age of seventy-eight, still had the panic vitality to clamber twice daily down from the Villa Borselli, high on the rocky center of the island, to the Marina Piccola and back up again. In a day's tour of Sorrento, he added one more to the local legends about him—a Socratic promenade that started at six, in the early daylight, and ended in the late dusk, at nine, and included a large share of eleven litres of southern wines.

Other figures from the legendary past emerged in ink, at least, with the appearance, after all these years, of an Italian translation of Compton Mackenzie's once scandalous Capri classic, "Extraordinary Women." The Italian title is "Donne Pericolose," which is not the same thing. The few copies that have appeared in the bookshops here have been gobbled up. The only item of even quasi-literary significance our soldiers have been interested in is small silver souvenir bells for their lapels—miniatures of the bell from San Michele, the San Michele of Axel Munthe, of whom they seem not to have heard. Their only interest in local art has been to have their cameo portraits cut, from photographs, by the rather fine local lapidarists—fragile likenesses of pilot Butch or Bill, Air Corps cap cocked over one eye, to send home to Mom for a brooch.

There are eight thousand natives of Capri, most of them poor, hard-working, and pious. In the recent Republic vs. Monarchy vote, the island's fishermen, peasants, and artisans voted in an enthusiastic, overwhelming majority, and with a certain amount of encouragement from their priests, for their King. The exceptions were the island's six hundred Communists, whose party chief is a popular *carrozzella* driver named Peppino. Capri's cliffs, garden walls, and breakwater still bear election slogans ("*Viva Savoia*" is the most frequent), which political energy painted on overnight months ago but which only time will take the trouble slowly to efface. Fearing that the hammer and sickle, which the more godly peasants actually regard as symbols of the evil eye, would do the Communists harm rather than good, Peppino's men merely tried to counteract "Up with the King" scrawls by "Down with the King" scrawls. These they achieved by painting upside down the two "V"s of "*Viva*," which are the symbol for up and which in their topsy-turvy position indicated down. It was not very direct action.

Postscript to Nuremberg

DECEMBER 7, 1946 A postscript to the Nuremberg trials is being written in a makeshift courtroom in the ancient Sapienza University of Rome. There are, however, certain differences in the two proceedings. This time, the victims' widows, weeping among the court spectators, shout "*Assassini!*" at the prisoners. This time, the German generals in the dock are von Mackensen and Maelzer. But the fanciful, morbid, ghoulish German Army touch, so familiar at Nuremberg, also marks the war-crimes trial in Rome. The charge is that, in an over-generous ten-to-one reprisal for thirty-two Nazi soldiers killed in 1944 by Italian Partisans near the Piazza Barberini, the German S.S. shot three hundred and thirty-five Italians in the Ardeatine

Cave, on the Appian Way. With a stroke of national genius, the Germans, who were not quite sure that all the hostages had been shot dead, dynamited the entrance to the cave, sealing up it and its dead and possibly living contents, thus achieving sadistic cruelty, horror, entombment, a mystery, and even a perversion of their favorite Wagnerian underground *mise en scène* all in one. The Ardeatine crime, when finally it and its cave were opened to the light and air of day, produced anguish, shock, and fury in Rome, and the Sapienza trial has revived that state of mind.

Unfortunately for the Allied military authorities who are hearing the case, no sooner had the trial opened than the fugitive 1944 German S.S. chief of Rome, Commandant Eugen Dollmann, head of the troops who shot the hostages, was spotted by a Roman taxidriver as he was about to step into a cinema for some light entertainment, was detained by the Italian police, and was found to be carrying an Allied pass, made out to a Giulio Cassani. The pass entitled him to immunity from arrest—a reward, the Italian newspapers headlined next morning, for his having aided the Allies in *pourparlers* at which the German surrender in Italy was arranged. Also according to the Italian press, Dollmann had been in Rome for a long time, supposedly sheltered somewhere in luxury by an Italian prince. While Rome shouted that Dollmann too should be on trial, the Allies for ten days maintained a stiff-necked silence, before they grudgingly declared that Cassani-Dollmann was indeed the S.S. Dollmann, adding that he had once been arrested by them but had escaped, that he had had nothing to do with arranging the German surrender, and that even if he had, he would have received no immunity card such as the one he carried and which they were investigating. They did nothing about adding him to the list of defendants, however. The angry suspicion among the Italians that he is being protected by Allied higher-ups seems a natural effect of their bewilderment at the Allies' opening tactless silence, at their refusal to amplify or adequately explain or, indeed, make sense, when they broke that silence, and, above all, at their keeping him from the courtroom. In the American and British colonies in Rome, it is felt that the Allies have made the worst blunder of their Roman occupation, that they have weakened Italian faith in our democratic accessibility, that they would have done better to put all their cards, however smudged, on the table, and that, since Dollmann is not in court, the trial has lost all meaning. It seems laying it on thick that the president of the war-crimes court should be a British major general named Playfair, which is a combination of words that the vast numbers of Romans recognize and find bitterly funny.

Italian Art

DECEMBER 7, 1946 A minor benign result of the war is the number of exhibitions now being held all over Italy of works of art long ago taken from their homes to safety and not yet returned. In Venice, there is an opulent, beautiful show in a building overlooking St. Mark's Piazza and its fluttering population of pigeons. It contains more than three hundred *capolavori* of the province of Venice. Among them are saints, painted upon medieval gold, from the twelfth-century village altars; Giorgione's worldly, romantic masterpiece "The Tempest;" and, as a novelty, a roomful of canvases by the hitherto nearly unknown sixteenth-century Pietro Marescalchi, a painter who, though he antedated Tintoretto, nevertheless worked in what was later regarded as Tintoretto's unique fulminating style. Art dealers are now rushing Marescalchi as if he were a promising débutante.

General Mark Clark is reported to have said of his Italian campaign that nobody had warned him that he would have to fight in such a blankety-blank art museum. According to art experts, Italy's greatest aesthetic loss because of this fighting was four of the six panels of the fifteenth-century "Martyrdom of St. Giacomo" Mantegna frescoes in Padua's Chiesa degli Eremitani, on which an Allied plane made a direct hit with a bomb intended for a railway station. The roofless Eremitani's vast, rosy-brick Gothic nave, which is open to the sky, looks like a quadrangle. Workmen are busy on the apse, where the frescoes once were. (There is angry criticism, even among Catholics, at the Vatican's diligently rebuilding blasted churches while the Church's faithful, the pious Italian poor, still live and breed in ruins.) The two surviving Mantegna panels escaped destruction only because they had been removed for long-needed repairs before the bombing. They are now displayed in the nearby Chiesa St. Antonio—beauteous medieval youths, full-hipped and as carefully posed as ballet dancers, watching the painful martyrdom of St. Christopher. The four shattered panels, now approximately forty thousand bits gathered up in baskets, have been sent to Rome's Istituto Centrale di Restauro, where restorers will try to piece together what is today Italy's most famous jigsaw puzzle. Not until the Padua Mantegnas had been bombed were sandbags placed around Giotto's "Life of Christ" frescoes, in the little Capella

Scrovegni nearby. These and his "St. Francis" frescoes at Assisi are, in composition, color, and Christianity, the major proof of Giotto's genius. Then, early in 1945 (so the chapel caretaker says), two Allied bombs fell fifteen yards in front of the Giottos, and five more a few yards behind. The "Hell" side of "The Last Judgment," which is over the door, had long been in bad shape; now the "Heaven" side has an ominous crack as a result of concussion. Otherwise, these holy illustrations are intact.

Italy's second greatest artistic loss was Pisa's Campo Santo, whose outdoor Benozzo Gozzoli frescoes were bombed to smithereens, except for the grimly humorous "Triumph of Death" series, which seems only to have been irrevocably blackened, probably by incendiary bombs or by the melted lead of the protecting roof over it. In Milan, the da Vinci "Last Supper," which is not being shown to the public, reportedly suffered more from neglect than from blast. Between the men who were carefully trained to destroy things and the men who negligently let things rot, tourists to Europe won't hereafter get their money's worth of these artistic gems, which had survived several hundred years of earlier hard times.

Elections in Italy

APRIL 22, 1948   There were actually ninety-nine official, registered political parties in the Italian elections this week, but only twelve of them were major parties, so called. Of those twelve, only seven counted—the Popular Front (Communists and Left-wing Socialists), the Christian Democrats, the Socialist Unity (Right-wing Socialists), the Republicans, the National Block (Reactionaries), the Monarchists, and the Social Movement (Neo-Fascists). Of these seven, only two groups were of crucial importance to Italy and to the world at large: two great rivals, each with a famous, historical edifice as its background—the Communists and their Kremlin, the Christian Democrats and their Vatican. What the Italian elections really amounted to was a throwback to an early social revolution, the Revolution of 1848, which was fought sporadically not just in Italy but all over Europe—an uprising aimed at achieving the significant modernisms of that day, liberty and the ballot—and which failed. In the 1948 echo of that revolution, fought here precisely and successfully to preserve the ballot and liberty, the modern revolutionary side, which is Communism and in a sense is counterrevolutionary, lost once again. No one here, however, thinks that it will be the year 2048 before this war between Europa's mutating Left and Right is fought for the third time. Italy feels that it has victoriously voted itself into an anti-Communist five-year plan, for which there are in reality no Italian political plans at all, and which, if not interrupted, will make the country's history until the next Italian elections, in 1953.

Because nearly three out of every ten Italians cannot read, the electoral campaign was carried on mostly by fabulous, entertaining, and cruelly biassed political posters, whose brilliant colors, imagery, and party symbols inflamed the buildings and piazzas of Rome, seat of a Church whose literacy and learning have been awesome for centuries. Maybe as a braggart gesture of satisfaction, because Soviet Russia claims to have taught more of its population their alphabet than any other country on earth, Communist posters featured more text and finer typography than those of their opponents. Each poster pasted up was supposed, by law, to enjoy twelve hours of visibility before a rival poster was stuck on top of it, but few lasted more than one morning or afternoon; hundreds of thousands were posted every day; and no two days' posters were alike. To miss the latest posters was to miss the latest political news, maneuvers, gibes, and attacks. The Romans, in their passion for polemics, pictorial art, and endless talk, clogged the sidewalks from morning till night, reading the handwriting on the wall. And till dawn the bill-posting workmen could be heard on the streets, slapping together their rich stream of paste and politics, in readiness for another day.

No party poster offered any program or promised any reform. Italians are used to accepting what their government chooses to give, and, anyway, they are at once too cynical and too religious to have faith in the promises of men here below. The election was simply a geographic struggle between revolutionary Moscow, in the east, and conservative Washington, in the west, and the big question was which of the two could convince the electorate that it offered, for the next five years, the most good or the most harm to Italian voters and to Italy, sitting in judgment in between, on the Mediterranean. Both the Christian Democrats and the Communists quickly developed a Machiavellian poster technique that borrowed material belonging to the other side in order to attract the eyes of its believers, who were thus beguiled into reading some nasty facts about their own party and its Russian or American home base. The Communists put out a stunning poster with Biblical quotations printed in the form of the Cross, which read all right to pious women until they came to the finale, which, in smaller letters, detailed the Church's recent painful scandal involving a priest, since unfrocked, who had been running Vatican City's profitable

245

black-market money racket. A scorcher for pro-American Catholics was a Communist poster shouting, "Yes! Vote for America," and adding, in small letters, "the land of one million annual divorces and two million legalized abortions." The Communists' most impudent Machiavellism was borrowing a portrait of the Italian patriot Garibaldi, with his famous Zouave cap and flowing whiskers, and using it instead of the hammer and sickle as their party campaign symbol. They even resorted, in one poster, to borrowing the mastheads and lead paragraphs of year-old editions of the London *Times* and the *Economist*, in which one paper feared that the Christian Democrats looked weak and the other that the Communists looked strong, both of which fears were then justified. At the bottom of the poster were further apt quotations from the Washington *Star*.

To the illiterates, the Christian Democrats' outstanding poster must have been the one that displayed a huge, appetizing loaf of bread broken in two, the upper, smaller portion labelled "Forty per cent, Italian" and the lower, larger one "Sixty per cent, gift of the American Democratic people." But the Christian Democrats' all-around triumph was a cartoon strip entitled "One Day in Togliatti's Life." In the first panel, he was shown at breakfast drinking coffee sweetened with sugar labelled "American" and wearing a shirt labelled "American cotton" and a pair of U.N.R.R.A. trousers. Next he was seen at a railway station, meeting his wife, who was also wearing American contributions. The locomotive that had brought her in was labelled "Army U.S.A. War Surplus Supply" and was burning "American Aid to Italy" coal. Next he was off to his office, smoking an American cigarette, to write his daily diatribe against American help as the industrial enslaver of Italy. After a dinner of spaghetti and chocolate dessert made of American wheat and cocoa, he sneezed and went to bed with a cold, taking a dose of American penicillin.

The gayest propaganda looked like money falling from the sky—banknotes, fluttering down from airplanes, issued by the Bank of Inflation, Moscow, in the sum of five zeros, marked "good for a five-year plan of lost savings," and signed by Bank Governor Togliatti and Cashier Luigi Longo. The most pretentious effort, and one that appealed only to the highly literate, was a poster setting forth a classical ode in which alternate lines formed a scurrilous Latin description of Togliatti that was quite foreign to the tenor of the ode when read in normal fashion. The most inspired piece of anti-Communist propaganda was unquestionably one produced in Naples, where a loudspeaker and a gramophone record were wired to the city's statue of Garibaldi, who was made to beseech passersby all day, "For the love of God, and if you love me, don't vote for me." A major effort to squash Moscow's misuse of this nineteenth-century patriot as Communism's symbolic man was inducing his daughter, Signorina

Clelia Garibaldi, to run as a senatorial candidate of the Republican Party and introducing her from a speakers' stand in the Roman Piazza dell' Esedra. An elderly, stout, black-coated lady, with a proud and humorous face elegantly adorned with rice powder, she delivered the shortest, quaintest speech of the campaign. "My father," she stated categorically, "would disapprove of the use now being made of him by the Communists. He told me once, years ago, that a German professor named Karl Marx had attempted to interest him in his new party, but my father declined. *Viva la libertà, la democrazia, viva l'Italia, ora e sempre.*" This last phrase, "now and forever," was her father's political battle cry.

All the chiefs of the major parties were given an opportunity to make a public outdoor harangue in Rome, and in every case the meeting was formally dedicated "to the Roman people," as in the old Forum days of Julius Caesar. The dignity, calm, and tolerance of the vast audiences, massed, at sunset, against classical ruins, Renaissance churches, and palaces of ochre baroque, must have proved a disappointment to the outside world, waiting for operatic fisticuffs and melodramatic bloodshed. At the monster Communist meeting, held before the very steps of the Church of St. John Lateran, the mother church of the Catholic world, the great crowd of comrades acted as if they were at a spring fair—swapping jokes, munching the new green beans now in season, and pouring down orangeade. There was none of the fierce devotion to the speeches, the disciplined bigotry of attention, the angry affirmative shouts, the clenched fists that mark, for example, the Communist gatherings at the Vel' d'Hiv', in Paris. The fact that Moscow helped sour its campaign by snubbing the Allies' proposal to return Trieste to Italy is interpreted as possible proof that Moscow belatedly discovered that the Italian Communists, though the largest Communist Party outside Russia, are still, by inheritance, too humanistic to be trusted with a victory and the all-important management of it, which would set a standard for all the subsequent Western-democracy Communizations, if and when. Young, highly placed Communists boast of being less rigorous about doctrine than comrades they have met from France or Yugoslavia, and add, as if they were referring to an indulgent father, that Moscow says it is O.K. Their startling, unorthodox gentleness comes, or so they say, as a legacy from the founder of the Italian Communist Party, a scholarly, gifted, hunchbacked little Sardinian named Antonio Gramsci, who, after twelve years of prison under Mussolini, was finally ejected in 1937, when he was dying. His nineteen notebooks of prison thoughts, distinguished by his special qualities of equanimity, humanism, and morality, have recently been published here in a volume entitled "Historical Materialism and the Philosophy of Benedetto Croce."

It seems that they were salvaged after his death by a mysterious English lady, who sent them to Moscow. There—at least according to Ignazio Silone, who is no longer a Communist but was formerly Gramsci's close political friend and literary confidant—the Gramsci manuscripts were expurgated by the Russians, and the book thus omits everything that might make Gramsci look the pure Trotskyite Silone swears he had become.

It is significant that Togliatti was under the influence of Gramsci, who converted him from Socialism, and that Togliatti, before he became too engrossed in Party friends to continue to see his non-Party friends, had an intellectual amiability the latter regard as a curious attribute for a coming Communist chief. *La Rinascita*, a monthly magazine put out by Togliatti —there is a certain touch of bookishness in the family, one brother being Vice-Rector of Genoa University—prints rather good young verse, stories, and modern art along with its strict and stodgy articles on Marxist dialectics. Non-Communists point out that, whatever Togliatti was in the early Gramsci days, he avoided Mussolini's prison by fleeing during the middle twenties to Moscow, where his aptitudes eventually made him No. 2 in the Comintern, a powerful post he apparently still holds. No one here is soggy enough with the conservative Christian Democrats' victory to think that the Communist Party has not some occult plan, as usual, that it can use profitably in defeat. It is supposed that Togliatti is the man who knows the plan and will put it in motion.

Until the election returns were all in, the beautiful Piazza Colonna, with its fine palaces, was roped off from traffic, so that the Roman people might congregate there to listen to a loudspeaker blaring news from behind the column of Emperor Antoninus. During the final week of the election campaign, La Galleria (the huge pillared arcade on the same piazza) was packed each night with crowds that had come to see the posters and listen to the political arguments, and the arcade hummed, to its high, coffered ceiling, with the sound of talk. To a visitor accustomed to violent Paris street conversations, these nocturnal *stoa* gatherings seemed positively sheltered in calm. Yet more than once there came a sudden roar of sirens, and a trio of jeeps, bringing the *celere*, or riot squad, charged over the sidewalk and into La Galleria's pillared aisles. Before them and their menacing motorized antics, the crowds agilely dissolved, half of the people zooming across to Antoninus's column, where they might watch in safety, the others darting back into La Galleria's interior rotunda. Inexperienced stragglers flattened themselves against pillars as the jeeps darted up one aisle and down the next or scurried sideways in reckless exhibitions of chauffeurship. It was like a jeep rodeo, dazzling to see at close range. During this Tuesday night's raid, your correspondent found herself unexpectedly sharing a pillar with a lunatic beggar woman whose hands were full of wilted tulips she had been trying to sell. Throughout the five or ten minutes of the spectacle, she sang and waved her flowers while the jeeps went through their careening patterns. The half-dozen special police who filled each of these little open cars were uniformed and helmeted, like soldiers. All carried tommy guns in their hands. Their handsome faces were expressionless. These *celere*, like gangster police, are what the duly elected new Christian Democrat government has declared it will use against the Communists if the Communists try force. The use of force has become the world's gravest communicable disease.

MAY 6, 1948 For a fortnight now, the Romans have been digesting their electoral news with mixed sounds of surfeit and distress. Both come from the winning Christian Democrat side. Among its unexpected millions of supporters were deserters from the older, traditional, lay political parties, who, in the crisis between Communism and democracy, mugwumped for the Christian Democrats, and thus for the Church. These voters and Italy's many *mangiapreti*, or priest-eaters—though no more cannibal than France's Radical Socialists or, indeed, any nineteenth-century anti-clerical-Catholic bourgeois group in Europe—are now ruefully pondering the influence in state affairs that the Italian clergy can wield as a result of the inchoate, unlooked-for landslide. One of the satirical weekly magazines has run a cartoon forecasting the legislative scene on May 8th, the date of the new Parliament's opening. The picture, drawn in the worldly manner of the eighteenth century, when angels had become part of decoration rather than illustrations of faith, shows the stately Chamber surrounded by an angelic host of flying priests, winging it horizontally, like blackbirds, their loose robes buoying them up as they aim for the Parliament's portico and windows.

Certainly the priests were active during the electoral campaign. For the colony of American journalists quartered here over the electoral weekend, this was probably the first election in which Hell figured as anything more than an expletive. Premier de Gasperi himself reportedly played up eternal damnation, 1948 style, in one election speech, declaring that "Communism means Hell, and no help from Russia, either. A Christian Democrat vote means your choice of Heaven, and American help besides." The day before the Sunday election, the entire back page of the Communist daily *Unità* was a warning against priests and their power over lay life and its innocent joys, providing, as proof, a picture of a copy of Flaubert's "Madame Bovary," a photograph of Charles Chaplin as Monsieur Verdoux, and one of a young couple jitterbugging, all three of which items of entertainment, according to *Unità*, the clergy had already banned. And what wouldn't they ban tomorrow if they got a real, free-for-all, Christian Democrat chance?

The famous, unpopular Article VII of Italy's new Constitution renewed Il Duce's 1929 Concordat between Church and State, once more confirming Catholicism as a state religion. It was voted against last year in Parliament by almost every party except the Christian Democrats and the Communists, but it was pushed through by this odd pair—by the first because it believes in state Christianity and by the second because Moscow used to believe in no Christianity at all. Since the Italians are deeply religious even when they are noisily anti-clerical, Italian Communism felt that it must clear itself by making contact with the *mystique* of the faith, even in the political company of its archenemies, the Christian Democrats. On account of Article VII, the main post-election topic of conversation here is the prospect of clerical influence in the new government.

The second big post-election topic is what the new government will do about social reforms. One reform, which is agrarian, has been needed for exactly two thousand years. The great *latifondo* estates of the south were a scandal in Julius Caesar's time. They were owned by pagan Roman patricians, absentee landlords, like the later Episcopalian English lords in Ireland and like today's Catholic Italian princes, dukes, and duchesses, living and lunching distantly and comfortably in *palazzi* in Rome and Naples. The condition of the unfortunate peasants and hired hands on these estates is still feudal. Americans could best compare the misery of the peasants in southern Calabria, Puglia, and Lucania with that of our Southern states' poorest sharecroppers, white and black, plus the troubles of the old-time Northern coal miners in the days when their employers told them what to think, how many hours to work, and where to live. Except that here the misery is worse. On some Italian lords' lands, the peasants' homes, which are part cave and part stone, are often perched on hills weary kilometres away from the malarial, fertile fields in which they work. While *mezzadria*, or sharecropping, as enjoyed by the prosperous peasants of Tuscany, now rewards them, as a consequence of their organized pressure, with three-fifths of their production, instead of half, the backward southern Italians still struggle under the *gabellotti*, a medieval system of multiple-rent collectors. During the election campaign, the two landlords of the south most frequently and unfavorably mentioned were the Archbishop of Naples and the liberation Mayor of Rome, Prince Doria-Pamphilj. The southern peasants and the southern nobles are regarded as Italy's two most backward classes. The night before the election, some of

250

the Roman aristocrats and rich industrialists assembled at Passetto's, the city's most lusciously lardered restaurant, and ate what they laughingly called a Last Supper. Luckily for them, and for democracy, it was not.

Even though Communism was crushingly defeated at the polls, masses of voters, whose piety is the one thing greater than their poverty, still remember the election threats and promises of the Communists. Last month, in the southern agrarian districts, Communist leaders, equipped with detail maps of the region, told the land-starved peasants to choose for themselves whatever of their masters' acreage they and their families could reasonably work, then outlined the choices on the maps with a symbolically red pencil and declared that that land would be theirs if they helped the Party to win. The seizure of the nobles' estates in Poland four years ago was cited as proof that such political miracles can indeed happen on this old European earth. Any relief proposals offered by the Christian Democrats will be more sedate. Ever since Premier de Gasperi became Italy's government chief, two and a half years ago, he has been committed to two reforms—a confiscatory tax upon Italy's few plutocratically rich families, mainly industrialists, and a land reform involving the great inherited estates. These reforms, he has always said, must be achieved by "slow, cautious, legal procedure." On the other hand, Italy's Communists, in or out of Parliament, will continue to proclaim their offer of an immediate division of wealth. On the walls of the buildings in Trastevere, Rome's workers' quarter, the Communists' most appealing slogan is still to be seen, undimmed: "Vote for Communism and a Better Society to Live In." It is the promise of this quick and easy utopia that the Western democracies have to compete with, each on its own home ground. Otherwise, the election, by which all democracies everywhere benefited, will, in time, add up to little more than so many tons of Italian paper ballots cast in optimism in 1948.

Of the half-dozen major movements that the mind and heart of Western man have created in the past two thousand years, three (a high percentage) were born in or cradled in Italy. These three are Christianity, Humanism, and Fascism. That leaves two movements to the Teutons (Luther's Reformation and the Socialism of Dr. Karl Marx) and one (popular-revolutionary Democracy) to be divided about evenly between France and America. In any successful United Democracies of Europe, Italy must be accorded deep consideration, because she is poor, she is overpopulated, she is older than any other segment of Western civilization except Greece, and she sits strategically upon the Mediterranean. The worldwide concern over the Italian election still bewilders Italy, not accustomed in recent centuries to being courted. As many Italians bitterly recall, the last time their country was patted on the back by the democracies for having stopped Communism was when the loquacious Mussolini marched on Rome.

Agrarian Reform, Italian Style [*]

MARCH 12, 1949 The farmland laborers of the South are a dangerous social and political problem for all Italy, like our Southern share-croppers before Roosevelt spoke for them. Rome is now speaking about Italy's sharecroppers in Parliament, where the agrarian-tenancy-contracts bill, one of four reforms promised in the De Gasperi election campaign, is under discussion. Until all four are acted on, the landowners will not know where they stand. It will take many of the peasants even longer to find out, because they cannot read.

OCTOBER 7, 1950 Italy's land reform, which the Demo-Christians promised two years ago and which some Italians feel has been needed for centuries, actually got under way last Sunday, September 24th. It was a great day for a few peasants. The reform began on the ball of Italy's foot, at Santa Severina, a lofty, ancient Calabrian village on the mountain plateau of the Sila, near the Ionian Sea. In the festooned, parched village square, in the presence of national dignitaries and neighborhood crowds, a little girl in her Sunday best drew by lot from an urn the first of the slips of paper by which three hundred and ninety-six lucky peasant families became, for the only time in local annals, owners of land—about three hectares each. In a speech of thanks, the peasants' leader said, "Since the world began, we never thought to see so luminous a day," and tried to kiss the hand of Minister of Agriculture Segni. Signor Segni is the government agrarian expert and hard-headed idealist who this summer began pushing the reform scheme through. The peasants' three hectares were expropriated, with compensation, by government decree from two local baronial families, the Berlingeri and the Baracco, who own entire landscapes. This is the first time in modern Europe that land has been expropriated in a democracy according to a government plan of "public

[*] Editor's note: Agrarian reform in Italy, at this date (1978), has still not been achieved.

justice and good." Not all members of the government and not all citizens, by a long shot, favored such justice and good. Under last-minute pressure from landowning interests, the reform bill was nearly defeated by a hundred and fifty Deputies, including some Demo-Christians. Americans who wonder where on earth their Marshall Plan money is really going may be interested to know that E.C.A. put fifteen billion lire and a lot of advice into the Sila project. Most Americans in Rome administration circles think it is one of E.C.A.'s best political investments in Italy. In Calabria last year, the Communists successfully incited the land-starved peasants to rise and seize the earth. This year, the Communists might find the peasants less responsive.

Twenty-eight thousand hectares have already been expropriated for the Sila project, with seventy thousand more to come. Santa Severina was just the official beginning. Its peasants are reported to have knelt and kissed their land when they took possession. It is poor land, of clay, sand, and rocks, eroded, deforested, with little water, with mean pastures that were once rich fruit uplands, and with only occasional oases of green in the valleys. Like all Calabria, the land also includes magnificent scenery, art monuments, and malaria. All the dozen important Rome newspapers sent reporters to Santa Severina; the event absorbed the entire attention of the nation and its press. Regardless of their papers' political or class affiliations, the reporters used phrases like "medieval poverty" and "corner of rural desolation" to describe what had suddenly met their citified eyes. In his speech to the peasants, Signor Segni said, "Your ethical elevation to the dignity of man is the first aim of this work. From this earth you can gain not prosperity but only the modest protection of security." Italy's land-reform plan, which is complex, painful, hopeful, and incapable of bringing heaven on earth to such an overpopulated nation, has at last and at least started on its historic way.

Roman Christmas

JANUARY 8, 1949 Rome having been the highly organized cradle of Christianity, the Roman Christmas was this year once again celebrated as a strictly southern antique festival, unalterably suited, over the ages, to the mild Mediterranean climate of Jesus' birth. The arctic, red-wool person of Santa Claus, inappropriate to this holy latitude, is practically unknown to the Roman populace and has only recently become familiar to the Italian upper classes, to whom he is, like much else here, a modern American importation. Since Italians observe the original date for Christian generosity, as established by the Three Kings when they offered their perfumed gifts in Bethlehem, presents were not exchanged here until January 6th, or Epiphany, popularly called Befana. (To the children, Befana has become personalized as a witch who comes down the chimney to fill their Epiphany stockings.) The Via Condotti's luxury merchants have reported that rich gifts—such as solid-silver dessert plates, at a quarter-million lire a dozen, emerald solitaires as large as lozenges, and even a million-lire's worth of gorgeous Milan-silk brocade to replace wallpaper in the home—were bought in quantity by the former *borsari neri*, or black-marketeers, who have been setting themselves up as a flashy new middle class.

Fortunately for the poorer Italians, Christmas here does not feature Christmas trees. The right species, which apparently grows only in Tuscany, was on sale, beneath what used to be Keats' window, at the Spanish Steps flower market for five thousand lire—about nine dollars—a tree, for the Anglo-American colony. This year, in the booths of the annual toy fair on the Piazza Navona, there was a big assemblage of Nativity figurines, which, in elaborate or meagre display, are to be seen in every home at this season. The selection of little cows, donkeys, Saint Josephs, and Wise Men, molded in pottery or carved of wood—the unstreamlined, handmade output of gifted artisans from all over Italy—was the best since before the war. It is a good sign, for it means that the tension of replacing daily necessities, like pots and pans in use since before the war, is definitely relaxed and that people can risk producing modest articles to be used only once a year—a catchpenny trade devoted to real luxuries, like piety and children's pleasure.

"Rosalinda, O Come Vi Piace"

JANUARY 15, 1949 "Rosalinda, O Come Vi Piace," an almost unrecognizably diverting production of Shakespeare's ordinarily tedious "As You Like It," has just closed at the Teatro Eliseo. It ranks as the most lavish artistic offering of the season to date. The comedy was performed, between interludes of Early English music, almost as a spoken ballet. The accent was on the purely visual—the décors and the prodigal silken costumes, all designed in an arbitrary eighteenth-century manner (practically modern dress for Shakespeare) by Salvador Dali. It was presented on a revolving stage. The scenery represented the Forest of Arden on one side, then whirled around to become the courtyard of the Duke's castle on the other. The role of Jaques was played by Ruggero Ruggeri, yesterday Italy's great classic actor, now so venerable that he sometimes forgets his lines, though never his grand manner. The producer was Luchino Visconti, a wealthy young Leftist nobleman who has become Italy's outstanding prestige producer by following a special system of his own, which is based on his theatrical talent, his impeccable taste, and his ability to ignore costs and the box office.

de Chirico

FEBRUARY 5, 1949 An exhibition of recent canvases by Giorgio de Chirico is on view at Rome's most recherché small art gallery, L'Obelisco. Chirico is now in his seventies. For many years his name has so dominated modern Italian art that his painter brother, Andrea, meekly paints under the psuedonym Savinio. De Chirico has obviously changed both his art and his politics since the twenties, when he was popular with the extreme-Left Surrealists in Paris and painted stark arcades, mythological figures with heads like footballs, and fabulous rearing white horses. Today, his horses are mingled with warriors in sketchy medieval battle scenes. Using an oily brush, reminiscent of Renoir's, he has painted some enchanting canvases—appropriate, perhaps, to a dining room—of enormous quinces, pears, and grapes, sitting large as houses or figures in the foreground of glamorous, umber Italian landscapes. He has also painted a nude forest nymph of remarkable flesh qualities and romanticism. Of the seventeen pictures being displayed, three are self-portraits, two of them showing him in Renaissance armor. The paintings of his face are almost lithographic—amazing, smooth likenesses of his harsh, proud features and his thick silk cap of straight white hair. They are portraits for posterity, of which he is evidently thinking these days, and they cut him off completely from the modern art of his past. In "Memorie della Mia Vita," his autobiography, which he published three years ago, he began to take his stand. In it, he blasphemously declares that the Ecole de Paris, which he once ornamented, was really founded on the Munich Secession School; he refers to the "so-called masterpieces of Braque and Matisse and other authors of malodorous works," and says that Dali has the brain of a little chicken. De Chirico has just been invited to become a member of England's Royal Society of Arts, the first time an Italian has been so honored. His Obelisco show has been declared out of bounds by all the young Leftist painters in Rome, who, had they been in Paris a generation ago, would have looked upon him as a political and artistic fountain. Today, he is eschewed here as a turncoat reactionary.

Italy and the Council of Europe

FEBRUARY 12, 1949 From the viewpoint of both ancient and modern history, there have been a couple of remarkable changes in the Mediterranean scene in the past fortnight. Britain, the great Protestant empire, has just given *de facto* recognition to Israel, that final national form of Old Testament Jewry, and she has, furthermore, agreed (certainly under pressure from the New World U.S.A.) that Catholic Italy, the original seat of New Testament Christianity, should be admitted to the recently evolved Council of Europe. This invitation to Italy by the democratic allies has changed Western Europe's map. Politically, Italy is now conceded to be on it for the first time since her pre-Axis days. The invitation has been hailed here as Italy's first postwar diplomatic success, and, more important, it seems to be a move toward European common sense in general. With the realistic intelligence of a defeated people eager to be saved, the Italians have long been insisting that the string of Western European democratic states—compared with the bulk of Russia, her Eastern European satellites, and her chunk of China—was too insubstantial to omit anybody (namely, democratized Italy). As Italy well knows from her Fascist days, there are two geographic gaps in the south—Spain and Portugal—and in the north, where the Scandinavian trio dare not utterly ignore their fear of Russia, the string is in danger of unravelling.

Before the two World Wars, England had the subtlety, the time, the money, and the trained diplomacy to operate all Europe on a balance-of-power principle, that brilliant Congress of Vienna invention whereby somebody weak, like Italy, was set against somebody stronger, like France, while England retained the power. Today, the United States, which is unquestionably operating peacetime Europe, has the more un-

wieldy job of trying to make everybody in the Western European democratic group, including England, strong by 1952. As long as England's
empire included India, the Mediterranean had to be practically a British
lake, carrying what were almost British pleasure boats, so agreeable was
the rich colonial maritime trade. Since India has withdrawn into indepen-
dence, and England—Socialistic, austere, and weakened by her unfaltering
struggle against Germany—has turned her attention to other areas, the
Mediterranean has resumed its classic position as the intercontinental sea
connecting Europe and its increasingly vital food-producing African colonies. The Mediterranean now leads not just down to Suez and Mandalay
but up to what is left of Greece and, beyond it, to Russia. In the eyes and
budget of Washington, Italy has been accepted as important. Perhaps as a
result, Rome has been rising from its handsome ruins in a modern renaissance, which may or may not last.

Italian State Betting

FEBRUARY 19, 1949 The popularity of soccer and of the national
soccer betting pool are phenomenal. The pool, called Totocalcio, was
founded by a private syndicate in 1945 and over a year ago was shrewdly
grabbed by the state, as a money-maker. It has been estimated that nine
million fifty-lira Totocalcio tickets are bought every week, which means,
in theory, that one out of every five Italians, including mothers and babes,
feels competent to predict each Saturday how twelve of the many soccer
matches being played all over the country will come out on Sunday.
They have to be right on all twelve to win the big pot, which is usually
between one and two million lire (seventeen and thirty-four hundred dollars); being right on eleven brings a prize of fifty thousand lire or less; the
state takes all from those who are right on fewer than eleven. On the
weekend of February 6th, the state paid out a hundred and eighty-five
million lire in prizes. There are ordinarily a dozen Twelves, as the big
winners are called, in a city the size of Rome. On this occasion, there were
so many, not only in Rome but all over the country, that the individual
prizes were comparatively small. The state advertises that in the last four
months it has paid out two billion seven hundred and eighteen million lire,
or over four million dollars, in prizes. The state takes fifty-one per cent of
the profit, twenty per cent goes to the Italian National Olympic Committee
to foster athletic programs, the distributors of the lists get about five per

cent, and the rest goes to pay the lottery's bureaucratic overhead. Frequently, when a big pot is won by a Communist workman, he publicly renounces his Party. Italians are great believers in miracles; many follow Communism because it promises to free them miraculously from poverty. When Divine Providence and soccer drop a fortune into their laps, they needn't look further. Moscow can offer them nothing like it.

The Italian state also makes a success of its operation of *lotto*. This is a descendant of the famous old lottery established by the Genoese Republic in 1644; today it resembles, somewhat, the numbers game in Harlem. Each of several big cities has its own *lotto* pool. Every Saturday, in each of these cities, five numbers are drawn from a grab bag by a blindfolded state orphan. There being no logical method of figuring out what the orphan will do, Italians sensibly select their *lotto* numbers—they buy from two to five numbers, in combination, between one and ninety—on the basis of their dreams. Dream books, with a number for every variety of dream, are available for consultation wherever state *lotto* tickets are sold. According to these hoary books, blood is No. 18, a child is No. 1, Jesus Christ is No. 33, a drunk is No. 19, fear is No. 90, a full dinner table is No. 44, women's legs are No. 77, and the human posterior, regarded as very lucky indeed, is No. 23. The chances of a bettor's picking all five lucky numbers are forty-four million to one. A bettor recently accomplished that in Bari, and received a total of a little over forty million lire, or about seventy thousand dollars.

In Latin countries, the state has long been considered the citizen's natural enemy; it takes his son for war and his money for taxes. The son may be willingly given, out of patriotism, but in France, and especially in Italy, even patriots believe in representation without taxation if they can wangle it. Tax evasion today is a grave problem here. Only dream-book lotteries and soccer pools can help fill the state coffer and give the citizen pleasure, to boot.

Pompeii

MARCH 12, 1949 The postwar situation in Pompeii is special. On the erroneous tip that Germans were hiding in the excavated ruins, American bombers toured above the ruins in the summer of 1943. A hundred and ten bombs exploded on sixty edifices, including the beautiful and nearly perfectly preserved Casa Marcus Loreius Tiburtinus and the Marine

Gate. The hit on the latter could almost be classified as a lucky one, for it brought to light a deeply buried suburban villa. This was excavated last year. Its frescoes are in the most splendid late so-called Third style—Nero's period, and the last before the earthquake of 63 A.D., which started the destruction that Vesuvius completed in 79 A.D. They exquisitely report on the myths of Ariadne and her Minotaur and of those tragic early fliers Daedalus and Icarus. Two-fifths of the site of Pompeii, it is estimated, is still unexplored, mainly because in over two centuries of spading the excavators have walled themselves in by dumping the dug earth in mounds that now barricade their progress. Professor Amedeo Maiuri, Pompeii's noted archeological director, has a solution. As he points out, just north of the estimated limit of the site, on the side of Vesuvius, lies a barren lava track. With a hundred million lire, he could build a suspension cable railway and haul off the tons of invaluable, fertile old volcanic ash in the mounds and convert the lava track into farmland. This would reclaim land—the great goal in southern Italy—and would also clear the way to further unearthing of the buried city for the edification of modern man. It is not in many places that Marshall Plan money could serve art and grow vegetables, too. This is the spot.

Benedetto Croce

MARCH 12, 1949 A remarkable small seminar group, the Istituto Italiano di Studi Storici, has recently been established by Italy's most venerable philosopher-professor, Benedetto Croce. Classes are conducted in a wing of his Palazzo Filomarino apartment, which is ample enough also to hold his library of sixty thousand rare volumes, to which the students have access. The Institute's aim is exalted—not just to promote historical study but to create a nucleus of historians. A senator as well as an intellectual leader, Croce has, in his old age, a prestige so widespread that his institute's backers include, oddly, the Banca Commerciale Italiana, the Credito Italiano, and the Rockefeller Foundation. There are about thirty carefully chosen graduate students, mostly in their late twenties, among them fourteen scholarship-holders from Italian universities, and two Americans, one of whom is here on a fellowship given by, *mirabile dictu*, the Rotary International. The course, which lasts two years, calls for the writing of a thesis, awards no degree, and offers classes in ancient, medieval, and modern history, with lectures by three professors, one of them the young, incredibly learned Giovanni Pugliese, who also holds a chair in the University of Naples. And there are occasional remarks, or *conversazione*, by Croce. In his eighty-fourth year, he still reads indefatigably, without glasses. He has never lent one of his sixty thousand books. During the war, the Germans stole them all and apparently carted them off to Rome. In any event, they later turned up, neatly boxed, in the Vatican. Not a book was missing.

Artists of Rome

APRIL 19, 1949 There are today nearly four thousand painters and sculptors in Rome. The problems of these living artists amidst great defunct art are pretty trying. With a bare half-dozen modern-art merchants in all Rome, there is, unfortunately, nothing like the flourishing art racket of Paris and New York. Indeed, aggressively modern art has had a hard time getting a toehold in the middle of a population of Old Masters so fine that contemporary artists have not been able to resist keeping an admiring eye on them. Italian modernism began with a tentative metaphysical period, just before the First World War, and during the war turned toward Futurism in a movement dominated by a fabulous trio, now dead—Boccioni, whose "Football Player in Motion" is still the great, basic Italian Cubist picture; Martini, the sculptor of elegant semi-realistic figures; and the writer Marinetti, their mouthpiece, who put them on the map and got himself arrested for shouting "Down with Wagner!" at a Stravinsky concert in Rome.

After the war came neoclassical Mussolini. Unlike Hitler, he did not bother to fight *Modernismus* on the ground that it was decadent; his strict autarchy simply made importation of anything foreign, including art ideas and art magazines, quite difficult. Until very recently, many Roman artists had never laid eyes on a Picasso or Braque original; they say there are none in any public museum in Italy. They say further that they themselves managed to go modern, with interruptions, only through what they call world atmosphere, plus old art magazines, as welcome as manna since the Liberation. It is these historic delays that have kept Italian modern art in a state of almost pristine, unformalized freshness. It has just had another bang-up interruption, this time from the Communist Party. Last autumn, the first National Contemporary Exposition of Art, consisting mostly of art by the very Left Wing Alliance of Culture, opened in Bologna. In November, *Rinascita*, the weekly literary organ of the Communist chief Togliatti, termed the Bologna show "an exposition of horrors and silliness." Since most Italian artists are poor, many of them had long been Communists. In Rome, those artists who were Party members resigned, almost to a man, because of the *Rinascita* critique, and now call themselves anarchists, an old Italian euphemism for disgruntled utopians. A hundred artists, from all over Italy, have founded the Society for the Defense of the Dignity of Man and are spunkily giving their first show this month, in Milan, its slogan being "Quality Regardless of Tendency."

What the *Rinascita* article made clear is that Italy's official Communism is tightening up, in accordance with the Moscow Party line. The Togliatti critique stemmed from a laying down of the law by the Soviet art critic V. Kemenov, in an article entitled "La Pittura e la Scultura nell' Occidente Borghese," published in the monthly *Rassegna della Stampa Sovietica* (*Review of the Soviet Press*) in March, 1948. This particular issue is now so rare that it can be found here only occasionally, and at a high price. Considering Shostakovich's testimonial, at the recent Waldorf shindig, that the Party line helped him, off and on, to write better music, Kemenov's basic Kremlin aesthetics seem very timely. His lengthy, didactic article is a development of his opening question, "What is the cause of the catastrophic decadence in which contemporary bourgeois art now finds itself?" In brief, he answers thus: "The characteristic of the imperialist bourgeois era is its anti-humanism, intended to oppress the worker's sense of his human dignity. Capitalism sells its modern art like men's suspenders or Coca-Cola. The sculptor Lipchitz deforms the human imagination. The English Henry Moore cynically derides the human form. Cézanne took away light from painting and turned everything into a still life. Matisse and Braque deny that there is any conflict between art and its public. They all are detached from life, deny realism, and are indifferent to subject matter, which they wrongly consider the enemy of painting."

Even worse insults are heaped upon Party-member Picasso, whom the Paris Communists feature as their prize intellectual catch. His superb new drawing of a dove appears on the front page of this week's *Les Lettres Françaises* as publicity for the French Party's forthcoming World Congress of Peace Partisans, which will star the French Communists who were refused visas to attend the New York Cultural and Scientific Conference for World Peace. Kemenov, after admitting that Picasso's Blue Period still seems O.K. to him, declares, "Picasso's works are a maladive apology for capitalistic aesthetics that provokes the indignation of the simple people, if not the bourgeois. His pathology has created repugnant monstrosities. In his 'Guernica' [which the Party widely used as anti-Franco propaganda], he portrayed not Spanish republicans but monsters. He takes the path of cosmopolitanism, of empty geometric forms. Picasso's every canvas deforms man, his body, his face." Kemenov ends happily with a eulogy of "U.S.S.R. art aims—large ideas, popularity in the true sense, equality, brotherhood, patriotism, and the fight for individual liberty! Today, Soviet culture is creating works of world importance following the road laid down by the genius of Stalin."

In Rome, at least, of the leading Italian modern artists, who may or may not have been politically shaken by Kemenov but whose art has not been affected—such men as Tosi, Carrà, Campigli, De Pisis, Sironi, Carlo Levi, Birolli, Cassinari, Bartolini, Mirko, Afro, Marini, Mafai, and Manzù, not to speak of the venerable, utterly apolitical Morandi, noted painter of un-Cézannesque still-lifes of bottles—only the Communist Guttuso has openly accepted the Party's aesthetic ruling. His latest paintings, in strong, primitive colors, show strong, fine men realistically at their labor.

Botticelli Censored

JULY 9, 1949 Rome has been suffering from what people consider, depending on their viewpoints, a scandal, a wave of false modesty, or just the thing the anti-clerical intelligentsia prophesied at last year's spring elections would come to pass under a Demo-Christian, prelate-dominated government. The climax was the banning from the walls of Rome of its most exquisite, aesthetic poster, the nude figure (shown only from the elbows up) of Botticelli's famous "Birth of Venus." It was one of the official posters for the city of Florence's recent festival honoring the fifth centenary of Lorenzo the Magnificent. It is suspected that the order for the suppression was the idea of the chief of police—the already unpopular Minister of the Interior, Mario Scelba. When he was asked in Parliament if Venus violated the laws on pornography, he refused to reply, as is his Ministerial privilege. Prior to the banning of Botticelli, the government required Roman movie posters of no more than ordinary commercial daring to be bandaged with strips of paper, which, in most cases, turned out to be little signs saying "Great Success" or "Closing Soon," wittily pasted over movie stars' bosoms or knees; and some recent issues of several of the humorous cartoon weeklies, such as *Travaso*, which is the Italian *Punch*, have been seized.

Suitably, the Ninth National Congress for Morality has been sitting at the Campidoglio, attended by Premier de Gasperi, by some leading Demo-Christian senators and deputies, and also by the noted endocrinologist Professor Nicola Pende, a scientific supporter of Fascist Party Secretary Achille Starace's "Manifesto sulla Razza," to which Pende contributed the statement that Jews do not belong to the Italian race. Premier de Gasperi's rambling speech at the final Morality Congress meeting boiled down to the simple phrase "Be discreet." This seems feeble advice to a handsome population dwelling among beautiful antique public statues and paintings.

Oil in Italy

JUNE 28, 1949 If the Italian government's experts are to be relied upon, Italy has just struck it rich. She has made her first major discovery of oil, in the Po Valley, near the town of Cortemaggiore, which is next door to land once owned by Giuseppe Verdi, whose "La Traviata" has been a money-maker itself. The oil strike is the most surprising good news that Italy, as used to bad luck as she is to bright sunshine, has had in modern times. There is something comic and pathetic in the Italians' incredulity at this sudden, pleasant change in fortune. This nervous state of mind was perfectly exemplified by *Il Messaggero*, a leading independent Rome paper, which announced under a huge headline that it had "news destined to arouse enormous interest," and then stammered, "For once, it is good news, so good that at first one hesitated to believe it or was tempted instinctively to diminish its importance." Then *Il Messaggero* took a deep breath and said, "Oil has been found in the Po Valley, in our own motherland." The Milan *Corriere della Sera* was so excited that it managed to include its home town, the Deity, and the national destiny in one annunciatory sentence, which sent the Milan stock market soaring: "It will be Milan, used as a refinery center, that will exploit this enormous economic wealth that God has desired to reveal to Italy so that she may have the strength to rebuild after her tragic days of sacrifice."

The remarks by Enrico Mattei, vice-president of the Azienda Generale Italiana Petroli, or A.G.I.P., the state-owned oil corporation that made the strike, were less metaphysical. He said that the oil field covers thirty acres in the triangle between the medieval towns of Lodi, Piacenza, and Cremona; that after Finance Minister Ezio Vanoni paddled his hands, voluptuously and officially, in the crude oil, the first well was stoppered up, there being nothing at hand in which to store or transport the stuff; that the Cortemaggiore region also contains a huge deposit of methane gas, on which the industry of the entire country could function for the next three-quarters of a century; and that, to put it mildly, "a profound transformation of Italy's economy is about to take place." Under such gratifying circumstances, Italy, which today is always buying or borrowing from everybody else's coal or oil buckets, will tomorrow be independent, riding around on her own gasoline and cooking her spaghetti and running her industries on her own natural gas.

A.G.I.P.'s vice-president also sadly and prophetically commented that "petroleum, like gold, gives bad counsel," meaning that as a modern source of power oil rouses the old Adam in men, which it has, indeed, already done here. The battle for control is even now being viciously fought, with chauvinism and greed, on the national and international fronts, even though the latest figures for the area are somewhat dispiriting —an estimate of a yield of a mere hundred thousand tons annually, which is nothing like Texas. However, Italians cheerfully suspect that the rest of the Po Valley is richer than that, since they have read rumors of an E.R.P. threat to cut its aid to the national petroleum industries, whose "too ambitious program could ruin the world petroleum market"—or perhaps only America's dominance of it. Obviously, the political crux of the Po Valley discoveries is the widely held belief that, because they were made by a state agency, the oil and gas logically belong to Italy and her people. Among most citizens, the situation has caused boundless satisfaction and boundless worry. The Communist Party's sentiment that "the oil is the least of our troubles; now we must preserve it from the cupidity of the New York and London trusts" has been echoed in a multitude of non-Communist hearts. For it appears that Standard Oil (New Jersey) and Anglo-Iranian Oil between them own sixty per cent of I.R.O.M., S.I.A.P., and S.T.A.N.I.C., which are Italy's refinery groups; and that the British and Americans expect to have more than a still, small voice in the operations to come. Furthermore, British and American machinery will be needed to develop the oil field, and that fact alone could force A.G.I.P. to make certain concessions. Just now it looks to many Italians as if the oil will belong to the Italian people only as long as it stays underground.

The methane deposit has an older, less exciting story. At Busseto, Verdi's Cortemaggiore property, the Maestro forbade his peasants to smoke in

264

his fields near the vents through which natural gas poured, for fear they would blow him and his farm sky-high. The gas in this region has been used for years, but in drilling for oil the engineers discovered that the deposit was much larger than anyone had realized. The government plans to draw off three hundred million cubic metres of it during the balance of 1949. The expectation is that by 1955 the yield will be nine billion cubic metres a year, the equivalent in energy of more coal than Italy is at present importing.

Conceivably, the Po Valley oil will change Italy's position among the world powers. The Romans built Europe's first great roads, but ever since horses went out of style, after the industrial revolution, Italy has been able to travel forward only with difficulty. If the Po Valley really adds up to something big, Italy may be able to speed into the future on the only new European resource that has turned up since the start of the Marshall Plan.

The Italian Riviera

SEPTEMBER 7, 1949 This coast has just been animated by an astonishingly prosperous summer season, with the greatest crowds of visitors, Italian and foreign, that it has known since the end of the Second World War, or, for that matter, since the beginning of the Ethiopian War, when Italy's astringencies and unpopular adventures really started. From rocky, démodé, Anglican Bordighera, on the north—Queen Victoria once planned to visit it, but the outbreak of a similar colonial war, with the Boers, interfered—to the sandier, more fashionable beaches south of Genoa, the Ligurian Riviera's summer weather (which was actually a continuation of Europe's dangerous drought) was perfect, and the resorts were overflowing with vacationers. Everyone, of every nationality, including the austere British, had, it seemed, plenty of money, which nobody denied or could explain, except as the latest and the most unexpected postwar development—a mystery whose pleasantest solution lay in spending. At Ventimiglia, on the western border, the extravagant garden restaurant called La Motola, which was noted even before the war for its hundred and twenty hors d'oeuvres, has been serving consequential dinners for two at about eight thousand lire, or nearly fourteen dollars at the legal rate of exchange. Well-to-do Italians said that this was very high, but they paid it, which was strange. Visiting New Yorkers, between their monologues on the American recession and on their financial insecurity, said it was cheap, which Italians found stranger still. The eastern Levante end of the Riviera was the smart part this season. Worldly figures who wanted to make sure that they would have no rest went to Portofino, whose small, picturesque harbor was filled with neat yachts; to Rapallo; to Paraggi; to Santa Margherita; and, after dark, to the Nord Est, the grandee night club of the region, overhanging the surf on the foundations of an unfinished modern castle, begun some years ago by one of the baronial Franchettis.

The Ligurian coast has always been used as a neighborhood bathing beach by the rich and titled clans of Turin and Milan, cities that are only one Apennine mountain range inland. The aristocrats of Turin, which is the capital of Piedmont, whence the royal rulers of Italy sprang, still regard themselves as models of courtly elegance, now stranded by history amidst the powerful industrial outcroppings of the north. The textile families of Milan are the most obvious millionaires in all Italy. The rich Genoese, who were heavily represented here during the summer, are traditionally the most ornate; recently, the sunburned wives paraded on the beach in silken décolletage, blazing with jewels. The wealthy landowning nobles were also here in full force this year—families whose fortunes and names are so ancient that they are mentioned more often in the archives than on the financial page of the *Corriere della Sera*. All these men and women of the upper classes were equipped with elaborate wardrobes, handmade from scarf to shoes, of a taste and diversity that made the wearers the most splendidly and individually dressed, if not the most hauntingly chic, of all the people on both the Italian and the French Riviera. Italy, unlike France, had no prewar revolution; instead of a Front Populaire, she had Il Duce. And, unlike England, Italy chose to have, instead of a postwar labor government, Christian Democrats. The rich in Italy are unique in Europe, for they are still rich.

The other end of the social scale, also well represented on the Ligurian Riviera, was to be found principally at the casino in San Remo. The crowd there made up a democratic picture indeed. The players were mostly former black-marketeers who evidently had all started in contraband Parmesan cheese. Gamblers used to dress impeccably as they ruined themselves on a turn of the roulette wheel, but the cheese gentry dressed comfortably for their fun. In the casino's well-known handsome, old-fashioned mahogany central room, the men, who were usually fat, cautious, and sweating, sat in their shirtsleeves and suspenders, frequently fanning themselves with nice tortoise-shell fans. Their women stood modestly behind them, advising, nudging, sometimes moaning at a loss or laying little bets over the men's shoulders. At the chemin-de-fer tables, the croupiers were often forced to interrupt their spatulas' busy whisking of cards and chips to explain, tolerantly, the rules of the game. The bank rarely ran to as much as a hundred thousand lire. The cheese crowd lost neither its head nor much of its cash.

After the Liberation, Italy's new government felt obliged to pass new gambling laws, since Mussolini's were obsolete. In the beginning, he moralistically shut down all the old Italian casinos; after 1932, he reopened three, all on strategic frontiers. First, vaingloriously, he reopened San Remo, to compete with Monte Carlo and tempt French currency over the border into Italy, as an aid to his autarchy, which badly needed *valuta*. For similar reasons, the Venice casino was later permitted to reopen; it could bring in Austrian and Balkan money. Then the casino at Campione d'Italia—a bizarre fragment of Italy near Lake Lugano that is completely surrounded by Switzerland—was reopened, in order to nab Swiss francs and German marks. Mussolini later licensed a casino in Tripoli, as a catchall for British sterling from Gibraltar and the French colonials' pay, and then another one, on the Isle of Rhodes, to tap Egyptian cotton fortunes.

At the end of the war, the government called the licenses of the Mussolinian casinos in to Rome for inspection, and they were supposed to close down during this period. The casino crew at Campione d'Italia, which is so cut off from Italy and so surrounded by the Swiss that it remained republican even under Il Duce, continued play until a commissioner from Rome marched up to it one night and personally told them to shut down. Some casino Partisans then marched out with machine guns, left over from the Resistance, accused Rome of having stolen their license, ordered it returned instantly, and went on playing. Now the three big former Fascist casinos are going again. In addition, a brand-new casino opened this August near Venice, in the midget Republic of San Marino, which Italians call the Republic of Four People. It will probably snare the money of nobody, of any nationality, but apparently the four-person republic wanted it, in quartet.

Tourists and roulette aside, San Remo's serious income derives from its carnations. It is the carnation center of Europe. In the Continental florist trade, San Remo's roses are somewhat less important than the carnations, being less beautiful, although more highly scented and stronger-stemmed, than their English-hothouse competitors. Ligurian flowers grow in the open, on cliff terraces above the sea, which gives them a toughness, of commercial importance for long-distance shipping, and without any new-fangled refrigeration cars. The local gardeners boast, "Our flowers grow, bud, blossom, and in hard times even die, outdoors." The great San Remo flower trade was first carried on with Russia, about 1905, when the Grand Dukes Cyril and Alexis had Ligurian villas and wintered there annually. The Czar's court turned carnations into big business. After the First World War and the revolutions, when Russia was using only red flags for palace decorations, San Remo began to build up an Eastern trade with Prague. A carload of flowers was dispatched there daily on an express and, with the Czechs acting as middlemen, was then distributed to Budapest, Trieste, Belgrade, Vienna, and elsewhere. By 1936, because of Austria's new autarchic program, Italian carnations became taboo in Vienna, and the Czech market weakened, in consequence. The French market had always been poor, although French Riviera flowers are raised mostly for perfume-making at Grasse. After the Ethiopian War started, both the French and the English imposed sanctions on Italy; in more emotional England, these applied even to the Italian carnation trade. However, the Rome-Berlin Axis saved the flowers by shifting the export business to Germany. It continued throughout the war, despite bombardment at both ends. San Remo was bombed by planes or shelled by warships eighty-nine times in the four months before the liberation. The carnation gardeners were told by the German soldiers stationed here during the war that they found when they went home on leave a bunch of posies meant more to their romantic, blitzed-out sweethearts than a loaf of black-market Italian bread. During the war, there was some less poetic carnation business with Switzerland, where the Italians had arranged for the Swiss to block flower payments, so that the Nazis could not touch them. The money was released after the war and it helped put the San Remo carnation trade back on its feet.

Daisies also are raised around San Remo, but they are despised, because fools can raise them. A daisy gardener can sit twiddling his thumbs until cutting time and still get a sure, if frugal, living. Carnations demand hard labor and a troublesome horticultural technique. For the easygoing daisy growers, countless Ligurians worked hard centuries ago; they built the masonry of the cliff terraces, stiff and narrow as staircases, and then over the years brought up basketfuls of earth dug from the sea, and the rain rinsed it and slowly drained off the salt. But the carnation growers continue to work hard today. Their flowers are sturdy, long-stemmed, small, and not highly scented. The San Remo carnations provided the cheapest pleasure of the Ligurian season.

Holy Year

VATICAN CITY, FEBRUARY 15, 1950 The second beatification of the Holy Year, and the first to glorify a woman, was solemnized by the Pope at St. Peter's on a Sunday of impressive morning and afternoon ceremonies. Thus, between dawn and dark, the Church of Rome, after long scrutiny into the reports on her life on earth, which ended eighty-three years ago, and into two miracles she performed after her death, officially lifted to a level of "restricted public veneration" a humbly born Spanish nursing nun, María Desolata Torres Acosta, founder, in Madrid, of the Order of the Servants of Mary, which now has communities in many parts of the world, including both the Americas. In the afternoon, fifty thousand people, some of them pilgrims, easily crowded themselves into the pillared nave and side aisles and the ornate transept of the mammoth basilica. Only a few hundred notables, with seats of honor in the choir, could see the Pontiff enthroned and wearing his jewelled tiara, or observe whatever it was that took place at the altar. St. Peter's ecclesiastical ceremonies are among the most ancient and most sumptuous of the Catholic world, and since 1633 nobody in the main body of the church has been able to see them. For the past three centuries, Bernini's fastuous gold-and-black baldachino—a ninety-five-foot monument to baroque—has crouched, with its contorted pillars and clinging cherubs, beneath Michelangelo's dome, just in front of the choir, and by its peculiar beauty has blocked off any sight of the functioning high priests and the most revered altar in Christendom.

What most of us who were at St. Peter's saw of the beatification vesper service was principally the afternoon's special iconography, consisting of three lithograph-like pictures of the beatified, lowly indeed compared with the great art the church used to patronize. The main picture, which was high in the apse, simply shows the beata in Heaven on a cloud, and the two others, more detailed and hung outside the choir, depict her two miracles. In one, she is appearing in 1916 as a vision to a young nun of her order, who was thereupon cured of a chronic gastric ulcer. The nun in question, Sister Lucía Allende, was reported to be in St. Peter's, as, understandably, the chief Spanish pilgrim. In the other, she is curing the chronic otitis of a little Madrid girl, who is rather overshadowed in the picture by five members of her family and the family doctor, in a frock coat.

Squeezed together on the benches next to this correspondent, near the towering baldacchino, were two worried nuns with a half-dozen adolescent orphan girls in uniform. We were diagonally across the nave from the ancient bronze statue of Saint Peter, dressed for the ceremony in a gold-cloth cape, with a gold mitre on his metal curls. In front of the orphans were two Spanish women, pilgrims in black lace mantillas and high combs, talking German (which they smilingly explained they had learned in Madrid during the war) with a brown-robed German Franciscan friar, also a pilgrim, who in several languages eagerly asked all the people around him when they had arrived and from where. He seemed disappointed to learn that nearly everybody lived in Rome.

To hosts of the faithful craning and jostling in the side aisles, even the Pope's entering passage down the nave, which is the apogee of all great ceremonies in St. Peter's, must have been not a sight but only a sound—a long, gentle roar of acclamation, funnelled down the nave by the echoing acoustics of carved stone. Above the greetings of the thousands shouting *"Viva il Papa!"* could be heard the silver papal trumpets playing the Vatican hymn, a delicate, melancholy tune. The Pope, carried shoulder-high on his swaying gestatorial chair, was accompanied—or so the Rome newspapers said the next day—by nine cardinals in scarlet, by a Spanish archbishop in purple, and by bishops in purple and a retinue of white-vestmented priests. All that we in the center of the church saw of the procession was, in glimpses, the Pope's white cap and crimson-caped shoulders and his scholarly face, and, to one side, the ceaseless, sedate motion of his hand, its two apostolic fingers signing crosses on the air. Shortly afterward, in the vesper Mass, the Sistine's famous boy sopranos let loose their voices in shrill and beautiful Palestrina.

Anticlerical Romans, who are Catholic, anti-priest, and pro-republican, and who since 1870, when Rome became a temporal and not a papal city, have constituted a considerable intellectual residue, say with satisfaction that so far the pilgrims have not made even a ripple in Rome. Apparently, a Holy Year, like any tourist invasion, always causes a metropolitan irritation, especially if the tourists do not spend anything. Most of the pilgrims have been lodging and eating in Catholic hostels and buying nothing. The Communists have naturally been quick to decry the entire Holy Year as a failure. The opening phase has certainly disappointed shopkeepers and hotel men, who seemingly had inflated postwar visions of four million well-heeled, pious tourists coming to town. That is twice as many as was estimated by the Vatican, which has been holding these Holy Years since 1300 and, furthermore, wisely figured that this one would be *austero*. The

Vatican's *Servizio d'Informazione* has just stated that 15,546 pilgrims are registered to arrive during February, and 117,000 in the Easter month, but that three times as many unregistered pilgrims, mostly Italians, always turn up to swell the ranks of the faithful.

The best souvenir shops for the pilgrims are in the Via della Conciliazione. (It is perhaps worth noting that this wide promenade, cut through by Mussolini to provide a tasteless, naked perspective of St. Peter's that was deplored by the old Romans, is now being partially closed off at the basilica end by a pendant pair of new church office buildings, on opposite sides of the street, whose jutting façades form a screen that restores to the church some of its old air of gigantic privacy.) All the Via della Conciliazione novelties for this year's pilgrims are dated, to give them memorial value. There are silk pocket handkerchiefs with the Pope's face on a background of lemony gold, the official Vatican color. For the tea table, there are porcelain bells made in the shape of St. Peter's dome. Cake shops also offer the dome, made up as brioche. There are key rings with trinket telescopes through which you see the Pope's profile, glass hip flasks with his portrait in color, and white plaster busts of him with his name, the year, and his spectacles painted on in gold. The biggest combination for your money is a pocketknife whose enamelled sides show a potpourri of St. Peter's, Garibaldi on horseback, the Victor Emmanuel Monument, the Colosseum, Caracalla's baths, and Jesus ascending over the Tiber River, with the inscription "Ricordi di Roma 1950." The prettiest souvenirs are the Vatican City postage stamps marked "Anno Santo MCML." There is a handsome brown twenty-lira issue that shows Perugino's fresco "Christ Giving the Keys to Saint Peter," the original of which is in the Sistine Chapel. There is a purple thirty-lira issue with a medieval painting of Pope Boniface VIII, who proclaimed the first Holy Year. In modern poster style, there is a chic architectural stamp that shows the foreshortened exteriors of Rome's four major basilicas, as if seen from the air.

All four basilicas—St. Peter's, St. John Lateran's, St. Mary Major's, and St. Paul's Outside the Walls—must be visited by the pilgrims. On the doors of all the Roman churches are printed signs specifically telling pilgrims what they are required to do. They have first to be confessed and receive Holy Communion, after which, presenting themselves at the four basilicas, in turn, they must recite in each three Our Fathers, three Hail Marys, and three Glory Be to the Fathers, then recite one of each for the intentions of the Pope, and add the Creed. It is the reciting of these prayers at these Roman altars, and only during the *Anno Santo*, that gives the pilgrims what is called the acquisition of the Jubilee, the word "Jubilee" in its Holy Year connotation meaning "a solemn plenary indulgence granted to Catholics by the Pope for the remission of sins." Plenary indulgence can also be gained in any year by Catholics who climb on their knees the twenty-eight steps of the *Scala Sancta*, now situated across from the Lateran, which are believed to be the stairs Jesus walked up in the Jerusalem palace of Pontius Pilate. The *Scala Sancta* is the only shrine where the pilgrims are much in evidence. Especially in the mornings, the steps are covered with the faithful, young and old, painfully and penitently crawling in the direction of Heaven. In his *Anno Santo* Bull of Proclamation, the present Pope reminded his followers that pilgrims of old often came to Rome on foot. Most of today's pilgrims come on excursion tickets, with a fifty-per-cent reduction on their railroad fare. For a slight extra charge, they ride from basilica to basilica in chartered blue, streamlined buses.

Another extraordinary Italian film, "Cielo sulla Palude" ("Sky Over the Marshes"), which won three prizes in Venice last summer, just had Holy Year premières in Vatican City and in Rome. It is extraordinary for its pictorial beauty, its lucid tragedy, its news value, and its piety. It is a reconstruction of the peasant drama of the martyrdom of thirteen-year-old Maria Goretti, who will be canonized, as the first saint of this Holy Year, at St. Peter's in June. In 1902, she was mortally stabbed by a violent country youth, whom she piously forgave on her deathbed for one of those attempted crimes against purity that occasionally assume mystic significance in a lonely, impoverished old Catholic region. The girl's mother, now over eighty, will be the first person in Church records ever to see her child made a saint. The murderer, Alessandro Serenelli, after twenty-seven years of prison—Italy does not have capital punishment—became a penitent lay brother and gardener in a monastery near Rome and went to see the film, as "the most terrible part of my expiation." "Cielo sulla Palude," like the best neo-realistic Italian movies, shows the drama of life, as brought into focus by poverty, among the farmers in the malarial Pontine Marshes, a sick, highly photogenic landscape. Made with Church documentation but otherwise a normal commercial production, it was splendidly and sensitively directed by Augusto Genina, one of the noted film men of the silent days. The cast is made up entirely of Italian peasants, mostly illiterate, who are natural actors. The story, which is about a brutal, adolescent sex obsession, is wonderfully played out by the two young protagonists, with Mauro Matteucci, a young farmer in real life, as the murderer and Ines Orsini, a blond twelve-year-old country girl, as the helpless, ignorant little martyr. The film has been compared to "The Bicycle Thief" as a *capolavoro*.

During the last Holy Year, 1933, the Church officially urged its followers to combat Communism. It would be unhistorical, however, for anti-Communists anywhere to suppose that this Holy Year is a militant political-propaganda thrust against Communism, even though the inference is drawn by some Italian Communists. Most educated Italians think the Church has already lowered its spiritual appeal by mixing in politics, by which they mean the Demo-Christian Party. Only a few think that the Church should go into politics militantly, as it used to, and offer sweeping social reforms to combat Communism, as it once reformed itself, if somewhat tardily, against the equally crucial assault of the Reformation. The Church is the oldest, most experienced institution on earth. In the opinion of certain intellectual Communists here, Kremlin Communism is increasingly patterning itself on it, especially as regards man's mysterious devotion to indoctrination and faith. These Communists say that this is true in reinterpretative ways which are too numerous to mention but of which autocriticism and self-purging, taking the place of confession and martyrdom, are the most obvious examples. Not long ago, a French writer, discussing the Holy Year, pointed out another parallel. He said that the Church long since discovered that man cannot live by bread alone and the Communists have more recently discovered that he cannot live without bread enough for all.

ROME, APRIL 9, 1950   The Holy Year's Holy Week climax of celebrations and commemorations here started, in their great ritual rhythm, with the mournful Maundy Thursday afternoon services, which the faithful traditionally attend in nine churches in turn. Rome emerged *en masse* and *en famille*, with an estimated hundred thousand of the local populace, including aristocrats in limousines and parents with babes in arms, circling the city in its devotions. Since the last century, the favorite of the nine churches, for some, has been the previously neglected medieval, countryside, basilicalike St. Saba, on the Aventine Hill, now appropriately streaming with purple wisteria, the Church's mourning color. On Holy Saturday, before the white-flowered altars in all the churches lay small pots of bleached new wheat sprouts, traditional sign of life after death. Though all altar ornaments were shrouded, other treasures were on special display in various churches—priceless Oriental rugs, brought back from the Crusades; gilded rococo mats, braided as daintily as hats from oak straw; and exquisite baroque mirrors, brought out to reflect the paschal candlelight. In the drama of special services and processions, the rich historical mixture that is Rome was even more noticeable than it usually is—Stations of the Cross being made in the imperial Colosseum, which once roared with lions; a holy torchlight procession winding up the Palatine Hill at night above the Forum; and, inside the medieval churches, Gregorian chant echoing among pillars long ago stolen from pagan temples. From Maundy Thursday on, the pilgrims came in a sudden gush, a few hundred on foot, many on bicycles, some in country carts, one on horseback, thousands in buses and trains from all over Western Europe, and thousands more by planes from across the seas, and together they filled Rome.

"Norma"

MARCH 11, 1950 In Rome, the Druid opera "Norma" is being featured for the Holy Year spring season. Its title role is being sung by Italy's new diva, the twenty-six-year-old Caterina Mancini. She made her operatic début last year in Rome, in Rossini's "Mosè in Egitto," and has a phenomenal Rosa Ponselle type of dramatic soprano of great range; she can sing E flat above a high C that comes in "Norma," and usually does, just for fun. She was born in one of the hill towns outside Rome, and is plump, nice-looking, affable, bourgeois, and respectable. Some member of her large family always accompanies her to the theatre. Her contracts include a clause about her being chaperoned. She recently turned down an offer to appear in "Il Trovatore" in the provinces because no relative was free to go along at that moment.

"Botteghe Oscure"

MARCH 11, 1950 Postwar Italian literary magazines have had hard sledding. Founded to run on talent that was unfettered, at last, for the pleasure of free speech by Fascism's fall, most of them soon bogged down for lack of money. Naples, the first big city to be liberated, had the first liberation literary gazette, the short-lived *Arethusa*, edited, in part, by

Signora Elena Croce-Craveri, daughter of the famous philosopher and herself a critical writer of meticulous judgment. When Rome was freed, another woman editor, Signora Alba de Cespedes, had a go at it with *Mercurio*, whose opening number contained exciting accounts of Rome's liberation in a round robin by Rome's best-known writers. But Milan's Arnaldo Mondadori, one of Italy's biggest commercial publishers, soon had to lend a financial hand, and he finally killed the magazine because it was unprofitable. The most influential literary magazine is the *Botteghe Oscure*, a thick biannual, beautifully and privately published since 1948 by still a third woman, the American-born Princess Marguerite Caetani-di Bassiano. She is trilingual, and no novice at publishing. For almost ten years after the First World War, in Paris, where she then lived, she financed *Commerce*, that remarkably nourishing French-language magazine that decanted certain ripening works of such special-vintage writers as André Gide (who frequently mentioned her in his journals), Paul Valéry, Léon-Paul Fargue, Valéry Larbaud, and Alexis Léger, of the Foreign Office, who in that period began signing his poetry "St.-John Perse." Her present publication takes its name from Via Botteghe Oscure, or Dark Shops Street, a former medieval shopping center in which stands the massive sixteenth-century Palazzo Caetani, the Rome residence of her husband's family. Her new magazine is more international than *Commerce* was, printing the prose and poetry of both known and unknown Italians, French, English, and Americans, all in their own languages.

The fourth number of *Botteghe Oscure*, which has over four hundred pages and has just come out, contains a British short story by Angus Wilson, who seems to be quite the thing in London now, and twenty-five poems by English and American poets. Included are two lyric Mexican recollections by Tennessee Williams, a notable bedside saga by William Carlos Williams about his dying mother, and a wild beauty called "Over Sir John's Hill," about hawks and other savage birds, by Dylan Thomas. Earlier issues contained a typical Florentine fragment on the city's amorous side streets, by Vasco Pratolini, whose novel "A Tale of Poor Lovers" has been admired in America; poems by Edith Sitwell, Marianne Moore, and E. E. Cummings; a sonnet called "A Failure," by the late Lilian Bowes-Lyon, who was related to the Queen of England's family; and a grand, impudent apostrophe to Death, a rare thing among the worried poets of today, called "Praise to the End!," by the American Theodore Roethke, a professor of Old English at the University of Washington. The most discussed of the Italian *novelle* to appear in the magazine has been "La Giacca Verde" ("The Green Coat"), by Mario Soldati, a prominent film director. It is a cruel and comic tale based on a crazy incident of the war, involving a famous orchestra conductor whose identity was stolen by his kettledrum player. The magazine has discovered some good heretofore unknown Italian writers—whose manuscripts were first turned down by publishers here, then printed in *Botteghe Oscure*, and finally published by the publishers who had turned them down. As in the days of the Renaissance, creative Italian writing seems to demand an aesthetic-minded patron. Today, the patronage comes from farther away. Princess di Bassiano was born a Chapin, the Chapins being a family that helped settle Springfield, Massachusetts.

Movie Scandal

ROME, MARCH 27, 1950 It's almost certainly a fact that when, with bewildered Italian help, the thirty-odd American newspaper correspondents and press photographers regularly operating here started what proved to be their unsuccessful twelve-day February siege of Ingrid Bergman, while she was lying abed in the Villa Margherita Clinic, she was, however unwillingly, the leading news story in the world. She and her infant, an invisible pair, pushed even President Truman and his hydrogen bomb onto the second page of hundreds of American newspapers that evidently were more interested in love. Now, eight weeks after the peak days, when an exclusive picture of her with the infant was enthusiastically calculated to be worth five million lire, or about eight thousand dollars, to anybody able to snap it, by hook or crook (nobody managed it), an unexclusive picture of the baby, solo, is rated by New York agency editors to be not worth the thirty-seven dollars and fifty cents it would cost to transmit it by radio. All babies, especially on second editorial thought, look alike, and a photograph of Robertino can be sent more cheaply and fast enough by air mail. So the Bergman news crisis, which started with its vital statistic at 7 P.M. on February 2nd in the Villa Margherita Clinic, on the Via di Villa Massimo—a crisis in which hundreds of thousands of cabled words were ticked out from here, in which Miss Bergman said nothing, and in which Rome seemed closer to Hollywood than to the *Anno Santo*—has finally died down, and the Roman American press is awaiting other statistics or events, such as the wedding and the baptism. Right now, or so American newspapermen have said to this correspondent—and Miss Bergman has said to this correspondent that she believes what they said to be true, because she has looked carefully out the windows of the Rossellini apartment on the Via Bruno Buozzi, where she is living, and can see no loitering cameramen—she could walk out of her apartment at any time without being met by a battery of photographers or reporters, such as were stationed at the hospital. Today they would have to be alerted.

Miss Bergman does not subscribe to any clipping service, but friends and enemies, known and unknown, have supplied her with what must be a fairly complete file of the evidence of her incredibly widespread newsworthiness. It runs into millions of words, most of them silly. With more patience than rancor, she says that nearly all of what has been printed is trivial, inaccurate, and distorted, except, of course, the three or four major facts. In the vast, rather empty salon of her apartment, her clippings, whose bulk grew steadily as she and Rossellini made more and more intimate revelations in the year following her arrival in Italy, form a sort of cheap, extra upholstery laid out over the divans and chairs. She seems to have preserved them as a painful phenomenon that, she realizes with Nordic realism, was inevitable. Over most of the past three months, she received, in addition, two hundred letters a day. Since the excitement over the baby's birth died down, the number has dwindled to about fifty. Eight out of ten letters declare that she is "wonderful" or "courageous." Most of these are from movie fans, and often verge on the illiterate. Eight out of ten also mention Christ and casting the first stone. Some are obscene, a few threaten death, and quite a large number of the recent ones complain about the nosiness of the press.

On April 13th of last year, Hearst's society columnist, Cholly Knickerbocker, announced in the New York *Journal-American* what society columns call "rumors" of a Bergman-Rossellini romance. The rumors had been rampant, Knickerbocker said, ever since she flew to Rome in March —or somewhat earlier, Miss Bergman says, than they knew about the romance themselves. On December 12th, Hearst's movie columnist, Louella Parsons, announced in a special I.N.S. story, which appeared in most Hearst papers, including the New York *Journal-American*, that it was rumored Miss Bergman would have a child in March. On that day, cameramen began to encamp before Miss Bergman's home, and she has since left her apartment only three times, the last time in February, to have the prophesied March child. On the night before Christmas Eve, she went to the Fono-Roma studio to do some belated dubbing in of sound on "Stromboli." And on January 22nd, a fine, bright Rome day, seeing no cameramen, she ventured out to wait in the sunshine for Rossellini, who was going to drive her into the country for a pleasant, salubrious walk. As she reached the street, an ambushed photographer rushed toward her, snapped a couple of pictures, and pursued her as she ran toward the nearest corner, thinking to hide behind a newspaper kiosk there. She circled the kiosk one way and he circled it the other, so he was able to take another shot, while she burst into tears and he "smiled at her ironically," a phrase contained in a charge the furious Rossellini preferred against him at a police station. The Italian Civil Code's Article X, which deals with photographs taken and published without permission, forbids the publication of photographs of people "as a means of indicating some fact about their personal life." Two of these pictures, which showed Miss Bergman's condition, were copyrighted by the A.P., and one or both of them were printed in the Milan weekly *L'Europeo*, in *Life*, and in a number of A.P. newspapers in the United States, including the Los Angeles *Mirror*, which published one over the caption "Is she or isn't she?" These pictures are notable, being considered the unique, sizzling news scoop of the whole complex Bergman-Rossellini journalistic campaign. On being advised of Rossellini's angry police-station complaint and Miss Bergman's tears, the A.P. management gallantly sent her flowers and a note of apology, which quaintly explained that the photographer was just an Italian. By then the police had dropped the charge against him.

Oddly, there were no photographers on the sidewalk at four o'clock in the afternoon of February 2nd, when Miss Bergman hastily crowded herself—a tall and by this time heavy woman, in a heavy coat—into a small car belonging to her physician, Dr. Pier Luigi Guidotti, and started for the clinic. The press pack, caught off guard, didn't get on the scent till seven hours later. Most of its members had by then had a busy evening. They had been invited to a lavish gala première, at the Fiamma Cinema, of "Volcano," the eruptive competitor to "Stromboli," starring Anna Magnani, whom the American press had long tagged as Miss Bergman's archrival in Rossellini's personal and professional career. The evening's entertainment had been diverting because it had been so strange. Contrary to expectations, Signora Magnani had not turned up. Warned that the baby had been born and reportedly commenting that this was Rossellini's supreme sabotage of her film, she stayed at home. Soon after the film started, a bulb in the projector burned out, and while a boy was sent across Rome on a bicycle to forage for another, the author of the film, Renzo Avanzo, unexpectedly entertained the spectators by doing a tap dance before the blank screen. It was also strange, the press thought, that on the same night, in a private projection room across town, a preview of "Stromboli," which has still not been released here, was being run off for several bishops and four hundred priests; the reason was that the Vatican is interested in the film's salvational religious climax, which has been cut in the American version.

By nine o'clock that evening, the Italian news agency Ansa had informed its subscribing newspapers that the baby had been born, and when, where, and what it weighed. The American press didn't catch on until later. When it did, the reporting of the Bergman-Rossellini news became a mass assault upon the principals in the case—mother, father, and child. By ten-thirty, some of the American and British news offices had been alerted by private individuals. The U.P. apparently got its news from a Belgian Dominican monk, Father Félix Morlian, who is rector of the Università Pro Deo, one of the churchmen interested in film propaganda, and an intimate friend of Rossellini; Reuters from a friend of Rossellini's musician brother Renzo; the New York *Times* from another Rossellini family friend. The A.P., perhaps as punishment by Providence or by Rossellini's friends for the offending January 22nd photographs of Miss Bergman, got no tip at all. The U.P. thought its story was the first in New York by a few minutes—at 4:48 P.M. Eastern Standard Time (10:48 P.M. in Rome). According to Hearst's I.N.S., its Rome correspondent's dispatch was received in Manhattan at 4:35 P.M. In his followup story, the I.N.S. man said it had been easy to find where Miss Bergman was going when she left the apartment, since she was traced "by pre-arranged telephone communication set up along the route" to the hospital—an idea as fanciful as it was unpleasant, for the buildings are three kilometres apart, and Rome's maze of streets offers as many paths as the opening of a chess game.

It is to be noted that none of these early world-shaking press stories, of a few hundred words each, were based on official announcements by the Rossellini family, who spent a sleepless night, between the telephone-ringing and their denials, or by the two doctors—Dr. Guidotti and the *accoucheur*, Dr. Giuseppe Sannicandro—or by those in charge of the clinic, who had hastily locked its openwork iron garden gate on the crowd of newspapermen collecting outside and said they knew nothing. Through this garden gate, one of the unfortunate A.P.'s reporters had managed to ask a nun, one of the hospital staff who went down to try to quiet the racket, if she would swear on the Bible that Miss Bergman was not in the hospital. The nun, who had doubtless never been to a movie in her life and apparently had no idea who anybody was, including the mob of reporters, declared in good faith that there was no Signorina Bergman there. There was a Borghese, a Principessa Borghese, who had given birth that evening, but it was twins. So all night the A.P. continued gloomily filing bulletins to New York that the news of the birth remained unsourced, except by Ansa, and naming all the sources of denials—family, nun, clinic, friends, *e tutti quanti*. The rival New York editors began querying Rome was it true, wasn't it true, and what on earth was going on there? This confusion added to the press's job and also to its irritation. At 9 A.M., the A.P. chief here finally got an official source—one of the two doctors who assisted at the birth. Beaten by nearly eleven hours by the hares, the tortoise A.P. nevertheless won, in its exhausting, protocolar fashion. The A.P. chief was later complimented by some staid Middle West newspaper editors for the "restrained way"—the unrestrained way had already stirred disapproval in some breasts—in which he had handled the news. By papers that enjoy the unrestrained, such as the New York *News*, the New York *Mirror*, the Los Angeles *Examiner*, and the Los Angeles *Herald & Express*, the brief, unsourced stories were carried under blaring four-column and six-column heads. The Rome press, dazed by all the American hoopla about one more baby on earth, dutifully gave the story a biggish, if kindly and unsensational, play—except for the Demo-Christian organ, *Il Popolo*, and the Vatican's *L'Osservatore Romano*, both of which practically ignored the event. This is an outline of how the siege began. There were, of course, dozens of minor incidents, such as the Hearst reporter's referring, like a man in the know, to Miss Bergman's tears and laughter after the baby was born. As a matter of fact, when she heard the child's first cry, she asked, "What time is it?"

By midnight, Miss Bergman, as well as the other patients in the clinic, could hear the reporters and cameramen clamoring at the garden gate and trying to climb over the stone wall at both sides of it. The clinic called the Celere, Rome's jeep riot police. As time passed and it grew chillier, the press nipped branches from the live oaks and the pines of the park that had once belonged to the princely Massimo family, built a fire, and settled down for the vigil. (In lesser force, this was to last twelve days.) The clinic director was outraged by the American hunger for news, but the next afternoon he began to realize that it could give his hospital, which is new and self-conscious, publicity. On the street, crowds had collected and a radio van had arrived. At 5 P.M., newspaper reporters—Rossellini had warned the clinic that press photographers could mean havoc—were invited in to see the clinic's reception rooms, with a view to some public praise. Cameramen streamed in with them, their cameras hidden under their coats. A mild bedlam broke out. Photographers, pursued by truculent nuns and angry attendants, raced through the corridors and kitchens and into private rooms. A *Life* photographer, who had used an emergency back staircase, was collared on the second floor, and right where a man at the head of his profession should be—before the locked door of No. 34, Miss Bergman's suite. The carabinieri were called in to guard her door and to eject all members of the press from the building, and the cameramen (for photographs were what was wanted; news could be made up) started really organizing the siege. They hired a room across the street from the clinic, set up a battery of cameras in the window, stationed men to cover the back exit of the clinic, and arranged among themselves for a round-the-clock schedule of watches, refreshments, and so on. The majority of the photographers were Italian free lances, hastily hired by American and Italian agencies. They thought the siege was absurd, and were more interested in the pay than in the news. One of the Italians has said that the siege cost the agency that hired him a quarter-million lire. It produced no pictures of Miss Bergman and the child.

Being a very healthy woman and recovering splendidly in a room in which, during her fortnight there, the iron Venetian blinds were kept pulled down (except for the last two days, when the electric light began to hurt her eyes) to prevent photographers from taking telephoto shots from trees or walls, Miss Bergman was soon strong enough to know, and feel trapped by, what was going on. The nuns who were her nurses reported, shocked by the wickedness of the world, that they had been offered a million lire to open the door a crack so that a photographer could snap a picture. An Italian cameraman with a conveniently pregnant wife took a room upstairs in the clinic, but as her time was found to be weeks off, both of them were thrown out. A free-lance photographer for *L'Europeo*, which disclaimed all responsibility if he fell and broke his neck, shinnied up a rain pipe to the balcony of No. 34. The rival weekly *Oggi*, which also wanted a picture, at least got a picture of the *Europeo* man, halfway up. In addition, *Oggi* photographed photographers walking teeteringly in single file, cameras in hand, on top of the walls surrounding the clinic, but it missed getting a shot of one who fell off and broke his arm.

Since no legitimate photographs of Miss Bergman or the baby were forthcoming, improvised photographs began to turn up. A midwife in the hospital, who, like the director, enjoyed the publicity, willingly lent herself to the photographers' needs. The New York *Mirror* published a picture, which it ran as an exclusive but which had already been flashed all over Italy, of the midwife weighing a baby "born yesterday." The self-cancelling caption read, "Is this Ingrid's Little Roberto? Exclusive picture shows midwife who attended Ingrid Bergman at birth of her son Thursday weighing a child at Villa Margherita Clinic in Rome. Although midwife said not, photographer was led to believe baby was Ingrid's." A still from "Stromboli," showing Miss Bergman sad-faced and in coarse pajamas, was dug up and used variously, one caption reading, "In the Villa Margherita, Ingrid is not smiling now!" Another picture, taken off the "Stromboli" set, and showing Miss Bergman in the striped bathrobe used in the picture and looking dreary, with curling pins in her hair and Rossellini standing by, was captioned, "She is well protected in Villa Margherita." An old shot from her film "Notorious," showing her sick in bed from poison given her by German spies, was titled "Ingrid at Rest." A news photograph taken of Miss Bergman last year at the Ciampino Airport—her eyes wide with alarm, for she was being almost crushed by the crowd—was dragged out and captioned to indicate that she had looked frightened while "en route to the clinic." Rossellini was the subject of fewer improvisations, because he was irate, and he had already taken a swipe at a *Life* photographer in the clinic (and apologized). However, one picture of him was sent out, captioned as the latest shot of him in the hospital. The picture was taken before, he says, he became "fat, balding"—as certain sections of the United States press have described him for the past year. Another photograph of Miss Bergman, taken in 1949 outside a Trastevere restaurant, showed her in the sort of loose coat she apparently wears year in, year out; the caption implied that this was a maternity garment, and the picture was represented as one "taken a few days ago, for which our cameramen patiently waited a long time"—possibly because it was felt that the weary photographers by now needed at least a little praise. The siege group across the street from the clinic did get a real photograph of Rossellini's ten-year-old son by his former wife, and it was run with a supposed statement by the boy: "I hate the new baby. It has blond hair." Actually, the lad came out of the building excoriating the photographers, in an excellent imitation of his father.

On the evening of February 6th, the voice of Dr. Sannicandro, the *accoucheur*, was projected on the Italian government radio, answering a series of questions on the birth, stating that the anesthetic that had been given shortly before to Rita Hayworth in similar circumstances had been used, but adding "*credo*" to everything else he said—stale news about the child's weight, the hour of birth, and so on, which, after all, had been announced by the clinic director the morning after the birth. The interview had been recorded at the clinic. Dr. Sannicandro was indignantly criticized by Rome medical men for being publicity-mad.

Some of the cameramen-besiegers stayed on duty through the twelfth day, but the American Acme agency pulled its man out early, having reached the intelligent conclusion that nobody was going to get even a peek unless Rossellini wanted him to. Besides, Acme had shrewdly got Rossellini's permission to go to the hills near Lake Bracciano—where, when he had time for it, he was working on his film on the life of Saint Francis of Assisi—to take some snapshots of him there. The A.P., discouraged, also shortly withdrew its photographer from the weary battle group. *Oggi*, the most powerful weekly in Italy, which thought it was going to get a world-beating picture of mother, father, and child for its cover the week after the blessed event, delayed its appearance on the stands from Saturday to Sunday and came out with a picture of a trio, all right—a warmed-over photograph taken in the Farfa displaced-persons camp, where the opening "Stromboli" incidents were filmed, showing director Rossellini with star Bergman, who held a two-year-old D.P. in her arms. *La Settimana Incom*, an Italian news-and-picture weekly, came out, in desperation, with a frank photomontage of a Villa Margherita hospital group, posed by models, on which the faces of Miss Bergman, Rossellini, the *accoucheur*, and the obliging and ubiquitous midwife had been pasted. About this time, one of the American agencies started the rumor that Rossellini was going to auction the baby's photograph to the highest bidder. A visiting American photographer for one of the big American weeklies wrote to Miss Bergman quoting another rumor—that the reason no one was allowed to photograph the baby was that it was a monster who would be hidden away and substituted for. He begged Miss Bergman, in her own interest, to permit him to photograph her son and scotch this rumor without delay. At the end of the twelfth day, since force and ruse had failed, the photographers worked out a plan by which one man, drawn by lot, would take one picture of the baptism, whenever it should occur, this to be shared by all. Rossellini approved the idea, but the Hearst picture agency refused to come in, and the scheme, and the siege, collapsed. Miss Bergman, Rossellini, and the baby had won.

The writing part of the press was no more successful than the cameramen were, but at least the writers were soon allowed back in the clinic lounge, where they could the better think things up. It is incredible that, beginning a day and a half after a woman had been through childbirth, reporters of two of the largest American news agencies should have sent her whining, wheedling, or inciting letters, and in some cases—of all things, for up-to-date reporters—handwritten and running page after page. The agency men used different psychological approaches. On February 5th, one tried to butter up Miss Bergman by sending flowers that purported to come from Maxwell Anderson, in whose "Joan of Lorraine" she appeared. The man claimed he had recently seen Anderson in New York, and, of course, there were flowers from himself, too. He also said that since his wife had had two daughters in two years, he realized that briefness in bedside visits was necessary, so would she give him a two-minute bedside interview? On February 7th, another man from the same agency tried the helping-hand angle. He opened by mentioning the rising swell of opinion in the United States, which he thought was being misled about her; then, with all due respect, Miss Bergman, it was his sincere conviction that now was the time for her to state her true position; you are much loved, Miss Bergman, but in the eyes of millions this sentiment is becoming clouded; it is my suggestion that you could remove the clouds by issuing statements—three paragraphs of them, which he asked her to sign. On February 8th, a reporter sent Rossellini his New York editors' five pages of cables, in cablese jargon, deploring the unfavorable American attitude toward Bergman, which could be counteracted if permission given us to take human-interest photos of the new family soonestly, as you know how American public reacts to baby pix. Two days before that, one of the original botherers had been at Miss Bergman again, stating that she might like to see what was being done to distort her in the eyes of the world and enclosing a cabled agency report on the *Mirror*'s baby-on-the-scale photograph, which he called a fake. He soon came back once more, with a new suggestion: that she jot down what he called a quick yes or no to fifteen questions. He wanted to know if she was planning to go to America, Paris, or Sweden; if she was planning to be married; if she was planning to make another picture; if she hoped to be reunited with her daughter Pia. Question No. 15 was "The nurse says your new baby smiles all the time. Is this an accurate report?" However, one of his colleagues had already taken the panhandling prize with a two-page handwritten letter in which he whined as probably few men with good newspaper jobs have ever whined. He said that he was sure Miss Bergman had had struggles when young and knew the bitterness and hardship that come from defeat; he was in the same position in Rome, dependent on obtaining a few comments from her. He begged her to consider the position she had put him in. He said he understood her desire to be alone with her loved ones at this time (not quite forty-eight hours after childbirth), but couldn't she spare him a moment to tell him how she felt? He ended by respecting her courage to live and love with her heart.

Altogether, Miss Bergman has during the past year received between thirty thousand and forty thousand letters on her so-called private life. They make a strange library, to judge by a few hundred random examples. Ninety-nine per cent came from America, usually air mail, and often registered. Most of them were addressed just to Rome. There were hundreds of those gay American congratulation cards for a baby's birth, and hundreds of sacred medals. Many modest sums of money were enclosed to buy the baby a present. One letter, piously dated "February 6th, the Feast of Saint Titus," was from a young seminarian studying for the priesthood, who said he was praying for her intention and thanked God for a new young soul on earth. One Negro woman expressed her appreciation of Miss Bergman's stand on segregation in Washington theatres. There was a kind note, in German, from Austria, which had been opened by the censor. There were thousands of enthusiastic letters from New York Italian-

Americans. One of many angry anti-Italian letters contained a photograph of Rossellini on which a mustache had been sketched and the words "Wop wolf" had been written. There were two letters from Canadian farmers and a fantastic one from a female miner out West, which began, "Well, Ingrid, I bet you're surprised to hear I sold my old mine and am in a new shack now." There were begging letters. One woman in the Middle West sent a huge envelope containing the deed to her house, her husband's old-age pension card, her Social Security card, and other personal documents, and a request that Miss Bergman pay the mortgage on the house. A retired colonel wrote a courtly letter of good cheer, closing it, "I beg to remain, dear lady, respectfully yours . . ." An elegant old American expatriate in Nice wrote that he was thinking of Cosima and Richard Wagner and wished he could order a little orchestra to serenade Miss Bergman with the "Siegfried Idyll." Several letters mentioned Hawthorne's "The Scarlet Letter" and deplored puritanism. There was one note of congratulation from the boss of a modest Madison Avenue dress shop, and on the back of it the names of his eleven employees, each name being preceded by the word "Sincerely" or "Love." Several letters threatened Miss Bergman. The most vicious threat of death was typed with a red ribbon, in impeccable French, and was sent from Alsace by *"Un Homme Nordique,"* who ended with *"Craignez la justice divine. Je me sens l'instrument de cette justice pour vous châtier."*

A great number of the letters contained criticisms of the press—references to "filthy scandal sheets in our land," "the disgust and outrage I feel for the press," "contempt for a press which thinks we have to know all." There was a letter from a former *Time* writer, deploring what he called the disgraceful American press, "against which those who wrote for it were usually unable to rebel." One angry grandmother said, "I told Louella Parsons a thing or two about her nasty tongue." Along with hundreds of letters of insult, there were cables of friendship and kindness from public figures, among them Cary Grant, Phil Baker, Georges Simenon, John Steinbeck, Ernest Hemingway and wife, Billy Rose and wife, and Helen Hayes and Charles MacArthur, and one from a Canadian Member of Parliament and wife, both unknown to Miss Bergman, that ended with "Cheers."

The Swedish letters were unanimously harsh, as the Swedish press was. More than one Swedish newspaper dubbed Miss Bergman "a blot on the Swedish flag." Swedish journals had never been especially flattering to her as an actress until the birth of her son, when suddenly they claimed that she was a great artist who had been destroyed by an Italian. In discussing her now, they invariably bring in the fact that the Italians bombed a

Swedish Red Cross truck during the Ethiopian War. One paper has started a campaign to get the Swedish government to abandon its attitude of neutrality on the question of the return to Italy of her African colonies and to side instead with Haile Selassie. This paper concludes that if the Swedish delegate in the United Nations General Assembly votes against Italy on the colonial question, as he should, it will be all Roberto Rossellini's fault.

The private element in the making of "Stromboli" has been of much less interest to the serious Roman newspapers than the treatment of the film in the American version. Editorials have appeared denouncing R.K.O.'s cutting and switching around of the film as punishment and sabotage. The Church has been particularly exercised about the fact that the final speeches of the actress, in which she calls upon God for help, have mostly been put into the mouth of an unseen announcer, as if they were a news report. Rossellini's repudiation of the Hollywood version of "Stromboli" (the original version may be either good or bad, he says, "since, like all directors, I have made both kinds in my time") was one of the big stories about him in the Roman newspapers during the American journalists' Bergman-Rossellini Roman holiday.

For two months, the American journalists in Rome were hot to find out what Miss Bergman's plans were. It is noticeable, in conversation with her, that she keeps repeating (in her strongly accented Nordic English) the earnest statement "I am healthy. I am still young enough. I can work." To Rossellini, harried, frequently enraged by the tensions and intrusions of the past year, and known among Romans as a volatile temperament in any circumstances, an American newspaperman recently said, looking puzzled, "What are you kicking about? You got five million dollars' worth of free publicity."

Léon Blum

ROME, APRIL 15, 1950 The death of Léon Blum, the French Socialist leader, shook Italy, where in the past men have been martyred for Socialism, where men have recently developed it into something else, including a series of schisms, but where the memory of it has stirred even the *borghesi*, faced with a Leftism so much harsher that it gives Blum, in retrospect, a gentle halo. The Republican papers wrote of him with a curious undialectic, worried grief because Europe—already poor in eminent men—had lost an elderly man of good will. He was referred to as the spiritual head of European Socialism, a scholar of great culture, a loss to French democracy and the author of its rebirth, the greatest world Socialist since the assassination of his idol, Jean Jaurès, and the chief of what is left of dwindling European humanism. The Italians were pleased that his last international message had been sent to their government, even if it was a reproof for their handling of displaced persons, and they remembered that the last word in the message was "humanity." The conservative *Tempo* commented thoughtfully, "He sustained for half a century the rights of intelligence and the duties of brotherhood. He was the last socialist in bourgeois clothes in today's Europe." Concerned over today's disunity among liberal men, the liberal *Risorgimento* said, "France is in mourning. He had moral authority and prestige. Who will follow him as sage and mediator?"

Ironically, the Socialists gave Blum the least space and the least praise. *Avanti*, organ for the Left Wing, pro-Communist so-called Nenni Socialists, was the severest of all the papers. It grudgingly credited him with admirable conduct after France's capitulation to the Nazis—during his Riom trial and his imprisonment at Buchenwald. But it acidly criticized him for his postwar polemics against Communism, which it said had affected the French proletariat and had even caused repercussions in other countries—quite an angry compliment. Italy's so-called Saragat Socialists, who are of Blum's particular brand, said nothing at all in print, since their paper, *L'Umanità*, had folded shortly before his death. Oddly, the Communist *Unità* went fairly easy on the man whom French Communists had attacked as the chief betrayer of the workingman. *L'Unità* said that his death symbolized the mortal crisis of Western Europe's traditional Socialism. It mentioned his having headed the Tours congress minority rebels of 1921 but did not add that his rebellion against the Third International turned French workers toward Socialism instead of Communism for the next quarter century. It also accused him of betrayal, masked as nonintervention, in Spain without explaining that France was then financially tied to England's tail. All the papers mentioned his Popular Front government, in which, in 1936, he became France's first orthodox Socialist, and first Jewish, Premier. They all mentioned, too, that it brought an advance in working conditions—a French New Deal—to France. There was confusion in the comment on his recent decision to align himself with even the bourgeoisie, if necessary, to keep the French Republic alive, and on his invention of the Third Force to try to establish a balance of power in

Europe. Through the obituaries on Léon Blum, the French history he influenced over the past fifty years was traced for Italian eyes. The history in his obits was the greatest tribute he could have received.

Love Letters to Mussolini

ROME, APRIL 15, 1950 Pure Fascism is probably not a very live political issue here, but the way the Fascist dead are allowed to speak for themselves and each other in the thousands of words now being dug up from private letters and memoirs is certainly nostalgic. Clara Petacci's love letters to "Sweet Ben" Mussolini are, if possible, less amazing as amorous quasi-state documents than for the fact that they are being run by the columnful in a respectable Republican paper, *Il Messagero*. They are the amatory cream of her rough drafts of forty letters lately released by the government to any editor who wanted them—a selection from five zinc boxes filled with eighty-six packets of her letters to her lover, the rest having been retained for political reinterpretation, following the recent discovery of the correspondence in a villa on Lake Garda. This was the region, already famous for d'Annunzio's political and tender adventures, where Petacci stayed in the spring of 1945, until Il Duce called her, wearily enough—she had long since bored him to infidelity—to join him, for what turned out to be their assassination, near Dongo. She dashed her letters off daily, like editorials. On September 14, 1939, just after the war and their liaison had broken out, she wrote him what *Il Messagero* called "The Joy Letter," stating, "When you kiss me, I almost faint." In its thousand words she also dragged in the well-known rosy mist, tender tears, an opening flower, and seeing the beauty of the stars for the first time. A week later, she complained to the Italian dictator, now busy with Hitler's victories, that she was forced to write "because I have no chance to talk to you. Why? Not a caress, not a word from the soul." Petacci's epistolary style—she was a thesaurus of sentimental clichés—took on authority over the years, from her sheer voluminousness. Just after the first bombing of Rome and shortly before Il Duce's arrest in the midst of his disaster, she wrote him that he was her religion, that Sundays were sad, and that bombs and war were less painful than his decision to pry her loose from him "like a little cockleshell from a reef, being careful not to break it after having sucked out its heart and life." There are plenty of chauvinist high-school boys still scrawling "Viva Il Duce" in chalk on Rome's sidewalks, and they must be thrilled at one of Petacci's last statements to Sweet Ben, done in her best style: "You are great, you are a creature of God, all you have done will remain like an ocean of light."

Jesuit Left Wing

ROME, MAY 6, 1950 The middle-of-the-road Demo-Christian government is now trotting halfway through its four-year course, which runs until the 1952 elections. It is already being said that the Demo-Christians, although now firmly in the saddle, will then be overthrown at the polls by the power that elected them in 1948—the Church. Certain elements in the Jesuit order, always the most intellectual, worldly, and militant of the Church brains, are reportedly leading a Vatican Left Wing. It should be noted that the Demos already have three wings—the major Center Wing, led by Alcide de Gasperi; the minor Left Wing, led by the Chamber of Deputies President Giovanni Gronchi; and what is called the Left Left Wing, a minor group led by Giuseppe Dossetti, a sort of Christian Socialist who, it seems, cannot be a regular Socialist because Socialists are anti-Church, which he definitely is not. Dossetti and his dozen or more followers are both feared and respected within the Party as the best prepared in intellect, theory, and social consciousness to face up to the Italian problems of today and tomorrow. It is this Dossetti minority—nicknamed the Conventino, or Little Convent—that the Left Wing Jesuits are said to have made a connection with. The Conventino, apparently with the Jesuit Left Wing nodding thoughtfully behind it, has for two years been heckling its own Party's Center Wing for being too conservative, too loaded with bureaucracy, and too cautious in its good will. Only last week, Dossetti told de Gasperi, as he has told him before, that he was too slow in aiding the poor and finding work for them. Many Italians consider that there is only one important political issue in Italy—the complex matter of agrarian reform—and that de Gasperi has been slow as an ox in doing something about it. Many Italians also increasingly believe that the political struggle includes not merely the Demo-Christians and the Communists but the Vatican. Supposedly, the Jesuit Left Wing group desires to restore the Church to the intellectual, cultural, and social leadership of Europe it lost six hundred years ago. It is thought that through the brilliant, dissenting

Conventino group the de Gasperi Demos will be eliminated in the 1952 elections and replaced by purer Church types, developed by an organization called Azione Cattolica, or Catholic Action.

Azione Cattolica is a vast lay organization that millions of Italians belong to, that everybody knows about, but that the newspapers, except for the belligerent Communist press, rarely mention. Its chief is Luigi Gedda, professor of pathology and psychology at the Istituto Maria Santissima Assunta, in Rome. It is modelled on, and subordinate to, the ecclesiastical hierarchy, and its aim is to organize Catholics in such a way that they will live in a Christian manner. Its members include children preparing for catechism, Boy Scouts, and so on, up through men and women of all ages. Most of its leaders are Jesuit-educated. Its system is arterial—from the Vatican to the smallest country hamlet. Its house organs, which include even comic papers for children, are numerous. Its literary weekly, *La Fiera Letteraria*, is perhaps the best literary weekly in Rome, as the pro-Communist *Lettres Françaises* is the best literary weekly in Paris. Azione is interested in the cinema, in art, and even in abstract sculpture. Owing to proscriptions that were laid down by Mussolini's concordat with the Vatican and that are still in force, Azione is strictly apolitical. But simply by being anti-Communist, it nevertheless wields enormous political power. For the past two years, under the Commissione Pontificia d'Assistenza, it has been holding classes throughout Italy, and especially in the impoverished south, where the Communists have been making hay. In these classes, men are taught, among other things, how to read, how to drive tractors, and how to apply the latest agricultural principles. The classes are a significant and practical new touch in the Kremlin-Vatican struggle to satisfy the hopes of the Italian poor. There is a Roman saying that the Church reasons by centuries, never day by day. A basis exists, many Italians think, for supposing that some of the Vatican's ideas for the twentieth century may soon be unfolded here.

Festivals in Venice

VENICE, SEPTEMBER 12, 1950 There has been very little *dolce far niente* in this island pleasure dome lately. In the midst of Adriatic heat, accompanied by cerulean skies, sensational sunsets, and mosquitoes, the activities of the late-summer season have demanded a lot of energy of the visitor who wanted to see everything, on land and water, that was going on, or even half of it. There have been four overlapping international festivals, all involving gondolas or motorboats or footwork—the twenty-fifth Biennale di Venezia, Europe's most cosmopolitan summer modern-art show; the thirteenth International Festival of Contemporary Music; the eleventh Theatre Festival; and, most dynamic of the quartet, the eleventh annual International Exhibition of Cinema Art. For several years, the movie festival has been, in its fleshless fashion, a focal point for the international set that annually congregates here for the season and that considers every first night a matter of privilege and principle. Unfortunately for the moviemakers and their works, this worldly summer clan has a long, rich memory, if gained only by hearsay, of the fantastic Venice seasons in the late nineteen-twenties. Then, instead of a mere Technicolor melodrama that cost millions, there was the colorful, living violence of Diaghilev and his Russian Ballet distributing their corporate beauty to the point of bankruptcy among the *palazzi* of the great Venetian scene. Modern art was not academic in those days, and an item hanging on the Biennale's walls seemed ambulatory and alive, because the important artists visiting here were the men who, with their new ideas, came to dinner. The magnificent dilapidation that is Venice was animated by a real revival of taste and of pleasure in taste; public entertainments had the intimate qualities of art, and private entertainments the splendor of public fêtes. What Paris then offered in its cloistered salons during gray winters Venice presented alfresco amid its marble-walled canals in summer. Thus the two cities alternated seasonally as the center of the civilized surface of Europe in a peak period of art and patronage, which grandly flourished and then dwindled away. (It was a period when well-informed people thought the First World War was all there was to it.) Against this traditional background of personalities and performance, the presence here of clean-cut Robert Taylor, flown up from the papier-mâché sets of "Quo Vadis," now being filmed in Rome, seemed rather anticlimactic.

For visitors in Venice, the best part of this year's Cinema Festival, which was held mainly on the Lido, was the fun of going to the movies in boats—fast public *motoscafi* that streaked across the Lagoon between lighted buoys and darted down the Lido Island boulevard canals to deposit the movie fans, in evening clothes dampened by the delightful voyage. The official premiéres were held in the Lido's big, modernistic Palazzo del Cinema, near the Excelsior Hotel, at five-o'clock matinées or at ten at night. For the convenience of visitors who preferred to spend their nights gambling at the Lido Casino, the latter programs were repeated next afternoon at the San Marco Theatre. The festival, which began August 8th, ended September 10th with the awarding of prizes. The most coveted, the Prize of the Lion of Saint Mark, went to "Justice est Faite," a French film directed by André Cayatte and starring Valentine Tessier and Jean Deducourt. It deals with the euthanasia killing of a man by his mistress.

Many of the films would not seem to be sensible propaganda for the countries that made them, even if they had been understandable to the people of other countries who saw them here. Of the American films entered, three—"The Asphalt Jungle," "Caged," and "Panic in the Streets"—featured crime as though it were a main American export. The sad historical significance of another, "All the King's Men," was lost on the Europeans, who had never heard of Huey Long. The most appreciated British film was the Italo-American story about Brooklyn "Give Us This Day," based on Pietro di Donato's novel "Christ in Concrete." It was directed by Edward Dmytryk, one of the famous ten Hollywood men convicted of contempt of Congress. To the eye, which is what Europeans who do not speak English must go by, the film appears good, but to the ear its dialogue seems sentimental and forced. Another of Britain's entries, which will doubtless be a big commercial hit, was the romantic Technicolor costume opus "Gone to Earth," starring Jennifer Jones as a fey, fox-loving wanton who speaks Shropshire dialect with a strong American accent. "La Ronde," perhaps the only skillful sophisticated picture shown, is, unhappily, so Frenchily French that Italian censors probably will not license it, and certainly American censors won't. It is a fantasy version of Arthur Schnitzler's bitter "Reigen," the *Reigen* in the film being an old Vienna merry-go-around symbolizing the amorous dalliances of ten characters, each of whom, beginning with a streetwalker, gets to know two of the others but never the whole group; the story ends as it began, with the tart in bed, completing the vicious circle. It is meticulously directed and superbly played by a constellation of stars including Simone Simon, Danielle Darrieux, Isa Miranda, Jean-Louis Barrault, Fernand Gravet, and Gérard Philipe. "La Ronde" is an exquisite paste jewel.

Luigi Zampa, the famous Italian director of neo-realistic films who was responsible for the admirable "To Live in Peace" three years ago, scored a fiasco this year with "E Più Facile Che un Cammello" ["It Is Easier than a Camel"], which Venetian critics found neither droll nor penetrating. The work of only one other notable Italian director was shown—Roberto Rossellini's "Francis, God's Jester." It was enacted by friars of the Franciscan Monastery of Nocera Inferiore, near Naples. Saint Francis is played by Fra Nazario Geradi, a lively, exalted young novice who was formerly a village schoolteacher. "God's Jester" (the Saint's own phrase) was the only Italian film that anyone bothered to discuss. It struck Protestants as an imperfect but remarkable film, a flashback over centuries into a situation of purity, illustrated by photography that tries to match Giotto's frescoes. Catholics either revered it as doctrine or deplored its lack of pathos and grandiosity. Those of the second viewpoint were also vexed by its child-ishly gay monks scampering barefoot over the lovingly photographed land-scape, and by the silly follies of Fra Junipero, who must have been God's simpleton. The story ends suddenly, with Saint Francis's inspiration to dis-band his group temporarily so that all can go to the ends of the earth to preach peace. This constituted the only warning—offered in the words of a saint of seven hundred years ago—heard at the Cinema Festival.

The Festival of Contemporary Music got off to a feeble start. The opening night of the Marquis de Cuevas Ballet, which was considered no great shakes recently in Paris, was at least a fashionable sellout at the lovely, gilded old Teatro della Fenice. There was only one first-rate ballet, Jean Cocteau's newish "Le Jeune Homme et la Mort," danced by Jean Babilée. For the opening of the purely musical half of the festival, also at the Fenice, hotel concierges gave away tickets, for few had been bought. The first concert began with Paul Hindemith's Concerto for English Horn and Orchestra, which is pastoral and made up of kindly dissonances, and closed with an ugly little symphony by the atonal Austrian Ernst Krenek, of which a French visitor remarked, "*Tant de bruit pour faire une omelette* [So much noise to make an omelet]." Later programs included "Two Studies for 'The Trial,' by Kafka," by Bruno Maderna, a young Italian composer who uses the twelve-tone scale; "The Earth," by Gian Fran-cesco Malipiero, Italy's ranking melodic modernist; and Arnold Schoen-berg's "The Survivor of Warsaw," conducted by himself. What the Venetians liked best were the free tickets and the opportunity to dress up.
Italian women dress more elaborately during the Venice season than they do anyplace else any time in the year. Venetian ladies, successfully approximating in organdies and cottons the black-and-white elegance of the old-time laces and trains, sweep majestically up and down the Piazza or step sure-footedly from their gondolas. During this high season, the private gondoliers are equally elegant, in white broadcloth waistcoats and with colored armbands bearing their employers' coats of arms, and colored sashes and ribbons on their boyish straw hats. In case of great haste or grandeur, there are as many as four gondoliers to a boat.

The twenty-fifth Biennale di Venezia, at the Giardini Pubblici, which will continue until the middle of October, features retrospective exposi-tions of the French Fauves, the four French masters of Cubism, the Italian Futurists, and the Germanic Blue Riders Group, thus offering a rarely seen correlation of the four basic schools that made and molded modern Euro-pean art. Among the artists represented are Matisse, Braque, Derain,

Vlaminck, Dufy, Van Dongen, Gris, Léger, Boccioni, Balla, Severini, Klee, Kandinsky, and Kubin. Some spectators have protested that not all the pictures are really distinguished, which is indeed true. Now that war is in the air, many collectors are not letting their pictures go beyond their front door. Few collectors are, of course, as close at hand as Mrs. Peggy Guggenheim, now installed, with her sizable collection, on the Grand Canal in her permanently incomplete Palazzo dei Leone, from which she lent, along other things, her splendid Braque "The Waltz," a Gris, a Picasso ("The Poet"), and Balla's "Automobile and Noise." The Biennale also contains fascinating big retrospectives of Rousseau and Bonnard, and Seurat's drawings; a collection of the Belgian James Ensor, including his notorious satire "Christ Entering Brussels;" and the Mexican Pavilion, containing a huge show of those four monopolists of Mexican art, Orozco, Rivera, Siqueiros, and Tamayo, who had never been seen in Italy before. The United States sent a roomful of fine John Marins. In the British Pavilion are three shows—Constable, Joseph Smith, and Barbara Hepworth's drawings and sculpture. It is a treat to have all these works together within walking distance. The Biennale is nevertheless as weak as it is dull in the showing of today's younger big and little painters, who, instead of entering the show on a competitive basis, were simply invited to send in their offerings—a system that led to some queer selections. Thus the French Pavilion is dominated by two gigantic, unpleasant bile-yellow creations by someone named Bernard Lorjou, whom French visitors have never heard of. Venice has a Communist mayor, and the paintings of the official Party artist Renato Guttuso are well in the fore. Ten million lire were given in prize money to living painters by donors as various as the Venice Rotary Club, the Communist publishing house of Unità, and Perugina Candies.

The season's gayest festival, which dealt in brawn, not brain, was the annual gondola race for local gondoliers, always held the first Sunday in September, from the Lagoon down the Grand Canal. The race was first run in the year 900. As usual, the racing boats were preceded by a procession of picturesque outriders—*bissone*, great ancient skiffs, with prows of silver horses or golden goddesses, that trailed purple or scarlet silk hangings in the water and that were each manned by a dozen hearties, who stood to the oars costumed as blackamoors in yellow silk, as blue-velveteened linkboys with top hats, as silver fishes, or as muscular pageboys in crimson. It was a stunning aquatic picture as they swept, under a blue sky, down the curves of the canal. The racers, white-clad, two to a gondola, followed after the starting cannon boomed, and were feverishly cheered by Venetians packed on palace balconies, church landings, family scows, or vegetable barges. The Venice firemen acted as water-traffic cops. Instead of blowing whistles, they used their fire hoses, freely sprinkling traffic jams of excited, shouting onlookers. The race was won—or half won—by a gondolier named Stregheti, a popular fellow who had won, or half won, four times before, has ten children, and can use his share of the three-hundred-thousand-lire purse. The fourth prize was a suckling pig.

DDT is now being used in Venice instead of the old mosquito nets over the bed, and there are other improvements. The commercial waterfront in the Zattere district, beyond the Giudecca, has been completely modernized since the war and is said to be better than that of the great port of Genoa, whose bombed equipment was merely repaired. Behind Venice's big business of summer tourists is its year-round livelihood—its port, which is manned by workers (today mostly Communist) bred, as were their fore-fathers for centuries, in the squalid poverty of the Bragora and Marittima quarters of the city. Under the Austrians, Trieste was able to strangle Venetian shipping. Under international occupation, Trieste has become nothing, and Venice would have resumed its rich Adriatic trade with East-ern Europe if the Iron Curtain hadn't been lowered before Eastern Eu-rope. As it is, the Yugoslavs have developed the rival port of Pola, denying Venice its opportunity, and the long projected canal between Locarno and Venice, which would speed inland trade through the port from Central Europe to Africa, is still far from being finished. The state-owned railways have cut their freight rates below the steamer rates for the run down and around to Naples. Venice still has some of its age-old trade to the Far East, and will probably continue to have it as long as any part of that immense East maintains relations with the West. Venice, whose power and luxury had once towered as high as the sails of its ships, began to decline with the shift of world trade routes to the new Atlantic lanes, and by the eighteenth century the decline was complete. Today, Genoa's dominant position is not questioned. Genoa is the handier port for the U.S.A.

The American Academy

ROME, OCTOBER 26, 1950 On the heels of the nearly two million Anno Santo tourists who have swarmed through the Holy City this year, there has arrived a little band of Americans who have special impor-tance as sightseers in Rome. They are this autumn's ten Prix de Rome winners, who are at the moment settling down in the American Academy —two painters, two composers, one sculptor, one architect, three students of the classics, and one landscape architect, whose prize is endowed by the ardent Garden Club of America. On their first sightseeing trips here and in Florence and Venice, they have had as cicerone Mr. Laurance Roberts, the former head of the Brooklyn Museum, who for the last three years has been head of the Academy. Otherwise, they are on their own, to stare or to labor, as they choose. Until Roberts set this policy, the prize-winners, like those in other such national academies here (there are about a dozen), had to spend their time making copies of Botticelli and so on, or writing well-bred sonatinas and so on; they had to turn in a set quantity of conventional work, as if they were schoolboys. Today, the American laureate gets a free bedroom and studio at the Academy; three meals a day there, for which he pays about a dollar and a quarter; twelve hundred and fifty dollars to cover a year's expenses; a few hundred dollars to spend on European travel; and freedom to follow his own artistic bent at his own speed. He is also permitted to apply for two one-year extensions. To him, and to many envious prizemen in the other academies, the American Prix de Rome looks like clover.

The French Academy here, which was founded under Louis XIV and is the oldest, is housed in the famous Villa Medici, on the Pincio. Despite the fact that Paris later became the cradle of modern art, the French Academy ignores modern art. The American Academy, which is among the newest, was founded under President Cleveland and is housed in a Renaissance-style building on the Janiculum. It is unique among the academies in accepting *Modernismus* as a norm. The main influences, perhaps, on the American composers here have been Stravinsky and Nadia Boulanger. One of the prizemen now at the Academy—he is in his second year—is the Negro composer Ulysses Kay, who wrote the music for the film "The Quiet One." Living at the Academy along with the prize-winners are a couple of dozen holders of fellowships or scholarships from various colleges or the Guggenheim and similar foundations. In addition, some older men, whom the Academy calls "resident" artists and scholars, are invited to join the group—until recently the painter Henry Varnum Poor was here, at present the art historian Edgar Wind is here, and the composer Aaron Copland is soon to be here—and pinch-hit as counsellors if the younger set call for help.

The only antique fixture of the American Academy is the residence of its director—the lovely orange stucco Villa Aurelia, alongside the ancient Janiculum park. The villa was built as a garden casino for a Farnese prince in the late sixteenth century, passed to a rich family of commoners who made candles for the Vatican, was used by Garibaldi as headquarters during the Republic of 1849, and was bought by Mrs. Clara J. Heyland, an American lady who installed regrettable Colonial bay windows in 1886 and on her death, in 1911, left it to the Academy. The Academy was started in 1894 by Charles F. McKim, partner of Stanford White; he had participated in the classic revival popularized by the Chicago World's Fair buildings the year before and thought it was high time young American architects got the real thing in Rome.

The Prix de Rome was established for American male citizens under thirty years of age and unmarried, but love and feminism have changed all that. One of the current Prix de Rome sculptors is Miss Concetta Scaravaglione. Six of the year's ten prize-winners are married men, and five have their wives in tow. For two years, Roberts hospitably housed not only wives but babies, but the babies proved unpopular. As a result, the New York painter laureate Joseph Lasker and his wife and infant are doing the prize year from an apartment in Rome.

"Quo Vadis?"

ROME, OCTOBER 7, 1950 M-G-M's filming of Henryk Sienkiewicz's famed novel "Quo Vadis?," at the Cine Città studios here, is a gigantic sunshine, celluloid, and Technicolor event that for months has been involving lions, bulls, Christian martyrs, pagan slaves, Max Baer's giant brother Buddy, Robert Taylor in a gold breastplate, ten thousand costumes, and a replica of the Circus Maximus of Nero's day. One of the men in authority for the last three months has been Hugh Gray, a worldly, entertaining, forty-year-old Irishman, so erudite that M-G-M originally hired him simply as a script-writer. Gray speaks Italian, Spanish, Portuguese, French, German, Welsh, and Gaelic; knows Greek, Sanskrit, and Latin; was schooled at Oxford University and Louvain University; intended to enter the Church; and has written a novel dealing with Ovid. For much of the past two years, he has been inditing a four-volume "Quo Vadis?" guide for the correct presentation of Nero's times. M-G-M's notion of Technicolored antique history—to judge by what visitors see on the Cine Città's set—is that it should include, among other anachronisms, welters of red velvet, a fabric not invented till medieval times, but Gray has personally worked in the interests of authenticity, and has introduced some experts and gossipers that are new to Hollywood circles. For the guidance of wardrobe mistresses and others, his book draws on Juvenal, Suetonius, Ovid, Petronius, Tacitus, Daremberg, and Saglio, and provides hymns for the Christian extras to sing that were culled from Yemenite melodies composed during the Babylonian captivity (from which some Early Christian music sprang), and brings the news that, as a Roman intellectual snob, Nero preferred to speak Greek, had no fiddle (he had a Greek lyre), and was not a real pyromaniac. For stage carpenters building a set of Petronius' house, Gray's notes read, "We may dispense with the tablinum leading from the atrium to the peristyle." His research index covers more than a hundred thousand references, with everything from how togas were properly worn to Roman mob psychology, the protocol for seating guests at orgies, and the circus arrangements for martyrdoms. Gray's erudition is appreciated by the M-G-M moguls here. One of them recently said, "That man knows Nero's Rome like I know the Gimbel family."

"The Medium"

ROME, NOVEMBER 4, 1950 Gian-Carlo Menotti is filming "The Medium" at the Scalera Studio here. The production is being financed, like a Broadway play, by New York angels, the most generous of whom also had a big slice of the Broadway production of Menotti's "The Consul." The film will cost only a little more than twice as much as the production of the opera itself in New York. It is being recorded on four "stereophonic" sound tracks, to give the effect of sound coming from different directions. By this method, it is hoped, filmed opera will be made to sound natural, or as natural as opera of any kind can sound. The cast, except for Marie Powers and Leo Coleman, is new. Monica is now sung by Anna Maria Alberghetti, the Italian girl who astonished Manhattan critics at her concert in Carnegie Hall last spring, when she was thirteen. "The Consul" is to be produced as an opera at La Scala, in Milan, this winter. This is the first time La Scala has bothered with an American opera, even one written, like this one, by an Italian citizen.

Emma Gramatica

NOVEMBER 4, 1950 Of the grand old European actresses, the Italian
Emma Gramatica, who is now in her seventies, is the last still functioning. Her current reappearance in Rome is an event. Her touring repertory
company, in which she stars in fourteen plays, is playing at the Teatro
Valle. Her vintage art, body, and memory are equally phenomenal.
She is one of the two daughters of Duse's stage manager. Her late sister
Irma, who was tall and had a resonant voice, became notable in Ibsen
roles. Emma, who became famous in Shaw's plays, is not as large as Irma
was, has merely an intimate voice, and out of her limitations developed a
style unique in theatrical Italy—of underplaying and of speaking confidentially (this is hard on Valle audiences; people in the back rows have to
cup their ears). From her repertory of plays by D'Annunzio, Barrie,
Maugham, and Pirandello, she chose for the opening of this engagement
Maugham's "The Sacred Flame," a drama about a mother who gives her
favorite son, a paralyzed aviator hero, a fatal sleeping draught, so that he
will not know his wife has betrayed him with his brother. Today, Gramatica is a gray-haired, unbeautiful, but fascinating Duse. In Maugham's
dramatic scenes, she employed gestures of the head and hands that were
almost imperceptible. Of Europe's venerable great actresses, none has
seemed, in the memory of this writer, less theatrical or more of an actress,
with the exception of her father's employer.

Caravaggio

MILAN, JUNE 16, 1951 The current major art event in Milan,
which has drawn Italians and tourists from all over Italy, is the Palazzo
Reale exhibition of paintings—borrowed from museums and churches on
the Continent, in England, and on the Mediterranean islands—by the
swashbuckling sixteenth-century Bergamasco artist Caravaggio. Garish,

brilliant, sometimes only prodigious—he started studying art in Milan at the age of eleven, and at the age of fifteen, a young master, set off for Rome and his fame—Caravaggio has recently undergone a renaissance in popularity that has enchanted some lovers of Italian art and left others, like the venerable Bernard Berenson, grumbling. Caravaggio was remarkable for his chiaroscuro; for his realistic compositions of thighs, knees, and posteriors; and for his acute portrayal of facial expressions. One of his most famous canvases, "The Conversion of Saint Paul," consists chiefly of the rump of the horse from which the Saint has just tumbled. His genre pictures of low-life subjects, like "The Card Players," are much appreciated conversation pieces among the well-dressed. But his final churchly compositions, like "The Beheading of Saint John the Baptist," painted for the cathedral of Malta, and "The Burial of Saint Lucia," painted for her church in Syracuse, and other paintings from his grave Messina period (he had to flee to the provinces after murdering his Roman model's justifiably jealous lover), like "Lazarus Resurrected" and "Adoration of the Magi," are superb, ripe compositions, and all four are now in Milan. Caravaggio's turbulent life ended in 1609, in an attack of malaria; he died alone, in a small boat on the Mediterranean. The Milan exposition provides copiously for pleasure and instruction. It includes paintings by Rubens, Velásquez, La Tour, Ribera, etc., that demonstrate Caravaggio's influence on those artists. And it shows letters written about him in his lifetime by art merchants, praising his work to dukes who might buy it. There is also a letter from a Roman citizen complaining that Caravaggio had beaten him up for fun one moonlit night. That post-Renaissance period was a violent one, and Caravaggio was its appropriate painter.

"Miracle in Milan"

JUNE 16, 1951 The best film about Milan is a new one called "Miracolo a Milano," which was created out of fantastic whole cloth by those two noted cinema talents, the director Vittorio De Sica and the scenario writer Cesare Zavattini, who, the last time they worked together, made "The Bicycle Thief." Postwar Italian films formulated a neo-realistic approach by turning current events into small dramas. Now De Sica and Zavattini have rung a change on this by turning the climate of current events into high fantasy. "Miracle in Milan" is a fairy story set in a poor

Milan suburb. It starts with an old lady's finding a naked baby boy in her cabbage patch. After his graduation from an orphan asylum, he becomes a miracle-working optimist, played by Francesco Golisano, who is one of the few professional actors in the film. The main theme is his naïve leadership of some hoboes living in huts on a vacant lot, who accidentally strike what they hope is water, for hygienic purposes, but which proves to be oil. Here the theme diverges onto two levels, one an uproarious pastiche of fast-moving, plug-hat capitalists bent on grabbing the oil, and the other a satire on greedy human foibles among the poor. At this point, the miraculous enters the picture, in the shape of a dove that, when rubbed, acts like Aladdin's lamp, granting any wish. From then on, there are nothing but captivating fragments of the magical and the comforting, including Cinderella, Freud, hexes that turn policemen into opera tenors, and so on. It develops into a fantasy cops-and-robbers struggle that includes angels involved with street-traffic laws and ends with the poor escaping over Milan Cathedral on street-cleaners' broomsticks. In its naïve melancholy, "Miracolo a Milano" recalls Charlie Chaplin. In its use of the fabulous, it is somewhat René Clair. But in the multiple humane and funny scenes of classic mountebanks, it is strictly Italian *commedia dell'arte*, up-to-date Milan style. The film has not greatly pleased Italian cinema fans, who prefer Hollywood boys meeting girls. The heavenly dove, a very materialistic provider, has offended the pious, and Rightist politicos have been worried by the satire on big business and its sumptuous office fittings, which include two office cows for fresh milk in the event of war. But if you enjoy fantasy with a sting in its gauzy tail, and if you want to laugh hard, then "Miracolo a Milano" is the foreign film for you.

"Europa '51," and "Umberto D."

SEPTEMBER 6, 1952 Roberto Rossellini's new film, "Europa '51," starring his wife, Ingrid Bergman, will probably prove to be as controversial as anything they have ever done on the screen or off. It will make its first public appearance at the current Venice Film Festival, where it is purposely to be the last movie shown—though that will not necessarily prevent its being more argued about than all the previous films rolled together. This is its theme: A woman named Irene, a foreigner in Italy who is married to a dull, well-to-do American businessman in postwar

Rome, is the mother of a bomb-shocked son, about ten, whom she neglects in favor of what look like very dreary dinner parties. During one of them, the neurotic lad flings himself down the stairs and dies. In her remorseful effort to reassess her values in life, Irene turns to a politically radical writer who loves her, whom she does not love, and who squires her in visits to Rome's poor suburbs. In a rapid concatenation of encounters with a couple of impoverished families, her first real feeling for human beings— an exalted, penitent loving-kindness—begins to manifest itself in her relations with the families' children, includes aiding the flight of a man who has just committed murder (which makes her a criminal, too), and culminates in her sitting with a tubercular prostitute until she dies. After the death, Irene's next experience in loving-kindness is with the insane, since, to avoid prison, she is placed in a psychopathic clinic. This makes up the important, the fascinating, the terrible, and the serious and controversial last half of the film, and it is here that the Rossellini-Bergman talents come into their own. It is in this section that Miss Bergman, whose present physical plasticity and thinned beauty give her a metaphysical quality, uses her gift for portraying somebody being directed by the voice of conscience. It is in this section that Rossellini's scenes are breathtaking. By means of his camera, he forces acquaintanceship with mad passing faces, with clinic doors that open and close like eyes, and with that sense of civilized inquisition—the summing up between society and the individual—that is a clinic's fatal climate. In the final disposition of her case, made in the presence of a psychiatrist, a priest, the family lawyer, a judge, and her husband, the woman refuses to return home, because, she says, loving one family is not enough. In careful answers to the assembled gentlemen's questions, she declares that she subscribes to no dogma, is not a political reformer, does not want to be a nun, believes Christ came to save people as they are and not to change them, and that if she loves others, it is because she despises herself. The story ends with her decision, made in complete sanity, to stay with the insane, where she is free to feel love as the only unrestricting communication possible between human beings. It is a film starring Miss Bergman as a twentieth-century saint in a sweater, and a story difficult to make valid without costume values or wit, such as Shaw's "Saint Joan" has. Rossellini says the picture is partly a reflection of the Christianism in the recently published books of the late Simone Weil. His exposition in "Europa '51" is probably too brief, and the compressed results can fascinate or infuriate. But they are likely to be of harrowing interest to people worried to despair about the way humanity has been acting of late.

The only high-class box-office bull's-eye in the general crop of films in Rome is the intelligent, very funny comedy "Due Soldi di Speranza"

("Two Pennyworth of Hope"), with the female lead played by the ripe young daughter of a Rome day laborer and the male lead by one Vincenzo Musolino, nephew of a celebrated Calabrian bandit of that name but otherwise unknown. The story, filmed in a village on the slope of Vesuvius, is rather like the volcanic wines—volatile and heady. It is an account of an amorous young man's struggles to marry, struggles caused by the circumstance that how much he earns, rather than how much he loves, is the social basis for marriage. "Altri Tempi" ("Times Gone By"), directed by Alessandro Blasetti, who made "Four Steps in the Clouds," is an octet of period pieces, built around a bookseller whose modern customers won't read the famous regional *novelle* by the great Italian writers he admires, and which promptly constitute the film. Among the eight is Pirandello's Sicilian story of the maddened, unfaithful wife, Fucini's Tuscan dialect tale of the peasants who quarrel nearly to the death about fertilizer, and Scarfoglio's hilarious Neapolitan annal about the pretty murderess and the silly lawyer, the latter excellently played by Vittorio De Sica. All this makes for ably directed required reading but adds up to a great many short stories for anyone except a bookworm.

This year's De Sica–directed film is "Umberto D.," which is about a retired petty official, starving on his pension, whose only friend is his dog. Dog-lovers are either crazy about it or can't stand it. De Sica uses in it the same technique of detail that made a masterpiece of "The Bicycle Thief," but in this case he seems to use it less in the service of tragedy than in the service of mere unhappiness. In many ways, the year's most effective Italian film is, oddly enough, Russian—Gogol's "The Overcoat," in an international adaptation. This is a beautifully cinematographed satire on the modern bureaucracies we all inhabit—the tragicomedy of a little official who dies because he cannot afford to buy a warm coat and returns to earth to haunt everybody who had refused to raise his salary.

It is a pity that work on the most peculiar film of the year has only barely begun. Whatever it sounds like, it was thought up by the scenario writer Cesare Zavattini, who, after all, thought up "The Bicycle Thief." The film is called "Noi Donne" ("We Women") and is to consist of five living short stories, each an episode volunteered from the life of an important cinema star, who will play in her own episode, with, if possible, the persons involved in it. Alida Valli, who was the Viennese girl in "The Third Man," has just made the opening episode with her former masseur, who figured in it. Isa Miranda, Bergman, Silvana Mangano (who was the handsome wench in "Bitter Rice"), and Anna Magnani are the four women to come. There is, of course, considerable studio gossip and curiosity as to which private incidents, or which versions of them, these ladies will choose to publicize.

It is known that the Italian government, like Italians generally, found no entertainment value in the seamy-sided, neo-realistic films that made post-war Italian directors famous; their dramatization of Italy's poverty was, the Italians thought, awful propaganda, even when New York, Paris, and London hailed the pictures as artistic. The government hopes that some of this year's films will play in the big American movie houses, rather than in the small art theatres.

Congress of Nuns

ROME, OCTOBER 4, 1952 An influx of nuns of all orders has lately been noticeable on Vatican City streets, on foot in pairs, in taxis in pairs, and in private cars in pairs—Franciscans, Benedictines, Dominicans; in brown habits, in pleated blue ones, in black ones, in white ones, and all in starched coifs like small clouds. They have flown in from Egypt, Africa, America, and other distant points, and are the sixteen hundred delegates (representing the world's million two hundred thousand nuns) to the first general congress of nuns in Christianity's two thousand years—a meeting of the Superiore Generali di Ordini ed Istituti Religiosi Femminili. The plain purpose of the congress has been to present to its members, through Vatican spokesmen, the Church's modernizing plans for "a transformation of female religious existence, as regards conventual practices of prayer and meditation, movement and work, rest and sleep, and heating and clothing"—plans that the sisterhood delegates have spiritedly resisted. The reason given for the meeting was that a falling off in the number of priests and male aspirants dedicated to carrying on the Church's work makes it necessary for the sisters to take a larger part in it. The first theological university for nuns was even among the new plans. But it was on the feminine question of the nuns' habits, those picturesque, inconvenient, hot, trailing robes and troublesome starched coifs—a costume specifically cited by the Vatican as calling for change—that the sisters put up the stiffest resistance. Along with plans for finally installing heating in cold-climate convents, the Church took up the matter of personal cleanliness, remarking, "It is true that our grandmothers washed less, and today it is true that the general sensibility to cleanliness has augmented." Recommended by the Church was a bath every week, and even oftener in summer. In Rome, where there is a great deal of practical gossip about papal problems, it is freely asserted that getting on with the nuns has ever been one of His Holiness's weightiest concerns. Romans were startled at what they felt was the sharp tone of reproof in the discourse the Pope delivered to the congress in person. Stating that "feminine religious life was in full flower twenty years ago but today its numbers are reduced by half," he counselled, as a remedy, that "the habits worn, the kind of life, and the seclusion of the religious sisterhoods should not constitute a barrier or a cause of unsuccess" in encouraging pious young girls to join. He then added, with his infallible authority, the last masculine word on the dress question—that the habits the nuns wear should be more modern and should conform to "the exigencies of hygiene." The nuns' congress, and everything that went with it, has caused much comment in Rome.

Show at the Colosseum

ROME, OCTOBER 4, 1952 About fifty years ago, the Parliament here forbade as blasphemous a scheme to stage lively spectacles of the bread-and-circuses type in the Colosseum. It was sacred ground, the politicians declared, where Christian martyrs had shed their blood. Since then, the rare Colosseum shows have been quasi-religious, with just enough of the pagan touch to draw the crowd. An attraction now briefly showing there, called "Il Colosseo Nei Secoli" ("The Colosseum Through the Centuries"), thus carefully features both the Crucifixion and a bacchanalian ballet. To judge by the opening-night performance, it would be a better show if it could be seen and heard. Unfortunately, the twentieth century was the one epoch the producers ignored. Without the modernity of loudspeakers to carry the shouting actors' voices across the vast ruin cupped under a classic starry sky, and with insufficient spotlighting, the spectacle was like a succession of obscure museum paintings in need of cleaning and stronger light to reveal their scarlets and greens and their occasionally noble composition. A far-off saffron-dressed chorus was lined up dangerously near the Colosseum's top arches, from where their alternating shouts of "Thumbs down!" during the gladiatorial fights and "Hallelujah!" during the Christian episodes echoed faintly, as if over time. However, the Crucifixion and the Descent from the Cross, if unexpected in connection with the history of the Colosseum, were profoundly impressive, obviously having been modelled after Fra Angelico's paintings. Only two scenes were brilliantly visible—Christ's Resurrection from the Tomb, which was suddenly floodlighted, as if with glory, and, some minutes later, the astonishing sight, against the black-arched shadows, of Christ in light ascending to Heaven (or, at any rate, to the top of the Colosseum, on a pulley rope). This was a truly startling thing to see, and it seemed to surprise the Roman spectators.

Roman Fair

AUGUST 15, 1953 July 25th, the tenth anniversary of Mussolini's fall, was quietly celebrated here by night illuminations of the façades of great antique and Renaissance buildings—the Colosseum, St. Peter's, and the finest *palazzi*, including the one on the Piazza Venezia where he used to harangue crowds from the balcony. The next day, there opened outside Rome an agricultural fair, advertised to feature, among other attractions, rice paddies, with pretty peasants harvesting rice from them, and a *risotto* restaurant nearby. The important thing about the agricultural show is where it is being held, which is in and around an amazing, lonely, far-flung complex of marble buildings, some of them still unfinished, and all of them ordinarily empty and seen by the public only as a broken silhouette across the Roman campagna. They are the uncompleted remains of one of Mussolini's most grandiose building projects, begun in 1937 and obstinately continued into the war until 1941, when it was abandoned. The name of the project was "E-42," meaning "Esposizione 1942," which was to be Fascism's great international fair in Rome. This title has been officially changed this year to "EA-53," meaning "Esposizione di Agricoltura 1953," but Romans are too used to the historical irony implicit in E-42 to call it anything else now. Even incomplete, E-42 is the most presumptuous, imposing permanent fairground in Europe. It is located halfway between Rome and Ostia, facing the Alban Hills, and has a land surface the size of the city of Florence. The handsomest and oddest building of the complex, pure de Chirico in style, is the Palazzo della Civiltà, by the side of the River Tiber. Its façades consist of six high Romanesque vaulted galleries, set one on top of another, which run around the four sides of the building's central core. At a distance, owing to the arrangement of the galleries' bays and arches, the Palazzo looks porous—a huge cube with tunnel-like holes and vistas disclosing the sky behind. At night, each arched ceiling is illuminated with indirect yellow lighting, making the Palazzo on its barren hill visible for miles around, like a fulminating honeycomb.

The rest of the buildings, looked down on from the top gallery of the Palazzo della Civiltà, are a more melancholy mixture. There are pillared porticoes of gleaming marble, mosaics, decorative staircases behind glass walls, and travertine laid in *reticolare*, Rome's ancient diaper pattern for bricks; there are marble arcades, weedy holes in the ground for buildings never started, and foundations never built on; there are nearly finished marble buildings with mattings still serving as roofs, and incomplete buildings so far away that their desolate pillars rise from a heath of scrub; and near the superb polished black granite pillars of the Palazzo dei Congressi there is an unfinished obelisk, which was to have honored Guglielmo Marconi for his invention of the wireless. On one of the buildings Mussolini had carved an imperial-sounding inscription, in which he prophesied that "this Rome shall stretch over other hills by the banks of the sacred river to the beach of the Tyrrhenian Sea"—which on a clear day can indeed be seen from the fairground. EA-53 is not much to look at, but E-42 is still Rome's most interesting unfinished ruin of the Fascist Empire.

"Ben-Hur"

ROME, SEPTEMBER 27, 1958 The last of the big American film spectacles that will probably ever be made in Rome is "Ben-Hur," now still in the making at Cinecittà, the enormous *statalismo* film studio, soon to be torn down, that was built by Mussolini south of the city. In Rome's extraordinary expansion, hundreds of new apartment houses today surround the sets. There seems no doubt that this particular "Ben-Hur"—that old theatrical war horse that has had Ben running on its practically unrusted chariot-race treadmill since its first Broadway performance in 1899—has been set up here as the apogee of super-spectacles, with the highest cost to date of any movie, twelve and a half million dollars having already been spent on it, which is five and a half million worse even than "Quo Vadis," also made here. The circus for the chariot race covers eighteen acres, and drivers and horses reportedly did about a hundred miles of racing in the various rehearsals and heats, drawing vast crowds of tourists and racing fans from Rome. The nine teams of four chariot horses (some being extras, in case of accident) were mostly bought in Yugo-slavia, where they had modestly labored as farm horses, but the white ones with which Ben-Hur wins are Lipizzans, the famous breed used by Austrian nobility on parade. They have been trained in Rome by Holly-wood's Glenn Randall, who wears a real diamond horseshoe pin instead of a tie around the stables; Hollywood stunt riders and California cowboys trained the Roman chariot drivers. The movie's desert scenes were filmed in Israel; Nazareth was rebuilt at Foggia, south of Rome; and a new Jerusalem was constructed at Anzio, near the U.S. Army's former beach-head. Some of the Roman patricians in the mob of ten thousand extras have been played by contemporary, recognizable counterparts, working either for fun or frankly for money, among them the Princes Emanuele and Edmondo Ruspoli, the Duchess Nona Medici, and the Russian Princess Irina Vassilchikov, who has theatrical aspirations. The director is the meticulous William Wyler, who, it seems, was born in Alsace and directs his Italian mobs in French, translated by his bilingual assistant director. The noted British poet Christopher Fry is still in Rome working on the dialogue. Artifacts and other technical details are being supervised by Professor Moshe Gottstein, of the Hebrew University in Jerusalem, an expert on the Dead Sea scrolls, and the Roman priest Father Francesco Vattione is taking care of the Christian end. The young Israeli actress Haya Harareet, who starred in the prize-winning Israeli film "Hill 24 Doesn't Answer," appropriately plays the role of Esther. Of all the famous Ben-Hurs of the past, certainly none has been so well read, studious, and historical-minded as the present incumbent, Charlton Heston, who recently correctly referred to a magnificent gold-embroidered V-shaped garment he wore (in an orgy scene) as a *synthesis romana*.

IV

‿❧

The Infinite Pleasure: Sylvia Beach

OCTOBER 24, 1959 In the history of Joyceana, the importance of Miss Sylvia Beach is both supreme and basic, as the intrepid, unselfish, totally inexperienced, and little-moneyed young-lady publisher of "Ulysses" in Paris in 1922, when this masculine illicit masterpiece could not be printed whole in any English-speaking country and managed to become a book because her printers in Dijon understood French only. In "Shakespeare and Company" (Harcourt, Brace), her memoir of herself, her times, and her bookshop, she establishes her fundamentals in her opening sentence, stating, "My father, the Reverend Sylvester Woodbridge Beach, D.D., was a Presbyterian minister who for seventeen years was pastor of the First Presbyterian Church in Princeton, New Jersey." Woodrow Wilson was a member of the congregation while president of Princeton, and considered himself and his family members even after he became President; the Reverend Dr. Beach performed the marriage ceremonies at the White House of daughters Jessie and Eleanor Wilson, and, as his last duty, officiated at the ex-President's funeral. Miss Beach's mother was born in Rawalpindi, India, where her Pennsylvania father was a medical missionary. In 1919, Sylvia Beach cabled her mother that she was opening a Paris bookshop—"please send money"—and Mrs. Beach sent her life savings, thus inadvertently making possible the publication of the French-inked volume that burst the printed confines of the English language and loosed upon our literature the interior monologue, with its candid dark secrets of the mind and body. In two years, to Miss Beach's surprise, her bookshop and lending library, established at 12 Rue de l'Odéon, was as well-known a Left Bank literary landmark for the incoming crowds of American tourists as was the Café des Deux Magots, and to all of us Left Bankers of the time she was known simply as Sylvia—except to the Irish author, to whom she was ever Miss Beach, just as he, with the strange formality of a polyglot genius in exile, remained Mr. Joyce to her and to everybody.

Miss Beach explains the name of her bookshop by saying merely that she thought of it one night in bed, perhaps because Shakespeare had always been a best-seller, adding that her reason for arriving in Paris in 1917, during what then ranked as the world's worst war, was that she was interested in contemporary French writing. By good luck, her interest led her to the Maison des Amis des Livres, the French bookshop and lending library (soon to be the model for her own) of Mlle. Adrienne Monnier, at 7 Rue de l'Odéon, where amity for the current leading books of talent included their authors as well—such as Gide, Jean Schlumberger, the poets Valéry and Fargue, and the novelists Larbaud and Jules Romains— who frequented it to discuss each other's writings and, at special, reverent sessions that Sylvia attended, to read aloud from their manuscripts. The immediate compatibility of these two extraordinary women—Mlle. Monnier, buxom as an abbess, placidly picturesque in the costume she had permanently adopted, consisting of a long, full gray skirt, a bright velveteen waistcoat, and a white blouse, and slim, jacketed Sylvia, with her schoolgirl white collar and big colored bowknot, in the style of Colette's Claudine à l'Ecole—eventually had an important canalizing influence on French-American literary relations as they flowed, almost like a new major cultural traffic, up and down the Rue de l'Odéon. When the unknown young American writers began founding the American literary school of this century in Paris—expatriates all, suddenly at home in work together against a background of foreign language, Gallic liberty, good cheap brandy instead of prohibition bathtub gin, and municipal architectural beauty instead of Midwest cornfields—Shakespeare and Company served as their club, mail drop, meetinghouse, and forum. Practically all of them, after that inexplicably creative postwar 1920–30 period became historic, were to be written about, or at least footnoted, by official literary experts back home, who mostly knew them only through the distance of print. The charm and big value of Sylvia Beach's book is that she knew the American writers of the twenties in their young flesh and faces in Paris, and writes about them with truth and in the vernacular.

Her vignettes from memory make lively illustrations, particularly of Hemingway, then earning his living as the sports correspondent of the Toronto *Star*—taking off a shoe and sock on their first meeting in her shop, and rolling up his trouser leg to the knee to show her his war scars from the Italian campaign; using her shop as a place to baby-sit with his son Bumby, while Papa read the London literary periodicals; reading in one of them Wyndham Lewis's brutal attack on him called "The Dumb Ox" and getting so aroused that he knocked the heads off three dozen tulips (a birthday present) on Sylvia's desk, then writing out a check to pay for twice as many new flowers. Among the senior figures who were earlier expatriates was Ezra Pound, in the "velvet jacket and the open-road shirt" of the English aesthetes. "There was a touch of Whistler about him," Miss Beach says, adding that "his language, on the other hand, was Huckleberry Finn's." Shortly after she opened her shop, two women visitors appeared, of whom she says, in part, "One of them, with a very fine face, was stout, wore a long robe, and, on her head, a most becoming top of a basket. She was accompanied by a slim, dark whimsical woman: she reminded me of a gipsy. They were Gertrude Stein and Alice B. Toklas. . . . Alice had a great deal more finesse than Gertrude. And she was grown up: Gertrude was a child, something of an infant prodigy." Gertrude took out a subscription to the lending library, which, she complained, had no amusing books in it, though it must have been the only lending library in Paris that "had two copies of 'Tender Buttons' circulating." The three ladies became neighborhood friends, although Sylvia disagreed with Gertrude's teasingly disrespectful opinion of French writing as "fanfare," and also of some other writing—for instance, Joyce's. "She was disappointed in me when I published 'Ulysses,' " and called at the shop to announce that thereafter she and Miss Toklas would patronize the American Library on the Right Bank. The Left Bank was a crowded small world as far as international writers were concerned, yet Miss Stein and Mr. Joyce managed not to meet until 1930; then, at the studio of Jo Davidson, who had done busts of both, Sylvia introduced to each other those two most famed living artificers of the English language.

Miss Beach's book is intimate, not scholarly, and thus full of interesting information. Her reminiscences are literally an index of everybody in the twenties, and she knew them all, major and minor, Northerners and Southerners, photographers, drinkers, publishers of private editions, the rare married ones and the generally unmarried, and the stray musicians, but, above all, those born to write—the young men and women whom the war had freed and changed, so that their novice talent came forth in the strong form of our own modern American literature. Where her book is unique is in its two contributions to the literary history of our century, of which the first (and here, again, only she knew it all and could now set it down) concerns that legend of bookmaking martyrdom which was the publishing of "Ulysses," and the second is her illuminating, haunting verbal portrait —first physical, then almost confidentially psychological—of Mr. Joyce, the half-blind genius who wrote the book and kept on rewriting it for almost nine years, tortured beyond his own physical pain by the fear that it would never see the light of day in print, with readers' eyes taking it all in, in astonishment, on the fair page. Miss Beach first met Joyce on a summer Sunday in 1920 at the house of a French poet, where he had been brought by Ezra Pound and she by Adrienne Monnier. He was thin, stooped, graceful, with a "limp, boneless" handshake. "On the middle and third fingers of the left hand, he wore rings, the stones in heavy settings," she writes. "His eyes, a deep blue, with the light of genius in them, were extremely beautiful. I noticed, however, that the right eye had a slightly abnormal look"—the result of his glaucoma. With his tall head and wavy bright hair, his light skin, rather flushed and freckled, and his narrow, fine-cut lips, "he gave an impression of sensitiveness exceeding any I had ever known," and when a dog barked across the road he trembled with fear, for he had been afraid of dogs since the age of five, when one bit him, and he fingered his goatee, which he said he wore to hide the scar. He blushed scarlet at racy French conversation, although, by his own estimate almost ten per cent of "Ulysses" could be accounted legally indecent. The next day, he called at her shop, twirling his ashplant cane like Stephen Dedalus —"a black felt hat on the back of his head, and, on his narrow feet, not so very white sneakers. . . . Joyce was always a bit shabby." Because she worshipped him as the greatest living writer, she shortly afterward proposed that Shakespeare and Company publish his masterpiece, and he accepted with alacrity. Here it should be noted that "Ulysses" affected and even afflicted the lives of four American women who aimed at doing what no man risked—publishing it *in toto*. First, there was Miss Harriet Weaver, who, in her London review, the *Egoist*, had already published as far as the "Wandering Rocks" chapters; at that point, the protests of her subscribers became so strident that overnight she wiped out the review and started the Egoist Press, so as to publish the rest, whereupon the British printers refused to set the type, since by British law they, as well as the publisher, would be subject to penalty if the book ran into trouble. Then, in New York, Margaret Anderson and Jane Heap began publishing "Ulysses" in their *Little Review*, three issues of which were impounded by the United States Post Office; when a fourth issue was seized, at the instigation of John Sumner's Society for the Suppression of Vice, they were brought to court on the charge of publishing obscenity, and were fined, which wiped out the *Little Review*. It was Joyce's giving Miss Beach this sad *Little Review* news—adding tragically, "My book will never come out now"—that led her to make her offer, which almost wiped out Shakespeare and Company.

The shop flew the blue Greek flag, for Ulysses the Wanderer, during the finishing of the manuscript and the long publication struggle. Joyce wrote with soft black pencils; finding intelligent volunteers to decipher his exotic and erotic vocabulary and type the manuscript grew harder after one volunteer's husband, scandalized by the text, threw her typescript in the fire. Miss Beach became Joyce's secretary, editor, impresario, and banker, and had to hire help to run her shop. She organized international and local subscription lists for the book to help finance its publishing and the Joyce family of four. Across the street, at the Monnier bookshop, the bilingual French novelist Larbaud, who thought the book "as great as Rabelais," gave a public reading, with admission charged, of passages he had translated into French (but even the French listeners were warned that they might "be justly offended"), and Joyce selected an extract from the "Sirens" chapter to be read in English. After typesetting had begun at Dijon, Joyce, in a kind of postscript ecstasy, scribbled some ninety thousand words more on the costly, repeatedly reset proofs, making a 260,430-word volume, of which Miss Beach managed to have two copies printed for his fortieth birthday, on February 2, 1922—one for him, one for her. By the eighth edition, despite lost sales in England and the United States, where it was banned and seized (at purchasers' requests, her shop sold it wrapped in false dust covers, one bearing the title "Shakespeare's Works Complete in One Volume," the other "Merry Tales for Little Folks"), Joyce was living luxuriously. "Ulysses" was the investment of his lifetime after years of penury, Miss Beach justly writes. When we minor Left Bankers occasionally went to dance in Montparnasse at Les Trianons, we could peer into its elegant restaurant and see the Joyces still at dinner, he being served royally, for he tipped like a prince—"overtipped" like one, "knowing the circumstances," Miss Beach writes, since the penury was now hers. "I understood from the first that, working with or for James Joyce, the pleasure was mine—an infinite pleasure; the profits were for him. All that was available from his work, and I managed to keep it available, was his." What she mostly gained, besides fame, were unwelcome offers—and she a minister's daughter—to publish erotica as a steady thing, such as "Lady Chatterley's Lover," at the request of Aldous Huxley, and the spicy memoirs of a maître d'hôtel at Maxim's.

The details of the final severance of unbusinesslike business relations between Joyce and Miss Beach make brief, painful reading. They had started their labors together through shared appreciation of his genius, and without a contract. Late in 1930, he suddenly produced a contract that he himself had written, and they signed it, though it turned out to have no legal value for her whatever—a strange, Jesuitical document, printed in photostat in her book, by which he gave her, for the first time, world rights to publish and sell "Ulysses" and at the same time stipulated that she should abandon them "if deemed advisable . . . in the interests of the author," in which case the new publisher would acquire his rights from her, at her price. Desperate at the American pirating of his book, Joyce started arranging for its publication by Random House, in New York (he got a forty-five-thousand-dollar advance, he later said), without telling her. But others told her, adding that she was only standing in his way, so she telephoned Mr. Joyce to tell him to dispose of "Ulysses" in any way that suited him, without considering her claims, which he was apparently already doing. After all, as she writes, the book was his: "A baby belongs to its mother, not to the midwife."

By the middle thirties and in the post-depression, Shakespeare and Company was in such a bad way that Miss Beach told André Gide she was thinking of putting up the shutters. The response of the Monnier-bookshop French writers across the street was wonderful: first a demand to the French government to subsidize her shop (naturally refused), then the formation of a committee composed of some of the most important talents of the day—Gide, Duhamel, Maurois, de Lacretelle, Jules Romains, Valéry, Schlumberger, and others—who issued an appeal for two hundred subscribers who would contribute two hundred francs a year for two years, to tide the shop over. They also gave readings in her shop for the subscribers, at which Valéry recited some of his most beautiful poems—including "Le Serpent," at Joyce's special request, though no mention is made of Joyce's reading anything. Among the Americans, T. S. Eliot came over from London to give a reading, and even Hemingway consented to read aloud from his works when Stephen Spender agreed to make it a double bill. And so Shakespeare and Company was saved—only to be emptied of every book and article in it by Sylvia herself in 1941, after a German officer, on being refused her last copy of Joyce's "Finnegans Wake," threatened to return and confiscate it and everything else in the shop. So Miss Beach was sent to an internment camp for half a year, Joyce having once more played an important role in her life. Today, though the shop is still closed, she continues to live, with her recollections, in a little apartment above it.

Colette[*]

JANUARY, 1967 Of this curious volume, *The Pure and the Impure*, in several ways unlike any other that Colette wrote, she eventually said, "It will perhaps be recognized one day as my best book." Its genesis probably sprang from diverse events and a new influence which rose in the year 1925 when she and Maurice Goudeket first met in the South of

* Introduction to *The Pure and the Impure*, by Colette, translated by Herma Briffault (New York: Farrar, Straus & Giroux, 1967).

France, she approaching her fifty-third year, he just turned thirty-five, the digits for their respective ages being the same but reversed like mirror writing. Of her three husbands, only he, the last and the friendly favorite, served her literary genius with the devotion of a young neophyte. Her first husband, Henri Gauthier-Villars, considerably her senior and a Paris journalist of sorts, had stolen her opening four *Claudine* books, the first one published on the edge of the century in 1900, by publishing them under his professional pseudonym of "Willy." Indeed, it was not till a quarter of a century later, in 1926, that she finally established her literary rights to them by producing the original manuscripts, which she had saved, scribbled in durable copybooks such as French children used at school.

By 1925 she was divorced from her second husband, the handsome, worldly Henri de Jouvenel, editor of *Le Matin*, who had pointedly asked her why she could not write novels that were not immoral. In 1923 he had started the serial publication in *Le Matin* of her latest work, *The Ripening Seed (Le Blé en herbe)*, now considered a classic of adolescent love, which *Le Matin* readers found so shocking that he had to stop printing it, unfinished. From it came her famous melancholy phrase, "Ces plaisirs qu'on nomme, à la légère, physique"—"These pleasures which are lightly called physical," meaning that they can also shake the soul. The first two words, "Ces plaisirs," formed the original title of this book you are now reading, which during World War II she inexplicably altered in a small, privately published de luxe edition to *Le pur et l'impur*. As *Ces plaisirs,* and before its publication in book form, it began to appear serially at the end of 1930 in a Paris weekly called *Gringoire*, whose editor, after the fourth installment, discovered (just like Jouvenel) that his readers neither appreciated it nor liked it, and cut it off so short that the word *Fin*, The End, appears in the middle of a sentence that is never completed. Under either title, *Ces plaisirs* or *Le pur et l'impur*, this book has long been out of print except as part of the several definitive complete editions of Colette's works. It is a book that has led a life of its own.

When Colette met Goudeket, she was still at the high tide of her first fame. With the publication in 1920 of *Chéri*, her sensuously perfect, short tragic novel, at the age of forty-seven she had become one of the masters of French prose. She had also become a literary expert in verbal candor in her written portraits of female nudes, which on canvas had been one of the loose glories of French Impressionist pictorial art. In earlier books such as *The Vagabond* and *The Ingenuous Libertine*, and in certain pages of the last *Claudine*, she had wielded an inspired pen as an intimate writer about women, with special interpretations. From Goudeket she received the strength both of euphoria and of renewed creative energy. By this time the posthumous volumes of Marcel Proust's *Remembrance of Things Past*—

she had known Proust during World War I at his dinner parties at the Ritz—were appearing in Paris and his grand design as a writer had emerged, with its new specific sexual subject matter and its new masculine shape of love. Colette's favorite writing formula consisted of autobiographic novelizing. (In another two or three years she would write *Sido*, the chef-d'oeuvre in this manner, her all-embracing biography of her mother, and of herself in her countrified childhood.) But in her many short works and in her short stories she had already made use of most of her early life, except a certain portion of her middle-thirties, and its recollections. She now turned to these, without haste and at first not even boldly.

In 1928 a private press published her character sketch of the Sapphic poetess Renée Vivien, born Pauline Tarn, in London, of an English father and an American mother, a fragile neurotic figure who spent most of her short, self-destructive life in Paris, maintained in mysterious semi-Oriental elegance and living on spiced foods and alcohol in a garden apartment by chance next to Colette's, near the Bois de Boulogne. Colette doubtless chose her to write about first, in these pure and impure recollections of extraordinary women, because Renée Vivien was dead—had died two decades earlier, in 1909. This provided for Colette the long, useful, writer's retrospective so easily enriched by the passage of time as it began to shorten itself onto paper and to take its shadows from a pen dipped in ink. Renée Vivien's poetry, which included impassioned propaganda for the Mytilene myth, was symbolistic in style and touched by Mallarmé, as was natural to the period, but was carefully constructed and poetically valid, for her gift was genuine.

When she presented an occasional book of her poems to Colette, it was discreetly concealed in a basket of exotic fruits or flowers or wrapped in a length of Oriental silk. None of Colette's circle ever saw Renée's lover, or learned who she was, but she must have been very rich. She would send her carriage and coachman to Renée's apartment when Renée was giving a ladies' champagne dinner party, with an imperious command, always instantly obeyed, for Renée to leave her guests and come at once. The poetess repeatedly said she feared she would be killed by her, if only by a surfeit of love. Colette's study of Renée, which glows with brilliant writing and a certain pity, became the most vivid phantasmagoric portrait in *The Pure and the Impure* when it was finally published in Paris in 1932.

With its various contents assembled, its descriptions of the little bars and restaurants favored by these special women in smoking jackets and long trousers, "worn like guilty pleasures," as Colette wrote, after describing herself in "a pleated shirt, stiff collar, sometimes a waistcoat," and always a manly "silk pocket handkerchief," it became clear, at least on second reading, if not on the first, that Colette in this new book had written a serious analysis of sex, of the sexual response and of sexual variety and ambiguity.

The book opens with an extensive appreciation of a woman Colette called "Charlotte," a generous cocotte who simulated long, nightingale-like cries of satisfied love because they gave felicity and a triumph of manhood to her dying young lover. It was Colette's desire to add to the limited treasury of truthful insights into love, into the mysteries of love in its many forms. And in the new book she used her customary semi-fictional formula to report on the behavior, the *mores*, reflexes, instincts of women, especially as sentient, desiring creatures drawn to similarities and even to substitutes. Colette, as author, confronts the reader at the same time in a somewhat fierce intimacy, with her personal remembrances, observations, and exact images, all dealing basically with the phenomenon of eroticism. Colette's understanding of the male sex amounted to an amazing identification with man per se, to which was added her own uterine comprehension of women, more objective than feminine. One can think of no other female writer endowed with this double comprehension whereby she understood and accepted the naturalness of sex wherever found or however fragmented and reapportioned. She seemed to have a hermaphroditic duality in her understanding and twofold loyalties.

One of the female figures in this transvestite society of the "Pure and the Impure" was a woman whom Colette called "La Chevalière," since her real title was too weighty to be mentioned, a quiet person, "with the solid build of a man, reserved and rather timid." Stripped of all the fictitious trappings with which Colette loyally sought to disguise her, she was easily recognizable to Parisians as the ex-Marquise de Belboeuf, with whom Colette had lived for six years after the end of her first marriage. To earn her living, Colette had become a music-hall dancer and mime, playing in Paris at the famous Ba-Ta-Clan and touring the provinces in an act called "Desire, Love, and the Chimera," in which she was costumed like a cat, with a feline mask and whiskers and a velvet tail. At certain times when funds were low, her traveling companion, the ex-marquise, had played a minor male dance role in the troupe. The father of the marquise was the Duc de Morny, illegitimate son of Queen Hortense of Holland, who was the daughter of Josephine Beauharnais by her first marriage—the famed Josephine who afterward became Napoleon's empress. Morny was thus a bastard half brother, on the distaff side, of Napoleon III of the Second Empire. Morny married a Princess Troubetskoy, and they had three children, of whom the only girl was the Princess Marie, affectionately called by her governess the "Little Miss," which became "Missy" and her nickname for life. She had married the Marquis de Belboeuf, whose estates were outside Rouen. A French woman writer who as a child had known Colette and Missy at Colette's seaside home at Rozven, on the Brittany coast, still recalls Missy's astonishing appearance. She had fine features, her mother having been beautiful and her father handsome. She wore no make-up. Her face was oval, her teeth were pretty, and she had a very pretty nose. She looked like a distinguished, refined, no-longer-young man, for she always wore men's clothes, indeed wore quite a lot of them, which made her look plump. To hide what might have seemed her effeminate figure, she wore an assortment of woolen waistcoats and shirts, and because her feet were aristocratic and small, always wore several pairs of socks, so they would fill up her men's shoes. She was addressed as Monsieur le Marquis. In Paris in later life she lived in the Passy quarter, always as a man. At the funeral of one of her brothers, she attended in a mourning veil and a démodé black dress. She "looked like a man dressed as a woman," the younger members of the family said with disapproval, and they begged her to hasten back home and put on her male attire, which she refused to do, feeling somehow that it would be disrespectful to the dead.

At the bottom of the social scale in Colette's reminiscences in *The Pure and the Impure* came "Amalia X," a majestic, down-at-the-heels old actress she had earlier met in her theatrical career, still optimistically telling her own fortune with a pack of soiled tarot cards on a little café table and remembering aloud what her life had been. Of all Colette's offerings, this was the most realistic and the least pure, being comic, coarse, and basic in its simple sexual wisdom about women and their women who simulated to be men—basic on fundamental psychologies such as only the poor can afford to understand, with their indifference to convention and their patience on matters which in their experience ranked merely as kinds of odd love. Amalia, who had traveled, had lived as one of the Western women in the palace of a pasha in Constantinople, from which she would go out at night, and at some risk, to keep her rendezvous with some little French blonde. "I had everything," she affirmed to Colette, "beauty, happiness, misery, men, and women . . . You can call it a life!" she concluded and went on turning over the tarot cards to discover what could not happen tomorrow.

At almost the end of her book, Colette astonishingly turned antiquarian. She cited the long lives of two wellborn English ladies who in the spring of 1778 (just after the founding of the United States of America and just before the French Revolution, neither of which interested them) had run away together to live in reciprocal happiness and poverty for fifty-three years in Llangollen, a small town in Wales. The elder of the two, Lady Eleanor Butler, had kept their diary of continuous small joys, referring to Sarah Ponsonby, her companion, in substantive terms such as "my love," or "my Delight": "Read Mme de Sévigné. My Love drawing." Or: "At ten my Beloved and I drank a dish of tea. A day of most delicious and exquisite retirement." Or: "Sweet sunshine, blue sky, birds innumerable. My Beloved and I went a delicious walk round Edward Evans' field." Sir Walter Scott and other distinguished travelers finally began calling on them, for the grace of their elegant manners and concentrated tenderness. There is finally, in *The Pure and the Impure*, also a report on jealousy between women in which Colette remarks that "in an eternal triangle there is always one person who is betrayed, and often two."

And thus ends this curious concentrated volume which Colette herself said should one day be regarded as her best book. It would be heretical to argue. What one most misses in it is her voluptuous writing about nature, with which she was so impetuously and watchfully in love, writing which is necessarily absent here—descriptions of fleshy fruit buds and sharp green new leaves, of willow sprouts as yellow as hair, of colors and odors in spring or autumn hedgerows. All of this praise of animate speechless vegetal nature in fields and forests has perforce been omitted from this book whose concern is human passion and physical sexual love, which are customarily practiced indoors.

How long Colette has lived, even after her death!

A Life on a Cloud: Margaret Anderson

JUNE 3, 1974 The demise of Margaret Anderson in southern France in the autumn of 1973 removed the last standing figure from that small early circle of amateur American publishers—oddly enough, all female —whose avant-garde output a half century ago unexpectedly became a new kind of important international literature. Her most remarkable labor was the serialization—over three years, in the famous vanguard magazine *The Little Review*, which she had founded in 1914—of James Joyce's "Ulysses," that masterpiece of verbal shock and emotional repletion which slowly turned into what it immutably remains today: a literary classic and the guidepost marking the new territory of the twentieth-century English-language novel. She was first tinged by fame when it became known that it was she herself, with her exceptionally handsome hands, who had labored over the endless bundles of sullying proofs, includ-ing the libidinous sections—how was this possible for so pretty and feminine a creature as she looked to be? Her profile was delicious, her hair blond and wavy, her laughter a soprano ripple, her gait undulating beneath her snug *tailleur*. The truth was that within her lay the mixture and mystery of her real consistence, in no way like her exterior. Her visible beauty enveloped a will of tempered steel, specifically at its most resistant when she was involved in argument, which was her favorite form of intellectual exercise, as I, who knew her for many years, can attest. Argument was for her like a scale on which she weighed truth and supposition, being herself insufficiently educated academically to know in advance what the proper avoirdupois should be.

Born in a prosperous, staid household in Indianapolis in 1886, with a liberal-minded, intelligent father and a bigoted mother, whom she disliked, she early developed such a wayward, precocious infatuation with piano music that when she entered Western College for Women, a classic freshwater institution in Ohio, she was able to persuade the faculty to let her skip the regular freshman courses and major in piano-playing instead. But through indolence she never practiced her Czerny finger exercises, preferring instead to eavesdrop dreamily on the advanced-piano-playing girls, whose repertory of preludes and nocturnes she soon learned by ear and by heart. What she liked was not to perform but to listen to the performances of others. She was the born enemy of convention and discipline—a feministic romantic rebel with an appetite for Chopin and for indiscriminate reading. But conversation was her real passion. She had early the visionary conviction that only artists were capable of stimulating talk, and that she would be better off dead than failing to be a listener to such talk, if she could just find it—which she certainly could not in her native city. Indeed, she became such an addicted listener that in 1906, after three years at Western College, she persuaded her father to let her go for further eavesdropping to Chicago, then the American intellectual center of ferment for the Middle West.

Chicago, unpleasantly scented by its stockyards when the wind blew from the west, was an invigorating mixture of past, present, and future intellectual stirrings—a city of mounting skyscrapers stretching beside its magnificent Lake Michigan. Impressionism and fragments of Cubism were still preëminent in the classes of the Art Institute, on Michigan Avenue. Harriet Monroe was starting her influential magazine *Poetry*, which introduced such heretical newcomers as Ezra Pound, Vachel Lindsay (with his "General William Booth Enters Into Heaven"—the first American transfer of a historical character into iconoclastic verse), the explosive Carl Sandburg, and, from overseas, D. H. Lawrence and William Butler Yeats. There was also a rebellious group of local literary radicals, including Ben Hecht, Maxwell Bodenheim, Burton Rascoe, Witter Bynner, Harry Hansen, and Floyd Dell, who were giving the city a reputation as a center of creativity second only to New York.

Margaret moved into this maelstrom with alacrity. She took a job, at eight dollars a week, as a clerk in a bookshop that had been designed by Frank Lloyd Wright. It was managed by the two sons of Francis F. Browne, the editor of the literary review *The Dial*, whose staff she soon joined, and where she acquired a working knowledge of how a magazine was put together. She supplemented her income by reviewing books for a religious magazine and for the Chicago *Evening Post*. In her early twenties, she was eager to make use of her drive toward organized inspiration, which was to become the dominant force in her career. On an impulse, she decided to found what she declared loftily in advance would be "the best art magazine in the world." This was *The Little Review*, a monthly "devoted to the seven arts," which had as its truculent slogan "A Magazine of the Arts, Making No Compromise with the Public Taste." A male friend of hers who was on the staff of a modest agricultural magazine—and, furthermore, was in love with her—provided the initial funds for her reckless venture. He had little money but said that he could give her each month from his meagre salary enough to pay her magazine's printing bills and a small office rent, and he advised her to go to New York and Boston to solicit paid advertisements for the *Review*'s first number. On this trip, she miraculously collected four hundred and fifty dollars. Two old publishing houses, Scribners and Houghton Mifflin, each bought two pages in her coming review just on chance, for Margaret was a persuasive saleswoman. Thus it was that *The Little Review* was launched, in March, 1914. No one expected to be paid for a contribution, and no one *was* paid. Nor did anyone feel robbed. It was nine years later, and in Paris, that Gertrude Stein pointed out to her that she could never have accomplished such a penny-less miracle in Europe, especially in France.

The first number of the *Review* featured Margaret's exalted opinions on Paderewski's playing; on Galsworthy's new novel, "The Dark Flower;" on William Vaughn Moody's letters; and on the poetry of the visiting Rupert Brooke—the beauty of his profile like a portrait of his muse, it seemed to many. Vachel Lindsay contributed a poem, "How a Little Girl Danced." There was an article on "The Meaning of Bergsonism" by Llewellyn Jones, and George Soule wrote about "The Cubist Literature of Gertrude Stein," commenting on her "aversion to personal pronouns" and her "strict adherence to simple declarative statements, untroubled by subordinate clauses or phrases of any kind." A general coverage of everything of literary interest to Chicago readers was carefully included. In the second number, William Butler Yeats, addressing American poets, recommended "General William Booth Enters Into Heaven" for its "earnest simplicity" and "strange beauty," and predicted that it would end up in poetry anthologies, which it soon did. The third number, dated May, 1914, struck out in a dangerous and more profitable direction. Emma Goldman, the anarchist, had come to Chicago to lecture, and just as *The Little Review* was going to press the impressionable Margaret dashed off an article in which she denounced ownership of private property and lauded "the anarchist religion." Since Miss Goldman—an advocate, it was said, of free love and of a judicious use of bombs to assure universal brotherhood—was anathema to the majority of respectable citizens, the May issue created a scandal. Margaret's friendly and generous backer informed her that if his connection with her suddenly notorious magazine became known he would lose his job, and begged her to understand why he could no longer supply her with funds. Margaret, equal to any emergency, since opposition always stimulated her, assured him that nothing could stop *The Little Review*.

Indeed, nothing could, and nothing did. Margaret returned to part-time book reviewing to help pay the printer. Subscription campaigns were inaugurated. The poet Eunice Strong Tietjens brought her a diamond ring, saying, "I don't want this anymore. Sell it and bring out an issue." The influential Bert Leston Taylor publicized her and the magazine in his famous column in the Chicago *Tribune*. Frank Lloyd Wright contributed a hundred dollars. And the editor ate when she could afford to. Nor would she compromise her position. Harriet Monroe brought Amy Lowell to see her. The affluent, portly Imagist poet from Brookline offered to support the magazine if she was made poetry editor. Margaret firmly declined the offer; it was not possible for her to function "in association," she said. When Margaret could no longer scrape up the rent for further city living quarters, she and her divorced sister Lois, Lois's two small boys and the unpaid office assistant, Harriet Dean, set up tents on the shores of Lake Michigan, where they lived from the middle of May until the chilly middle of November. The *Review* was then running a series of articles on Nietzsche. A Chicago *Tribune* journalist interviewed Margaret and wrote a feature story about the revolutionary Nietzschean beachcombers. It brought in a host of welcome subscriptions. It also lost the group the use of a house that had been promised them; when the owner, a certain Mrs. Buckley, read the article, she said she wouldn't dream of lending her house to such a person as Miss Anderson, and what a great shock it had been to discover that a young lady who appeared so charming could be so depraved. The beachcombers were rescued from the probability of a freezing winter sojourn on the sands by a Socialist friend of Emma Goldman's, who put at their disposal a dismal vacant house of his on Indiana Avenue.

The following spring, the well-known Anderson restlessness began to reassert itself. Margaret moved *The Little Review* from Chicago to

California—to a dilapidated ranch house near Muir Woods, across the bay from San Francisco. Margaret had what she considered a strong passion for nature, and for living in it, if necessary, in discomfort. She had recently taken onto the *Review* staff a highly intelligent assistant named Jane Heap —an impressive-looking woman of Norwegian ancestry, whose father had been an alienist and the head of an asylum in the Middle West. Jane had spent her childhood and youth among the insane, whose company she found instructive, whose irrationalities and imaginations she was deeply interested in, and of whom she told wonderful stories. The first California issue of the *Review* became one of its most famous, and in a way its most notorious. It consisted of sixty-four blank pages. Since the contributions recently received by Margaret had seemed to her not good enough to put into print, the only words she found worthy of ink were those contained in her statement to that effect: No art was being produced, and she would make no attempt to publish anything second-rate. When Margaret spoke of art, what she usually meant was superior conversation or ideas on any one of the arts. In "My Thirty Years' War," the first volume of her memoirs, published in 1930, she states that she never knew why anyone should sneer at the phrase "Art for art's sake," which seemed to her ideal. "Should it be art for money's sake?" she asks. In her opinion, an artist was an exceptional person with something exceptional to say. Thus, Jane Heap was encouraged to put down on paper a series of eccentric monologues, signed "jh," which were to become characteristic and regular inclusions in *The Little Review* in its later phases, and among its best. Only by exception did the magazine print fine prose as such. Mostly, it featured superior aesthetic arguments, and only occasionally did it print examples of especially good writing—these usually having been brought to light by the European editor, Ezra Pound, whom the magazine acquired in 1917, when Margaret impetuously moved herself, Jane, and *The Little Review* to New York.

Indeed, it was Pound who sent over the manuscript of "Ulysses," which was to be the high point of *The Little Review*'s fame and the beginning of its eventual destruction. Pound highly recommended the Joyce work, with the warning that it might get the magazine in trouble with the censors. When Margaret read it, she is reported to have exclaimed, "This is the most beautiful thing we'll ever have! We'll print it if it's the last effort of our lives." In a way, this is what it proved to be. The "Ulysses" excerpts ran for three years, with very little appreciation from readers, and four times the magazine was burned for alleged obscenity by order of the United States Post Office. "It was like a burning at the stake, as far as I was concerned," Margaret later wrote in "My Thirty Years' War." "The care we had taken to preserve Joyce's text intact; the worry over the bills that accumulated when we had no advance funds; the technique I used on printer, bookbinder, paper houses—tears, prayers, hysterics, or rages—to make them push ahead without a guarantee of money; the addressing, wrapping, stamping, mailing; the excitement of anticipating the world's response to the literary masterpiece of our generation . . . and then a notice from the Post Office: BURNED." Despite the early hopes for what *The Little Review* considered Joyce's masterpiece, the public reactions to "Ulysses" on the whole were cold, when not inimical. Indeed, for a number of months—and, in some cases, for years—there was little enthusiastic response from the world's intellectuals. Occasionally there came some desultory appreciation, usually from the Far West in America. New York was particularly indifferent, and the *Times* was the worst. "Indeed, the *Times* took pleasure in insulting us roundly as purveyors of lascivious literature," Margaret declared. These were heroic days for the editors. It was one of the periods when they were sometimes without any money at all. By this time, Margaret and Jane Heap were living at 24 West Sixteenth Street, in the old William Cullen Bryant house. At one point, they had nothing but potatoes to eat, having providentially bought a barrel of them from a Long Island farmer. Another time, they had only flour in their kitchen, so they ate biscuits. They had the cheapest printer in New York— a Mr. Popovitch, whose mother had been poet laureate of Serbia—and on Sundays Margaret and Jane often went to his East Side printshop and helped set type, correct proofs, and fold pages for the binder. However, they eventually had an intermission of good luck—an introduction, courtesy of Ezra Pound, to John Quinn, the noted Tammany Hall lawyer and collector of modern pictures and manuscripts. After telling them how they should run their magazine, he arranged to endow it to the extent of sixteen hundred dollars; he himself contributed four hundred dollars, and he asked three rich friends, Otto Kahn among them, to do the same. For at least eight months thereafter, the two women lived, worked, and even published their magazine without panic—but not without letters of insult, which continued to pour in from a section of the public that passionately disliked the Joyce opus. Indignation was principally caused by the episode in which Mr. Bloom indulges in amorous musings about Gertie MacDowell and her underclothes, and the complaints were frequently more obscene in language than anything that Joyce had written. They also heralded the difficulties the editors were to have almost immediately with the Society for the Suppression of Vice. The hue and cry began on October 4, 1920, when the Washington Square Bookshop notified *The Little Review* that the store had been served with papers by the Society for having sold a copy of the magazine's July-August issue to a minor, who turned out to be a little girl just entering her teens. John Quinn denounced the editors as "damned fools" for thinking that they could publish a book like "Ulysses" in such a "Puritan-ridden country" as the United States. He said that he would fight the injunction against them but that it was a lost cause. He was doing it for Joyce himself, he said, and not for them, because "you haven't got an ounce of sense"—probably the truest thing that had been said about them up to that time. Margaret Anderson and Jane Heap came to trial in the Court of Special Sessions before three judges—two with white hair, who slept during the major part of the proceedings. The third, presumably Norwegian by heritage or inclination, said afterward that if he had known that Jane was of Norwegian descent he would have changed his decision. It may be that Quinn fumbled his handling of the trial. Basing his case on Joyce's prestige in the world of letters, he scored government officials for their cultural ignorance, which prevented them from distinguishing between literature and pornography. The judges did not want to hear anything about James Joyce's literary standing; for them, the discussion was to be exclusively on the question of obscenity. At one point, one of the sleeping judges awoke and, regarding Margaret with a protective air, refused to allow the objectionable passages to be read in her hearing. The verdict returned was, of course, against *The Little Review*. The magazine was fined a hundred dollars, and, despite John Quinn's furious protest, Margaret Anderson and Jane Heap were led off to have their fingers printed. Throughout the trial, not one New York newspaper came to the women's defense, or to the defense of James Joyce. No one wished to be identified with the "Ulysses" scandal. Only the women's devoted friend Mary Garden spoke up. "I'm disappointed in you," she said. "I thought you'd go to jail." Not until two years later, when Sylvia Beach published "Ulysses" in book form in Paris, did *The Little Review*'s enthusiasm for and devotion to the Joyce work begin to be shared by Americans generally. That is to say, increasing numbers of our countrymen returning from Europe would smuggle in a contraband copy (along with the customary contraband bottle of Scotch). At first, it must be admitted, the only motive was the titillation of owning something rare and illegal, but later there was an increasing awareness of the importance of "Ulysses" as literature. Finally, even the then sanctimonious *Times* devoted columns to the Joyce masterpiece.

By then, however, Margaret had had enough of *The Little Review* and was impatient for something new. In one of the colloquies she was fond of printing in the magazine as a sort of cathartic exercise, she wrote:

> "I am definitely giving up *The Little Review*," I told Jane.
> "You can't give it up. You started it."
> "Are you mad? I started it. I can give it up."

"You have no sense of responsibility."

"Self-preservation is the first responsibility."

"You certainly can't give it up."

"I certainly can give it up. I'll give it to you."

With this abdication, Jane became the sole functioning editor, although Margaret retained the title until the *Review*—it became a quarterly, then an annual—sputtered to its final issue, in 1929.

It was Margaret's meeting with two disparate personalities that indicated to her the direction from which her desired new element of change was to come. William Butler Yeats, an early *Little Review* contributor then on a visit to the United States, ignited her curiosity with anecdotes about European writers, which made her eager to be with them on their home grounds. Her meeting with Georgette LeBlanc, French former companion of Maurice Maeterlinck, proved even more fateful. From the first, they formed an attachment with all the signs of permanence. Mme. Maeterlinck, a diseuse and singer of exceptionally fine sensibilities, had given a series of New York recitals that failed to arouse much interest; her enthusiasm for Americans as a vigorous new race had not engendered a corresponding enthusiasm on their part for the refinement and delicacy of her Gallic artistry. She was now planning to return to Paris, and offered Margaret a career as her piano accompanist. At last, Margaret's passion for the piano showed signs of being useful.

In the spring of 1923, Margaret and Georgette along with Jane Heap, sailed for France. In Paris, the editors went first to see Ezra Pound. "It will be more interesting to know him when he has grown up" was Margaret's sharp reaction after meeting the thirty-eight-year-old Pound. She invariably wanted the immediate and full development of any relationship or personality that she had had the genius to discover or the percipience to employ. This impatience was at once a sign of her prophetic feeling about newly ripening gifted creators and a source of a great deal of irritation to her friends and contributors. Had she known how to cook (she never learned, though she did know how to eat well), she would have been the kind of cook who is always opening the oven door too soon to see if the apple pie is done. Her curiosity was always a fraction too ardent. Of Francis Picabia, who had become the French editor of *The Little Review* in 1922, she said tartly, "We had never had anything from him except a Picabia number"—vanity being the dominant quality *he* had developed. However, Margaret had an almost geographic sense of where new talent was to be located. Long before Picabia supplied her with enough of his own material to fill a complete *Little Review* number, she had seen to it that the magazine printed works by Louis Aragon, André Breton, Philippe Soupault, and Paul Morand, as well as by the best of the younger Frenchmen—René Crevel, Paul Éluard, Tristan Tzara (a Rumanian who had turned himself into a Parisian), and Pierre Reverdy. Margaret and Jane also met Joyce, of course, who told them that because of constant interruptions the practice of sustained conversation had become impossible for him, adding, "In my books I have my revenge."

The Little Review had published a Brancusi number two years before, and the editors went to dine with Brancusi in his stone studio in the Rue de Vaugirard. Margaret straightened the cigarette in her holder before lighting it.

"Can't you smoke it if it's crooked?" asked Brancusi.

"With less pleasure," said Margaret.

"*C'est une idée comme une autre,*" said her host.

They met Erik Satie, and Margaret asked him to write an article about Les Six for *The Little Review.*

"How long?" Satie asked.

"As long as you like," she answered.

"*Ah, non,*" said Satie. "*Ce sont les limites que j'adore.*"

They visited two earlier American writers who had become Paris fixtures—Ernest Hemingway and Gertrude Stein. *The Little Review* had published two short experimental pieces by the unknown Hemingway, and he now read them a story with the title "Mr. and Mrs. Eliot," which they also took for publication. Margaret's admiration for Gertrude Stein focussed on Gertrude's warm nature and the contagious sound of her extraordinary, abdominal laughter. But in "My Thirty Years' War" she was constructively critical of Miss Stein's writing: "To me, Gertrude Stein's style can be regarded as having two aspects. She has (1) a way of saying things which presents perfectly her special matter; she has (2) a way of repeating those things which detracts from her special manner." Gertrude's use of repetition as a way of underlining the importance of some particular statement was a technique that Margaret perfectly understood but did not condone, since she usually found it boring. Gertrude (and her alter ego, Alice Toklas) liked Jane Heap, it turned out, but cared little for Margaret. One of the things that made Margaret insupportable to other women of spirit was a belief she had developed in her own infallibility, which, of course, made her unbearable. Probably it was inevitable that Gertrude and Margaret would not get along, since both were outstanding egotists. Quite often, they would meet in a country house at Orgeval, outside Paris, invited by a mutual friend for Sunday lunch. In such meetings, it was

Gertrude's psychology that dominated. Gertrude talked only when she had something to say of definite interest—to herself, and thus, by extension, to her listeners, because she was intelligent and a splendid talker. Her nature was so solid that it reduced Margaret to the two opposite elements always uppermost in her own personality—violent agreement and violent disagreement, both accompanied by characteristic spirals of her taunting laughter. She meant to taunt no one, however, as her nature was affectionate, but she had a split mentality, based on her addiction to argument. The Orgeval lunches invariably developed, by the second cups of coffee which ended them, into small verbal wars. These were Margaret's particular delight, and if she was able to say, as she drew on her topcoat to go home, that she'd never had better conversation, it was her way of acknowledging that she had been involved in battles with almost everyone at the table and felt that she had triumphed in most of them.

As it happened, I, too, was at those lunches in Orgeval. I had by then known Margaret for a relatively short time, having first met her soon after she came to Paris. This was rather early in her worshipful friendship with Georgette LeBlanc. Georgette's ethereal nature, her psychological and spiritual perfections, as described by Margaret, gave her the seeming character of an archangel, which in reality she rather resembled. However, these heavenly superiorities could have been explained more rationally as consisting of Georgette's exquisite French manners, full of consideration for and courtesy toward all the people surrounding her. The second volume of Margaret's memoirs, "The Fiery Fountains," published in 1951, is devoted almost entirely to her enveloping life with Georgette. Just before they left New York, a rich friend had promised Georgette an endowment for life, with which she was urged to buy a château in France (to be used as a pied-à-terre, Margaret wrote). Inexplicably, the proffered endowment was suddenly withdrawn, and Margaret found herself in her familiar penniless condition. Georgette's sister was the chatelaine of an eleventh-century château in Normandy—the Château de Tancarville—and, at Margaret's urging, the two descended on the sister and her husband. They were to be, off and on, permanent boarders for the next twenty years.

Living in a château was a realization of Margaret's long-established yearning for a romantically framed existence. She was a peculiarly complicated and inflated personality. In *The Little Review*, she had been leading readers onto a superior plane of appreciation of the new, constrictive, detonating, and deflating twentieth-century art, but her psychic self was still housed in an elaborate old-fangled euphoria, embedded in her nature like a mild, incurable malady. By her own statement, she "lived her life on a cloud and was the happiest person she knew." It is a pity that no one ever made an early analysis of her character, untempered by the accumulating devotions of her friends and by the eccentricities that eventually upholstered her personality and performances. "At this time we had less money than anyone in the world (including those who have none at all)," she boasted in "The Fiery Fountains," "but we spent twenty years in five of the more celestial French châteaux." The Château de Tancarville was the first of these. Now *un monument historique*, it is a spectacularly intricate white stone pile, of varied towers and architecture, built above the River Seine on the outskirts of Saint-Romains de Colbus. Its legend declares that it once sheltered Richard the Lion-Hearted and that Queen Elizabeth I of England lived for a summer in its square tower. The windows of its rooms are twenty feet high, and in Margaret's day each bedroom had a canopied bed and an appended dressing room. The château was so enormous that many of the rooms were not even used. This generosity of space was in direct contradiction to the lack of generosity of Georgette's sister and her husband. They were very rich, but they had had avarice preached to them and practiced before them for years. (Of the family's many economies, its practice of sex economy was perhaps the most startling. One branch had three sons and three châteaux; the father engaged one mistress for all three of them, and included himself in the bargain.) The rooms at Tancarville were usually kept in semi-obscurity in order to control the electricity bill. Also to save electricity, the owners would sit in the salon after dinner in complete darkness. Once, when Margaret asked for a brandy for a guest of hers and jokingly handed the servant five francs in payment, the servant returned with the liqueur but without the money, informing her it had been retained by the master, who had measured out exactly five francs' worth. Georgette's sister demanded of them the regular hotel charge—six francs—for each bath they took, and checked their hot-water heater to see that they didn't cheat. Margaret, recalling how she and *The Little Review* had lived on American generosity for years, was appalled by her new intimacy with the brutality of French thrift.

Whenever Georgette and Margaret could afford it, they broke away and found nests, free of niggardly relatives, in small, cheap French hotels. Margaret once shamed Georgette's brother-in-law into parting with fifteen hundred francs—he kept complaining of Margaret's insolence in demanding it while he suspensefully doled it out, a few hundred francs at a time—with which they rented an apartment on the Left Bank of Paris; there they spent eight agreeable months, with Margaret usually going out only at dusk, because her one suit was too worn to be exposed to daylight.

Another time, near Tancarville, they found and rented a lighthouse, but winter came, the lighthouse was too cold to live in, and back they went to the relatives' château. In 1930, Margaret, desperate for some money of her own, wrote "My Thirty Years' War," and Georgette, in a similar spurt of diligence—perhaps it was contagious—wrote "Souvenirs," a memoir of her life with Maeterlinck. Margaret's book was a success, Georgette's less so, but with their combined royalties they were able to live in comparative luxury for another period, and Margaret even bought a little car. Of the three autobiographical volumes she eventually wrote, "My Thirty Years' War" is today the most readable and interesting, detailing as it does the events that led to the founding of her inflammatory magazine, which shattered complacent literary customs, aroused curiosity, and became a kind of monthly cult among its devotees. She was not a good writer, but she was an animated memorialist of what had made her life vivid and unforgettable. She was easily moved to rhapsodies and a sense of well-earned triumph when she recalled the trailblazing years. In the second volume, "The Fiery Fountains," she unexpectedly became an invaluable writer on the emotions. She writes on the classifications of love, on the varieties of love, on romantic love, on amity, on perfections of friendship, furnishing an extremely interesting and rare analysis of these states of feeling. In a section subtitled "The Art of Love," she remarks, with aphoristic felicity, "In real love you want the other person's good. In romantic love you want the other person." In her long years of devotion to Georgette LeBlanc, she combined or separated categories of love with the fluidity of mist or rain or sunshine, like climates of the heart. Georgette was the most important and influential of all Margaret's emotional friendships. The concerts that Georgette gave in Paris on her return from America achieved extraordinary appreciation. When she recited poetry, she literally moved her listeners to tears—tears of pleasure, tears of tenderness. It was, in part, with the skill of an actress that she played upon the susceptibilities of her auditors. After all, this was her professional art—a miracle of aural communication that Margaret, in her book's fervid prose, was able to recommunicate to her own audience.

A section of "The Fiery Fountains" deals with Georges Gurdjiev, the Russo-Greek mystic who, surprisingly, had become an important part of their spiritual lives. They had first heard of him in New York early in the nineteen-twenties, when his disciple and publicist A. R. Orage, former editor of the English philosophical magazine *The New Age*, came to America to spread the Gurdjievan doctrine. In 1924, when they were new in Paris, they learned that Gurdjiev was accepting a small group for special teaching at his Institute for the Harmonious Development of Man, as he called a retreat he had established in a château at Fontainebleau-Avon, outside the village of Moret. This, renamed by him the Château du Prieuré (another of Margaret's "celestial châteaux"), had once been inhabited by Mme. de Maintenon, and Margaret and Georgette lived there, at intervals, for several years. Gurdjiev was at this time much discussed in international circles. People from all over the world—female mostly, well-to-do mostly —were living in his Institute in order to learn of what they called his cosmology, which his devotees—among them Katherine Mansfield, who spent her final years there and died there—supposedly practiced as a way of life. Gurdjiev had stated in Margaret's hearing that there existed a super-knowledge and a super-science—phenomena guaranteed to bring her curiosity to the burning point. Life at the Prieuré consisted largely of discussions, which would also have made of Margaret a ready disciple. ("What can Gurdjiev give that the Bible doesn't give? I would say, Everything. The Bible doesn't give it, only shows it. . . .") Beginning as eager converts, Margaret and Georgette soon became proselytizers; indeed, all those involved with the Gurdjiev tenets seem never to have completely dropped their relation with his systematized thinking. In the touching final pages of "The Fiery Fountains," when Margaret has us live through with her the sudden discovery, on the eve of the outbreak of war in 1939, that Georgette has a cancerous growth, then through Georgette's painful illness and her death from the disease in 1941, Gurdjiev and his precepts keep reappearing like apparitions. Toward the end, Margaret reports, Georgette became obsessed with the idea that the savant was coming to say farewell, and kept inquiring if he had arrived. Finally, a card from Gurdjiev's group was delivered, with the message that Gurdjiev had said that she possessed "*beaucoup de courage,*" and Georgette made her last, mysterious statement: "*Alors . . . nous allons mourir sans mourir?*" ("Then we will die without dying?")

Fearing German bombing of Paris after the declaration of war, Margaret and Georgette had moved to the South of France, to the small village of Le Cannet, near Cannes, where they remained during the early days of the Occupation. The United States was urging its nationals to return home, but Georgette, a French citizen, would not go, and Margaret refused to leave without her. After Georgette's death in Le Cannet, Margaret was finally prevailed upon to sail for New York. Her close Paris friend Solita Solano, who was already here, told Ernest Hemingway of Margaret's penniless plight, and he sent four hundred dollars to pay for the trip.

The third and last volume of memoirs, called "The Strange Necessity" —a title she conceded she had borrowed from Rebecca West—is devoted mainly to retrospection and what she calls "ruminations." Its text has an improvisatory quality, as if she were thinking out loud. Although she admits that she no longer remembers facts, only emotions, new additions to her life history of necessity seep through. Her life had been ornamented by strong relationships, and was now about to include one more. In June, 1942, eight months after Georgette's death, Margaret sailed from Lisbon on the Drottingholm, bound for New York. Early in the voyage, Dorothy Caruso, widow of the singer Enrico Caruso, introduced herself, saying, "I hear you published *The Little Review*." By the time the boat docked, they had become friends—"the last great friendship of my life," Margaret wrote—and they were domiciled together until Dorothy Caruso's death, in 1955. Margaret left for France the next year, returning to Le Cannet, where she lived as a recluse until her own death, seventeen years later. Those final years she spent mostly listening to her favorite Chopin records and herself playing the music she had loved best. She also continued to write her highly charged feuilletons—passing thoughts arrested on slips of paper—some of which were published in the new American semi-annual *Prose*, a comforting return for her to the familiar little-magazine formula. In the last of these, published posthumously, she wrote, "I am ill, with a bad heart, bad lungs (emphysema), and seven other alarming symptoms, which I ignore. I have been having a three-month attack of shingles, and have just learned that Henry James, at seventy, had them for four months." (Henry James—she must have been pleased to include him!) She then went on, the prey once again of her habitual euphoria, "I am 83 (84?) years old, and I am the happiest person I know," ending, characteristically, "And I am not 83 years old. . . . I have just learned, from a reliable source, that I am 86."

She concluded "The Strange Necessity" with a final summation: "I wonder why I have wanted to write this story of my life. I know it at first hand, but so incompletely that it has little meaning. It has been so happy and so sad, as happy as flowers, as sad as moonlight—a happy life that loves the saddest music. It has been a striving and a failing; a development and a diminution; it has been proud, and egotistic, and modest; aggressive and unassuming; alert and unconscious; hopeful and, I fear, lost. It has overflowed with thankfulness and remorse—a life like any other, but which has seemed to me so different, so special, and so blessed as to be unique. The blessings I wanted were love and music, books and great ideas and beauty of environment. I have had them all, and to a degree beyond my asking, even beyond my imagining."

She died at Le Cannet in the night of October 18, 1973.

Cézanne

PARIS, SEPTEMBER 9, 1974 The great art attraction in Paris has been the exhibition at the Orangerie of the thirty Cézannes that belong to France's various national museums. After the imperial golden treasures at the Petit Palais, the Cézannes seem a republican comedown, but they form a splendid sampling of the best-known French modernist. Cézanne had prophesied that he could astonish Paris with an apple, and certainly it was his paintings of apples that gave him his first fame. In his search for stylization of form and the rendering of volume through color, he found apples the most appropriate subject. In one canvas on display, called "Apples and Biscuits," there are eleven of them, carefully painted. All his life, Cézanne worked with discouraging slowness. He devoted a hundred sessions to painting a mere still-life, and a hundred and fifty sittings to each of the portraits of his wife. His passion for work was almost morbid. Even after his early artistic success, he feared that his remarkable new painting style was due to a defect in his eyesight. Socially ill at ease with people, if by chance he met an old friend, such as Zola, he would signal to him not to speak.

The suppression of concise contours in his early landscapes was what led him to Impressionism. Of rival painters he said they painted only likenesses of nature, whereas his aim was to paint a portion of nature herself. To the intensity of his vibrant colors he added a use of blue in perspectives, which he felt that science itself authorized. Certain of his flower paintings, greatly admired by van Gogh, are featured in this exhibition, as well as the famous landscape of Estaque, with its vivid blue sea. In the version of "Les Baigneurs" in the Orangerie show, the blue shading of the bodies has the peculiar quality of enamel. To the public, the canvas of greatest interest is certainly "The Hanged Man's House," that fascinating yellow, angular section of a dwelling in Auvers-sur-Oise, viewed at a street corner that pitches downhill—a picture repeatedly exhibited even in Cézanne's lifetime. The Orangerie catalogue characteristically fails to explain who the hanged man was, or why hanged. Always a violent and melancholic man, Cézanne toward the end of his life was convinced that his mind had long been decaying. Yet what marks this great exhibition is precisely the vigor of his genius and the logic of his organizing brain.

Memory Is All: Alice B. Toklas

DECEMBER 15, 1975 Gertrude Stein, the mortal center of Alice B. Toklas's existence for the thirty-eight years that the two women lived together in concentrated amnity in Paris, died on July 27, 1946, leaving Alice companioned by two dominant preoccupations. One was vast in its scope, encompassing the New Testament belief in life after death, by which, in her interpretation, she and Gertrude were to be united again in Heaven for eternity. The other preoccupation was merely mundane, and thus much more bothersome. It was to prepare literary immortality for Gertrude by seeing that all her unpublished manuscripts were printed; this project would require considerable cash, while the first would require only faith, which cost nothing.

Four days after Gertrude's death, Alice was writing from the apartment they had shared, at 5 Rue Christine, to their friends Carl and Fania Van Vechten, in New York: "I'm here alone. And nothing more—only what was." Two days later, on August 2nd, to Carl Van Vechten: "She gives the Picasso portrait to the Metropolitan—the rest to me—and then to Allan's children—so I definitely stay on." On August 5th, to another pair of old New York friends, W. G. and Mildred Rogers: "I went to the country and got Basket [her and Gertrude's white poodle] Sunday, and he and I will stay on here." And to Bennett Cerf, Gertrude's publisher, thirteen days after that: "And now Basket and I are in the flat alone, where we definitely stay on."

"Staying on alone"—Alice's description of the twenty-one remaining years of her life without Gertrude—is both the heart-catching theme and the title of a book subtitled "Letters of Alice B. Toklas" (Liveright, edited by Edward Burns). It is a rich, emotional volume. The broad sweep of information derived from family and household letters, from letters to prospective publishers of Gertrude's work, and to biographers of Gertrude and to old and new friends on both sides of the Atlantic, gives us a picture not only of the major items in Gertrude's and Alice's lives together, viewed retrospectively, but also of what would likely be the items of prime importance in Alice's future. "I wish to God we had gone together as I always so fatuously thought we would—a bomb—a shipwreck—just anything but this," she wrote sombrely to one intimate New York friend a little more than a year after Gertrude's death. But though she had been left bereft, she was not left without occupation. Gertrude had willed her manuscripts and papers to Yale University, and Alice obediently sorted and packed these and shipped them off. "When I've finished sending things to Yale and done some typing and cleaned the flat and caught up with darning and patching," she wrote another old friend, early in her bereavement, "well, then it will be spring, and Basket and I will take walks and be in excellent form." Yale held an exhibit of Gertrude's correspondence, and Alice wrote to Donald Gallup, curator of the university's collection of American literature, "I am so thrilled with your description of the exhibition of the letters. What a variety there is of human nature in them. And your including the rejections—the refusals—how Gertrude would have appreciated that. You must know how those refusals hurt at the time they were received, but one day Blanche Knopf outdid even all Knopf's Knopfishness, and then Gertrude forgot our hopes and bitter disappointment and burst into that loud laughter." Another bequest—the 1905-06 Picasso portrait of Gertrude, which was given to the Metropolitan Museum—elicited from Alice, "They took the Picasso portrait for the Metropolitan ten days ago. It was another parting and completely undid me. Picasso came over to say good bye to it and said sadly—*ni vous ni moi le reverra jamais* [neither you nor I will ever see it again]. It was all there was left of their youth."

Whether dead or alive, Gertrude always had a domesticating influence on her admirers, of whom I was one. At the Stein-Toklas parties, the gentlemen would congregate loyally around Gertrude, while we ladies would be grouped around the tea table presided over by Alice, so we could get the gossip. Alice was a very entertaining purveyor of news. She gave it to you adding item to item, as if she were detailing the recipe for a fruitcake. You always knew where Gertrude was in the room, because she would let out her whoops of laughter; curiously, I don't remember ever hearing Alice laugh, although she had an acute and sharp sense of humor, which, since it was bordered with wit, was quiet in tone. Her conversation had its own pattern—she obtained a variety of effects by setting forth the opposite of what anyone else might have said. Her voice was soft, her California accent agreeable, her vocabulary precise, rhythmic, and possessed of its own sense of speed, with allegro touches. A great deal of this personality, this domestic intimacy, comes through in the printed letters. Alice had adopted the childish clan name of Woojums for Carl Van Vechten, which thereafter figures in their correspondence. The very first letter in the book begins, "Dearest Fania and dearest Papa Woojums," and is signed "Mama Woojums." In subsequent examples, Fania Van Vechten is Madame W., and sometimes the Empress. Gertrude, whenever mentioned to the Van Vechtens, is Baby Woojums, or Baby for short. Other close friends have their own cozy sobriquets: Mr. and Mrs. W. G. Rogers are the Kiddies—Rogers was one of the first doughboys she and Gertrude had met during the First World War, and to show their familiarity with American slang they called him the Kiddie, which afterward was extended to "Dearest Kiddies," or "Dear Mrs. Kiddie" when Alice is writing only to Mrs. Rogers, thanking her for a gift and, in return, presenting her with a recipe for an "old old French pastry called Massillon . . . They should be frosted all over with a white rum frosting with chopped pistachio sprinkled on the top but I don't bother to do so."

Gertrude was likely to plunge into intimacies like a bear cub, but with new acquaintances Alice observed the formalities until the friendship had ripened to a first-name basis. Thus, Mina Curtiss, who had been introduced to her in 1948, after Gertrude's death, as a friend of Virgil Thomson and Carl Van Vechten, progressed gradually from "Dear Mrs. Curtiss" to "Dear Mina dear." Referring to Gertrude by her first name was more easily achieved. "Oh but you must say Gertrude—it wouldn't be friendly to do otherwise," Alice wrote Mrs. Curtiss. "You know, it was the very young who explained that, when they started the habit twenty-five years ago. It was quite shocking at first, but they finally convinced me, and in no time it was accepted—historical and no further trouble. It was contagious, so that the G.I.s spoke not of but to her not as Gertrude but Gertie—those at the station when they came—the Seventh Army replacements—through our village. Here in the flat she was very ceremoniously Miss Stein. Afterwards on the stairway? . . ."

Like Gertrude, however, Alice could be ambivalent about friends old and new. To one of the latter—an Italian translator of "The Making of Americans," who had graduated from "Miss Pivano" to *"Nanda dear,"* she wrote in 1950, "Paris has been full of Americans—two million—at least—have come to see me—they bore and exhaust me—though I only see those who were friends of Gertrude whom she would have wanted to see . . . but then in spite of wanting to see them all—some of them used to bore her. Did I ever tell you she once said she was going to put an advertisement in the *New York Herald Tribune* saying Miss Gertrude Stein does not desire to see any friend she has not seen for fifteen years?" Alice also had a gift for keeping the heat on under smoldering vendettas. One was against the Museum of Modern Art, which Gertrude "loathed and despised." When the Metropolitan, in an arbitrary private transaction, agreed to "deposit" the Picasso portrait of Gertrude with the Modern for a period of ten years, Alice coldly informed the Metropolitan that Miss Stein had very deliberately chosen it to receive the portrait, and, had there been any other choice, "the Museum of Modern Art would not have been an alternative . . . indeed [Miss Stein] thoroughly disapproved of its policy and aims." Alice kept up such a vigorous campaign, through lawyers and friends, that the Metropolitan was finally goaded into reclaiming the picture. Having won her victory, Alice yet continued her gibes. To a casual acquaintance, she wrote, some years later, "Please do not ask me to chide your wife about the Metropolitan's giving the portrait to that frightful Museum of Modern Art for ten years—since it got back to where it belongs much more quickly than one had reason to hope for. . . . Is your wife possibly connected with the Museum of Modern Art? If she is she is saving it from damnation." And some years after that, in another letter—Alice could be really hard—she reports that three people from the Museum of Modern Art were brought to see the pictures in her apartment, and said of the Picassos that "they had never seen such fine Braque painting." She goes on, "I held my tongue—that was in the other room. Then they came in here and repeated their error. *Silence de ma part.* They appealed to me—was it not—pointing to the big picture over the fireplace. It would be if it were—I permitted myself to answer. And I plied them with sherry—*pâté brioche* and my best little cakes—allowing myself to tell the story—*sans discrétion*—to anyone who will listen."

Early on, Gertrude, and therefore Alice, had taken an aesthetic stand favoring Picasso's work against that of Matisse, which the latter, not unnaturally, had resented. When Gertrude, in "The Autobiography of Alice B. Toklas," wrote that the beautiful Mme. Matisse was beautiful like a horse—meaning it as a compliment—the comparison was misunderstood. Then the Paris newspapers aggravated the issue, the fat was in the fire, and "there was no further acquaintance" with Matisse. However, with Alice, to be out of sight was not necessarily to be out of mind. In 1950, some seventeen years after the *malentendu*, she was still snipping away, writing to Donald Gallup that Matisse was "amongst the majority—the commonplace majority as Gertrude called him—of the sad and mistaken." Even when she is quoting for her own advantage something the painter had said, she cannot resist a sneer: "It's as true and trite as most of Matisse's reflections." About Ernest Hemingway, another of Alice's objects of ill will, she was also implacable: "Did you see *The New Yorker's* profile of Hemingway???!!! Nothing he has said since—not even his novel—will be as complete an exposure of all he has spent his life hiding. It's strange that he should be taking so much pleasure in destroying the legend he worked so patiently to construct. Someone . . . sent an A.P. man to see me, and I got into a frightful row with him about Picasso's painting and Hemingway's new book (as if they could be mentioned in one sentence)—he the A.P. man said he thought Picasso was painting carelessly and Hem was writing carelessly! . . . I liked defending Hemingway—it was the first opportunity I've ever been offered—it will no doubt remain a unique experience." And a few days later, after she had been sent some uncomplimentary reviews of Hemingway's new novel, "Across the River and Into the Trees," she wrote, "People seemed to think they would please me. Far from it—the whole Hemingway legend—which we saw him create and *soigner*—going to pieces as it is under one's eyes is the most pitiable embarrassing thing imaginable. The present Hemingway crack up—one must borrow from the vocabulary of the greatest of his victims—has far too much old-fashioned biblical punishments and rewards for comfort to those living in the present. But of course that is just what he doesn't do—he is hopelessly 1890—and one can damn him no further. He wears like the New Look but he is in the tradition of Kipling."

Interspersed with Alice's malice is Alice the dedicated housewife. "Amateur art isn't satisfactory—is it?" she inquired rhetorically of one correspondent. "When I used to bake a cake for Gertrude I never asked is it good, I always said does it look like one that came from the baker's—it should have tasted better because the material it was made of was of a superior quality to what the baker used but wasn't mixed and baked in a professional way, which was what would make it look like the baker's. Well it was often that Gertrude thought it did. Finally some one said one looked as if it had come from a Women's Exchange and Gertrude said that should satisfy me." She fulminated against the new, postwar indifference in Paris to giving or receiving small change, so atypical of the French: "Having learned the value of *petites économies* in '15, it leaves me flabbergasted —how can one save *sous* (that is present francs) if they aren't returned to one—it's very confusing if not immoral."

Unavoidably, since *la bien-aimée* is never far from her thoughts, Alice reveals certain of Gertrude's personal, eccentric preferences. For instance, Gertrude could not bear having anyone read aloud to her—a habit French authors were addicted to. "I read with my eyes, not my ears," she told Picasso. "Ears are inside me." To which Picasso, who could be as elfin as Gertrude, said, "Of course writers write with their eyes, painters paint with their ears. And further neither painters nor writers have ever been painted with their mouths open." We learn that "Gertrude wouldn't have been amused with the present glorification of Melville—not even of 'Moby Dick'—she thought that he was being grossly overrated. He was not one of the writers whom she chose as examples of expressing our sense of abstraction." Nor did the Joyce novel "Ulysses" please Gertrude: "She once said it was rather more than she could manage of the Irish fairies—that Irish fairies were even less palatable than German fairies." Gertrude did, however, have an "unfailing appreciation" of F. Scott Fitzgerald's work. Ulysses S. Grant she considered our greatest eminence—"not second to Lincoln but first." Picasso she thought of as a younger brother. "They understood each other in spite of saying dreadful things when they were irritated," Alice writes. And, least surprising in this list, it was, Gertrude felt, *un*familiarity that bred contempt.

Gertrude's will stipulated that her executors pay to Carl Van Vechten such sums of money "as [he] shall, in his own absolute discretion, deem necessary for the publication of my unpublished manuscripts." All the rest and residue, "of whatsoever kind and wheresoever situated," was left "to my friend Alice B. Toklas . . . to her use for life" and, "insofar as it may become necessary for her proper maintenance and support," the executors were authorized "to reduce to cash" any of the paintings in the Stein collection, which, at the time the will was drawn, in July, 1946, included twenty-eight Picasso paintings and a portfolio of his drawings, as well as seven Juan Gris canvases. Permission for the sale of any of these art works was to be obtained from a Baltimore-court-appointed estate administrator. Upon Alice's death, the remainder of the estate was to go to Allan Stein, only child of Gertrude's oldest brother, Michael, and, after him, to his three children. Gertrude had told Alice that she wanted everything—every manuscript of hers—published, and Alice quickly set out to implement her desire. Although diminutive in size and rather bent, Alice had the strength of a giant when it came to organization; in her years with Gertrude, she had already made it her function to coördinate the conveniences of daily living to accommodate Gertrude's hours of writing, even when they took place at night. Five weeks after Gertrude's death, Alice informed Carl Van Vechten that the first publication, by the Yale University Press, would be "Four in America," one of the "difficult" Stein manuscripts (the four subjects were George Washington, Ulysses S. Grant, Wilbur Wright, and Henry James), for which Thornton Wilder had offered to write a long introduction. The book appeared in the fall of 1947. "Isn't 'Four in America' perfect?" Alice wrote to Dearest Kiddie. "Isn't Gertrude the essence of U.S.? How I wish she could have seen the book—it was always the happiest day of the year (way back it was of the decade) when a new book of hers came in the post and she spent the morning or the whole day reading it. And then when it was read she would say *oui, c'est cela*." Eventually, through her penury and self-denial, plus her driving determination, Alice saw eight volumes of the unpublished works printed by the Yale University Press. She also helped support herself during some trying times by writing an idiosyncratic, chatty cookbook, which sold well, and "What Is Remembered," a less successful volume of memoirs but, in my estimation, her most entertaining book.

The Baltimore court had appointed an elderly lawyer, Edgar Allan Poe—the poet's great-nephew—as administrator of Gertrude's estate.

Gertrude had been precise about how her funds were to be spent, but, unaccountably, Poe proved to be an obstructionist and parsimonious in fulfilling her wishes, of which he seemed to disapprove, although it was none of his business. Alice cajoled and threatened, Poe sent money in driblets, and in 1954 Alice, who was desperate, finally sold about forty Picasso drawings without informing Poe—and, upon what now seems the poor advice of Daniel-Henry Kahnweiler, Picasso's dealer, for considerably less than their market value. The plot machinations that followed would have done credit to a Victorian novel. In Alice's orderly existence with Gertrude, there had never been any melodramatic or violent eruptions. But with Gertrude gone, the difficulties so often attendant upon the inheritance of property and interpretation of testaments were inflicted upon her relict, Alice. Allan Stein's wife, Roubina (referred to scornfully in these letters as the Armenian, although she was in fact Rumanian), kept a beady eye upon the pictures in the interests of her minor children. In 1951, Allan Stein died, and the children were in line to inherit after Alice died. In 1961, while the increasingly infirm Alice was absent in Acqui, Italy, taking a mud-bath cure for her arthritis, Mrs. Stein procured a court order to have the pictures removed from the Rue Christine apartment to a Paris bank vault, on the ground that their security was endangered by Miss Toklas's absence. When Alice returned from Acqui she found the walls bare. "The pictures are gone permanently," she wrote a friend pathetically. "My dim sight could not see them now. Happily a vivid memory does. . . . Don't worry about me—I am 84 years old. All old people fall—an aunt skating on the ice—a granduncle jumping off a streetcar. (Alice's imagination was always lively.)

In going over an inventory of the pictures, Roubina Stein had discovered the Picasso drawings missing. She accused Alice of illegal behavior, which was true enough, since she had not sought Poe's permission before she sold them. Alice, on her side, insisted, with equal truth, that she had been within her rights, according to Gertrude's will. To aggravate the tension, Poe was inexplicably three months behind in Alice's monthly allowance. "My eyes are a great trouble," she informed Russell Porter, the Paris lawyer she had engaged to protect her—and little enough help he was able to be. "I can write only by holding the paper within about ten inches of my eyes under a strong light. . . . It is urgent that he [Poe] sends me the money by wire at once—for I am down to bedrock. . . . Gertrude Stein—in her generosity to me—did not foresee that such an occasion could arise." Her financial situation was so precarious that some of us among her old friends raised a fund for her maintenance. Alice was hospitable; she took to inviting us in turn to *bec-fin* restaurants for lunch, after which, in settling the bill, she was inclined to leave the equivalent of twenty dollars as a tip, in addition to the regular service charge. We also discovered that she would send her servant to Fauchon's fancy shop to buy her weekly groceries. (She thought the best was none too good and, as a matter of fact, sometimes not good enough. One November, I troubled to find her a fresh peach she had requested, vainly hoping she would not notice its flaws.) To protect her—and ourselves—from such civilized improvidence, we were finally forced to dole out her income weekly.

The final calamity was still in store. The building at No. 5 Rue Christine was sold, and each occupant was offered the opportunity to buy his apartment. Alice ignored this opportunity, being of the optimistic opinion that she would not be evicted, because of her advanced age. While she was in Italy for her annual arthritis cure, the new owner of her flat sued for possession and won the case. Although powerful friends intervened—even André Malraux, then Minister of Culture, for Gertrude Stein's name was still potent, and Alice was regarded as her official survivor—the French law was adamant. To rehouse her, the musician Doda Conrad and I, after a fruitless search for the kind of old-fashioned Left Bank quarters she was accustomed to, finally had to settle for a comfortable and modern, if unpicturesque, apartment at 16 Rue de la Convention—a noisy commercial street, several miles from the Rue Christine flat which had been so perfectly peopled with her recollections of Gertrude. Alice was eighty-seven when she was forced to move—bedridden, partially deaf, and almost blind. From her pillow in the new apartment, the only view she had was, ironically, that of the local parish church from which she was to be buried three years later. As a little girl in San Francisco, she had been created a Christian in the most casual way by a Catholic friend of her unorthodox Jewish parents; the friend, Alice once told me, had sprinkled her with holy water, which, with childish faith, she had regarded as a valid baptism. In late 1957, after receiving instruction from a very obliging English priest, who supplied her with a missal and a rosary (which she thereafter wore looped around her left wrist), she was officially admitted into the Church and received Holy Communion. She was now ready to meet Gertrude in "the peopled heaven."

The last letter in "Staying On Alone" was written fourteen months before her death, to a young New York couple, Harold and Virginia Knapik, long devoted to Alice. It reads, "I don't know what is to become of me. . . . The Armenian's lawyer is trying to make some sort of settlement without selling any of the pictures. But how he's going to manage it I'm sure I don't know. Do come back soon. I shan't last forever." She died on March 7, 1967, just before her ninetieth birthday, and was buried in the tomb that she had purchased for herself and Gertrude in the Père Lachaise Cemetery. "Dead is dead but that is why memory is all and all the immortality there is," Gertrude had written years earlier in "The Making of Americans." It is a quotation not often mentioned, and surely it would not have been Alice's choice as the epitaph for their mutual earthly devotion.

With the death of Alice, Gertrude's cherished picture collection, which Alice had fought so bitterly to keep intact as a memorial to her, became the property of Allan Stein's children and was dispersed by them without sentiment. A major selection was purchased for about six and a half million dollars by four trustees and one patron of the Museum of Modern Art, the institution that Gertrude and Alice had so detested, and became the nucleus, in December of 1970, of a spectacular exhibition there— "Four Americans in Paris: The Collections of Gertrude Stein and Her Family." The preview night for privileged members, held in a great storm, with the rain falling in sheets, predictably was a fashionable affair, the ladies and gentlemen arriving in their dampened finery to be greeted by a long, formal receiving line that included the new official owners of Gertrude's art. The smart public atmosphere could never, of course, have substituted for the ambience of the Rue de Fleurus studio, where Gertrude's pictures, discovered by her and bought modestly, and now worth a millionaire's ransom, had originally hung, where they had had the benefit of her pure and sacred passion before price became one of their miraculous merits. In their new, sleek museum showcase, the major value that seemed lacking was private love.

Pablo Picasso

APRIL 21, 1973 Pablo Picasso was born and died a phenomenon. "What is a painter?" he once asked, in front of others, while talking to himself. Having asked his question, he then answered it: "He is someone who founds his art collection by painting it himself." Picasso was that kind of painter. Another time, he overheard someone say, "I don't like Picasso," obviously referring to his paintings, and intruded to ask, "Which Picasso?"

During his career, Picasso, according to André Malraux, produced well over six thousand paintings. Of the multiple art styles that were then employed in France, he made use of all, especially those most filled with his own deformations. When he was approaching his eightieth birthday, he decided that, having gone through so many years, he should have the privilege of choosing for the rest of his life the age he preferred. "I have decided," he said, settling the problem, "that from now on I shall be aged thirty." His energies were so great that even in his bogus-thirties period his habitual creation continued pouring out, though it was mostly audible in his wit and visible in his psychological showmanship and legerdemain, all of which were trivialities compared to what he had produced in his previous era. Many of the wittiest things he said occurred in conversations in which he had the opportunity to cap what someone else had said. During the nineteen-thirties, when the fabrication of counterfeit Picassos was at its height—his works being the most often counterfeited because they rated the highest prices—an old journalist friend took a small Picasso painting belonging to some poor devil of an artist to Picasso himself for authentication, so the impoverished artist could sell it. "It's false," Picasso said. The friend took him another little Picasso, from a different source, and then a third. "It's false," Picasso said each time. "Now, listen, Pablo," the friend said. "I watched you paint this last picture with my own eyes. "I can paint false Picassos just as well as anybody," Picasso replied. He then bought the first Picasso at four times the price the poor artist might have hoped it would fetch. When another person took Picasso a counterfeit etching to sign, he signed it so many times that the man was able to sell it only as a curiosity to an autograph dealer.

When Stalin died, Picasso, who had by then joined the Communist Party, drew an imaginary portrait of a young Stalin with a neck like a column of steel and a brooding Georgian look on his face, and it was published in the Communist *Lettres Françaises*. It drew a chorus of complaints from the weekly's loyal readers, who sensed that this sketch was unofficial and therefore disloyal. On being asked by a friend who was a French Party member what he would do if France became Communized and he found himself forbidden to continue working as an artist except on Party cultural lines, Picasso answered, "If they stopped my painting, I would draw on paper. If they put me in prison without paper or pencil, I would draw with spit on the cell walls."

A remarkable description of the young Picasso came from the pen of Fernande Olivier, who was a member of the Montmartre Bateau-Lavoir group of artists and writers, to which Picasso belonged. She wrote, "Small, dark, thickset, unquiet, disquieting, with sombre eyes, deep-set, piercing, strange, almost fixed. Awkward gestures, a woman's hands; ill-dressed, careless. A thick lock of hair, black and glossy, cut across his intelligent, obstinate forehead. Half bohemian, half workman in his clothes; his hair, which was too long, brushing the collar of his worn-out coat." With time, his large, impressive head became a bronzed, hairless dome. An artist friend described Picasso's way of beginning a new picture: "His eyes widen, his nostrils flare, he frowns, he attacks the canvas like a picador sticking a bull."

Picasso painted his world, and often his people, to suit his own style, which, of course, rarely looked natural to the eyes of others. He said, "We all know that art is not truth. Art is a lie that makes us realize truth—at least, the truth that is given us to understand. People speak of naturalism's being in opposition to modern painting. I would like to know if anyone has ever seen a natural work of art. Nature and art, being two different things, cannot be the same thing. Through art we express our conception of what nature is not. There is no abstract art. You must always start with something. Afterward, you can remove all the traces of reality; the danger is past in any case, because the idea of the object has left its ineffaceable mark. Academic training in beauty is a sham. When we love a woman, we don't start measuring her legs."

Picasso was a great conversationalist, and especially a noted solo talker. His recollections of his poverty in his early Montmartre days still make warming, valiant tales. Once, he and Fernande Olivier, who lived with him, had had no food for a day or so when some early Picasso admirer rapped on the studio door. Opening it, they found leaning against it a long loaf of bread, a bottle of wine, and a tin of sardines. In a few years, Picasso's pictures began selling at magically high prices. Thus, he was able to fulfill one of his earlier stated desires: "I should like to live like a poor man, with a great deal of money."

Picasso will rank as the most prodigious artist of our time. He was a man fortunately composed in terms of excess. Even as a genius, he had more gifts than he needed.

Letter from Paris

SEPTEMBER 16, 1975 If you saw Paris last summer, you saw it the way it looks today, for in most respects it has not changed an iota. Old cities are monuments to themselves, not easily altered, and with difficulty even repaired. The major scenic corners of the Place Saint-Germain-des-Prés are preserved immutably by their invaluable resistance to improvement. Some of us passed fragments of our youth sitting out-of-doors on the broad, hospitable terrace of the Deux Magots café, facing the elderly church and its open gardens of stunted trees, and we participated with our eyes in the processions of young brides and grooms, whose future we could not guess but irresistibly wondered about, with vagrant curiosity. Next door to the terrace was an opulent old-fashioned jewelry shop—still there —where some of the richer brides' presents came from, according to René, the headwaiter and general gossip of the Deux Magots.

In the warm Seine Valley, where I have been spending my vacation, in a house inside a walled garden west of Paris, there is an unexpected paucity of fruit on the familiar trees, usually loaded in the early autumn with small pears, which, when ripe, are succulent eating with a bite of cheese. The local farmers—or those who still exist—declare that this is not a good fruit year, although the cherry trees were overburdened in June, and the thieving *merles*, France's singing blackbirds, were so numerous as to be ranked as a pest.

The new freak rose creations are what the local growers call "bicolor." They have been bred to produce petals that are red on their outer side but white toward the flower's center, the white parts being thick-looking, like a white kid glove. Another breed is a dramatic yellow and red. There are also new colors in roses, including a well-formed lavender one, called Sissy, that is much talked about. It is a true lavender, and by next summer we may see lavender roses as a normal novelty in Paris flower shops. The first of the lavender roses was called Saint-Exupéry, after the French writer.

The final rose square of our own garden is behind the house, and thus farthest from immediate inspection, as a kind of floral apology. It blooms with a medley of colors and confusions—a garden of errors and survivors of mistakes, left to chance and to their floral fate, frequently bursting with inappropriate rich colors, like bad embroidery. There are tiny bushes of miniature red roses, their flowers like scarlet pennies. There is everything you might want and decide against as not worth your time or your hope or the space it would occupy in the rich ground. These roses grow helter-skelter in the narrow, rotted foundations that once supported the old barn. Their backdrop is a high hedge of gigantic rosebushes, as tall as a man but named Queen Elizabeth—garlands of coral-pink blooms so rich that they sway heavily in the wind. Above their invisible roots grow small, fertile weeds, which we have not had time to discourage. Among them there are such perpetual survivors as the little blue star-faced flower known in Shakespeare's time as love-in-a-mist—and still so called, for what could be a better performer without constant sunshine? Of all parts of our rose garden—so impoverished when compared to the great lines of incarnadined blossoms in the well-tended gardens of our neighbors—this final mixed garden, collected over the years in our rich rural corner of the Île-de-France, is my favorite floral harvest.

Index

Holy Year in, 269–74
modern artists of, 260–62
in 1945, 231–34
1948 election and, 247
Prix de Rome winners, 295–97
Rome *Il Globo*, 232
Rome *Il Messaggero*, 263, 288
Rome *Il Popolo*, 280
Römerbad Hotel, Badenweiler, 157
Ronde, La, 292
Roosevelt, Franklin D., 118
Rosalinda, O Come Vi Piace, 254–55
Rose, Billy, 203, 285
Rosenberg, Alfred, 110–11
Rosenkavalier, Der, 128
Roshanara (dancer), 192
Rossellini, Renzo, 279
Rossellini, Roberto, 234–36, 237, 292, 301
Ingrid Bergman and, 276–86, 301–2
Rossellini, Roberto, Jr., 276, 279–80, 283
Rossini, Gioacchino, 274
Rostovtzeff, Michael, 212
Rotenberg, June, 217
Rothmere, Lord, 105
Rothschilds, 43, 54
Rotterdam, Holland, 123
Rousseau, Jean Jacques, 294
Royal Highness (Mann), 170
Royal Society of Arts, 256
Rubens, Peter Paul, 300
Rudenko, Roman Andreyevich, 106, 118, 119
Ruggeri, Ruggero, 255
Rumania, 116, 123, 164
Runciman, Lord, 46
Ruspoli, Prince Edmondo, 308
Ruspoli, Prince Emanuele, 308
Russia, 108, 135, 154, 158, 159, 164, 228, 268
enters Poland, 47–48
Germany's attack on, 112–13
post-war Germany and, 143–44
post-war Poland and, 133–34
Russo-German alliance, 106, 186

sector of Berlin controlled by, 142–43
Russians
at Nuremberg trials, 106–7, 109, 118, 119
Western Allies unite to stop, 109

Sacher's, Vienna, 44
Sacred Flame, The, 299
St. Blasein, Germany, 157
St. Francis frescoes, 244
St. Gereon Church, Cologne, 97
"St.-John Perse," 275
St. Peter's, Rome, 269, 270, 271, 272, 306
St. Saba, Rome, 273–74
Saint Stephen's Cathedral, Vienna, 128
Salm, Count Alfred, 33
Salmhofer, Franz, 128
Salome, 128
Salon Carré, 62
Salsomaggiore, Italy, 230
Salzburg, Austria, 38, 217
1936 Music Festival, 32–34
1938 Music Festival, 40–42
Sandburg, Carl, 320
Sannicandro, Dr. Giuseppe, 279, 282
San Remo, Italy, 266–68
Sarcey, Francisque, 201
Saroyan, William, 209
Sartre, Jean-Paul, 240
Satie, Erik, 327
Saturday Evening Post, 154
Sauckel, Gauleiter, 107–8
Scala Sancta, 272
Scalera brothers, 234
Scalera Studio, Rome, 298
Scaravaglione, Concetta, 297
Scarfoglio (Italian author), 303
Scelba, Mario, 262
Schacht, Hjalmar, 110, 121
Schaub, Adjutant, 7, 8
Schiller, Friedrich von, 15, 168, 174
Schirach, Baldur von, 107, 110
Schloss Artstetten, Austria, 45
Schlumberger, Jean, 310, 314
Schneider, Alexander, 217

363